Basketball Empire

Basketball Empire

France and the Making of a Global NBA and WNBA

Lindsay Sarah Krasnoff

BLOOMSBURY ACADEMIC
LONDON • NEW YORK • OXFORD • NEW DELHI • SYDNEY

BLOOMSBURY ACADEMIC
Bloomsbury Publishing Plc
50 Bedford Square, London, WC1B 3DP, UK
1385 Broadway, New York, NY 10018, USA
29 Earlsfort Terrace, Dublin 2, Ireland

BLOOMSBURY, BLOOMSBURY ACADEMIC and the Diana logo are
trademarks of Bloomsbury Publishing Plc

First published in Great Britain 2023

Cover design: Graham Robert Ward
Cover images: charlesdeluvio (unsplash) and Pongnathee Kluaythong/EyeEm,
Leonello Calvetti and Digital Art (Getty).

A catalogue record for this book is available from the British Library.

A catalog record for this book is available from the Library of Congress.

ISBN: HB: 978-1-3503-8418-7
       PB: 978-1-3503-8417-0
       ePDF: 978-1-3503-8420-0
       eBook: 978-1-3503-8419-4

Typeset by RefineCatch Limited, Bungay, Suffolk

To find out more about our authors and books visit www.bloomsbury.com
and sign up for our newsletters.

For Jackie

CONTENTS

FIGURES

ACKNOWLEDGMENTS

This project began life the night of September 22, 2013, when I watched Les Bleus win the EuroBasket title. I was stationed in Paris, deep into a research project on how actions of the US diplomatic community in France during the First World War impacted the bilateral relationship. One early takeaway was the critical role that individuals played to foster closer ties on a citizen-to-citizen level, even as the political or military situation caused strain between France and the United States. One century later, watching the French team celebrate their continental crown on television, knowing half of them played in the NBA raised questions around which this book is based.

Basketball Empire owes everything to the women and men on both sides of the Atlantic Ocean who contributed their time and shared their experiences. You'll find them featured throughout these pages, and I cannot thank them enough for their patience as work to get *Basketball Empire* across the finish line took far longer than anticipated. I'm also privileged to work with the phenomenal team at Bloomsbury Publishing, including Maddie Holder and Meg Harris. But this book would not be possible without the larger team efforts of so many who have served as sounding boards, cheerleaders, editors, and more.

It would be remiss to not begin with those whose advice and tutelage have guided and inspired. My thanks to Evelyn Ackerman, David Nasaw, Herrick Chapman, and Bob Edelman, my sporty academic north star. Moreover, I would not be who I am today without the magic of my late mentor Jackie Simon.

The basketball world in France, the United States, Senegal, and beyond has been immeasurably welcoming throughout the entire process. I could not have undertaken this project without the guidance of French Basketball Federation Archivist Daniel Champsaur and members of the federation's cultural patrimony commission, including Michel Rat, Fabien Archambault, Jean-Marie Jouaret, and Christelle Bertho. NBA International has also played an important role, as have the communications departments at the Los Angeles Clippers, Oklahoma City Thunder, Orlando Magic, Utah Jazz, Washington Wizards, and French Basketball Federation.

I've gained greater insights thanks to exchanges with colleagues near and far. Thank you Yann Casseville, Sylvère-Henry Cissé, George Eddy, Sylvian Fian, Arnaud Lecomte, Paul Odonnat, Bakary Sakho. I owe much to Jonathan Johnson and Simon Kuper for helping me to kick around some of my fledgling ideas, as did the late Grant Wahl, who encouraged me to return to my journalism roots to test the waters for this project. Grant also introduced me to Alexander Wolff, whose experiences, ideas, and writing are a guiding force. Isabelle Genest, Vince Gennaro, David Hollander, Daniel Kelley, Brianna Newland, and my New York University students have also helped shape how I approach *Basketball Empire*'s themes.

Thank you to my sports diplomacy network, who over the years have helped me better refine understandings of this framework, how it is used past and present, and its real-life implications. My sporty partners in crime, I couldn't do it without you Trina Bolton, Nabila Dekkiche, Heather Dichter, Aashika Doshi, Katia Foucade, Jose Gigante, Carole Gomez, Sarah Hillyer, Stuart MacDonald, Travis Murphy, Morgan O'Brien, Jason Parker, Verity Postlethwaite, Gavin Price, Simon Rofe, Sarah Solémalé, Chris Young, Tom Zeiler. A special thanks to Laurent Dubois, Amy Garrett, Sarah Federman, Taylor Mills, Darley Newman, Alex Wieland, Louise Woodroofe.

Images help to tell stories in different ways than words can. My deep thanks to the Musée du Basket for contributing images from their archives, as well as to the related FranceAndUS website (www. franceussports.com), to *L'Équipe Magazine*, and to the YMCA Paris. Honorable mention to FranceAndUS intern Messiah Wambo Fiase, who worked on the data visualizations depicting French players into the NBA and WNBA.

Lastly, to my family, especially my parents, I couldn't do any of this without you—thank you for all that you do.

GLOSSARY

BAL	NBA–FIBA Basketball Africa League
CFBB	Federal Basketball Center (also known as Pôle France or just INSEP)
CUC	Clermont Université Club
D1	Division One, top division of the National Collegiate Athletic Association
DTN	National Technical Director
FFBB	French Basketball Federation
FIBA	International Basketball Federation
INSEP	National Institute for Sport, Expertise, and Performance
IOC	International Olympic Committee
LBF	Feminine Basketball League
LNB	National Basketball League
NBA	National Basketball Association
NCAA	National Collegiate Athletic Association
Pôle Espoir	Elite basketball training programs for U14 and U15
Pôle France	Elite basketball training program for U18 located at INSEP (also known as CFBB)
ProA	Top division of the National Basketball League
ProB	Second division of the National Basketball League

PUC	Paris Université Club
WNBA	Women's National Basketball Association
Les Tricolores	National teams' nicknames pre-1980
Les Bleues	National women's team nickname post-1980ish
Les Bleus	National men's team nickname post-1980ish

INTERVIEW SUBJECTS

Basketball Empire features project-specific oral histories and on-the-record journalistic interviews conducted for published media pieces with the following people:

Tariq Abdul-Wahad, *former French international, NCAA and NBA player*

Christian Baltzer, *former French international and Director of Le Mans-Sarthe Basket (MSB)*

Nicolas Batum, *French NBA player and present captain of Les Bleus*

Gérard Bosc, *former French international and FFBB National Technical Director (DTN)*

Jacques Cachemire, *former French international who idolized Bill Russell's defense*

Bill Cain, *former French international and MSB professional player*

Carmine Calzonetti, *former American player and coach in France*

Patrick Cham, *former French international and CFBB Coach of Diaw-Parker-Turiaf, Director of CFBB in Guadeloupe*

Vincent Collet, *national team coach, former professional player at Le Mans*

Philippe Desnos, *director of the youth academy at Le Mans*

Boris Diaw, *fourteen-season NBA veteran and Champion, former captain of Les Bleus*

Jean-Pierre Dusseaulx, *former L'Équipe basketball journalist*

Chris Ebersole, *Associate Vice President and Head of Elite Basketball, NBA*

George Eddy, *basketball journalist and former player and coach*

Paoline Ekambi, *first French NCAA Division 1 player, former French international*

Camille Eleka, *childhood best friend of Batum and French professional basketball player*

Martin Feinberg, *second American basketball player in post-1945 France*

Henry Fields, *former American player and coach in France who introduced Bill Russell-style defense in France*

Isabelle Fijalkowski, *former French international, NCAA player and first French to play WNBA*

Katia Foucade-Hoard, *former French international, and first French player to complete four years on scholarship playing NCAA D1 basketball*

Evan Fournier, *French NBA player*

Fabrice Gautier, *national team osteopath who treats many NBA players past/present*

Mickaël Gelabale, *former French NBA player and international*

Rudy Gobert, *French NBA player*

Kenny Grant, *former American coach in France and current basketball agent*

Sandrine Gruda, *all-time best scoring player for Les Bleues; former WNBA veteran and 2016 WNBA Champion with the LA Sparks*

Marine Johannès, *French WNBA player and international*

Arthur Kenney, *former American player in France*

Pascal Legendre, *basketball journalist*

Terry Lyons, *former Vice President of NBA International*

Olivier Mazet, *basketball agent*

Frank Ntilikina, *French NBA player*

Crawford Palmer, *former Duke and Dartmouth player, former French international*

Sam Presti, *Oklahoma City Thunder General Manager and former San Antonio Spurs official*

Johan Rat, *former NCAA D1 player; current French TV analyst for NCAA March Madness tournaments, and son of Michel Rat*

Michel Rat, *former CFBB Director and former French international*

Élisabeth Riffiod-Diaw, *one of France's best female basketball players in history*

Jean-Pierre Siutat, *FFBB President*

David Stern, *former NBA Commissioner*
Mark Tatum, *NBA Deputy Commissioner*
Diandra Tchatchouang, *former NCAA D1 (Maryland) and French international player; activist and representative on the Paris 2024 Players' Commission*
Gabby Williams, *WNBA player and French international*

Introduction

Neither cold weather nor a transportation strike deterred the throngs that gathered the night of January 24, 2020, to be part of history as the National Basketball Association (NBA) played its first regular season game on French soil. A sold-out crowd of nearly 16,000 filled the Accor Arena in Paris to watch the Milwaukee Bucks tipoff against the Charlotte Hornets. The majority clearly favored the Bucks and their European-born star Giannis "The Greek Freak" Antetokounmpo, but their support for hometown hero Charlotte forward Nicolas Batum was deafening.

"Ba-tum, Ba-tum," the crowd chanted whenever the national team captain made a play and again after the final buzzer, replete with standing ovation. Although his team was frustrated and ran out of momentum in the fourth quarter for a 103–116 loss, Batum was all smiles for the match marked a triumphant finish to a week of basketball. For eight Januarys, starting in 2011, the NBA's midwinter European matchup was hosted at London's O2 Arena. The sold-out spectacle made business sense as the anglophone global sports axis runs through the British capital. But it was not a natural fit, because basketball struggles for relevance within the United Kingdom.

France, however, is a different story. The country, often referred to as the *hexagone* for its six-sided geographical shape, is the oldest basketball-playing country in Europe. The Continent's first match was played at the Parisian YMCA in December 1893. Over the decades, France has developed a deeper, more ingrained basketball ethos than most people suspect, despite lacking a sports culture similar to that of Britain, Germany, or the United States. Indeed, many, including Jean-François Martins, Sports Advisor to Paris

Mayor Anne Hildago, argue that Paris is a natural fit for the NBA. "There is a real basketball culture, as well as [Paris] being a symbolic city," he told influential sports daily *L'Équipe*.[1]

The NBA's Paris sojourn was a ray of light during a difficult year for Batum. The previous March, he was demoted from the Hornets' front five after starting the previous 280 games of his career; in November he struggled with an injury.[2] Moreover, Batum's twelfth NBA season was marred by the mental strain of his father's ghost. Richard Batum, a Cameroonian-born professional basketballer in France's second division, collapsed from a heart ailment on-court during a 1991 game aged just thirty. Two-year-old Nicolas was in the stands, traumatized. The memory haunted Batum and his family grew apprehensive that, just like Richard, Nicolas wouldn't live to see his 31st birthday on December 14, 2019.[3] Then the milestone passed without incident, and lifted a millstone from Batum's neck.[4]

Thus, by January 2020 the Normandy native had a lighter step even as his role on-court evolved. Batum was now a play-creator but took few shots, an average of 3.5 per game, and an infrequent scorer. "I make 'Diawesque' matches," he joked to *L'Équipe*, a nod to retired NBA Champion and former Team France captain Boris Diaw, a player known for his altruism and game IQ but not for his high-scoring.[5] Batum took after Diaw, but recalled the day seventeen years earlier when he sat in Accor Arena for his first NBA experience, a preseason game between Hall of Famer Tony Parker's San Antonio Spurs and the Memphis Grizzlies.[6]

Parker was not the first Frenchman to play in the NBA. That distinction rests with Tariq Abdul-Wahad (né Olivier Saint-Jean), an NCAA defensive specialist drafted by the Sacramento Kings in 1997. But it was not until Parker arrived as a nineteen-year-old prodigy in 2001 that being French in the NBA began to have cachet. That Parker earned his way into a starting position on Spurs Coach Gregg Popovich's roster within his first five games made US officials and scouts take note. Parker changed the metric.

While Parker cemented the concept that France can produce high-level players it is his good friend Diaw who personifies the country's basketball empire. A fourteen-season NBA veteran and fan favorite, Diaw was an athletic, intellectual player whose game balanced off-court passions for photography, food, and more. His father Issa, a high jumper from Senegal, met his mother, celebrated basketball heroine Élisabeth Riffiod (later, Riffiod-Diaw), while they both trained at France's elite sports facility and school, known today as the Institut National du Sport, de l'Expertise et de la Performance (National Institute for Sport, Expertise, and Performance, INSEP). But few know that some of Diaw's earliest memories are of following his mother around the court, a basketball in his hands.

It's a surprising story for neither Élisabeth, Boris, nor their homeland were destined for basketball greatness. Riffiod-Diaw began playing in her late teenage years and became the first Frenchwoman to land a one-handed jump shot after studiously watching video of her idol, Boston Celtics legend Bill Russell. Diaw fenced, practiced judo, and only specialized in basketball once he was recruited to play at INSEP in the 1990s. There he met fellow future NBA Champions Parker and Ronny Turiaf; later, their careers illustrated to kids back home that they, too, could play in the league and as a result helped internationalize the NBA's labor force. Similar trends developed within the specters of the WNBA, which include ever-more international players, many of them French.

Since Diaw's national team retirement in 2018, Batum has carried the flame as Les Bleus' captain and the embodiment of France's basketball empire. He serves as elder statesman, speaks out against racism, represents his French identity and Franco-Cameroonian cultural heritage, helps the next generation, and comes off the bench to help the collective. Batum's NBA Paris game was Diawesque, and as he exited the court that bitter January evening, he wondered: which kid tonight will be inspired to make it to the NBA?[7] This book introduces some of the basketball stars and shows how they've contributed to cultural, technical, and knowledge exchanges between France, the United States, and Africa through the game.

* * *

France today is a basketball empire, a breeding ground of the game that has helped internationalize and globalize the NBA. The league's Frenchmen are part of the larger European and international cadre that changed player demographics, influenced the NBA's style of play and off-court culture, and contributed to its overseas growth. But what sets the French case apart is how this hoops-swishing empire is built on the twin pillars of the unique Franco-American relationship and the complicated Franco-African postcolonial legacies.

In his influential 2010 work *Soccer Empire*, Laurent Dubois argued that France's football fortunes were deeply interconnected to its former empire, and that its future similarly rested with the tentacles that bind the *métropole* (mainland) to the Antilles and Africa. Moreover, this football empire dared France to reexamine itself. "Like the runners John Carlos and Tommie Smith, who famously raised their fists in a salute to black power as they received their medals for the United States in the 1968 Olympics, the French team simultaneously represented and challenged the nation," he wrote of Les Bleus' politicization and subsequent symbolism.[8] Basketball plays a similar, albeit far less tension-filled role.

Basketball Empire owes much to Dubois' work and argues that basketball, too, is deeply indebted to the country's colonial and postcolonial history. Women and men with roots in the Antilles and francophone Africa play a pivotal basketball role as athletes, coaches, referees, officials, and grassroots organizers. In this sense *Basketball Empire* treats empire as a geographic space from which France nourishes its overall game while also reinvesting and developing the African game and market.[9] But this book is also about the creation of a cultural empire. Here, the lines are blurred because it's an enterprise subtly crafted, heavily informed by American connections and the generations of US players who plied the game, and oftentimes remained, in France. Yet, over time these influences have been reworked into a "French" hoops platform and exported through players to the United States.

*   *   *

France's basketball empire is an exemplar, albeit hidden, story of the NBA's globalization. Since 1997, it's become a major pipeline for international NBA and WNBA players. No other nation outside of North America has sent more young men to the league (forty-one to date).[10] There were nine French players on October 2022 NBA opening night rosters, while in September 2022 Iliana Ruppert became the second Frenchwoman to hoist the WNBA's championship trophy. But this pipeline also supplies other rungs of the basketball spectrum, including the NCAA and the NBA's developmental G-League.

Some play team roles, while others are among the NBA's best.[11] Thus, as part of the larger European influx, the French have helped change the league's style and techniques. They're known for teamwork, passing, and technicality, including players like Minnesota Timberwolves center Rudy Gobert, who prove that the tallest players can be agile and tactically articulate. Michael Jordan, one of the game's greatest players, highlighted the ways that this cadre has contributed to the game:

> The European players have expanded the style of basketball because of the versatility they brought to the game, which I think is good for the game, which is increasing scoring . . . it forces us Americans now to play a much more rounded basketball game. That's what the European players have taught us as individuals in the States.[12]

With so many players in the league, the country has become an important commercial focus. The NBA views France as an entry point into Europe and is one of its "best" global basketball markets, according to NBA Commissioner Adam Silver.[13] France is one of the largest European marketplaces for NBA merchandise, and the second biggest subscription base for the NBA League Pass, an internet-based streaming service.[14] But the relationship deepened in October 2022, when the NBA started streaming games of French ProA club Boulogne-Levallois Metropolitans 92 (Mets 92) on League Pass to familiarize its US and global audiences with the team's young star, Victor Wembanyama. The decision was taken because this talented "unicorn" of a player was widely regarded to be among the top prospects at the June 2023 NBA Draft.[15] The resultant silver lining was that Wembanyama, as well as his teammates and the French ProA teams they competed against, gained new exposure on an NBA platform during the 2022–3 season.

It is helpful that over time the league has built a working relationship with the French Basketball Federation (Fédération Française de Basket-Ball, FFBB). There were longstanding FFBB fears in the 1990s over the NBA's potential to strip its basketball of its identity, players, and fans. Moreover, there was anxiety that television broadcasts of NBA games came at the expense of the domestic league. Today, the two bodies cooperate on a range of initiatives, including player availability for national team duty and youth programs like the Jr. NBA league, although it can at times be a complicated relationship. That's not to say that all of the French basketball establishment is open to or enamored of the US-based league; there were and likely remain critics who fear that kids' emulation of the NBA's flashier game elements will detract from the tactical, technical, and game IQ-building work needed for young players to flourish. Still, it's clear that the NBA has helped influence basketball and kids in France.

France's youth basketball system also influenced the NBA's own global elite youth development training program, the NBA Academy institution, in an interesting twenty-first-century twist. Much in the way that the country's youth football programs are recognized as top-flight, developing and exporting an astonishing number of footballers, its basketball academy system is recognized as best-in-class by industry experts.[16] Part of the formula is the feeder system that identifies promising talent and recruits youths into regional training schools, the professional clubs' youth academies, or, for the elite of the elite, the Federal Basketball Center (Centre Fédérale du Basket-Ball, CFBB) at INSEP.

Moreover, the *hexagone* is a portal for the NBA into francophone Africa, one element of the league's growing African footprint. French players with roots in Africa invest in basketball and development programs on the continent and have represented Team Africa at the NBA's Africa Game. Meanwhile, the media who cover them, notably Canal+ Afrique's Paris based coverage, help the NBA reach new audiences. In doing so they stoke greater African fandom and participation, especially in West Africa. That's translating into home-grown players and consumers, many of whom support the Basketball Africa League, the NBA's first professional league outside of North America. It's a hoops tie with deep roots for African players have long marked French courts, increasingly so in the 2000s as professional opportunities in France proliferated, notably within the Ligue Féminine de Basketball (LFB), which has attracted some of the African continent's top female hoops talent.[17] But it was not always this way.

*   *   *

When David Stern took over as NBA Commissioner in 1984, it was an era of renewal. Teams worked to overcome the fiscal insolvency that threatened to shutter the enterprise and a public image tarnished by players' perceived drug use. The league received a lifeline when Magic Johnson and Larry Bird were drafted by the Los Angeles Lakers and Boston Celtics, respectively, in 1979 and created a rivalry that injected new vivacity and relevance. The June 1984 draft class, which included future stars Jordan, Charles Barkley, and University of Houston Nigerian ace Hakeem Olajuwon, gave birth to a new NBA.[18] But a domestic renaissance alone was not enough.

Part of Stern's vision included building the NBA's global profile. There was a concerted effort to make league broadcasts available overseas to cultivate international interest. With players like Olajuwon, it seemed that there were a few foreign players who could compete and possibly attract fans and consumers from back home. One such contender under Stern's nose that summer was French wingman Hervé Dubuisson. That July and August, the star of Les Bleus led France in its first Olympic men's basketball tournament appearance since 1960. While the team failed to win a single official match at the Los Angeles Games, Dubuisson caught the attention of scouts and signed to play NBA Summer League for the New Jersey Nets, the first European-born and trained player to sign an NBA contract. But Dubuisson's American dream ended abruptly for the French season was set to begin and the Nets were unable to guarantee any future with the team.[19] "I could not take the risk," he later said of his decision to ditch a shot at the NBA.[20] Despite this storyline, France was not on Stern's radar. Instead, he focused on potential pipeline countries for players and fans like Italy, where the professional league was financially strong and attracted high-quality players.[21] Nobody could fault Stern, for France was not among the world's basketball powers, contrary to the country's rich hoops history.

Sport in France

France's basketball empire is a hidden story because the country's export emphasis on high culture—food, fashion, literature, art, cinema—obscures its role in sports. Yet, in some ways, it shouldn't be a surprise. After all, the modern Olympic movement was founded by French aristocrat Pierre de Coubertin in 1894, two years before he helped implement the modern Olympic Games. France was a founding member of FIFA in 1904, while Frenchman Jules Rimet served as its longtime president from 1921 to 1954 and launched the FIFA World Cup in 1930. Meanwhile, French Football Federation (FFF) Secretary-General Henri Delaunay, alongside *L'Équipe* editor

Gabriel Hanot, dreamed up what has become one of the world's sporting mega events, the UEFA European Championship.[22]

Yet, this footprint was disconnected from culture back home. In the late nineteenth century, physical education in schools was mandatory but predicated on the German-style calisthenics and physical culture then popular for preparing future soldiers and mothers for the nation. Coubertin, on the other hand, favored team sports like rugby and football popularized by the English public schools as more ideal for forming citizens and leaders of the empire. Similarly, he was a fierce advocate of amateurism and thus inculcated a notion that playing sports for money—professionalism—was a taint upon sports' mission to educate and form a healthy, sound body for the nation, therefore reinforcing class politics in the early promotion of sports.

The First World War began to puncture these attitudes. It became clear that physical culture wasn't best suited to prepare for modern warfare, as the dead across the fields of northern France and Belgium testified. Gymnastics and calisthenics drills didn't teach traits that the trenches required: reacting to constantly changing on-field conditions, thinking and responding quickly.[23] Moreover, football and basketball proved useful helping men to convalesce, rebuild their bodies and strength, and pass the time.

Team sports gained new currency in the post-1919 period for (re)building the national body, but Coubertin's ideal of amateurism prevailed until the 1960 Olympic Games in Rome. That summer, in front of a live television broadcast audience, French Olympians failed to live up to the image of a powerful, youthful, influential country perpetuated by President Charles de Gaulle with their twenty-fifth-place overall finish.[24] Part of the problem was that the majority of youth weren't terribly interested in sports. A leisure-orientated consumer culture geared towards the baby-boomers didn't bode well for convincing them to practice sports. Access to places to play and practice remained difficult. Moreover, the country lacked a national sports culture.[25] As basketball legend Christian Baltzer noted, "sport wasn't as important then as it is today."[26]

What's remained constant is the perception that sports can help to assimilate newer arrivals into the Republic's fabric, thus the country's sports heritage is enriched by generations of immigrants and migrants. For centuries, France has been a destination for those seeking political and religious freedom or better economic opportunities. Following the First World War, thousands of Poles arrived to help rebuild, particularly the industrial and coal-rich regions of the northeast, while Russians found refuge from the revolution back home. Italians, Spaniards, Jews and others from Central and Eastern Europe fled political and religious persecution, while post-1945 waves of Portuguese, Antilleans, and former colonial subjects from Africa and Indochina arrived in pursuit of better economic opportunities.

Thanks to *jus soli*, citizenship of the soil, if one outwardly assimilates to "French" norms in public life, then one can become French. Historically, the institutions used to forge citizens were the public schools, the military, and the transportation-communications networks that bound the country together since the 1870s.[27] Sport also played a role. The Tour de France, created in 1903, was a way for citizens, including school children, to learn about the country.[28] Team sports, especially football, the country's most popular, populous, and consumed sport, were also used to create Frenchmen and, to a lesser extent, Frenchwomen.[29] The values that sports teach are compatible with republican concepts of citizenship: meritocracy, learning to play by the rules, fair play, teamwork. Sports arguably foster community and remain one of the Republic's more democratic milieus.[30]

For those good enough to represent the country on the world stage, the act of donning the French uniform and being fêted as a national representative creates a sense of citizenship. Legendary national team and Real Madrid midfielder Raymond Kopa, the son of Polish immigrants, noted how he consecrated his sense of French identity on the field when his compatriots shortened his family name from Kopaczinski to the more French-sounding Kopa.[31] In the 1980s, midfield magician Michel Platini, the grandson of Italian immigrants, led Les Bleus to new international success, while a decade later Zinédine Zidane, whose parents were born in what was then French colonial Algeria, helped France capture its first-ever FIFA World Cup victory (1998) and second European title (2000).[32] The heroes from France's 2018 World Cup winning team reflected this background: Paul Pogba's parents are from Guinea, N'Golo Kanté's parents from Mali, and Antoine Griezmann's maternal grandfather was a Portuguese football player while his father's family originally came from Germany.[33] This rich tradition, Dubois argues, helps make France a football empire.[34] Yet despite football's appeal for the popular and immigrant classes, it remains a site of non-belonging to the larger elite cultural and opinion-making circles.[35] That's why the country's immigration and migration patterns enriched basketball in markedly different ways.

Towards a New Type of Empire

France's basketball empire is founded on Franco-American, Franco-Antillean, and Franco-African pillars, but hinges on an openness to outside cultural influences and, subsequently, the impacts of sports diplomacy. French culture has been shaped by numerous outside ideas and influences derived from its centuries-long status as a crossroads of peoples from around the world. While it can at times be insular, French culture has flourished by taking a foreign cultural construct, reworking it, and exporting it as something identifiably French.[36] Musicians Serge Gainsbourg and Johnny Halliday were heavily influenced by American blues, jazz, and rock 'n' roll.[37] The horn-shaped Austrian *kipfel* roll was transformed by nineteenth-century pastry chefs into the ethereal croissant.[38] Thus, it's no surprise that recent scholarship builds out a more decentralized approach to older narratives to show the role of global contacts and cultural exchanges.[39]

Sports are no different. INSEP, a centralized statist approach, was influenced by the East German and Soviet models, designed to rectify the sports crisis by providing training facilities, technical experts, schooling, and other support for the country's elite and aspiring young athletes.[40] The FFF's famed football training academy at Clairefontaine was molded by Romanian coach Stéfan Kovacs who, from 1973 to 1975, served as manager of Les Bleus.[41] Replicated in slightly different ways by the FFF's professional clubs into an academy structure, the French system is long known to produce and export high-caliber talent.[42] Others have copied the French blueprint, and the FFF is engaged in exporting its hard-won savvy, teaching other national federations how to train coaches and players *à la française*.

Basketball similarly profited from global contacts and cultural exchanges. The CFBB is influenced by the same European roots as INSEP but also by the tactics, techniques, and athletic style of play that's infused French basketball in recent generations. Professional club youth academies also turn out talent exported to some of the world's elite leagues, including the NBA and EuroLeague, while the French style of play has earned Les Bleus the moniker "the United States of European basketball" for their ability to adopt and spin an American-inflected fast, aerodynamic game.

That's why sports diplomacy, the cultural, knowledge, and technical exchange between France and other countries in and around the arena, provides a vital framework for this story. The intersection of the sports world with the diplomatic one, sports diplomacy, is best understood as the communication, representation, and negotiation that occurs in and around the sports arena.[43] Traditionally, sports diplomacy is understood as being conducted by governments or government representatives, but today it's the far more visible form of nontraditional sports diplomacy, that undertaken by a wide range of non-government actors, that also facilitates international sport.[44] That's to say, when everyday citizens within the global sports industry engage in cultural, technical, or knowledge exchange, they blur the line between diplomat and sportsperson and engage in a form of citizen diplomacy.[45] Thus, the role of individuals in informal sports diplomacy plays an outsized role in France's basketball empire.

The intersection of sport and diplomacy has a deep history. The emergence of fin-de-siècle international competitions centered on bringing athletes together to celebrate peace and unity but the sports world emerged from the Great War democratized and increasingly politicized. Benito Mussolini and Adolf Hitler both harnessed the growing influential soft power of sports success and hosting sporting events like the FIFA World Cup (Italy, 1934) and Olympics (Germany, 1936) as ways to broadcast the triumph of fascist ideology in the 1930s.[46]

But things were different after 1945. Nations increasingly utilized sport for a range of goals, including solidifying regime or ideological legitimacy or supremacy to currying political favor.[47] What differed in the postwar era was not just how many more governments latched onto sport for a variety of foreign and domestic reasons, but also how much athletic victory could inform global public opinion. It could do so because sports were amplified by technology breakthroughs, increased dissemination of television broadcasts and, in the 1960s, satellite transmission.[48] As a result, countries sought to cultivate foreign public opinion through sports.[49]

It wasn't just nation-states that recognized the viability of sports as a tool of persuasion; international governing federations also seized on their newfound status. After 1945, many of the largest sports federations reorganized, independent of the bipolar polemics of East–West, and thus gained new degrees of autonomy from the larger diplomatic transformations that shaped geopolitics, such as FIFA, which became a different kind of diplomatic ecosystem.[50]

Alongside this change, a new era of public diplomacy provided athletes with the power to serve as diplomatic ambassadors, representing their country and sport to the world at large. Countries integrated sports into their diplomatic toolboxes through cultural exchanges of teams and coaches in the late 1950s and 1960s. The United States dispatched some of its best-known African American athletes to represent the country and dispel public opinion about its racial segregation and discrimination. Such attempts by the US Department of State tried to illustrate how the Civil Rights Movement forced change, albeit slowly.[51] More broadly, the United States sought to culturally contain the Soviet Union through sports.[52] France also attempted to harness the potential of sport. Yet, soft power success was often evasive given the sport crisis of the 1960s and 1970s in which elite athletes failed to capture major international accolades.[53]

Within this context, formal basketball diplomacy played an ever-more important role. The US–USSR rivalry was deescalated by basketball exchanges but these were not purely neutral endeavours. US basketball Cold War supremacy was perceived to be in decline and its 1972 Olympic gold medal loss to the USSR, set against the context of the controversial Vietnam War, illustrated the erosion of the US game, its pride, masculinity, influence in the game, and the wider world.[54] The Fifth Republic also used formal basketball diplomacy. Paris cemented its 1964 opening of diplomatic relations with Beijing by sending its men's team to China for a two-week tour at the height of the Cultural Revolution in summer 1966, one of the first Western national sides to do so since 1949.[55]

But France's basketball empire owes far more to the informal sports diplomacy fostered by the Franco-American relationship. It's a little surprising for this form of cultural, technical, and knowledge exchange relies on individual people-to-people interactions and, despite ties dating to the 1770s, the two nations have no mass immigration history. Yet, generations crisscrossed the Atlantic in discovery of one another. It is this mythic ethos of "America" for the French, and "la belle France" for Americans that forged symbolic, formative experiences and migrant stories of transformation.

Pivotal figures left France to explore "America" over the centuries and brought certain "American" ideas and practices back home. This included Alexis de Tocqueville in the 1830s and Simone de Beauvoir in the late 1940s. More recently, Parker and Batum, who arrived as nineteen-year-olds to chase their NBA dreams, illustrate the continuity of this *rapport*.

There was little migration in the opposite direction until the Great War changed the dynamic.[56] For the first time, large numbers of young American men and women went to France to serve in the military and medical corps and got to know everyday French people on an intimate basis thanks to wartime duties. Their first-hand experiences, as well as the thousands of letters they wrote home detailing their new lives, introduced many more everyday Americans to France and the French in new ways, delving more deeply than the stereotypes fostered by business, fashion, food, and art. Many remained after demobilization in 1918–19 and many more arrived during the 1920s and 1930s as the comparatively lower cost of living in France allowed a better lifestyle than back home. Among them was an expatriate colony of writers, musicians, and artists that included Ernest Hemingway and F. Scott Fitzgerald. Another wave of Americans flooded back to France after the German defeat of 1945.

Despite a propensity towards attraction and admiration, this relationship is also one of critique and contempt, based at different points in time in an asymmetry between the two countries. Through the 1910s, France arguably had the upper hand in world affairs and cultural dominance, but the tables turned in the first half of the twentieth century. In the post-1945 era, there's a sense that for the French, US culture is alluring, especially for the youth, but that Americanization, whether of processes, institutions, or business, is not. Conversely, Americans view French culture as exotic and full of the allure of freedom, even if in reality that's not exactly the case. And there's also a sense of US condescension toward French sport, which helps to explain why the NBA's internationalization and globalization via the French market is often overlooked. Through it all, informal basketball diplomacy has bridged the gap.

Another factor in this basketball empire is France's role as a longtime beacon for African Americans who, since the 1840s, found greater freedom as expatriates in the *hexagone* than back home.[57] France and the urbane center of Paris provided greater cultural and intellectual freedom for Black Americans than back home where Jim Crow laws stultified and stigmatized.[58] In France, such barriers did not exist—or at least, that was what was communicated about interactions with the French. Black Americans' experience of respectful treatment by local French Caucasians provided expatriates with an unprecedented sense of liberation and belief that they were treated better.[59] Reality, however, was sometimes different, for many did not write home about the subtle racisms they encountered, thus lending credence to a color-blind French myth that became popular within Black American culture.[60] Regardless, cultural arbitrators from music, art, dance, and other *milieus* garnered new-found success in France, including writer James Baldwin, dancer Josephine Baker, intellectual W.E.B. DuBois, and jazz musician James Reece Europe, thus leaving their imprint on the Black American idea of France.[61]

Sports, too, were an area where Black Americans found success in France. While these athletes' experiences and their mark on sports culture are overlooked by scholars, a few known examples shed light on this complex equation. Take Major Taylor, one of the first global African American sports celebrities who in the early twentieth century captured imaginations, hearts, and records as a speed cyclist.[62] Taylor was a winner on the track yet found that the French viewed him as curiously "different," treated well but one of the few Black people, aside from Chocolat the clown, circulating in society at the time. French media coverage painted the cyclist as having a leg up on the Caucasian competition, a reference to the era's stereotypes about Black athletes' physical dominance but lesser intellect.[63]

As impressive as Taylor's accomplishments were, he was a visitor and never formed a deep attachment to France the way that others did. Two US consuls better illustrate the role and rapport between African Americans and French sport. The late nineteenth and early twentieth century was an epoch where African Americans made progress and entered the diplomatic rungs of the US Department of State, even as their civil rights declined, and a small number were dispatched to France.[64] Dr. George Henry Jackson arrived in La Rochelle to serve as US consul in 1898 and played an integral role developing and presiding (1904–11) over rugby club Stade

Rochelais.[65] Nearly a decade later, another African American consul, William H. Hunt, made his mark. During his tenure in St. Étienne (1907–27), Hunt was president of local rugby side Racing Club Stéphanois and used sports to integrate into and become part of the local community.[66] Jackson and Hunt used what we would now call sports diplomacy as a way to connect with local constituents and become part of the community.[67]

In the post-1945 period, its basketball, not rugby, that's served as a beacon for subsequent generations of Black Americans to pursue their passions and livelihoods in France. Today this basketball diplomacy framework has helped turn the tables for French NBA and WNBA players now teach their French fans about the leagues and US culture. They serve as informal ambassadors of France in the United States, and representatives of the WNBA and NBA to France, roles that they did not volunteer for, but which most of them understand and seek to fulfill. As Parker relayed to *L'Équipe*,

I always took this role [of representing France, of being an unofficial ambassador] very seriously to be sure that France was well represented in the United States. I always had this idea, to show Americans that the French know how to play basketball.[68]

The French–African and French–Antillean connections have also played decisive roles in creating this hoops empire in numerous ways. First and foremost, it counterbalanced US cultural basketball imperialism. One of the reasons why then-FFBB president Robert Busnel could promote US-style basketball techniques and practices as he sought to revitalize basketball during the Cold War was that, from a foreign perspective, the US game was intimately tied to African Americans.[69] After all, the most celebrated US basketball team on earth from 1950 until perhaps the 1980s was the Harlem Globetrotters, the first entirely Black basketball club to tour France. Thus French basketball's embrace of Black players, whether they were African Americans, from the *métropole*, or the empire (and after 1960, the former empire), was a way to counter the optical problem of appearing too close to the Americanization of basketball.[70] So, while basketball wasn't unique in its embrace of players of color, its reasoning for doing so was perhaps more singular.

The former empire helped France counterbalance US influence in international sport in other ways. During the 1960s, France worked with its former African assets to grow and retain the *métropole*'s soft power reserves.[71] But it also harnessed the sports diplomacy framework to build a francophone bloc as a way for Paris to contest Washington's cultural supremacy, especially via the Olympic movement.[72] Thus the tensions over US cultural imperialism played out within the French sports world to basketball's ultimate benefit.

Basketball Empire is the story of the NBA's internationalization and globalization through one exemplar market, as well as the impact of French players on broadening and diversifying the WNBA. It is not a story of Americanization of basketball; rather it is the story of France's response to globalization. *Basketball Empire* is also a "window" into how France built a new position in the twenty-first century world order through the soft power and cultural cachet of sports diplomacy. Although the "Made in France" model popularized through football is more widely known, *Basketball Empire* demonstrates that the hoops version is more intertwined in today's globalized world and the symbol of France's sustainable future.

*   *   *

Diaw noted in 2017, "a lot of people [in the United States] don't even know we play basketball in France."[73] This book seeks to rectify this popular misunderstanding. *Basketball Empire* takes a chronological approach to establish the key characters, plotlines, and events that mold this story. But because it is such a recent story, one that features the role of the individual in sports diplomacy, it is the story as told through the lens of players past and present whose international experiences bring *Basketball Empire*'s themes into greater relief.

The roadmap is divided into three sections. Part One focuses on the foundations set primarily in France as transnational forces reshaped the country's basketball, systems, style, and results. Each chapter uses the experience of French and American voices to build a portrait of these transformative evolutions, denoting how cultural, technical, and knowledge exchange through the sport set the stage for France in its most global sense to become a basketball breeding ground, even if they didn't capture the media spotlight.

Part Two centers upon the twenty-first-century French experience in the United States, taking a deeper dive into how individual players engaged in informal sports diplomacy because of their professional (or collegiate) careers. These stories illustrate the different pillars at work within the basketball empire, and the intergenerational cultural, technical, and knowledge exchange gained from living US hoops dreams that's impacted French basketball.

Part Three puts the basketball empire into the global context. It delves more deeply into the themes at work since the 2010s that help to explain the global impact and appeal of the NBA and WNBA as told through the French example and its US, African, and Antillean pillars. This includes a look at how French and African basketball have long "rubbed shoulders" in inextricably linked ways, which feeds into the NBA's own Africa-centric efforts, like the Basketball Africa League. It picks apart the twenty-first-century growth and appeal of the NBA in France and also delves into how the transformations at work in *Basketball Empire* led to the creation of a budding basketball rivalry between France and the United States with a focus on the national teams' competitions.

The epilogue centers on the NBA's return to Paris in January 2023, teasing out implications of *Basketball Empire*'s findings for the forthcoming 2024 Paris Olympics and the 2028 Los Angeles Olympics in the run-up to the 250th anniversary of the official Franco-American alliance that year. While *Basketball Empire* crescendos with these two significant Olympiads for the French–American story, it is an ever-green story that shows no signs of slowing down, as each year's NBA and WNBA drafts include newer generations of French basketballers eager to live their own hoop dreams.

Notes

1 Yann Ohnona, "Jean-François Martins: 'La NBA à Paris ? Un Événemenet d'Envergure Mondiale,'" *L'Équipe*, March 28, 2019, https://www.lequipe.fr/Basket/Actualites/Jean-francois-martins-la-nba-a-paris-un-evenement-d-envergure-mondiale/1003274.

2 "Nicolas Batum: 'L'ASVEL, la Future Salle, Tony Parker, l'Équipe de France, l'Interview Vérité," *Le Progress*, March 23, 2019, https://www.leprogres.fr/rhone-69-sport/2019/03/23/nicolas-batum-l-asvel-la-future-salle-tony-parker-l-equipe-de-france-l-interview-verite; Nick Friedman, "Record Overall Eastern Western," n.d., 23.

3   Rick Bonnell, "How Hornets Forward Nic Batum Faced His Father's Death and His Own Fear of Dying Young," *Charlotte Observer*, January 21, 2020, https://www.charlotteobserver.com/sports/charlotte-hornets/article239440933.html.

4   Bonnell.

5   Yann Ohnona, "Nicolas Batum, Ailier Des Bleus: 'Un Changement d'Ère,'" *L'Équipe*, January 22, 2020, https://www.lequipe.fr/Basket/Article/Nicolas-batum-ailier-des-bleus-un-changement-d-ere/1101550.

6   Eric Michel and Julien Lesage, "Nicolas Batum: 'J'ai Vu Mon Premier Match NBA à Paris,'" *Le Parisien*, January 22, 2020.

7   Michel and Lesage.

8   Laurent Dubois, *Soccer Empire: The World Cup and the Future of France* (University of California Press, 2010), 3–4 (23–24 in ebook).

9   As Nico Bésnier argues, these migratory lines are much more complex than a postcolonial power taking and profiting from their former empires. Niko Besnier, "Sports Mobilities Across Borders: Postcolonial Perspectives," *The International Journal of the History of Sport*, 32, no. 7 (May 3, 2015): 854.

10 NBA International to Krasnoff, "All-Time International NBA Players," July 2022.

11 As Silver noted, "they are disproportionately represented based on their population in the NBA . . . as you all know, we have some of our very best players who are from France." NBA International, "Transcript: NBA Pairs Game 2020 Press Conference" (NBA Communications, January 24, 2020), https://mediacentral.nba.com/transcript-nba-paris-game-2020-press-conference/.

12 "Transcript: NBA Paris Game 2020 Press Conference" (NBA Communications, January 24, 2020), https://mediacentral.nba.com/transcript-nba-paris-game-2020-press-conference/.

13 See NBA International, "Transcript: NBA Pairs Game 2020 Press Conference" and Ohnona, "Jean-François Martins."

14 Patrick Murray, "Why Is the NBA Headed for Paris This Week?," *Forbes*, January 21, 2020, https://www.forbes.com/sites/patrickmurray/2020/01/21/why-is-the-nba-headed-for-paris-this-week/#73a2bed711ee.

15 Tatum, Written interview for the author, via email, December 27, 2022.

16 Lindsay Sarah Krasnoff, "Made in France: How 52 Players Born in a Single Country Made It to the World Cup," *The Athletic*, June 24,

2018, https://theathletic.com/406527/2018/06/24/made-in-france-how-52-players-born-in-a-single-country-made-it-to-the-world-cup/.

17 FIBA, "African Women Creating a Legacy in France," FIBA. basketball, October 7, 2020, http://www.fiba.basketball/news/african-women-creating-a-legacy-in-france.

18 Filip Bondy, *Tip Off: How the 1984 NBA Draft Changed Basketball Forever* (Da Capo Press, 2007), x.

19 Dubuisson was under contract with Parisian club Stade Français.

20 Maxime Malet, "L'histoire des Français en NBA: Les Pionnieres Entre Rêves et Rendez-Vous Manqués," *L'Équipe*, January 23, 2020, https://www.lequipe.fr/Basket/Article/Les-pionniers-francais-en-nba-entre-reves-et-rendez-vous-manques/1100905.

21 David Stern, Interview with the author, telephone, March 17, 2016.

22 Although Delaunay first conceived of a pan-European national team competition in 1927, the tournament was not implemented until 1960, five years after his death, when it was hosted in France. For more, see UEFA.com, "EURO 1960."

23 For more, see Lindsay Sarah Krasnoff, "How the Great War Made Soccer the World's Most Popular Sport—and Led to Its First Viral Moment," *The Athletic*, November 16, 2018, https://theathletic.com/653722/2018/11/16/how-the-great-war-made-soccer-the-worlds-most-popular-sport-and-led-to-its-first-viral-moment/.

24 Lindsay Sarah Krasnoff, *The Making of Les Bleus: Sport in France, 1958–2010* (Lexington Books, 2012).

25 For more on youth, sports, and government initiatives of the 1960s, see Krasnoff, *The Making of Les Bleus*; Jobs, *Riding the New Wave*.

26 Baltzer, Interview with Christian Baltzer, April 18, 2017.

27 Eugen Weber, *Peasants into Frenchmen: The Modernization of Rural France, 1870–1914* (Stanford University Press, 1976).

28 Christopher S. Thompson, *The Tour de France: A Cultural History* (University of California Press, 2006).

29 The first official women's football match in France occurred in 1917. Although more Frenchwomen began to play in the 1920s and 1930s, the game was prohibited by the Vichy Government after 1940 and thus fell out of favor until its revival in the late 1960s and 1970s. As a result, there have been comparatively few Frenchwomen who played football, although that is starting to change in the 2010s and 2020s. For more see Krasnoff, "The Up-Front Legacies of France 2019"; Laurence Prudhomme-Poncet, *Histoire Du Football Féminin au XXe Siècle* (L'Harmattan, 2003).

30 Lindsay Sarah Krasnoff, "How Football Offers Hope for France," *CNN International*, November 16, 2015, https://edition.cnn.com/2015/03/11/football/charlie-hebdo-france-football/index.html.

31 Raymond Kopa, *Mes Matches et Ma Vie* (P. Horay, 1958), 129.

32 For more on Zinédine Zidane and his family's connections with Algeria, see Dubois, *Soccer Empire: The World Cup and the Future of France*; Yvan Gastaut and Steven Apostolov, "Zinedine Zidane's Return to the Land of His Ancestors: Politics, Diplomacy or Something Else?" *Soccer & Society*, 15, 2014, 685–95.

33 In the aftermath of the 2015–16 terrorist attacks that strafed French society, French rapper Black M, with family ties to Senegal, released a song that celebrated France's varied immigrant and double-culture background. The video, "Je Suis Chez Moi," featured prominent cultural icons who, although they identify as "French," boast a double-culture thanks to their family immigrant history including comedian Gad Elmalah and Griezmann.

34 Dubois, *Soccer Empire*.

35 See Stéphane Beaud, "'Le football est le sport des classes populaires'" (Le Cavalier Bleu, 2019); Stéphane Beaud and Frédéric Rasera, "Introduction," *Repères*, 2020, 3–6.

36 Such was the case with the tourism industry, and how French hoteliers were trained in postwar American hotel tastes and expectations, then returned home and worked these realities into their own concept of hospitality, becoming the number one destination for American tourists and the world. For more see Elizabeth Becker, *Overbooked: The Exploding Business of Travel and Tourism* (Simon & Schuster, 2013).

37 Yves Bigot, *Je t'aime, Moi Non plus. Les Amours de La Chanson: Les Amours de la Chanson Française et du Rock* (Don Quichotte, 2016).

38 Jim Chevalier, *August Zang and the French Croissant: How Viennoiserie Came to France* (Chez Jim Books, 2010); Lawrence R. Schehr and Allen S. Weiss, *French Food: On the Table, on the Page, and in French Culture* (Routledge, 2013).

39 See Pascal Blanchard, Sandrine Lemaire, Nicolas Bancel, and Dominic Thomas (eds.), *Colonial Culture in France Since the Revolution* (Indiana University Press, 2013); Patrick Boucheron and Stéphane Gerson, *France in the World: A New Global History* (Other Press, 2019).

40 Krasnoff, *The Making of Les Bleus*.

41 Krasnoff, *The Making of Les Bleus*.

42 Krasnoff, "Made in France."

43 J. Simon Rofe, *Sport and Diplomacy: Games within Games* (Manchester University Press, 2019), https://doi.org/10.7228/manchester/9781526131058.001.0001.

44 For more, see Stuart Murray, *Sports Diplomacy: Origins, Theory and Practice*; Stuart Murray and Geoffrey Pigman, "Mapping the Relationship between International Sport and Diplomacy," *Sport in Society*, 17, no. 9, October 21, 2014, 1098–118.

45 For more, see Murray and Pigman, "Mapping the Relationship between International Sport and Diplomacy"; Geoffrey Pigman, "International Sport and Diplomacy's Public Dimension: Governments, Sporting Federations and the Global Audience," *Diplomacy & Statecraft*, 25, no. 1 (2014): 94–114.

46 As Barbara Keys notes, there's a distinction between sports as global events and as a state's mobilization. See Keys, *The Ideals of Global Sport: From Peace to Human Rights*.

47 Robert Edelman and Christopher J. Young, *The Whole World Was Watching: Sport in the Cold War* (Stanford University Press, 2019).

48 For more on the impact of television on the Olympics and the image of sports in and after 1960, see David Mariniss, *Rome 1960: The Olympics that Changed the World* (Simon & Schuster, 2008); Robert Edelman, Alan Tomlinson, and Christopher J. Young (eds.), *Sport and the Transformation of Modern Europe: States, Media and Markets, 1950–2010* (Routledge, 2011); and David Hand and Liz Crolley (eds.), *Football, Europe and the Press* (Routledge, 2013).

49 For more, see Edelman and Young.

50 Grégory Quinn, Nicola Sbetti, and Philippe Vonnard, "FIFA's Reconstruction after the Second World War: A Matter of Diplomacy?" (Sport & Diplomacy: Message, Mode and Metaphor, SOAS University of London, 2015), 3.

51 Damion L. Thomas, *Globetrotting: African American Athletes and Cold War Politics* (University of Illinois Press, 2012).

52 Jérôme Gygax, "Diplomatie culturelle et sportive américaine : persuasion et propagande durant la Guerre froide," *Relations internationales*, 123, no. 3 (2005): 87–88.

53 The few exceptions were in swimming, skiing, and track and field, where French athletes like Jean-Claude Killy and Michel Jazy brought home hardware.

54 Kevin B. Witherspoon, "'Fuzz Kids' and 'Musclemen': The US–Soviet Basketball Rivalry, 1958–1972" in Heather Dichter and Andrew L.

Johns, *Diplomatic Games: Sport, Statecraft, and International Relations since 1945* (University of Kentucky Press, 2014); For more on the United States' use of basketball in the Cold War, especially via the Harlem Globetrotters, see Fabien Archambault, "La politique des bloc(k)s," *Materiaux pour l'histoire de notre temps*, 106: 2, October 2012, 33–9; Archambault, "Tournées Des Harlem Globetrotters en Europe dans la Seconde Moitié Du XXe Siècle (Les), in *Encyclopédie pour une histoire nouvelle de l'Éurope*, https://ehne.fr/article/civilisation-materielle/circulations-sportives-europeennes/les-tournees-des-harlem-globetrotters-en-europe-dans-la-seconde-moitie-du-xxe-siecle."

55 Lindsay Sarah Krasnoff, "Rétro 1966 et 1980 Les Bleus En Chine: Basket, Propagand, et Diplomatie," *Basket Le Mag*, September 2019.

56 While some nineteenth-century Americans traveled to France as part of the Grand Tour or for Parisian fashions, it was not until after 1880 that more arrived on French shores, particularly artists, students, and businessmen, and played critical roles in exporting back to the United States certain ideas of France. For more, see Nancy L. Green, *The Other Americans in Paris: Businessmen, Countesses, Wayward Youth, 1880–1941* (University of Chicago Press, 2014)

57 For more on the American expatriate experience in France see Green, *The Other Americans in Paris*; Ronald Weber, *News of Paris: American Journalists in the City of Light Between the Wars* (Ivan Dee, 2006); and Michel Fabre, *La rive noire: les écrivains noirs américains à Paris, 1830–1995* (A. Dimanche, 1999).

58 Bettye J. Gardner and Niani Kilkenny, "In Vogue: Josephine Baker and Black Culture and Identity in the Jazz Age," *The Journal of African American History*, 93, no. 1 (Winter, 2008), 89. Also see Tyler Stovall, *Paris Noir: African Americans in the City of Light* (Houghton Mifflin, 1996).

59 Stovall, *Paris Noir*, xiii.

60 Rached Gillett, "Jazz and the Evolution of Black American Cosmopolitanism in Interwar Paris," *Journal of World History*, Cosmopolitanism in World History, 21, no. 3 (September 2010): 472.

61 For more on the Black American experience in Paris and France, see Stovall, *Paris Noir*; Trica Danielle Keaton, T. Denean Sharpley-Whiting, and Tyler Stovall (eds.), *Black France / France Noire: The History and Politics of Blackness* (Duke University Press, 2012); Michel Fabre, *La Rive Noire: les écrivains noirs américains à Paris, 1830–1995* (A. Dimanche, 1999) ; James Campbell, *Americans Exiled in Paris: Richard Wright, James Baldwin, Samuel Beckett and Others on the Left Bank* (Scribner, 1995); Rashida K. Braggs, *Jazz Diasporas:*

Race, Music, and Migration in Post-World War II Paris (University of California Press, 2016); and T. Denean Sharpley-Whiting, *Bricktop's Paris: African American Women in Paris between the two World Wars* (SUNY Press, 2015).

62 For more on Major Taylor, see Major Taylor, *The Fastest Bicycle Rider in the World: The Autobiography of Major Taylor* (S. Greene Press, 1972); Andrew Ritchie, *Major Taylor: the Extraordinary Career of a Champion Bicycle Racer* (Johns Hopkins University Press, 1996); and Todd Balf, *Major: A Black Athlete, a White Era, and the Fight to Be the World's Fastest Human Being* (Crown Publishers, 2008).

63 Michael Kranish, *The World's Fastest Man: The Extraordinary Life of Cyclist Major Taylor* (Scribner & Sons, 2019), 167.

64 The administrations of William McKinley, Theodore Roosevelt, and William Taft promoted Black Americans into what was then the US Bureau of Consular Service. Between 1880 and 1920, some 50 Black Americans were assigned as US Consuls overseas, although the majority were appointed to posts in the Global South. See Justesen, "African-American Consuls Abroad, 1897–1909," 72.

65 Today, the Stade Rochelais' Marcel Deflandre stadium has a grandstand dedicated to Jackson in honor of his service to the club. See Lindsay Sarah Krasnoff, "Spotlight on George H. Jackson," Office of the Historian Tumblr, US Department of State, February 2015, https://historyatstate.tumblr.com/post/112149978083/spotlight-on-dr-george-henry-jackson; "Histoire du Club" Stade Rochelais, https://www.staderochelais.com/club/histoire/histoire-du-club.

66 Hunt was the long-serving president of Rugby Club Lindsay Sarah Krasnoff, "The Ruby-Loving US Consul at St. Étienne," *Huffington Post*, February 27, 2015. https://www.huffpost.com/entry/the-rugbyloving-us-consul_b_6764064 For more on William H. Hunt, see Adele L. Alexander, *Parallel Worlds: The Remarkable Gibbs-Hunts and the Enduring (In)significance of Melanin* (University of Virginia Press, 2012); and Lindsay Sarah Krasnoff, "Views from the Embassy: The Role of the US Diplomatic Community in France, 1914–1917," US Department of State, Washington DC, 2014. https://history.state.gov/departmenthistory/wwi

67 At the time, rugby was a sport of the elites and perceived to build strong bodies, strengthen minds, and build character, part of the "muscular Christianity" belief that sports prepared young men to be future leaders. Cycling, on the other hand, was one of the earliest sports to professionalize in France and thus tainted with money in a society that long clung to Pierre de Coubertin's ideals of sports amateurism. The discrepancy in images between the two, one of the

elite amateurs the other of the lower-class professionals, was also likely a factor in how and why Taylor was viewed through different lenses than Jackson or Hunt.

68 Xavier Colombani, "Tony Parker : 'Il y a Un Vrai Amour de La NBA En France,'" *L'Équipe*, January 23, 2020, https://www.lequipe.fr/Basket/Actualites/Tony-parker-il-y-a-un-vrai-amour-de-la-nba-en-france/1101881.

69 Archambault, "Tournées des Harlem Globetrotters en Europe dans la Seconde Moitié du XXe Siècle (Les)."

70 Archambault, "Tournées des Harlem Globetrotters en Europe dans la Seconde Moitié du XXe Siècle (Les)." Also see Archambault, "La politique des bloc(k)s."

71 Pascal Charitas, "A More Flexible Domination: Franco-African Sport Diplomacy during Decolonization, 1945–1966," in *Diplomatic Games: Sport, Statecraft, and International Relations since 1945*, ed. Heather L. Dichter and Andrew L. Johns (University of Kentucky Press, n.d.).

72 Pascal Charitas and David-Claude Kemo-Keimbou, "The United States of America and the Francophone African Countries at the International Olympic Committee: Sports Aid, a Barometer of American Imperialism? (1952–1963)," *Journal of Sport History* 40, no. 1 (2013): 69–91.

73 Diaw, Interview with the author, February 26, 2017.

Prologue

Each summer, with the iconic Eiffel Tower in the backdrop, thousands gather in Paris for what has become the world's largest outdoor basketball festival. Since 2003, Quai 54 has served up a high-energy street basketball tournament that blends music, fashion, art, and entertainment as amateurs and professionals alike gather to play and enjoy the game. Influenced by the famed Rucker Park, New York street ball, as well as a dose of francophone African culture, and in partnership with Jordan Brand, it celebrates the best of the global game, including a globally inspired hoops identity. In July 2022, France's iCanPlay team snagged top honors with its women's tournament victory; the winners were treated to a short trip to New York to absorb the city's hoops culture first-hand.

This portrait of basketball is vastly different from its fledgling origins, for the game was not terribly popular in twentieth-century France. Invented in December 1891 by James Naismith, a Canadian-born educator at Springfield College, which was then affiliated with the Young Men's Christian Association (YMCA), a Protestant-oriented educational organization, basketball was born global.[1] Two years later, twenty-two-year-old Melvin Rideout, one of Naismith's original basketball players, introduced the game to Paris, and by 1900, Rideout's former classmates brought the game to Brazil, Australia, and China, among others.

Basketball's early association with the YMCA hindered its appeal during an era of intense public discourse about the role of religion in public French life. The controversy led to the 1905 Emile Combes Law that established *laïcité*. While *laïcité* does not have an exact translation in English, it is a form of secularism in which the

official public religion is that of the republican state.[2] Basketball
was thus stigmatized.[3]

The Great War changed the sport's fortunes. The arrival of
basketball-playing US doughboys in 1917–18, nicknamed
"Sammies," infused the game with a certain sense of cultural
modernity while also introducing locals more broadly to US sports
culture.[4] During the interwar period, it was embraced by the
schools, particularly the ecclesiastical schools, as a tool to develop
healthy bodies, thus the sport was stigmatized anew in a laic era.
Basketball was used by the military to rebuild bodies devastated by
years of trench warfare. It was also viewed as good for women and
girls to strengthen bodies while maintaining an idealized feminine
grace and morality thanks to its non-violent, non-contact traits.[5]
Thus since the 1920s, basketball is viewed as an educational tool,
whereas football after its 1932 professionalization is regarded as an
economic endeavor.

Class attitudes towards basketball have long marked its place in
French culture. The sport was played by the middle classes and
those in the provincial cities and towns, especially in southwest
and western regions, a byproduct of its post-1919 development.
It was thus well regarded by opinion-makers and elites, including
government officials, who celebrated the national teams'
performances on the international stage.

Despite basketball's lofty status, it remains a "closeted" sport,
meaning that it lacks media visibility. As early as the 1890s, local
media covered basketball, but it was quickly overshadowed by
other commercially driven sports.[6] L'Équipe's success in the 1950s
and 1960s, for instance, was driven by the commercialization of
professional football (as well as cycling).[7] Basketball, in contrast,
did not professionalize until 1987.

From its very beginnings, Gallic basketball has had an intimate
bond with the United States. Construction of the YMCA's Parisian
outpost, completed May 7, 1893, contained an exact replica of
the basketball court used in Springfield, Massachusetts, the first
hoops-specific structure outside of that hallowed hall.[8] The deep-
seated friendship and symbolism of the Marquis de Lafayette
and the Statue of Liberty, a gift by the people of France to the
United States in 1885, was part of the original motivation for why
American YMCA educators justified their interest in and work
with France.[9]

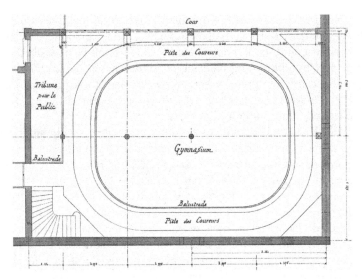

FIGURE P.1 *YMCA Paris gym plan, 1892, revised 2020. Design of the world's oldest existing basketball court at the Paris YMCA on Rue de Trévise. Credit: Association YMCA Paris Archives.*

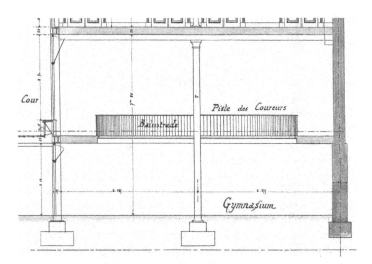

FIGURE P.2 *YMCA Paris gym plan, 1892, revised 2020. Design of the world's oldest existing basketball court at the Paris YMCA on Rue de Trévise. Credit: Association YMCA Paris Archives.*

Even in the early years, individuals played a critical role fostering Franco-American basketball diplomacy. Rideout introduced tactics, techniques, and game know-how, as did the influx of basketball-playing US military and medical personnel in 1917–18.[10] The first organized international basketball tournament took place in June 1919 as part of the Inter-Allied Games and featured three teams: the United States, Italy, and France.

Then basketball lost a bit of its cultural association with the United States. It was appropriated by the French during the interwar period, no longer considered American as rivaling Catholic factions embraced the sport as part of their youth outreach.[11] French rules vied for dominance across Europe while the *ripopo* style of play developed.[12] Coined by *L'Auto* journalist Robert Perrier, *ripopo* constituted an unbridled, inconsistent style of passing game that neglected the balance of a floor game.[13] Perhaps *ripopo* wasn't a surprising style, for at the same time journalists began to describe the style of football played by the French as "football champagne" for its effervescence, lightness, and spontaneity despite its seemingly complicated passes.[14]

The return of American G.I.s in 1944–5 ushered in a renewed interest, but the French game remained markedly different from its *ami américain* until the American, Antillean, and African pillars that fueled its revitalization and return to international relevancy began to change the game.

Notes

1 Lindsay Sarah Krasnoff, "How the NBA Went Global," *Washington Post*, accessed November 28, 2020, https://www.washingtonpost.com/news/made-by-history/wp/2017/12/26/how-the-nba-went-global/.

2 The idea was first ushered in by the revolutionaries of 1789 who broke the Catholic church's centuries-long chokehold on power, but coined during the 1870s under the Third Republic. For more on *laïcité*, see Jean Bauberot, *Laïcité, 1905–2005, Entre Passion et Raison* (Paris: Seuil, 2004); France was not the only Western European country to go through bitter public debate over the role of religion in official public life of the state in the early twentieth century; Italy, Spain, and Portugal also endured similar fights for laic secularism.

3 Fabien Archambault, Loic Artiaga, and Gérard Bosc (eds.), *Le Continent Basket: L'Éurope et Le Basket-Ball Au XXème Siècle* (Peter Lang, 2015).

4 For more, see Fabien Archambault and Loic Artiaga, "Introduction: Balle au panier et impérialisme boomerang," in Archambault, Artiaga, Pierre-Yves Frey (eds.), *L'Aventure des "grands" hommes: Études sur l'histoire du basket-ball* (Limoges: Presses Universitaires de Limoges, 2003).

5 For more on what was, and was not, viewed as idea for Frenchwomen's bodies under the Third Republic, see Mary Lynn Stewart, *For Health and Beauty: Physical Culture for Frenchwomen, 1880s–1930s* (Cambridge University Press, 2001).

6 See Gérard Bosc, "L'apparition du basket en France (et en Europe) à la fin du XIXe siècle," in Fabien Archambault, Loic Artiaga, and Pierre-Yves Fray (eds.), *L'Aventure des "grands" hommes* (Presses Universitaires de Limoges, 2003).

7 Gilles Montérémal, "L'Équipe: Médiateur et Producteur de Spectacle Sportif (1946–1967)," *Le Temps Des Médias*, no. 9 (February 2007): 107–20.

8 Today the Trévise court is the oldest original basketball terrain in the world. For more, see Lindsay Sarah Krasnoff, "The Untold Story of Basketball's Hidden Sporting Treasure," CNN International, January 24, 2020 https://edition.cnn.com/2020/01/23/sport/nba-france-paris-basketball-spt-intl/index.html.

9 Lafayette was the French aristocrat who fought alongside George Washington against the British during the American Revolution. Sabine Chavinier, "Introduction et Diffusion du Basket-Ball en France: Le Temps des YMCA," in Fabien Archambault and Loic Artiaga (eds.), *Double Jeu: Historie du Basket-ball entre France et Amériques* (Vuibert, 2007), 69.

10 YMCA leisure foyers and aid groups like the Comité d'action en faveur des regions dévastées (CARD), established by Ann Morgan to help the northern and eastern regions of the country destroyed by trench warfare, showcased sports like basketball and baseball.

11 Chavinier, "Introduction et Diffusion du Basket-Ball en France."

12 Éric Claverie, "Le Ripopo ou la Naissance d'un Style Français: 1920–1939," in Fabien Archambault, Loic Artiaga, and Gérard Bosc (eds.), *Double Jeu: Histoire du Basket-Ball Entre France et Amériques* (Paris: Vuibert, 2007), 155–65.

13 Ibid., 160.

14 See Chs. 5–6, Lindsay Krasnoff, *The Making of Les Bleus: Sport in France, 1958–2010* (Lexington Books, 2013).

PART ONE

Foundations

1

"I Didn't Go to France to Play Basketball," 1954–60

Martin Feinberg arrived in Paris on a bitterly cold January day in 1954 to study journalism at the Sorbonne courtesy of the G.I. Bill. "I was very innocent," the Cleveland cab driver's son said of his desire to cross the Atlantic Ocean. "I didn't know much about politics or the world, so I wanted to get to Europe."[1] After a short tour of the Continent that included Germany, Italy, and Spain, Feinberg returned to Paris, rented a room on rue Casimir Delavigne in the fifth arrondissement, and began his studies. In many respects, the twenty-seven-year-old was like other postwar arrivals in the French capital: keen to enjoy life. The city, and the country more broadly, was buoyed by postwar rebuilding and growth, even as the Fourth Republic and its empire teetered on the brink.

"I didn't go to France to play basketball," Feinberg maintained decades later. But the game found him, providing opportunities to meet and interact with the local student population while simultaneously infusing the game with new tactics and techniques. Within the student-centric Latin Quarter, Feinberg met Jacqueline and Madeline Cator, twin sisters who played basketball for the national team. The women convinced their new American friend to try out for the basketball section of Paris Université Club (PUC), then considered the best squad in the country. "I had a big desire to enjoy life," he reasoned. "I had played a lot of basketball, even in the Navy. I didn't know anything about the PUC, but they asked me to come out, and I said sure."

Feinberg set up a meeting with PUC's coach, Emile Frézot. Nicknamed "Le Barbu" (the bearded one) by his players, Frézot was reportedly delighted with Feinberg.[2] "The men's coach was thrilled to have a six-foot-three American," Feinberg recalled of first meeting Frézot, who also led the national men's team, Les Tricolores (today known as Les Bleus). The American was older than most of PUC's roster and had more on-court experience, so Frézot invited Feinberg to play during a friendly international game in two weeks' time.[3]

That first game in 1954 was a wakeup call. The team traveled by car and stopped en route for lunch, replete with wine mere hours before tipoff. It amazed Feinberg, who wasn't allowed to smoke or consume alcohol while playing basketball in the States. He was also taken aback by the stadiums, which were vastly different from back home; instead of dedicated arenas, basketball was played in multi-purpose structures with slippery floors, both a reflection of the sport's amateur status as well as its transition from being played outdoors prewar to indoors after the war.[4] "There was no comparison," Feinberg said, "and that's one of the reasons why I wanted to bring the PUC [to the United States] to see this wondrous of stadiums to play basketball in."

That's how PUC became the first French basketball team to visit the United States in December 1955. The landmark trip introduced PUC to how Americans perceived and resourced the game, including the ways that basketball, and sport more generally, was part of the country's culture. It provided a means of technical exchange, as the team acquired various tactical manuals which they later translated and served as reference points.[5] The Frenchmen gained new knowledge of different US playing styles through their competition against Mid-Atlantic and Midwest NCAA and American Amateur Union (AAU) teams. They also experienced the United States and its people first-hand; this was important as it was the first time that the team, save Feinberg, visited the country and thus countered certain French stereotypes about their sister republic. But the young men of PUC also represented postwar France to the Americans they met. The team was composed of university students, including Bamako-born Roger Antoine, who served as captain of Les Tricolores for most of the 1950s, and thus defied US stereotypes about who was French.

The cultural and technical knowledge exchanged as a result of this trip helped the team strengthen its game and that of France as its players went on to serve different influential basketball functions.[6]

It was an example of informal sports diplomacy, but it was not the only one that helped basketball blossom. Feinberg's good friend and roommate during PUC's away games, Antoine, embodied how France's complex relationship with Africa enriched its basketball fortune. Another transatlantic experience foretold a different trend as Jean-Claude Lefebvre left greater Paris for Gonzaga University in Spokane, Washington. The twenty-year-old Frenchman was the first known to play US collegiate basketball. These three men may not have been the most pivotal personalities in basketball's evolution, but their stories illustrate the impact of informal exchanges through basketball.

Scouting Report

The early evolution of postwar basketball and its growing international influences occurred at a time of general rebuilding and recalibration. The Fourth Republic (1946–58) was the era of French history most molded by transnational pressures thanks to contraction of empire and reconfiguration of the global order under the Pax Americana.[7] France of the 1950s was a country in flux in numerous ways. To start with, its geopolitical role was reframed as its days as a Great Power ended, superseded by superpowers the United States and the Soviet Union. Paris thus navigated a tenuous line between nuclear-armed Washington and Moscow as the Cold War coalesced into a bipolar axis that pitted capitalism against communism.

The French also contended with the thorny question of how to interact with and position policies with respect to the United States. Allies since 1778, historically Paris held the upper hand in the transatlantic partnership, but the dynamic with its sister republic after two world wars was very different. They worked together to stem the spread of communism in Indochina, even as they competed for influence in other theaters such as Africa and the Middle East. But at home, throughout the 1950s, there was a need to mediate relations between American servicemen posted on US army bases throughout the *hexagone* and the local population.[8] This fed into anxiety about the invasion of American culture through Hollywood movies, Coca-Cola, or the rock 'n' roll music of performers like Elvis Presley, and revived the cyclical anti-Americanism that long shaped Franco-American relations.[9] Like it or not, many French seized upon closer interactions with their American counterparts as part of the rebuilding process.[10]

Yet, crisis after crisis confronted the state, notably over its colonial empire. The first materialized in 1946 as communist leader Ho Chi Minh sparked a broader Indochinese quest for independence by force. The French army suffered an embarrassing defeat at Dien Bien Phu by Vietnamese nationalist forces in May 1954, and the resultant Evian Accords that July ended French rule in Southeast Asia. Mere months later, in November, a second bloody war of decolonization broke out in Algeria, one that raged throughout the 1950s, toppled the Fourth Republic, paved the way for the Fifth Republic (1958–present) under General Charles de Gaulle, and deeply divided families. The 1956 Suez Crisis, which forced French and British governments to relinquish control of the Suez Canal, further contributed to a sense of France in crisis internationally while pressure mounted for full decolonization of francophone West Africa.

It wasn't just France's place in the world that was reconstructed in the 1950s; the country itself had to be revived. Parts of the countryside, especially in Brittany and Normandy where the heaviest fighting of World War II occurred, were rebuilt. In need of economic stimulus, the Elysée Palace opted into the American-funded Marshall Plan, a program for postwar economic recovery and investment to rebuild Europe. It helped launch an economic boom that propelled the country to new modernization and prosperity from 1945 until 1975, commonly known as the Thirty Glorious Years (*Les Trente Glorieuses*).

The social fabric was also in dire need of mending. Fractured by wartime roles and debates over resisters, bystanders, and collaborators, postwar the country came together over the fabricated memory that the majority resisted Nazi occupation and supported the Free French led by de Gaulle.[11] The population also recalibrated as France experienced new waves of immigration. During the interwar era, Poles, Italians, Spaniards, and Jews from Central Europe settled in search of economic opportunity or to escape political or religious persecution. They joined recent arrivals from the empire in Africa and Asia, who came to the mainland to help wartime industry and remained to rebuild the country's factories and farmlands. Thus, after 1945, there was the need to assimilate more diverse populations into public life through the institutions of the state, the language, and culture.

Demographically, the country expanded in other ways. The unprecedented number of births starting in the 1940s through the 1960s produced the generation known worldwide as the baby-boom generation. For France, which long suffered from some of the lowest birthrates in Western Europe, the youth surge helped reinforce the sense of national rejuvenation but strained the state's institutions, notably the schools. In other ways, however, the baby-boom generation helped the state return to an era of prosperity; for example, parents had to purchase new clothing, toys, strollers, etc. for their children. This consumer demand stimulated production and fed into *Les Trente Glorieuses*.[12]

Consumerism increased with greater prosperity, and in turn drove sports. Matches and events were broadcast over the radio and increasingly on television, even though more widespread television ownership did not materialize until 1960s.[13] Consumption also helped propel influential sports daily *L'Équipe*, born in February 1946 out of the former *L'Auto*, to new postwar success thanks to its coverage of the era's two most popular professional sports: cycling and football.[14]

The first team sport to professionalize in 1932, football was a lightning rod for the acrimony over the professionalization of sports. Well into the 1950s, many of the country's elites hewed to the ideal of sporting amateurism enshrined in the values of Olympic founding father Pierre de Coubertin. Even as opinion-makers looked down upon professional football as a sport of the working and immigrant classes, it was the most popular, widely consumed, and mediatized sport. It thus served as a tool of assimilation and facilitated the integration of recent waves of immigrants into the social fabric.

This history was stitched into the national football team. On February 15, 1931, Raoul Diagne became the first player of Black African descent for France when he suited up against Czechoslovakia, a role he reprised several times throughout the 1930s; he also played for Racing Club de Paris. The Paris-raised Diagne did not receive any negative critique for his on-pitch service for France, although he had to contend with the disapproval of the Under-Secretary for the Colonies Blaise Diagne, his father, who wanted his son to pursue a more desirable career in the professions.[15] By the 1950s, a new generation of players suited up for France reflective of the empire, such as Setif-native Rachid Mekhloufi, who played for the national team four times before his defection to represent the nascent Algerian Front de liberation nationale (FLN) team in 1958. Then there were the men who took France to third place at the 1958 FIFA World Cup, many of them first-, second-, or third-generation immigrants, including Roger Piatoni (Italy), Just Fontaine (Spain), and Raymond Kopa (Poland), one of the country's all-time football legends. The mélange was also reflected in professional football, as men left North and Sub-Saharan Africa to play in the *hexagone*.[16]

Basketball was still an amateur endeavor, even though it, too, served as a tool to assimilate newcomers. But it also contended with more transnational forces, starting with the country's wartime ally. In the immediate post-war period, the United States was increasingly ensnared in a clash with the Soviet Union, and each side sought to portray its power and influence others through their cultural endeavors. The public diplomacy efforts shaped by US foreign policy specialists after 1945 increasingly turned to sports to facilitate relations where US soldiers remained stationed on European soil, like in France.[17]

Yet, basketball's numbers remained small. In 1940, there were just 28,206 licensed basketball players, a number that grew over the decade; by 1952, just 94,725.[18] In France, as in other countries, individuals must obtain a yearly license from their sport's national governing federation. The system gauged where to supply resources but also served to indicate which sports were played, where, and by whom.

This was important for, throughout much of its history, basketball was a sport of the provinces and midsized urban areas. It was played predominantly by the bourgeoisie for, in the amateurism era, not everyone could afford to play and practice basketball. The sport was not as popular as football or rugby, although within certain regions local basketball clubs were rallying points for the community and often reflected their original roots tied to Catholic patronages.[19]

Unexpectedly, basketball provided a ray of light as it entered a golden era for the national teams. The men, then known as Les Tricolores, won the European Championship silver in 1949, and bronze in 1951 and 1953; it clinched silver at the 1948 London Olympics following a David versus Goliath matchup against the United States, then finished in sixth place at the 1950 inaugural

FIBA World Championship. The women's team won the country's first FIBA World Championship medal when they snagged bronze at the 1953 tournament in Chile. Even though both teams won recognition for France internationally, basketball was far from the mind of the average citizen in a country that lacked a sports culture.[20]

Across the Atlantic, basketball also struggled for in the United States it had only recently professionalized. There was an abundance of amateur and semi-pro teams across the nation, but the professional game was tainted with an association of poor player comportment, as a rough game that lacked class, was regionally focused and centered on barnstorming (perhaps racially coded perceptions by an audience of white opinion makers and businessmen).[21] Moreover, teams played in lackluster arenas, often small and darkly lit and relied on exhibition games to draw crowds.

The NBA rose out of this uncertain cauldron of immediate postwar dynamics. The Basketball Association of America (BAA) was formed in 1946, with eleven teams.[22] Most were under the ownership of ice hockey team owners who wanted to maximize arena profits. As such, the BAA operated with limited financial means as teams found it difficult to draw paying spectators away from other professional sports, college basketball, or the Harlem Globetrotters.[23] In 1948, the BAA absorbed several teams from its competitor, the National Basketball League (NBL), and rebranded as the National Basketball Association (NBA). Yet, the nascent league continued to face difficulties throughout the 1950s as it sought financial solvency, team stability, and popularity with the ticket-buying public. The NBA thus began to introduce new efforts to win over fans, such as introduction of the twenty-four-second shot clock and a series of other rule changes in the 1954–5 season designated to make the game more dynamic.[24]

There were a few early notables. Minnesota Lakers George Mikan, arguably the NBA's first famous star, was a crowd favorite. But until the emergence of a new generation of stars in the late 1950s, the league lacked a personality to drive growth.[25] In fact, the NBA's popular successes would thereafter be driven by stars, players whose on-court panache infused the game with entertainment and an emphasis on individuality, even as it was evident that one player alone could not carry a team throughout a championship season. The reliance on stars set the NBA apart from its French siblings (and remains a distinction today).

Another early issue was that of integration. Black basketball teams produced stellar players, with the New York Rens and the Harlem Globetrotters the two most well-known by the 1920s and 1930s. Yet, although Harry "Bucky" Lew was the first African American to play professionally with an otherwise all-white team in 1920 when he suited up for the Lowell Pawtucketville Athletic Club, there were few opportunities for Black players to be paid for their on-court skills.[26] Unlike the Negro Baseball League, which provided a forum for Black baseballers to play professionally, there was no equivalent for basketball; the Rens and the Globetrotters were among the rare opportunities to do so.[27] The war forced some professional teams to integrate out of necessity in December 1942 as so many men served in the armed forces. Despite an abundance of talent, the NBA did not break the color line until 1950 when Earl Lloyd, Nat Clifton, and Chuck Cooper entered the league.[28]

Even so, by the early 1950s, US leagues were known among the French basketball world as having players to emulate. Tactician and head coach of the national teams Robert Busnel began to contribute regular articles to the French Basketball Federation's (FFBB) monthly publication, *Basket-Ball*, which pulled apart plays and tactics of American college and NBA players like Mikan, University of Kentucky's Bill Spivey, and New York Knicks' Dick McCurie.[29] Busnel clearly had access, albeit likely limited, to video footage and, more likely, heavily relied on scouting notes for his opinions and transmission of the US game.

That's why the Harlem Globetrotters were highly regarded and served as a reference point in France. This legendary club launched its first overseas tours in 1950 and played across Europe, including Paris, the south of France, and Nancy.[30] They played in front of crowds that numbered into the thousands, including some 75,000 Germans at their 1951 stop in Berlin.[31] The Globetrotters served as unwitting tools of US public diplomacy, as a way to "sell" US foreign policy while countering that of the Soviet Union.[32]

The Globetrotters may have cultivated the image of the United States overseas, but they also demonstrated to French audiences the potentials of the game. Their 1951 tour included dates in Limoges to display their "art" of basketball.[33] Busnel considered the American players nearly perfect in form, if not a little silly in some of their on-court acts.[34] In 1952, Les Tricolores played the Globetrotters in Paris, an on-court humiliation for the home team in front of a sold-out crowd of 16,000 as the Americans handily outplayed them.[35] According to longtime basketball journalist Pascal Legendre, the Globetrotters were "truly magicians."[36]

The Globetrotters represented a different kind of basketball than the type played in France. Theirs was a more aerodynamic, spectacle-centric game. Although Busnel admired these US players, it was not without an awareness of the larger cultural issues at play; one of the reasons why he promoted US-style basketball techniques and practices was that, from a foreign perspective, the US game was intimately tied to African Americans.[37] Thus, French basketball's embrace of Black players, regardless of where they came from, was a way to counter the optical problem of appearing too close to the Americanization of basketball.[38] Moreover, American players like the Globetrotters helped stoke interest in the game—and the more people who were interested in basketball, the more people might play the game and provide a wider net of potential players to feed the national teams. It was thus not an embrace of Americanization of basketball, but a French response to the changing dynamics of the global game.

Keeping France competitive internationally was a constant premise of Busnel's work. At the inaugural 1950 FIBA World Championship, hosted and won by Argentina, France finished sixth, but it was a useful endeavor. As Busnel wrote in *Basket-Ball*, it was necessary to learn new combinations, rapid executions of plays, and keep up a fast pace of counterattacks.[39]

Even the federation recognized that there were problems with the French game. The men's team lacked a sense of timing, which resulted in missed opportunities and, perhaps, missed medals. "The French [player] was always an individualist," lamented *Basket-Ball* following the May 1951 European Championships. "He likes to shine, he likes praise, he likes being the star. Thus, he tends to be too slow in his actions if he sees a player better placed [to make a play]." This trait, it noted, was part of society's larger emphasis on the player who scored, whether in basketball, football, or rugby. "We forget that the scorer does nothing but concretize teamwork, work important to easily end attacks." In contrast, teamwork, even at the expense of individual on-court personalities, was a key strength for the Soviet team.[40] Such statements are surprising to twenty-first-century readers, for the strength of French players in the NBA and WNBA is their polyvalence on-court and sacrifices of personal glory for the best interests of the team.

Busnel's focus on enriching the game helped propel the national teams in international competition throughout the 1950s. But it was the cultural, technical, and knowledge exchanges of three early pioneers that sowed the seeds on which the future empire flourished.

The Captain

The French basketball community, at least around Paris, welcomed those who might help improve the game, including a student from Bamako, Roger Antoine. Born June 28, 1929, to a Caucasian French mother and a Black father, Antoine went to Paris to complete his university studies in electrical engineering.[41] A track and field specialist known for hurdles and a lover of football, Antoine was discovered by chance on April 18, 1951 in Paris's Salle Japy. That afternoon, the main draw of PUC versus Barcelona was preceded by a match that pitted journalists against a team of student-athletes from different sports to entertain the crowd. A twenty-one-year-old Antoine took to the floor and scored thirty points.[42] Awed by the young man's prowess, PUC invited him to play with the team.[43] Months later on December 1, he debuted with the national team during a friendly match against Belgium, the first player of color on the men's team, thirteen years after Sokela Mangoumbel became the first player of color on the women's national team.[44] For Antoine, 1951 began a decade-long sixty-six-game career *en bleu* in which he averaged 8.2 points, and served several years as team captain, including for the 1956 and 1960 Olympic Games.[45]

Antoine was an example of the early waves of young men (and later, women) from sub-Saharan Africa who played basketball in the *métropole* alongside their university studies. The game was played in the overseas territories postwar.[46] Senegal had strong players and the FFBB began to invest more attention and resources into developing the game after 1953. Although the region lacked terrains, coaches, and referees, Busnel noted that there were good athletes who should be developed.[47]

Antoine was considered to be one of France's best players.[48] A leader on-court, he was a known "ball thief, lively and sober at the same time," according to *L'Équipe*, and developed an acute sense of timing and anticipation.[49] Busnel admired Antoine's technique, his speed on-court, and the relaxed way that he executed plays, claiming that the young player could comfortably compete in all five posts on-court.[50] In short, Antoine exhibited many of the traits that Busnel identified for success at the international level, and was recognized for his storied career. He was named to and captained the 1964 Europe Team and, the following year, honored as a laureate by the Académie du Sport, the first basketballer to enter the storied institution.[51]

In his longtime leadership of the national team, Antoine was an official representative of France and thus engaged in formal sports diplomacy. The uniform he wore reflected the colors of the country and displayed the national symbol of *le coq*, while his leadership as captain spoke to the perceived ideals and values of the republic at that juncture.

Meanwhile, throughout his PUC career, Antoine played important roles on- and off-court. Because PUC played internationally, he served as an informal sports diplomat representing, communicating, and negotiating foreign public attitudes about France and its basketball on the European stage. He was the team's most high-profile player of color, but Antoine was not its only one. He was joined by Senegal-born Samba Sow, a twenty-three-year-old student who played the 1957–8 season with PUC. Sow and Antoine traveled with PUC to Moscow to contest the 1957 World Youth Festival. Teammate Michel Rat recalled that journey and the foreign reactions to his two friends, as "women and children came out to touch [them] because they had never seen Black people."[52]

Antoine's personal reflections on how these travels impacted or influenced his game are lost to time, not known to have been recorded. But former teammates Feinberg and Rat noted how Antoine was part of the team, whether PUC or Les Tricolores, and just as excited as everyone else to travel, learn, and represent through basketball, including on a groundbreaking 1955–6 trip to the United States.[53]

"Our American"

PUC opened its arms to another outsider, Feinberg, three years after it embraced Antoine. Born in New York on April 16, 1926, Feinberg's family moved to Cleveland during the Depression. Feinberg started to play basketball during high school, a game popular in his heavily Jewish neighborhood. Once the United States entered the war in December 1941, he enrolled in the Navy and attended officers' school to train as a pilot at the University of Michigan, where he also played for the now famous basketball team. Back then, however, things were different. "Nobody was interested in it," he said of basketball's place on the Ann Arbor campus. "They were interested in [American] football and the war, so there wasn't much emphasis on basketball."

The war ended before Feinberg served, but basketball remained a constant in his routine. He played semi-professionally for the Twentieth Century Fox basketball team and traveled with them across the country. It was a resurgent era of sorts for US hoops. The collegiate game flourished during the 1940s, if not at the University of Michigan, then certainly at many campuses across the country, even though its deceptively squeaky-clean image masked the game's problems with gambling.[54]

In Paris, basketball found Feinberg. He forced himself to communicate with his teammates in French. "I had a terrible accent, but I understood French fairly well," he said of the start of his cultural exchanges. The first time he suited up for PUC in 1954 was another learning moment about the place of basketball in France, from a difference in stadiums to the game's social perceptions and more, reflective that the sport wasn't terribly important within the wider public.

Thus, Feinberg dreamed of introducing his French friends to basketball back home, so they could understand that their sport didn't have to be consigned to the closet. He also wanted to expose PUC to how other Americans played the game. Many learned new US techniques and style from playing with Feinberg, who was noted for being able to change rhythm to cement a play, having good on-court visibility and game IQ, and to shoot ambidextrously.[55] But that was a poor substitute for more comprehensive exposure. Thus Feinberg hatched an idea: to take the first French basketball team to the United States. He had a willing partner in Frézot who thought such a trip could be useful from a technical and cultural standpoint, not just for PUC, but for the future of French basketball.[56]

The pre-departure build-up naturally involved a few stressors over last-minute obstacles, including one posed by the armed forces. French military authorities called up Antoine for mandatory

FIGURE 1.1 *Martin Feinberg with Paris Université Club. Credit: Musée du Basket.*

military service. They had already issued his uniform, but a little persuasion from all sides released him from duty, temporarily, to make the much-lauded trip. Of equal importance, Antoine's visa came through at the last minute.[57]

Feinberg realized his dream as PUC departed Le Havre on December 21, 1955.[58] The team traveled in third class aboard one of the luxury liners of the day, the SS *America*, but the cold, choppy Atlantic waters left many listless in their bunks, too seasick to move. Despite the tempestuous crossing, PUC was excited to begin their American adventure as they boarded a flight from New York to Chicago. They wanted to sample the myths of "America." The team experienced a night at the famed Chicago Pump Room restaurant, where Jacques Huguet, a medical student who later steered FFBB's medical policy, gave an impromptu comedic monologue.[59] For Feinberg, it was a successful cultural outing. As he told a reporter, "I'm very much interested in them liking America. That, for me, is the idea."[60]

FIGURE 1.2 *Paris Université Club (PUC) in Chicago, 1955–6. Credit: Musée du Basket.*

The PUCistes were also curious to see how they fared against US teams. They lost their first game, a 43–68 drubbing in Wheaton, Illinois, but rebounded to win over Lake Forrest College, 69–64, and North Central Iowa, 67–58.[61] If the trip was an opportunity to observe the US game, then PUC also provided American audiences with a taste of its French sister, to the chagrin of several journalists. According to *Sports Illustrated*, the Frenchmen "played a game that looked absurdly old-fashioned" and "concentrated on ball control, an occasional well-executed fast break, and set plays off the double-pivot offence."[62] For the *Milwaukee Sentinel*, the team's 43–74 loss to Marquette University illustrated a silver lining for "what the Parisians lacked in cage know-how and finesse they tried to make up with *ésprit de corps*."[63] Days later on January 9, after being bested by the University of Baltimore, 68–76, the *Baltimore Sun* reported,

> Baltimore, like most United States college teams, utilizes the shoot-and-run offense and zone defense. Paris, on the other hand, has a tight and very effective man-for-man defense and, in spite of a height deficiency, grabbed more than its share of rebounds.[64]

After nearly two weeks in the United States, the Frenchmen were exhausted and practically broke. They left their interpreter, Feinberg, behind in a Cleveland hospital to recover from a torn Achilles tendon. Yet the trip was a resounding success despite the box scores. For Frézot, it was a scouting trip *par excellence*, for it provided ample opportunity to watch the variety of different tactics and styles played by their opponents. "American basketball is much more virile than ours and much more athletic in the sense that their players play from one bout to another in a match with the same speed," he told *L'Équipe*.[65] This technical knowledge was later deployed by Les Tricolores at that summer's Melbourne Olympics.

Time-Out

The Melbourne Games of 1956 proved fertile ground for French basketball. Les Tricolores' fourth-place finish behind the United States, the Soviet Union, and Uruguay respectively, was an improvement over its eighth-place finish four years earlier.[66] Busnel proudly touted that the French had nothing to learn from other countries and, aside from the United States, managed to show its strength over other countries during the marathon of competition.[67]

Importantly, the Games featured a young up-and-coming star for Team USA, twenty-two-year-old center Bill Russell. A legend-in-the-making, Russell helped the University of San Francisco Dons to back-to-back NCAA championships in 1955 and 1956 before graduation that June. Now he had the chance to fulfill one of his long-held desires, to compete at the Olympic games.[68] In Melbourne, Russell exulted in the camaraderie amongst international athletes, and was unexpectedly touched by the symbolism and pageantry of the Opening Ceremony.[69] On-court, he blocked shots and helped set a rapid tempo while giving his all for the team on its way to a gold medal finish, winning hearts and minds around the world in the process. Russell helped elevate the game, literally moving it more into the vertical stratosphere and away from the longitudinal on-court passes.[70] Although his influence on the French game in the late 1950s was minimal, Russell later inspired young French players while his defensive techniques made their way on the *hexagone*'s hardcourts in the early 1960s, irrecoverably shaping the game.

Les Tricolores' fourth-place finish at Melbourne was a success. As *La Petit Gazette du Musée* argued, "[basketball] could pretend to serve as a sports symbol for a country reborn from the ashes."[71] In fact, an undated report prepared by officials at the National Institute for Sport, the country's elite sports school now known as INSEP, on how to best prepare for the Rome 1960 Olympics noted the new importance of sports. "Too many young French have the sentiment, founded or not, of living in an era of decline," it noted. "The best of them must be able to prove in international competitions the continuity of the French figurehead and, if it was true that it has faltered, its rebirth."[72] Although the author remarked on France's middle-of-the-road status at the time, no longer a Great Power or economic locomotive, it proposed a plan for sports success in 1960 to counter the image of decline. "We produce smart athletes," it boasted.

> Let us say at least that the young Frenchman is of a cerebral vivacity superior to that of most of his foreign competitors …

Our basketballers are among the best in the world . . . our most favourable Olympic sports are basketball (and fencing) . . . as basketball is the most intelligent team sport.[73]

While the report noted a lack of time and opportunity to address the country's sports weaknesses, it argued to focus on its strengths, including "absolute priority to fencing and to basketball."[74]

Given such attitudes, Busnel constantly sought to maintain French competitiveness in international competition. When he received a phone call in 1955 alerting him to a potential seven-foot-three basketball talent, he was more than just intrigued; Busnel became entirely invested.

The Eiffel Rifle

The player in question was basketball novice Jean-Claude Lefebvre, who after two years of Busnel's tutelage grasped enough to become the first French player to play US collegiate basketball on scholarship, and later the first Frenchman drafted by the NBA. Lefebvre's story was unusual, from his height to the even more extraordinary experience of being recruited to play in the United States. He engaged in cultural exchange through the game during his two-year adventure with Gonzaga University in Spokane, Washington, but did not impact the game back home. What Lefebvre's story did do was illustrate what was possible for a French player, even if they never reached the rungs of critical success in the game.

Lefebvre was an eighteen-year-old basketball novice when he was unexpectedly recruited to the game by Busnel. Born in 1937, the second of four children, Lefebvre was raised on the family farm in Épais-lès-Louvres, a small village of approximately one hundred people on Paris's northeastern periphery.[75] As a kid, he and his youngest sister were teased because of their height; despite his physique, he wasn't terribly sporty even though he loved the cycling races at the Vel d'Hiv and enjoyed reading athlete biographies.[76] One day in April 1955, he went to see the family doctor, Michel Andrivent, about a sore knee.[77] Dr. Andrivent, who was affiliated with INS and physician for the national basketball teams, called his close friend Busnel to tell him about the tall young patient. The tactician was so intrigued by the teenager's potential to help France be more competitive on the international stage that he personally trained Lefebvre four hours a day in order to school him in the game.[78]

As journalist Legendre noted, "Busnel himself estimated that [Lefebvre] could be the decisive arm of the Olympic Games of Rome."[79] It was an era of change in the international game. The *ripopo* style played by French teams of the 1920s, 1930s, and immediately postwar, an unrestrained free passing game, was outdated and no longer an advantage.[80] Instead, countries fielded ever-taller, more athletic players. And, as Russell's 1956 Olympic performance illustrated, vertical games were increasingly competitive. Busnel recognized the growing dissonance between these new "athletic armaments" and a French side still playing small ball, despite his increased focus on counterattacks and other tactics designed to speed up the game.[81]

Lefebvre was a willing student, although one sensitive about his height.[82] As he told the *Miroir Sprint* in January 1957, "I didn't want to play basketball because it was a sport for tall people. I didn't want to be used like a freak, I wanted, and want, to be a young man like everyone else."[83] Still, he trained with Busnel and gained a sense of freedom through sport.[84]

Busnel's protégé progressed. Lefebvre began to play with the national team, first called up for a February 2, 1957 friendly match against Czechoslovakia, but did not earn playing minutes until that June's European Championship. At the same time, he was engaged in a six-month-long recruitment effort, spearheaded by US basketball agent Jim McGregor, which is how the twenty-year-old Frenchman arrived at Gonzaga University to study literature and play basketball early that September.[85]

Spokane, Washington was an enormous change of scene and full of cultural shocks at every turn. For starters, Lefebvre didn't speak much English, so he first lived with Bulldogs head coach Hank Anderson then moved into DeSmet Hall.[86] His classes were in French, but he planned to enroll in business classes once his English improved.[87]

Lefebvre became just another student. One of his closest confidants was teammate Richie Williams, and their shared love for the game and for dancing helped bridge divides.[88] He socialized with others and was well-liked, even as the Frenchman was a source of wonderment for how he towered above the masses.[89] Although it's difficult to reconstruct the kinds of cultural exchanges that occurred between Lefebvre, friends, and teammates from existing records, it's easy to imagine conversations by both sides curious to learn more about each other in an era in which information traveled more slowly. It's likely that the Frenchman shared some of his love of literature and theater, as well as his admiration for US singers like Frank Sinatra, Elvis Presley, and Gonzaga alumnus Bing Crosby.[90]

Much more is known about "The Eiffel Rifle's" basketball abilities thanks to the nation-wide media attention he attracted from the start. As the first Frenchman to play basketball on scholarship, his story tantalized with the promise of what other international recruits could do for the game.[91] Yet, despite Anderson's tutelage, Lefebvre's on-court game did not live up to the hype. His scored fourteen points for the Bulldogs in the November 1957 season opener against the College of Idaho but did not demonstrate consistency. He could dazzle, as he did in a February 1958 game against Whitworth in which he netted twenty field goals, ten of twenty-one free throw attempts, and fifty points, a school record as Gonzaga bested their cross-town rival, 75–72, in the game's last seconds.[92] But often Lefebvre's game was mediocre, which by his sophomore season became a source of frustration. He had difficulty picking up the pace to match the speed of the US game, which ran the ball whereas the French game was based on passes and shots.[93] He was also hampered by health issues that ranged from conditioning to anemia-related difficulties.[94]

After his second season ended in spring 1959, LeFebvre withdrew from Gonzaga and returned to France. He rehabilitated a left knee injury, became increasingly comfortable back home, and decided to remain to train with the national team that summer ahead of the Rome 1960 Games.[95] During the June 1960 NBA Draft, the Frenchman was selected sixty-fourth *in absentia* by the Minneapolis Lakers; however, Lefebvre's Olympic and NBA dreams were shattered when he was hospitalized for tuberculosis.[96]

Lefebvre set a precedent for a French player to be scouted, recruited, and play collegiate basketball in the United States, as well as to be drafted by an NBA team, even if his on-court results were a disappointment. Despite a gap of nearly twenty-five years before the next wave of young French hopefuls hit American shores to fulfill their hoops dreams, Lefebvre's story stands out for it dovetailed with the end of France's first golden era of basketball.

Post-Game

The mid-to-late 1950s was the beginning of the end of French basketball's golden era, even if officials were unaware of the shadow that loomed on the horizon.[97] In fact, May 1959 proved to be a point of optimism for Les Tricolores as they engaged in two different types of what today would be recognized as basketball diplomacy.

First was a special clinic with legendary Boston Celtics coach Red Auerbach and star point guard, the French-American Bob Cousy, who were in Paris after a trip to Dakar. Organized by Feinberg, the two Celtics attended France's pre-European Championship training camp, offered game advice, and exchanged with the team.

"Monsieurs, you're too technical," Cousy observed in French. "The important thing for a basketball player is to score points. If he scores, why modify his gestures? . . . the 'natural' must prevail over the 'prefabricated.'"[98] He refrained from discussing social issues, perhaps reasonable given the environment. Months earlier, de Gaulle was inaugurated as the first president of the Fifth Republic after war in Algeria felled the previous government. Moreover, American anti-communism sentiment may not have sat well with some of the French at a time when the Parti communiste français (PCI) still held sway.

Among the players who interacted with Cousy that day were Michel Rat, Feinberg's PUC teammate, and Lefebvre. On May 21, the team began a second exercise in sports diplomacy as they sought to ascend the podium once again at the European Championship. They began the campaign in Istanbul with a devastating 48–80 loss to the Soviet Union. Les Tricolores rebounded to win their next six games before they fell to Hungary, 60–62, on May 30 and the Soviets again the following day, 72–88.[99] But it was enough to clinch the tournament's bronze medal, the team's last podium finish until 2000.

Notes

1 All Martin Feinberg quotes in this chapter, unless specified, from Martin Feinberg, Interview with the author, interview by Lindsay Sarah Krasnoff, December 7, 2014.

2 Feinberg; "Huit du PUC et l'ex-Barbu," *Basket-Ball*, May 1, 1955.

3 Feinberg, Interview with the author; "Huit du PUC et l'ex-Barbu."

4 Philippe Cazaban and Daniel Champsaur, "Le Basket s'enracine en France, 1914–1932," in *Géants: Tout l'histoire du Basket-Ball* (Chronique Éditions, 2015), 41–57.

5 Michel Rat, Interview with the author, September 24, 2021.

6 Lindsay Sarah Krasnoff, "Barnstorming Frenchmen: The Impact of Paris Université Club's US Tours and the Individual in Sports Diplomacy," in J Simon Rofe (ed.), *Sport and Diplomacy: Games within Games* (Manchester University Press, 2018), 130–46.

7 Tyler Stovall, *Transnational France: The Modern History of a Universal Nation* (Taylor & Francis, 2015), 363.

8 François Doppler-Speranza, *Une Armée de Diplomates, Les Militaires Américains et La France, 1944–1967* (Presses universitaires de Strasbourg, 2021).

9 For more, see Victoria de Grazia, *Irresistible Empire: America's Advance Through Twentieth Century Europe* (Harvard University Press, 2006); Richard Kuisel, *Seducing the French: The Dilemma of Americanization* (University of California Press, 1993).

10 One example of this was the tourism and hospitality industry which, starting in the 1950s, learned from best practices in the United States in order to revive and promote tourism to France. For more, see Elizabeth Becker, *Overbooked: The Exploding Business of Travel and Tourism* (Simon & Schuster, 2013).

11 The scabs of reality, that the majority were in fact bystanders and thus bore varying degrees of responsibility, would not be torn away until the 1970s reckoning forced by American scholar Robert O. Paxton and a new generation taking their parents to task for their wartime decisions, roles, and repercussions. Michael R. Marrus and Robert O. Paxton, *Vichy France and the Jews: Second Edition* (Stanford: Stanford University Press, 2019); Herrick Chapman, *France's Long Reconstruction* (Harvard University Press, 2018).

12 For more on the postwar changes to French economy and its impact on society and youth, see Richard Ivan Jobs, *Riding the New Wave: Youth and the Rejuvenation of France after the Second World War* (Stanford University Press, 2007); Kristin Ross, *Fast Cars, Clean Bodies: Decolonization and the Reordering of French Culture* (MIT Press, 1995).

13 M. F. Lévy and E. Cohen, *La Télévision Dans La République: Les Années 50* (Complexe, 1999).

14 Gilles Montérémal, "L'Équipe: Médiateur et Producteur de Spectacle Sportif (1946–1967)," *Le Temps Des Médias*, no. 9 (February 2007): 107–20; "L'Auto devient L'Équipe," *L'Équipe* (blog), July 21, 2014, https://blog.lequipe.fr/histoire/28-fevrier-1946-lauto-devient-lequipe/.

15 FIFA, "Diagne Blazes a Trail with Les Bleus," FIFA, https://www.fifa.com/news/origin1904-p.cxm.fifa.comdiagne-blazes-a-trail-with-les-bleus-2765374.

16 Claude Boli, "La migration des footballeurs africains en France. Le cas des Ivoiriens (1957–2010)," *Hommes & migrations: Revue française de référence sur les dynamiques migratoires*, no. 1285 (May 1, 2010): 58–64; Claude Boli, "La perception des joueurs africains en France. Projection et imaginaire colonial," *Hommes & Migrations: Revue française de référence sur les dynamiques migratoires*, no. 1285 (May 1, 2010): 124–32; Stanislas Frenkiel, *Le Football Des Immigrés France-Algérie, l'histoire en Partage* (Artois presses université, 2021), http://apu.univ-artois.fr/Revues-et-collections/Cultures-sportives/Le-Football-des-immigres-France-Algerie-l-histoire-en-partage.

17 Part of the US public diplomacy policy in France during the 1950s was to promote American sports, notably basketball and baseball. These efforts impacted French public opinion but did not play a direct impact on French basketball at the time. For more, see François Doppler-Speranza, "'Shooting Hoops with Foreign Teams' Basketball Ambassadors on US Military Bases in France (1916–1961)," in *Beyond Boycotts: Sport during the Cold War in Europe*, ed. Philippe Vonnard, Nicola Sbetti, and Grégory Quin (De Gruyter Oldenbourg, 2017), 135–56.

18 "Licenses" (Fédération Français de Basket-Ball (FFBB), July 1, 1952).

19 Loic Artiaga and Fabien Archambault, *Double Jeu: Histoire Du Basket-Ball Entre France et Amériques* (Paris: Vuibart, 2007); Cazaban and Champsaur, "Le Basket s'enracine en France, 1914–1932."

20 Lindsay Sarah Krasnoff, *The Making of Les Bleus: Sport in France, 1958–2010* (Lexington Books, 2012).

21 David George Surdam, *The Rise of the National Basketball Association*, Kindle (University of Illinois Press, 2012), sec. 79; Douglas Stark, *Breaking Barriers: A History of Integration in Professional Basketball* (Rowman & Littlefield, 2019), 100–2.

22 "A Chronology of the Teams in the NBA," Boston Celtics, accessed April 22, 2022, https://www.nba.com/celtics/history/nba-teams-chronology.

23 Surdam, *The Rise of the National Basketball Association*, 79.

24 "NBA Rules History" (NBA, n.d.).

25 Surdam, *The Rise of the National Basketball Association*, sec. location 92.

26 Stark, 1–2.

27 Stark, 14–20.

28 Stark, 102; NBA, "Top Moments: Earl Lloyd, Chuck Cooper, Nat Clifton Blaze New Path in NBA," NBA History, accessed April 12, 2021, https://www.nba.com/history/top-moments/1950-nba-pioneers.

29 Robert Busnel, "Les Enseignements Techniques des Championnats du Monde," *Basket-Ball*, February 1, 1951; Robert Busnel, "À Chacun Son Style, Mais Il Est Bon de Copier ou du Moins de s'inspirer des Gestes des Grandes Champions," *Basket-Ball*, March 1, 1951; Jacques Huguet, "Vedettes 1950: Regards sur les USA Riches en Champions et en Scandales," *Basket-Ball*, March 1, 1951.

30 Ben Green, *Spinning the Globe: The Rise, Fall and Return to Greatness of the Harlem Globetrotters* (Amistad, 2005), 224–5.

31 Green, 239–40; Damion L. Thomas, *Globetrotting: African American Athletes and Cold War Politics* (University of Illinois Press, 2012).

32 Green.

33 Pascal Legendre, "Wilt Chamberlain, les Globies et la France (1ère partie): Les Harlem Globe Trotters n°1 mondial," *Basket Europe*, December 25, 2018, https://www.basketeurope.com/livenews-fr/434572/wilt-chamberlain-les-globies-et-la-france-1ere-partie-les-harlem-globe-trotters-n1-mondial/.

34 Legendre.

35 Philippe Cazaban and Daniel Champsaur, "Les Harlem Globetrotters au Pied de la Tour Eiffel," in *Géants: Toute l'histoire du basketball* (Chronique Éditions, 2015), 155; Legendre, "[REDIFF] Wilt Chamberlain, les Globies et la France (1ère partie)."

36 Pascal Legendre, Interview with the author, August 11, 2017.

37 Fabien Archambault, "Tournées des Harlem Globetrotters en Europe dans la Seconde Moitié du XXe Siècle (Les) | EHNE," in *Encylopédie Pour Une Histoire Nouvelle de l'Europe*, accessed October 4, 2020, https://ehne.fr/article/civilisation-materielle/circulations-sportives-europeennes/les-tournees-des-harlem-globetrotters-en-europe-dans-la-seconde-moitie-du-xxe-siecle.

38 Archambault, "Tournées des Harlem Globetrotters en Europe dans la Seconde Moitié du XXe Siècle (Les) | EHNE." Also see Fabien Archambault, "La Politique des Bloc(k)s: Basket-ball et Guerre Froide," *Materiaux pour l'histoire de notre temps*, 106, no. 2, October 2012, 33–9

39 Robert Busnel, "Triomphe du Basket Modern: Base sur l'offensive," *Basket-Ball*, April 1, 1951.

40 "VIIe Championnat d'Europe," *Basket-Ball*, June 1, 1951.

41 "Huit du PUC et l'ex-Barbu."

42 "La Disparition de Roger Antoine," *L'Équipe*, August 13, 2003.

43 Pierre Tessier, "Roger Antoine Successeur Désigné de André Buffière au Capitanat de l'équipe de France," *L'Équipe*, September 20, 1955.

44 Born in Nantes on April 23, 1911, Bangoumbel was the French team's shining start during its first international tournament, the women's European Championship of 1938, according to national team coach Paul Geist. "Death Record Sokela Mangoumbel" (INSEE (Government of France)), accessed May 10, 2021, https://deces.matchid.io/search?q=Sokela+Mangoumbel&size=n_60_n; Paul Geist, "L'Opinion Du Manager," *Basket-Ball*, October 27, 1938; Dominique Wendling, "[Portrait] Roger Antoine a ouvert la voie," *Basket Retro* (blog), January 14, 2021, https://basket-retro.com/2021/01/14/portrait-roger-antoine-a-ouvert-la-voie/.

45 "La Disparition de Roger Antoine."

46 FFBB, "Ligues d'outremer" (Fédération Français de Basket-Ball (FFBB), October 1, 1952).

47 Robert Busnel, "Premier Stage à Dakar," *Basket-Ball*, June 1, 1953.

48 Pascal Legendre, "Roger Antoine, Pionnier du 'Black Power' dans le Basket Français," *BasketEurope*, October 7, 2016, http://www.basketbeurope.com/livenews-fr/ffbb/edf-homme/3816. . ./roger-antoine-pionnier-du-black-power-dans-le-basket-francais/.

49 "La Disparition de Roger Antoine."

50 Legendre, "Roger Antoine, Pionnier du 'Black Power' dans le Basket Français."

51 Fédération Française de Basket-Ball (FFBB), "Roger Antoine," French Basketball Federation, accessed May 12, 2021, http://www.ffbb.com/http%3A//www.ffbb.com/ffbb/patrimoine/academie-du-basket/academiciens/roger-antoine; "Les Laureats," Académie des Sports, accessed May 12, 2021, https://academiedessports.com/evenements/les-laureats/.

52 Michel Rat, Interview with the author, October 20, 2015.

53 Feinberg, Interview with the author; Michel Rat, Interview with the author, October 26, 2014.

54 Surdam, *The Rise of the National Basketball Association*, sec. 79.

55 "Huit du PUC et l'ex-Barbu."

56 Feinberg, Interview with the author; Gérard Edelstein, "Le PUC Est Parti pour Les États-Unis," *L'Équipe*, December 21, 1955.

57 Edelstein, "Le PUC Est Parti pour Les États-Unis."

58 Pierre Tessier, "Le PUC s'embarquera le 21 Décembre pour Les États-Unis," *L'Équipe*, December 6, 1955.

59 Feinberg, Interview with the author.

60 Robert Chromie, "Paris Athletes Say Oui Oui on Chicago Visit," *Chicago Tribune*, December 29, 1959.

61 S. I. Staff, "French Fried," *Sports Illustrated*, January 16, 1956.

62 Staff.

63 Rel Bochat, "Marquette Routs Paris 'Five,' 74–43," *The Milwaukee Sentinel*, 5 January 1956, 11.

64 Walter F. Herman, "Baltimore U. Holds Off Late Rally to Top Paris, 76–68," *Baltimore Sun*, 10 January 1956.

65 Cornelius Ryan, "Le PUC a Courageusement Résisté à l'Université de Baltimore (76–68)," *L'Équipe*, January 11, 1956.

66 "Melbourne / Stockholm 1956 Basketball Men—Olympic Basketball," International Olympic Committee, November 30, 2020, https://www.olympic.org/melbourne-/-stockholm-1956/basketball/basketball-men.

67 Robert Busnel, "Remarquables Pendant La Moitié de La Compétition, Les Français Doivent à Leur Cran et à Leur Volonté une Excellente 4è Place," *Basket-Ball*, January 1957.

68 Aram Goudsouzian, *King of the Court: Bill Russell and the Basketball Revolution* (University of California Press, 2010), 055.

69 Goudsouzian, 59–60.

70 Goudsouzian, 2.

71 "C'était en 1955, Zoom Arrière," *La Gazette du Musée*, January 2013.

72 Institut National des Sports, "Notes Soumises à Monsieur Le Directeur Général de La Jeunesse et Des Sports à Propos de La Préparation Aux JO 1960" (Institut National des Sports, Undated), Centre des Archives Contemporaines (CAC) 19780586 Art 100.

73 Institut National des Sports, 8–10.

74 Institut National des Sports, 10–11.

75 Vincent Janssen, "Jean-Claude Lefèbvre: A jamais le pionnier. Épisode 1 : La découverte," *Basket Retro* (blog), April 6, 2021, https://basket-retro.com/2021/04/06/__trashed-8/.

76 Janssen.

77 Janssen; Jerry O'Brien, "Ah, Quel Homme! Oh, Quels Feet!," *Sports Illustrated*, December 9, 1957.

78 Pascal Legendre, "Lefèbvre, le 1er Français drafté en NBA," FFBB, April 16, 2013, http://www.ffbb.com/lefebvre-le-1er-francais-drafte-en-nba.

79 Legendre.

80 Éric Claverie, "Le Ripopo ou La Naissance d'un Style Français: 1920–1939," in *Double Jeu: Histoire Du Basket-Ball Entre France et Amériques*, ed. Fabien Archambault, Loic Artiaga, and Gérard Bosc (Vuibert, 2007), 155–65; Archambault, "La Politique des Bloc(k)s"; Janssen.

81 Lindsay Sarah Krasnoff, "Developing Athletic 'Atomic Armaments': The Role of Sports Medicine in Cold War France, 1958–1992," *Performance Enhancement & Health* 2 (2013): 8–16.

82 O'Brien.

83 Sacha Rutard, "Une histoire sur Jean-Claude Lefèbvre, le géant de 2,18m qui fut drafté en NBA | Basket Europe," *BasketEurope*, April 7, 2021, sec. Livenews, https://www.basketeurope.com/livenews-fr/544041/une-histoire-sur-jean-claude-lefebvre-le-geant-de-218m-qui-fut-drafte-en-nba/.

84 Janssen.

85 For more on Lefèbvre's recruitment to Gonzaga and his first weeks in Washington, see Vincent Janssen, "Jean-Claude Lefebvre: A jamais le pionnier. Épisode 2 : Le grand saut," *Basket Retro* (blog), June 2, 2021, https://basket-retro.com/2021/06/02/jean-claude-lefebvre-a-jamais-le-pionnier-episode-2-le-grand-saut/; Mike Schmeltzer, "Jean Claude Lefebvre Brought National Attention to Zags," *The Spokesman-Review*, February 21, 2017, https://www.spokesman.com/stories/2017/feb/21/jean-claude-lefebvre-brought-national-attention-to/; Legendre, "Lefèbvre, le 1er Français drafté en NBA"; O'Brien.

86 Schmeltzer.

87 "Lefèbvre Etudiera Les Arts et Le Basket à l'université Gonzaga," *Miroir Des Sports*, September 23, 1957.

88 O'Brien.

89 Schmeltzer.

90 Janssen.

91 LeFebvre's scholarship included tuition, room, and board. In addition to playing basketball he also held an on-campus job installing shelving in the library, for which *Sports Illustrated* reported he was

paid $10 per week. For more, see O'Brien; Legendre, "Lefèbvre, le 1er Français drafté en NBA."

92 Schmeltzer.

93 Plowman, "The Eiffel Rifle Zags First 7 Footer Jean Claude Lefebvre Debuted in 1957 to International Fanfare | Gonzaga University."

94 Schmeltzer; Krasnoff, "Developing Athletic 'Atomic Armaments': The Role of Sports Medicine in Cold War France, 1958–1992."

95 Plowman.

96 Plowman.

97 "C'était en 1955, Zoom Arrière."

98 Henri Chapuis, "Robert Cousy: "L'équipe de France Devrait Jouer Pour J.-C. Lefebvre," *Miroir Des Sports*, May 19, 1959.

99 FFBB, "Historique Des Matches FFBB," FFBB History Database, accessed June 29, 2020, http://www.ffbb.com/edf/historique-des-matches.

2

Basketball in Crisis, 1960–68

In June 1960, the Harlem Globetrotters toured France, mesmerizing the countryside with their entertaining, lively game. One player stood out: Wilt Chamberlain, a late roster addition fresh off an award-winning rookie season with the Philadelphia Warriors and eager to rejoin the European tour.[1] That month, the Globetrotters wowed fans in the small Normandy town of Courgeoût. In the stands was seventeen-year-old Jean-Pierre Jarry, who later recalled for *L'Équipe*, "you cannot imagine what this represented to us to be able to watch African American athletes just 15 years after Liberation. They were immense, had allure, and brilliant uniforms."[2]

For the French, it was a remarkable chance to witness first-hand Chamberlain's basketball abilities, skills he plied in the NBA. Although tacticians like Robert Busnel were aware of these traits, it was the first time for many to see for themselves what elements of the US league and its style of play were like. It was, as basketball journalist Pascal Legendre later noted, a pivotal point as the country discovered "the magic of American basketball."[3]

But it wasn't the only sports revelation that summer. Barely two months later, on August 25, the Olympic Games opened in Rome and punctured the myth of French basketball fluency. It was the first Olympiad widely mediatized through broadcast television.[4] Moreover, expectations across the *hexagone* were high for success, thanks in no small part to a press that stoked nationalistic chauvinism on the court.[5] French officials, whose hopes were somewhat tempered by the late 1950s sports report a few years earlier, remained optimistic about their basketballers, fencers, swimmers, and track and field athletes.[6]

Yet, Rome 1960 was a watershed moment, a "zero hour" for French basketball, and sport more broadly, as its Olympians failed to meet expectations. The country's twenty-fifth place finish on the medal table underscored in hard numbers that it was no longer a Great Power; countries such as Hungary, Poland, Denmark, and Japan all fared better thanks to gold medal wins, something the French lacked. Two silver and three bronze medals, hardly the marker of a great or even middle-ranking country, deepened the humiliation. Such results were in flagrant contrast to the image of revival, rejuvenation, and *grandeur* put forth by President Charles de Gaulle of a victorious, strong France.

The basketball tournament was dispiriting. Les Tricolores qualified directly thanks to their international record and fielded a team that consistently won results since its 1948 Olympic silver medal. Roger Antoine continued his captaincy and was joined by national team mainstay Christian Baltzer and a new generation of rising stars. But the team could not catch a break. Les Tricolores lost their first match on August 26 against Czechoslovakia, 53–56, while their second match against Yugoslavia the following morning was a heartbreaking 61–62 loss after leading at the half. They won their third match against Bulgaria, 73–72, two days later but the effort was not enough to keep their hoop dreams alive. France was eliminated within three days of first tip, even as they continued to play for an eventual tenth-place tournament finish.[7]

Les Tricolores were outmatched, a performance that diverged from their perceived rung in world basketball. The 1960 Olympics launched a basketball crisis defined by a lack of competitiveness at major international competitions. Despite Busnel's efforts to incorporate new tactics, the men's team did not qualify for another Olympiad until the 1984 Games; although France placed fifth at the 1963 FIBA World Championships in Brazil, that was its last appearance until 1986.

Part of the equation was the larger evolution of the game during the 1960s, both internationally and at home. NBA players like Chamberlain and Bill Russell literally took basketball to new heights, playing a more vertical game, whereas the French iteration focused on a passing style that more resembled a ballet on the court than the airborne maneuverings of the US and NBA game.[8] Moreover, teams throughout the Eastern Bloc enlisted ever-taller players to exert physical dominance on-court. Combined with their coaching tactics and techniques, this often translated into off-court soft power through their ability to garner wins, influence, and respect from the game's glitterati.

Basketball's crisis, notably on the men's side, continued into the 1980s but the 1960s were a turning point. Despite the inability to qualify for the Olympics and FIBA World Championship, Busnel and others worked to improve results thanks to people-to-people cultural, technical, and knowledge exchanges in and around the hardcourt. Even as it took time for them to take root and thrive, these basketball diplomacy encounters built around French–American, French–Antillean, and French–African ties paved the groundwork for the future.

Scouting Report

Rome 1960 illuminated more than just a basketball crisis. It highlighted that French sport more broadly was in cardiac arrest. The lack of Olympic results touched a nerve at the Elysée Palace, for it heightened anxiety about the country's place in the world as the recalibration begun under the Fourth Republic continued during its successor.[9] De Gaulle navigated an independent path from the superpowers, a long-standing objective that was reinforced by development of a *force de frappe* (nuclear program) in 1960.[10] Despite this goal, at critical junctures, such as the October 1962 Cuban Missile Crisis, France proved a solid ally to the United States. But that didn't mean that de Gaulle didn't challenge Washington as he crafted French foreign policy. In January 1964, he reestablished diplomatic relations with Beijing, long before the United States thawed relations with the People's Republic of China, and in 1966 withdrew troops from the NATO alliance, which extended to removing NATO bases from French soil.

These efforts occurred alongside the Quai d'Orsay's renewed focus on Africa. By the end of 1960, the sub-Saharan empire ceased to exist thanks to the decolonization process begun by referendum two years earlier. Paris thus embarked on policies to maintain close ties to the region, including within the realm of sport; at times this meant preventing US influence in the sporting realm in the region.[11] The bloody colonial war to retain Algeria continued to split families apart until eventual Algerian independence via the Evian Accords of

1962. These shifts further underscored how France needed to create a new path in international affairs.

Decolonization and the continued need of labor to fuel postwar economic prosperity translated into new waves of immigrants and migrants to the mainland. North and sub-Saharan Africans, Spanish, Portuguese, and French Antilleans filled jobs that many established French citizens didn't want, cleaning buildings and offices or working in factories or other menial jobs. Many sent money back home, brought families to France, and began new lives on European soil. France's *jus soli* citizenship provided routes for newcomers to become French provided they assimilated into public life, just as was expected of previous generations. This influx ultimately changed notions of who was "French," but this issue had not yet reared its head.

Sport continued to serve as a means of assimilation although French performances at Rome was perceived as a humiliation. De Gaulle himself was reportedly enraged and, according to *L'Équipe*, stated that,

> If France shines abroad thanks to its thinkers, its sages [scientists], its artists, it must also shine through its sportsmen and women. A country must be great through the quality of its youth and you cannot conceive of this youth without a sporting ideal.[12]

He launched the country's first government investigation of sport to discover why its Olympians had underperformed. Four problem areas arose: a lack of sports terrains; no time during the school day for youths to engage in sport; a youth uninterested in sports as leisure-time activity; and the difficulty of elite athletes to train while holding regular jobs to maintain livelihoods. In response, the government launched a series of multi-year sports plans designed to address each problem area.[13]

Thus, during the 1960s de Gaulle instigated an unprecedented attempt to democratize sport and become further ingrained in citizens' lives. The Fifth Republic worked to make sport more accessible through the construction of new sports terrains and increasing facilities' operational hours so that they were available outside of work or school commitments.[14] Greater attempts were made to engage youth, especially teenagers, in organized sports outside of school to inoculate interest in playing and provide supervised leisure time to counter anxieties over juvenile delinquency.

This focal point spoke to adult fears that the large baby-boom generation was more interested in the growing global youth culture. Adults worried about how to integrate this unprecedentedly large demographic into the institutions and cultural fabric of the nation. There were far more students than the country's classrooms and universities could accommodate, to say nothing about the extra teaching personnel needed to educate them. As the baby-boomers matriculated into the university system and early professional careers, they forced structural changes that extended to long-held cultural norms about what was "French" culture. The US cultural influences of the 1950s were replaced by British influences like the Beatles or Mary Quant miniskirts. Moreover, European youth of the 1960s were increasingly bound by a budding sense of shared history and identity as increased opportunities to study and travel across borders forged new friendships.[15]

The intertwined youth and sports crises came to a head during the "Events" of May–June 1968. Sparked by a student revolt, country-wide protests and strikes rocked the political and social realm and threatened to overturn state institutions. In the immediate aftermath, and with a series of lackluster basketball results and sense of deepening crisis in mind, the French Basketball Federation (FFBB) instituted a critical change in June 1968 that paved the way for a slow revival. Without the basketball crisis, the French game would likely not have been as open to the outside influences that have since served as its foundations. The basketball crisis, part of the larger concurrent and intertwined youth and sports crises, thus set into motion a revitalization.

The Gentleman

One strand of basketball diplomacy's technical and cultural exchange that enriched the game in the 1960s came once again from PUC's American, Martin Feinberg. Given the club's history of being open to outside influences, it wasn't a surprise that they embraced not just Feinberg, who by the early 1960s coached the team, but other cosmopolitan forces. In 1962, Feinberg introduced his latest recruit, the American-born Henry "Gentleman" Fields, a power move with lasting repercussions.

For Fields, basketball was a way to see the world, just as for Feinberg and generations of players since. Born in New York in 1938 and raised in North Carolina, the six-foot-five Fields played basketball at the University of Elizabeth City (North Carolina) where he earned all-conference honors. While finishing his studies, Fields read the 1957 *Sports Illustrated* feature on Jean-Claude Lefebvre, then in his freshman year at Gonzaga, and was inspired. "[Lefebvre] spoke of French basketball," Fields told *La Depeche*. "At the time, I had to do my military service. If you remained in the army for three years you were able to choose your assignment. So, I chose France."[16]

Fields was posted to the US military base in Orleans in 1960, where he plied his game. He helped the US military team to the European and World Military Basketball Championship. But he also traveled to Germany to attend a basketball clinic run by Adolph Rupp, coach at the University of Kentucky. Despite Rupp's record of racial exclusion, Fields admired his teaching abilities and considered him the father of modern basketball. "The first fifteen minutes [of that clinic], I learned more basketball than I had learned all my life," Fields later recalled. "Everything Adolph Rupp taught was so simple."[17]

His reputation on-court caught the attention of several clubs, but it was PUC that tweaked his interest, in part through Feinberg. PUC's "American" saw Fields play at a Supreme Headquarters Allied Powers Europe (SHAPE) NATO tournament outside of Paris and approached with an offer to join the team, which Fields joined once his military service ended. Although the team was technically amateur, he received a subsidy of 450 francs a month and use of an apartment.[18]

With PUC, Fields was an effective defender who blocked and rebounded shots with finesse rarely seen on at the time. "My idol was Bill Russell," Fields confessed.

> I studied his movements, watched him when he played. I worked on that when I was in the Army, I worked all day on that, I worked eight, nine hours a day, a lot of the times by myself, just to work on different moves I see the player does.

For Fields, the ultimate end-goal was to coach basketball, and the more time he spent in France, the more he wanted to remain in-country. It was a plan that had first percolated during his army service when he spent dedicated time in the language lab to learn and perfect his French so that he could coach.

Fields brought the same work ethic that he used to learn Russell-esque techniques to the hardcourt. "I played the Bill Russell-type defense," he said of his idol.

> When I went to PUC, all they said about American players, was "oh, all Americans want to do is shoot." And I said, "I'm going to impress them because I'm not going to shoot. I'm gonna pass. I'm gonna block shots and pass the ball and let the other guys shoot." We had guys who could shoot. And people loved me because I passed the ball. That made [PUC] strong.

The aerodynamic and defensive style of play pioneered by Russell was, through Field's transmission, a form of technical exchange that laid the groundwork for future French defenders.

During the 1962–3 season, Fields put this finesse into play when he teamed up with Roger Antoine for a title. "People didn't talk about rebounding, blocking shots, defense, that wasn't talked about," he recalled of the team's victory over Bagnolet, 66–57, for the league championship on May 3, 1963. But Fields put on a defensive masterclass each time he took to the court for, "with me, nobody came to the basket."

It was just the second time that PUC was crowned Champion of France, a title their opponents had previously held. Bagnolet were known for their speed and improvisation, but the defensive techniques introduced and perfected by Fields defined the game. PUC brought an "impeccable defense, a superior athleticism, an organized attack, a tactical surety, and a grand bonhomme," Robert Busnel wrote in *Basket-Ball*, with a note that Fields, Antoine, and teammate Michel Rat were among the game's best players.[19]

The French tactician applauded PUC's efforts and noted the impact of their two American sages. He credited Feinberg for the win, "well done Monsieur Feinberg!" Busnel also praised Fields:

> The only foreigner operating in France who has been able to comply with the discipline of a team, instead of forcing the team to comply with his game. A model teammate who reminds me of someone . . . Let's see, let's see! Perfect positioning, vision of the game, model teammate, intelligence . . . But [Fields reminds me of] FEINBERG, naturally.[20]

FIGURE 2.1 *Henry Fields with Paris Université Club. Credit: Musée du Basket.*

Among the more than 5,300 spectators in the Stade Pierre de Coubertin stands that evening was a young man, Jean-Pierre Dusseaulx, who watched Fields orchestrate PUC's victory.[21] Dusseaulx was in the habit of attending PUC's matches for he lived near their home stadium, Stade Charlety; it was only later in the decade that he began to cover basketball for *L'Équipe*, the start of a decades-long career chronicling the sport's evolution and revolution. "Of the players of that era," he said, "Henry was perhaps the first real professional. He was a true pro."[22]

Fields was embraced by the basketball establishment, such as it was, and helped impart his style of play through clinics and workshops. "He was a model," former National Technical Director Gérard Bosc told *La Croix*.[23] He was eventually asked to work with French, Swiss, and German national teams and coaches to teach these defensive actions and help make players more technically sound. "They didn't know this type of training existed," Fields recalled. "I was giving them what I learned at the basketball clinic with Adolph Rupf. They thought I was a genius because they had never worked on those types of techniques [like faking and driving]."

He also introduced them to his basketball work ethic, putting on-court drills and preparation over leisure-time relaxation. At the time, French players trained once or twice a week, whereas Fields was used to the American-style workouts of two to two-and-a-half hours per day. The difference was stark and, in his mind, helped explain why France wasn't better internationally.

> I've said from the first time I came to France: France should be the second-best basketball country in the world, because they have a mixed culture, they have all these Black guys from the Antilles, they have the guys [of Polish heritage] in the northern part of France, they've got the Spanish; they can probably go back and forth, they're running, they have everything. The only thing they were missing was coaching. The basic individual techniques.

An American Half-Time

The country's cosmopolitanism and immigration heritage translated into a culture open to outside influences, a phenomenon that extended to basketball and, notably PUC. The team was the first French one to visit the United States in December 1955 and January 1956 but was otherwise well versed in playing abroad. It often traveled internationally to play matches, especially in Eastern Europe, including Moscow, and Africa for tournaments in Senegal, Morocco, and elsewhere.[24]

For Fields' teammate Rat, "PUC was one of the spearheads" of integrating outside influences in its basketball, one that also fed Les Tricolores.[25] Rat was recruited to PUC as a nineteen-year-old student during the 1956–7 season while studying to become a physical education teacher specialized in basketball. Within three years he began to play with the national team and won bronze at the 1959 European Championship, a victory he credited to learning to play better with PUC. "I didn't know what a block or a screen was, and I learned all of that from the PUC. It was a school of learning," Rat recalled decades later. "We were playing elaborate basketball.

We learned to defend, we learned to play with tall centers, I learned basketball. This is how I became an international player."

In December 1962, PUC again returned to the United States, a trip organized by Feinberg to further expose his players to US basketball culture and tactics. This informal sports diplomacy initiative helped a new generation of players to improve their game while at the same time learning first-hand about American culture and society, even its uglier facets. As Feinberg later confessed, "I loved the United States and wanted them to learn about basketball and Americans."[26]

On December 15, members of PUC, which included Fields and Rat, flew to the United States. Three days later, the team tipped off a series of games through the mid-Atlantic with a 42–39 win against Gallaudet University in Baltimore. A 37–87 loss to Oglethorpe two days later and shortly thereafter to AAU team Brownston, 66–68, dampened spirits slightly, but the team focused on the overall experience, not the game outcomes.

Part of the exercise was to learn new game techniques and tactics. Rat recalled how once again the team was given copies of technical documents, which he translated, to take home and incorporate into their repertoire. During this trip PUC also learned the shuffle offense, a system to move the ball via all five players through a series of screens. This was just one example of people-to-people sports exchanges that helped to enrich French basketball's technical know-how.

Another aspect was learning about US basketball cultural phenomena, such as sneakers. Although the French market began to feature basketball-specific kicks, such as the Busnel, according to Feinberg these models couldn't compare with the lighter, nimbler Converse. Thus, he strategically booked the team to conduct a radio interview after which they would receive a pair of the iconic sneakers for free. "They were very generous, the Americans, wherever we asked for the tennis shoes [basketball sneakers], we got them," he recalled. Such gestures were not lost on the visitors. As Rat later articulated, "everyone was crazy for Converses because they were American products."

The team also was indoctrinated into the realities of Jim Crow racial segregation. The supposedly "separate but equal" division of public spaces between those who were white and Black, from restaurants and hotels to drinking fountains and public transportation seating, such as on buses, was known of in France. But it was different to directly experience it and have a teammate targeted. In 1962, with Fields in tow, the French had a first-hand crash course on American racial attitudes when they traveled to the South.

After PUC won against Gallaudet they took a bus to Atlanta to play Oglethorpe. It was a long ride and when the bus driver stopped to refuel, the team took the opportunity to get out, stretch, and search for food. The roadside restaurant looked promising but, when the team entered, they were stopped by the proprietor. "The lady [owner or server] said nicely, 'I'm sorry we can serve you [referencing the white players] but we can't serve him,'" Fields recalled of how he was singled out.

It was the French players' first encounter with Jim Crow segregation. As Rat recalled, "we were profoundly shocked at [Fields' treatment.]" Feinberg tried to ease the awkwardness by declaring that he didn't want to eat there. "I was embarrassed," he remembered of the situation. "Henry Fields, of course, knew exactly what was going on." The team left and went elsewhere, the bad taste of the Atlanta-area experience the only such difficulty encountered on the trip.

For Fields, it was just another encounter in the Jim Crow South, but it wasn't as if he escaped racism entirely by building a life in France. There, too, racism was alive, albeit in different, more subtle ways. "[The government] made French people believe that you aren't racist, you don't have any problem against the coloreds, that only Americans are racist, and you aren't like the Americans," he recalled. "I suffered from it, because I walk out and people said, 'Ah! You are happy to be in France? You know we're all the same.'"

Despite such sentiments, Fields sensed that he was considered different because he was a basketball player. Still, the slights were real.

> You get on the metro and sit down and the people get up and go across the car. You go to a discotheque or a night club, and you have to have a card to get in; you sit at a table and wait a long time to be served . . . they weren't aggressive, it was just special.

Fields thought PUC's US trip was successful in that it proved that not every American was racist. "They were expecting Blacks on one side of the street and whites on the other," he said of television and print media portrayal of Jim Crow. "But the only time they saw that there was a problem was in Georgia . . . they expected that to be happening all the time."

This sports exchange, organized at the grassroots level by Feinberg, illustrated the power of people-to-people interactions through sport. PUC's French contingent came away with a more intimate understanding of the United States' complex culture, just as its Americans better comprehended France by playing the game and integrating with local communities, not just the expatriate crowd.[27] It's important to note that PUC wasn't representative of many of their generation; as basketball players, a sport that wasn't part of mainstream French culture, they were open to American influences and were already well disposed towards the United States—aside from the issue of its race relations. As these PUC players matured into professional careers around the game, they recalled with relish their US trip and what they learned from Fields and Feinberg, incorporating some of the elements learned (training, tactics, gear) in their work to overturn the basketball crisis.

The Changing Game

French basketball began to change. The ball was different, evolving from a "hard little white ball that would stick to your hand," as Fields later told *The New York Times*, to "real basketballs."[28] The game itself changed too. There was more rebounding, more blocking of shots. Teams trained more, and greater commitment was given to upskilling coaches to better teach and train their players from earlier ages. Fields was credited with helping to begin this revolution. As *Le Monde* later wrote:

> Henry Fields was not, has never been, in French basketball, an American like the others. The fact remains that Henry Fields will have given to French basketball as much as he received, not only through his talent as a player, but also by working as an educator in the clubs and by creating basketball schools."[29]

Such changes came at a time when Russell himself revamped the US game and helped place the NBA on firmer footing. The league had muddled through its first decade of infancy and by the 1960s stars such as Russell, Oscar Robertson, and Chamberlain attracted fans. Their bravado and flair helped gain attention, such as Chamberlain's 100-point game with the Warriors on March 2, 1962.[30] Games were more fluid and faster as Russell and his contemporaries played higher into the air.

The game also started to evolve in post-colonial Africa. In 1961, FIBA created an African division and within a few years the premier pan-African competition, the African Basketball Championship (today known as AfroBasket), was established for men (1962) and women (1966). These first tournaments were dominated by North Africa on the men's side with the short-lived United Arab Republic (1962, 1964) and Morocco (1965) crowned victors before Senegal began its long dominance of the African podium in 1968. Similarly, UAR dominated the women's 1966 and 1968 competitions before Senegal became the perennial African champions.

Some francophone African basketball federations retained working relationships with the FFBB after 1960.[31] This was part of a broader effort by French officials to influence their former African holdings in the growing Cold War balance.[32] Moreover, after decolonization, some of these federations, like Senegal, benefitted from continuity; they kept the governance structure originally implemented by the FFBB. This helps to explain in part why Senegal was one of the more dominant basketball powerhouses in African competition early on for they did not have to build from scratch.[33]

Basketball was also in transition across the Atlantic Ocean in the French Antilles. The state implemented new sports policies in Martinique, Guadeloupe, and French Guiana, constructed facilities and terrains, and increasingly encouraged Antillean youths to engage in sports. Thanks to their geographical proximity to the United States, the Antilles had more American sports cultural influences, especially in basketball.[34] Impressionable youths in Guadeloupe in particular cut their teeth on basketball courts, some who tried to emulate NBA players.

While the game and its influences changed in the mid-1960s, so did the FFBB's efforts to be more competitive internationally, a reflection of continued inability to make a mark at major competitions. The basketball crisis deepened as the men's team failed to qualify for the 1964 and 1968 Olympic Games or the 1967 FIBA World Championship. Following a fourth-place finish at the European Basketball Championship in 1961, the team's best finish across the next several tournaments was ninth place in 1965.

Busnel and the FFBB wished to regain an edge in competition and launched Operation Grande Taille, a campaign to recruit tall players.[35] Since the 1950s, Busnel was convinced that tall players were the key to sparring against height-advantaged East European teams. Thus, basketball authorities sought to improve young elite players' nutritional diets, increased musculation and weightlifting regimens, and recruited unusually tall boys and girls to the game.[36]

1968

All of this coincided with the "Events of May 1968," which announced the maturation of the baby-boom generation. The student-led revolts stemmed from their desire for greater freedom, cracked the older patriarchal social order of their parents, and liberated social mores. Once workers joined the student protests on May 13 to demand better wages and working conditions, the country's economic life came to a standstill. Although events did not result in a political revolution, they led to legislative elections that June and de Gaulle's eventual resignation the following year.

The sports world was implicated in the May 1968 events. The country's professional footballers went on strike to demand better working conditions and wages, while elsewhere there were calls for sports to be taken with greater seriousness as a constructive part of society. *L'Équipe* ceased publication from May 23 until June 10 and, following its return, ran an editorial that emphasized how

> sport is also, and above all, freedom. Sport is also the field of human reconciliation; the stadium is the crossroads where the various classes of society, without denying their convictions, learn to esteem and understand each other."[37]

The strikes forced a liberalization of sports and basketball. That June the FFBB acquiesced to a rule change that increased the number of foreigners that a team could field from one player to two. According to journalist Dusseaulx, Busnel's rule change had nothing to do with the "Events of 1968" or the demands for labor liberalization. "It was two totally different worlds," he said. "[Busnel] considered that French basketball wasn't as strong. He told himself, 'it's necessary to strengthen, and for French teams to be better, it isn't a spectacle.'"[38] The alteration of the number of foreign players allowed per team did exactly that: it set in motion a chain of events that further opened the game to outside influences. The resultant sports diplomacy of cultural, technical, and knowledge exchanges in and around the hardcourt improved talent and results.

Notes

1 Chamberlain was elected MVP and Rookie of the Year that season. Prior to entering the NBA, he played with the Globetrotters from 1958 to 1959, and greatly enjoyed discovering Europe. See Pascal Legendre, "Wilt Chamberlain, les Globies et la France (2ème partie): Wilt amoureux de l'Europe," *Basket Europe*, December 26, 2018, https://www.basketeurope.com/livenews-fr/434650/wilt-chamberlain-les-globies-et-la-france-2eme-partie-wilt-amoureux-de-leurope/.

2 Ken Fernandez, "Quand Wilt Chamberlain et les Harlem Globetrotters Débarquaient dans un Village Français," *L'Équipe*, March 20, 2020, https://www.lequipe.fr/Basket/Article/Quand-wilt-chamberlain-et-les-harlem-globe-trotters-debarquaient-dans-un-village-francais/1120738.

3 Fernandez.

4 David Maraniss, *Rome 1960: The Olympics That Changed the World* (Simon & Schuster, 2008).

5 Lindsay Sarah Krasnoff, *The Making of Les Bleus: Sport in France, 1958–2010* (Lexington Books, 2012).

6 Institut National des Sports, "Notes Soumises à Monsieur Le Directeur Général de La Jeunesse et Des Sports à Propos de La Préparation Aux JO 1960" (Institut National des Sports, Undated), Centre des Archives Contemporaines (CAC) 19780586 Art 100.

7 IOC, "Official Report of the 1960 Olympic Games, v.2," 1960, 633–40, https://digital.la84.org/digital/collection/p17103coll8/id/21636/rec/27.

8 Jean-Pierre de Vincenzi, Interview with the author, September 22, 2016.

9 For more see Krasnoff, *The Making of Les Bleus*.

10 For more on French foreign policy and objectives to ensure French independence under the Fifth Republic, see Christian Nuenlist, Anna Locher, and Garret Martin, eds., *Globalizing de Gaulle: International*

Perspectives on French Foreign Policies, 1958–1969 (Lexington Books, 2010); Philip Gordon, *A Certain Idea of France: French Security Policy and Gaullist Legacy* (Princeton University Press, 1992); Frédéric Bozo, *French Foreign Policy Since 1945: An Introduction* (Berghahn Books, 2016).

11 For more, see Pascal Charitas, "A More Flexible Domination: Franco-African Sport Diplomacy during Decolonization, 1945–1966," in *Diplomatic Games: Sport, Statecraft, and International Relations since 1945*, ed. Heather L. Dichter and Andrew L. Johns (University of Kentucky Press, n.d.); Pascal Charitas and David-Claude Kemo-Keimbou, "The United States of America and the Francophone African Countries at the International Olympic Committee: Sports Aid, a Barometer of American Imperialism? (1952–1963)," *Journal of Sport History* 40, no. 1 (2013): 69–91.

12 Anouk Corge, "Charles De Gaulle, le sport en porte-drapeau," *L'Équipe*, June 13, 2020, https://www.lequipe.fr/Tous-sports/Article/Charles-de-gaulle-le-sport-en-porte-drapeau/1143151.

13 For greater details on the government's findings, see Krasnoff, *The Making of Les Bleus*.

14 The government estimated that some 4,000 gymnasiums, 1,500 swimming pools, and 8,000 sports terrains were constructed by the state from 1961 to 1975. Marc Falcoz and Pierre Chifflet, "La construction publique des équipements sportifs : Aspects historique, politique et spatial," *Les Annales de la Recherche Urbaine*, 79, no. 1 (1998): 14–21.

15 For more on the topic, see Richard Ivan Jobs, *Riding the New Wave: Youth and the Rejuvenation of France after the Second World War* (Stanford University Press, 2007); Richard Ivan Jobs, *Backpack Ambassadors: How Youth Travel Integrated Europe* (Chicago: University of Chicago Press, 2017).

16 Cyril Doumergue, "Henry Fields, un Géant Américain à Auterive," *La Depeche*, September 9, 2018, https://www.ladepeche.fr/article/2018/09/09/2865295-henry-fields-un-geant-americain-a-auterive.html.

17 All Henry Fields quotes in this chapter, unless specified, from Henry Fields, Interview with the author, June 30, 2015.

18 Rémy Dessarts, "Le Commerce des Basketteurs Américains," *Le Monde*, September 29, 1980.

19 Robert Busnel, "Le Paris Université Club: Incontestable Champion de France," *Basket-Ball*, May 1963, X.

20 Busnel, XI.

21 *PUC/Bagnolet Finale Championnat 63*, 2021, https://www.youtube. com/watch?v=cQlOZ8Ccezw; Jean-Pierre Dusseaulx, Interview with the author, October 16, 2015.

22 Dusseaulx, Interview with the author.

23 Pascal Charrier, "Henry Fields, le Basket de New York à Auterive," *La Croix*, September 19, 2009.

24 Yannick Deschamps, "La Diplomatie Sportive Entre la France et l'URSS, des Années 1920 à l'année 1991. Acteurs, Échanges et Stratégies" (Université de Strasbourg, 2020).

25 All quotes in this chapter, unless specified, from Michel Rat, Interview with the author, June 29, 2015; Michel Rat, Interview with the author, October 26, 2014; Michel Rat, Interview with the author, September 24, 2021.

26 All Martin Feinberg quotes in this chapter, unless specified, from Martin Feinberg, Interview with the author, interview by Lindsay Sarah Krasnoff, December 7, 2014.

27 Lindsay Sarah Krasnoff, "Barnstorming Frenchmen: The Impact of Paris Université Club's US Tours and the Individual in Sports Diplomacy," in J Simon Rofe (ed.), *Sport and Diplomacy: Games within Games* (Manchester University Press, 2018), 130–46.

28 G. Dryansky, "American Jumpshots in Europe," *The New York Times*, November 28, 1982, sec. Magazine, https://www.nytimes.com/1982/ 11/28/magazine/american-jumpshots-in-europe-g-y-dryansky-is-an-american-writer.html.

29 Dryanksy.

30 David George Surdam, *The Rise of the National Basketball Association*, Kindle (University of Illinois Press, 2012), sec. 106.

31 J. Simon Rofe and Lindsay Sarah Krasnoff, "Transcript: Interview with Carmine Calzonetti and Kenny Grant" (SOAS University of London, May 2020), "Basketball Diplomacy in Africa: An Oral History from SEED Project to the Basketball Africa League (BAL), https://eprints. soas.ac.uk/32908/1/BBDipAF2020%20Carmine%20Calzonetti%20 and%20Kenny%20Grant.pdf; Johan Rat, Interview with the author, September 24, 2021.

32 Pascal Charitas, "A More Flexible Domination: Franco-African Sport Diplomacy during Decolonization, 1945–1966," in Heather L. Dichter and Andrew L. Johns (eds.), *Diplomatic Games: Sport, Statecraft, and International Relations since 1945* (University of Kentucky Press, n.d.).

33 Rofe and Krasnoff.

34 Jacques Cachemire, Interview with the author, 2015.

35 "Operation Grande Taille," *Basket-Ball*, April 1983.

36 For more on this and the evolution of sports medicine of the era, see Lindsay Sarah Krasnoff, "Developing Athletic 'Atomic Armaments': The Role of Sports Medicine in Cold War France, 1958–1992," *Performance Enhancement & Health* 2 (2013): 8–16.

37 Editorial, "15 Jours Après," *L'Équipe*, June 10, 1968.

38 Jean-Pierre Dusseaulx, Interview with the author, October 16, 2015.

3

Emulating an Idol, 1968–84

The women's European Basketball Championship was held in Italy in July 1968, but until the very last minute the French team wasn't sure that they would participate. Given the "Events of 1968" that May and June, which rocked the country to its core, there were doubts as to whether there was enough stability at home to send the team abroad. Head coach Joë Jaunay wrote in *Basket-Ball*, "personally, I was against participation," even as he acknowledged how much he wanted his team to compete with the continent's best talent. "Without being prepared, the team approached the tournament with ambition."[1]

But it was not sufficient. The team was more technically advanced and taller than in recent selections, but whether due to a lack of full preparation or the instability back home, Les Tricolores couldn't hold their own in competition. France lost all three of their group matches. Eliminated from the tournament's more competitive stages, France lost to Czechoslovakia, 49–54, Hungary, 36–42, and Romania, 48–59, then won a 91–47 blowout against West Germany and against the Netherlands 60–55 to round out classification.

France finished eleventh out of thirteen teams while the Soviet Union won the championship title thanks to the scoring of its sixteen-year-old prodigy Uljana Semjonova. Yugoslavia, Poland, East Germany, and Bulgaria were the top five finishers, respectively, a deception for West European teams who, except for Italy (sixth) and Belgium (seventh), finished last.

Jaunay's tournament autopsy noted that the East Europeans had a three-month preparation period in the lead-up to competition. They had more time to learn to play together, to build team chemistry and problem solve on-court. In contrast, he noted,

Western counterparts' national team training was "often hasty and, in any case, never analogous." Thus, he argued, "this means that they cannot win, that they will never be able to win until they fight with equal preparation."[2]

But what if France were able to bring together some of its best talent, the core elements of the national team, to play together on one club season-in and season-out? That was the solution that Jaunay and other basketball officials worked towards. It was implemented in Clermont-Ferrand, located in central France, and one of the city's women's clubs, Clermont Université Club (CUC), emerged as the unofficial hub of women's basketball.

The revitalization was aided indirectly by the June 1968 FFBB rule change that increased the number of foreign players on rosters from one to two. The informal sports diplomacy it unleashed via knowledge and cultural exchanges helped the women's game flourish at the continental club and elite levels. CUC and the national team's improved results were built on the know-how cultivated by generations of home-grown coaches and technicians and facilitated by basketball's longstanding cultural role as an "acceptable" endeavor for women. But they were also influenced by male players and coaches who arrived in the *hexagone* and introduced the tactics and drills popularized in the United States.

A certain US vibe thus informed women's basketball. The experiences of CUC and national team center Élisabeth Riffiod illustrate how the NBA effect rippled across the Atlantic Ocean. Meanwhile, the exchanges forged through the basketball friendship between US coach Carmine Calzonetti and the legendary CUC star Jacky Chazalon led to the first US-style basketball camps for kids, an instrumental development.

Scouting Report

The ascent of French women's basketball to the peaks of European club and continental competition occurred against the backdrop of a realigning world in which sport increasingly took greater import. The uprisings of 1968 were part of a larger global phenomenon that unleashed liberalization of societies and cultural attitudes, with ripple effects into foreign policy. In the fifteen years that followed, terse relations between the two nuclear-armed superpowers eased into a brief *détente*, a warming of relations that provided Paris with greater flexibility overall, including towards its American sister republic.

Charles de Gaulle's presidential successors Georges Pompidou (1969–74) and Valery Giscard d'Estaing (1974–81) continued a foreign policy designed to maintain French independence yet became more activist. Franco-American relations at first under Pompidou were unprecedentedly warm. US President Richard Nixon acknowledged France's role as a "major strategic partner," and it seemed a new era of transatlantic *amitié* was at hand.[3] But the 1973 Arab–Israeli War once again tested the friendship as Paris's position was not congruent with Washington's. Ultimately, France sided with the United States when the conflict threatened to escalate into a larger test between the superpowers. Within Europe, French diplomacy focused on strengthening relations with West Germany and expansion of the European Economic Community (EEC) to include the United Kingdom. Its policies vis-à-vis the Middle East curried favor with oil-producing Arab states, which France relied upon for inexpensive oil, while closer cultivation of ties with Africa sought to repair an image tarnished by France's role in the Algerian War.

The country increased its fingerprints on international institutions during the Giscard d'Estaing administration. Paris laid the groundwork for what eventually became the Group of Seven (G7) with the 1975 Rambouillet summit, pushed for a stronger European community, and worked to bring the heads of Europe closer together through the European Council, which first met that same year.

But the 1973 Arab–Israeli War ignited an oil and energy crisis that brought the thirty years of postwar economic growth to a halt and cast a shadow over domestic concerns. Economic stagnation combined and new waves of immigration, predominantly from former areas of empire in Africa, was kindling for the return of a far-right-wing political movement. The Front National (FN), led by Jean-Marie Le Pen, capitalized on insecurities bred from a sense of socioeconomic instability and a turn away from older cultural mores to scapegoat immigrants and gain a political toehold.

At the same time, the second wave of feminism gained traction. Despite roots in the Revolution of 1789, notably through Olympe de Gouges' influential *Declaration of the Rights of Woman and of the Female Citizen*, the feminist movement floundered until the post-1945 era. Women finally gained the right to vote in 1944, and five years later Simone de Beauvoir's *The Second Sex* planted the seeds of modern feminism. But it took 1968 and a more militant movement, led in part by the Women's Liberation Movement (MLF), to catalyze greater change. Throughout the 1970s, sexual mores eased, contraceptive pills became widely available (for free), abortion was decriminalized (1972) and legalized (1975), and equal pay institutionalized (1972) as more women entered the workforce.[4]

Within this context, sport provided one possible solution to knit society's various strands together in the post-1968 anti-elitist climate. Although the state recognized sport's ability to serve as a domestic as well as foreign policy tool, continued lack of French results hindered using sports to cultivate soft power or court the country's youth. The continued basketball and sports crisis highlighted by the 1960 Olympics prompted the French government and the French Basketball Federation (FFBB) to reevaluate efforts. After 1968, there was increased focus on rectifying the problems flagged eight years earlier in recognition that such efforts were not yet effective.

It was clear that a new blueprint was needed and in October 1975 the Mazeaud Law was enacted. The legislation was named after then-Secretary of State for Youth and Sports Pierre Mazeaud, an elite alpinist who in 1978 was part of the first French team to scale Mount Everest; he pushed to reset society and government's relationship with sport in the belief that it was a national obligation. The resulting law inscribed sport as part of French culture for the first time and attempted to create sports heroes, something Mazeaud fervently felt necessary in order to inspire new generations of kids. The Mazeaud Law also laid out the republic's obligation to its elite athletes. Not only did it pledge to support their training with the rechristening of the national sports school into the National Institute for Sport, Excellence, and Performance (INSEP), where they could train, it also established the grounds for a youth sports development program as another part of the equation to fix the sports crisis. It thus sought to confer government legitimacy on sports in new ways.[5]

But legislation and training programs alone were insufficient; it was necessary to make sports more attractive to younger generations. It was crucial to inspire and maintain kids' interest to pursue sports to its highest levels, thus the law also committed the state to the promotion of sports for all.[6] Three years later, creation of the National Committee of Elite Sport (CNSHN) established a system of youth detection that scouted promising young talent and fed them into the country's new sports training systems.[7]

But not for football. Instead, the French Football Federation (FFF) founded its own youth talent detection and training system, which later served as a blueprint for other sports federations like the FFBB. In 1972, the FFF established the National Football Institute (INF) at Vichy to centralize training of its most promising talent to finish school so that, in the event that they failed to become a professional footballer, they could fall back on another career. The following year, the first professional football club youth academy was launched at Nancy with the FFF mandating that all top division clubs have an academy by the 1977–8 season. Inspired by National Technical Director Georges Boulogne, these academies encompassed the recommendations of national team coach Stephan Kovacs, a Romanian who coached Dutch giant Ajax to two European Cups before joining France in 1973, to start teaching technical skills at younger ages.[8] The academies provided small financial stipends to pay young players to board, train, and complete their scholastic education with the club. Many professional clubs had an academy on paper until the late 1980s, when brick-and-mortar academies were constructed.[9] They later became models of inspiration for basketball clubs as they crossed the line from amateur and semi-professionalism into professional status.

While there was an increased reference to US basketball after 1968 thanks to the young men who came to France to coach and play, the game remained far apart from its American counterpart. The NBA, for example, was not well known, even by basketball journalists like *L'Équipe*'s Jean-Pierre Dusseaulx. "One knew it existed, that it had the very best players, but that was the extent of it," he said. "The NBA was another world."[10] Interestingly, the women's game began to benefit from the US and NBA transatlantic influences of the post-1968 era as it, too, came out of isolation vis-à-vis its American cousin.

Since its earliest years, basketball was played by women in the United States. It was thought of as well suited to cultivate a feminine physique, build moral fiber, and aid in overall education.[11] In France, the situation was a little different. The late nineteenth- and early twentieth-century development of sports was predominantly viewed as a masculine activity but there were a few outliers.[12] Tennis, calisthenics, and dance were all deemed suitable for Frenchwomen, and many took up bicycling despite great public furor.[13]

World War I changed attitudes and opened more opportunities for women to play sports, including basketball. The first women's championship was contested in 1920, and within a few years several women's athletic clubs founded basketball sections.[14] At the time, the French Feminine Sports Federation (FFSF) organized and promoted women's sports. Its influential founder and president Alice Milliat focused more on football during the interwar years out of personal preferences, but the FFSF organized the first women's basketball league in 1928; Saint Maur club Linnet's was the first French champion, a title they reclaimed five more times in less than a decade.[15] The game was further inscribed when in 1936 women's basketball was integrated in to the FFBB, which has run the French women's championship since 1937.

Basketball also grew internationally, providing yet more opportunities for Frenchwomen to play.[16] France was one of five teams to compete at the first-ever women's European Championship staged in Rome in October 1938. Its fourth-place finish with just one win over Switzerland, 43–18, wasn't entirely a surprise. Several key players, including captain Lucienne Velu, missed the tournament as they could not take time off from their jobs. The resulting roster, cobbled together in last-minute fashion, lacked chemistry. Some critics blamed the lackluster record on the absence of an attacking offense.[17] Other observers, including team manager Paul Geist, overlooked the fourth-place result and instead viewed the tournament as an excellent testament to the growth of international competition and the public's interest.

"Our players proved that they know how to fight with admirable heart, they learned a lot and that is essential," he wrote in *Basket-Ball Magazine* after the tournament. "Our best player, the calmest, who played the most appropriately," Geist noted, was Sokéla Mangoumbel.[18] The twenty-seven-year-old Nantes native, a player full of joie de vivre, predated Roger Antoine as the first Black player for France.[19]

The women's national team did not compete again until after World War II, even as the game developed. Importantly, it avoided the social taboos and negative stereotypes as being "too masculine" for women to play that football was subjected to. Moreover, women's basketball has, historically, been better regarded in France than in neighboring countries like Spain and Italy.[20]

The immediate post-1945 era enabled France to flex its muscle. The women's side improved in international competition with a fourth-place (out of twelve) finish at EuroBasket 1950, its best result of the decade. France was one of two European teams to contest the first FIBA Women's World Championship (today's World Cup), held in Santiago, Chile, in 1953; the eight other sides were from the Americas.[21] Coached by Robert Busnel, Les Tricolores, as the team was then known, fought hard and notched a third-place finish, its first medal.

Notably, the team was perceived by French male basketball and diplomatic authorities to be a success less on court than in terms of what their style of play and comportment communicated to the larger world about France and femininity. French Ambassador to Chile Jacques Baeyens cabled the Quai d'Orsay on March 14, 1953, to inform them of the team's service to the state. "Our players managed to secure the prestige of French sport and to give the Chilean public an excellent impression of French female youths," he wrote while effusing how other athletes should be able to so brilliantly represent the nation as the team.[22] FFBB president Charles Boizard acknowledged the team's sporting success. "You have served French sport well and you have served France well," he wrote.

You have defended your colors with an admirable heart, but moreover, by your kindness and the correctness of your behavior, you have contributed to destroying a monstrous and undeserved conception of the French woman, which unfortunately prevails abroad.[23]

Then the sports crisis hit and engulfed basketball. The women's team failed to qualify for the 1960 European Championship, finished in eighth place in 1962, and did not place better than tenth at the 1964, 1966, and 1968 editions. The team failed to qualify for the 1957 and 1959 FIBA World Championships, placed tenth at the 1964 tournament, and again failed to qualify for the 1967 event hosted in Czechoslovakia.

A downwards spiral of French results must also be placed within the context of the rise of Eastern Europe's women's teams. The

Eastern Bloc's investment in state-sponsored sports programs and the use of international sporting wins to reaffirm the valor of communist ideology was particularly noticeable in basketball. From 1950 until 1960, the European Championship was held in and dominated on the podium by communist regimes. Hosted by Western Europe in 1962 (France), 1968 (Italy), and 1970 (the Netherlands), Eastern European teams finished in the top three consistently until 1970, such as the Soviet Union, Czechoslovakia, and Bulgaria.

France's track record wasn't one that inspired. "In 1970, nobody believed in the French women's team, except those who were part of it," wrote Dusseaulx in *L'Équipe Basket Magazine*.[24] Set against this backdrop was the rise of a young talent and her future teammates who wrote history and firmed the foundations for the future basketball empire.

Landing the One-Handed Jump Shot

Élisabeth Riffiod was part of this basketball transformation. Born July 20, 1947 in Besançon, by October 1966, she came to the attention of her physical education teacher, Suzanne Viguier, for at six-foot-one, nineteen-year-old Riffiod, then in her senior year of high school, stood out.[25] Viguier, a licensed coach, also captained local basketball team Vesontio Femina, a storied women's club founded in 1922.[26] She was thus privy to the FFBB's Operation Grande Taille initiative to recruit tall youths to the sport.[27]

The coach approached Riffiod with the suggestion to try basketball. The idea took Riffiod by surprise for, since she was a young girl, she suffered from a health issue that often left her tired.[28] But she took to the game, and later told *L'Équipe Magazine* that "rather quickly, I gave my captain reasons to believe in me."[29] She had height, a tall vertical jump, and a slow heart rate (38 beats per minute), which were an attractive package. But she had an even more important quality: dedication, drive, and a desire to work hard.

Riffiod's immersion into basketball also provided a strong dose of self-confidence. "Until then, I suffered from my height," she recalled to *L'Équipe Magazine*. "Basketball allowed me to value my height, to no longer be ashamed by such a long body, and to instead use it to the best way possible."[30]

Viguier coached Riffiod's first months, but word of the tall teenager rapidly spread to Jaunay. As a young player in the early 1940s, he was influenced by the tactics and techniques of Michael Ruzgis, an American who played and coached in France. This early exposure through informal sports diplomacy left a lasting imprint, for Jaunay remained attuned to developments in the US game. But he was committed to improving the French game. The Frenchman served as National Technical Director from 1964 to 1980, spearheading the general direction of elite basketball development, coached the men's team from 1965 until 1974, the women's team from 1966 to 1976, and CUC for four seasons beginning in 1972.

One of the first things he did upon taking the reins was to instruct each region's technical advisor to give him the names of girls taller than six feet.[31] He was preoccupied with finding players who had physical qualities that could lend themselves well to the game. Increasingly, the focus was on creation of versatile centers for, after 1960, such positions required athleticism, agility, and speed to lend a competitive edge to teams.[32] When the technical advisor from the Besançon region submitted Riffiod's name, there was a note that, while tall, she was still quite new to the game.

Yet, despite the improbability, she earned her first cap with the women's national team mere months after she started to play. It was a March 11, 1967, friendly against Czechoslovakia that Les Tricolores lost, 69–57. The Besançon native had no impact on the game. But it was the start of a new phase in her development, one in which her basketball IQ began to flourish for playing with the national team was entry into a new world. "Because I found the best atmosphere there, I agreed to comply without reservations to the requirements represented by wearing the tricolor jersey," she later told *L'Équipe Magazine*. "For me, the E[quipe] D[e] F[rance] is the most beautiful of adventures. An adventure worth living, which sometimes escapes sportswomen who do not realize the full benefit that can be derived from it."[33]

That year she was also recruited to be part of the first cohort to train and study at what is today INSEP. Although Riffiod wanted to attend university to become a biology teacher or to teach natural sciences, Jaunay informed her that attending classes in Paris was out of the question, for the commute was too far from campus. Instead, she took correspondence classes to become a physical education teacher while she trained on campus.

Her basketball regimen was by and large an individual one overseen by Jaunay, even though she continued to play with her home team on Sundays. And, as that was in the eastern part of the country, it meant she traveled quite a bit, particularly for away games.[34] "Very often, I trained alone," she said, although there were three or four players who came out from Paris a few times a week to practice with her.[35]

A big part of Riffiod's development was influenced by hoops developments across the Atlantic. "[Jaunay] was inspired by US basketball and insisted that the fundamentals were important," she recalled. At his suggestion, Riffiod began to watch game tape of the Boston Celtics versus Cincinnati Royals NBA finals. The ritual may seem self-evident to twenty-first-century audiences but in 1960s France it was not typical. The dominant perception was that, while the league was spectacular in its athleticism, it wasn't a style of basketball that was terribly intelligent or well constructed, and that it was too individualistic.[36] Yet it was through this ritual that Riffiod discovered Bill Russell. "Speaking of Bill Russell, for me, it's something very strong emotionally because he's always been my idol," she said.[37]

By this time, the player was a key foundation to the Celtics' dynasty. After Russell's 1956 Olympic gold medal with Team USA, he forged a career in Boston as one of the era's dominant shot blockers and rewrote the script for defenders around the basketball world. By the time Riffiod began her tutelage at INSEP, Russell had won nine out of an eventual eleven NBA championships and racked up numerous individual awards, including multiple Most Valuable Player, All-Star, and All-Star Game MVP accolades. Thus her studious analysis of Russell was instructive for how to play defense and to do it well.

Russell was an informative reference in another way: his jump shot. At the time, female players shot the ball with two hands to take long-range shots. But not Riffiod. Because she began playing so late, "I didn't shoot from far, I didn't have a two-handed shot," she recalled. So Jaunay had her watch that tape over and over to absorb the American's shooting tactics. "[Jaunay] told me that I will learn to shoot directly with one hand, a one-handed jump shot," Riffiod recalled of these technical lessons. Which she did, becoming the first French woman to do so.[38] While her teammates started to increasingly play around with taking the shot small steps at a time,

FIGURE 3.1 *Élisabeth Riffiod with Clermont Université Club (CUC).*
Credit: Musée du Basket.

Riffiod jumped and stayed in the air with her jump shot. "He really inspired me," she said of watching Russell.

Yet, for all that she emulated her idol, Riffiod credited her career to Jaunay:

> If Joë Jaunay hadn't had this idea of wanting [me] to play with his team, to build the women's national team, to look for tall girls, I would never have played basketball ... I would have stopped playing basketball. I owe a lot, my whole career and my whole future and my whole life, to this coach.

Riffiod completed her studies to become a teacher in 1971, and played for two years with Evreux Athletic Club (1970–2). Then, in fall 1972, she signed with CUC.

The Demoiselles de Clermont

CUC, the most storied female basketball team in France, owes its success to crosstown rival AS Montferrand (ASM). In 1949, ASM won its first national championship with its junior women's team who, as they aged into the senior rungs, proved to be one of the country's best, winning the 1958, 1959, and 1962 French championship and two French Cups (1957, 1958).[39] They were led by Edith Tavert, a 1953 FIBA World Cup bronze medalist who parlayed a storied on-court career into a legendary one coaching. From 1950 until 1964, she was both player and coach but left to assume head coach duties with CUC after a falling out with ASM officials.[40] Many of ASM's best players followed Tavert, including a young Chazalon. ASM had to rebuild nearly from scratch, an effort facilitated with Tavert's return to the head coach position in 1975.

In the interim, CUC filled the vacuum. In 1967, it disputed the French final and within three years imprinted itself on the larger European scene. There were several ingredients that helped CUC's success. First, it had Tavert then, after 1972, Jaunay at the helm, which helped set CUC apart. So, too, did the rapport that the women's players had with their male counterparts, including several Americans. Third, at Jaunay's direction, the team was stocked with some of the country's best talent, a move designed to allow national team players to play together regularly to build chemistry, familiarity, and compete against some of the best. Lastly, CUC's storybook plot was completed by a talented foe, Semjonova, of cross-continental rival Daugava Riga.

These elements made CUC the most dominant French side of the era. From 1968 until 1981, the team won thirteen national titles and contested five European finals (1971, 1973, 1974, 1976, 1977), four of which were against Daugava Riga. But its on-court successes led to court-side problems. Often the team could not accommodate its fans, for its 6,000-seat stadium was frequently sold out.[41] Off-court, its players became some of the more recognizable athletes of the era, for CUC was one of the most mediatized sports teams.

The team's undisputed star was Jacky Chazalon. Born March 24, 1945, in Alès, Chazalon was known for her precision of play, fluidity of movements, and her ambition to excellence, influenced by the US players who began to play in France after 1968. Combined, these traits were credited with bringing new technical dimensions to women's basketball.[42]

Chazalon, Riffiod, and CUC put women's basketball into the sports media pages, popularized the game, and translated wins together into wins for the national team. The September 1972 European Championship, held in the Netherlands, was the first time that Les Tricolores demonstrated how the chemistry and familiarity fostered by playing together with CUC could translate into a podium finish. Following a close first match against Poland on September 11, in which the French squeaked out a 68–67 victory, the team notched wins against Italy (63–58) and the hosts (69–50) before a 41–77 loss to the Soviets. Triumphs over Hungary (54–49) and Bulgaria (69–64) set up a gold medal match against the USSR on September 19. The final was a shattering disappointment as the French were outclassed 33–94, although Riffiod put up a game-high eight points. Nonetheless, it was a silver medal finish, the country's best in an international women's competition, one that was televised to the French public back home.

It was a contrast to women's basketball in the United States. Despite the passage of Title IX of the 1972 Education Act, which prohibited gender-based discrimination in providing sporting opportunities within federally funded education institutions, women's basketball at US universities in the 1970s was engaged in an uphill battle. Players across the country had to sell T-shirts and engage in other entrepreneurial endeavors, like bake sales, in order to fund their teams.[43] As *L'Équipe Basket Magazine* reported in January 1976, "American women's basketball remains if not a circus phenomenon—what it was—at least a marginal, minority phenomenon."[44] The publication noted that the tides were slowly turning in the United States, and while European and Soviet club teams were still better, they would not have an advantage for long. "Jaunay thinks [the women's basketball gap between Europe and the United States] won't last."[45]

Half-Time

In 1976, France hosted the women's European Championship, fittingly in Clermont-Ferrand. The hosts aimed for second place, "simply because there is the USSR and nobody actually pretends to win over the Soviets," Dusseaulx wrote of French chances.[46] He pointed to the exemplary Soviet record at European competition: they had won every single biennial tournament but one since 1950.

> The USSR is invincible. And not just because of the presence of Semjonova. The Soviets know how to play very well, even without their giant . . . To watch the USSR is a pleasure, for this team approaches the ideal. We are persuaded that even the men's teams of Nationale 1 [top men's league in France] would lose against the USSR, despite their athletic advantage.[47]

As Jacques Marchand, editor of *L'Équipe Basket Magazine*, observed in May 1976, "today, more than ever, women's sport can be and must be understood as a social phenomenon."[48] But such hopes were short lived. The tournament was not a popular or a basketball success and the hosts finished fourth. One month later, many of CUC's players rejoined the Tricolores to compete in qualification for the first women's Olympic basketball tournament. It lost to the United States (71–59), to Poland (65–61), and won against Mexico (55–35), but it was not enough to secure an Olympic berth.[49] Tensions erupted and Chazalon left CUC, as well as the national team.

The start of the 1976–7 season brought winds of change as twenty-nine-year-old US coach Bill Sweek took over at CUC.

"When my friends from France knew that I was going to train CUC they called me crazy," he told *L'Équipe Basket Magazine* in January 1977, four months into his tenure. "It was a team of stars, the only one in France on the women's side, and the coach wasn't the actual boss."[50]

Sweek arrived to find a team of hard workers, but players who were constantly asked to perform. That year alone, many team members vied for the European Club Cup, the European Championship, and Olympic qualification. "The amount of work to prepare for these three competitions was considerable, and left physical and moral traces," he told the publication. His players trained every day even though they didn't seem to derive the same desire or pleasure from playing.[51] So Sweek brought in some younger players to rejuvenate the team and reignite fire for the game.

Even as CUC reset, the team's impact had deep ripple effects that helped stimulate the game across the *hexagone*. They stoked greater interest and participation in basketball.[52] By 1976, basketball was the top sport for women, with some 100,000 licensed players whereas seven years earlier there were only 20,000, driven mostly by CUC.[53] While local clubs benefitted from interest in the sport, a new phenomenon facilitated kids' tactical know-how, one imported from the United States by one of CUC's coaches and implemented by one of its female hoops heroines: the summer basketball camp.

Merlin the Wizard

The Jacky Chazalon basketball camps were revolutionary developments in youth sport when they debuted in the late 1970s, a collaboration between Chazalon and her good friend Carmine Calzonetti. The American, born February 9, 1947, grew up outside of Philadelphia in New Jersey and crafted a collegiate career at Saint John's, where he played from 1966 until 1969. After graduation, Calzonetti signed with agent Jim McGregor and that summer received an invitation to play in Italy.

Calzonetti's French story began some eighteen months later, when McGregor told him that the team in Nantes was in need of a guard. Calzonetti agreed to a tryout, jumped a train to the western port city and arrived with just a pair of clogs on his feet.[54] He played barefoot against properly shod French players during his tryouts, was offered the position, and for the next five years haunted the Nantais hardcourt.[55] Nicknamed "Merlin the Wizard," Calzonetti helped Nantes to the Nationale 2 championships and served as player-coach from the 1972 season on.[56]

In early 1974, CUC tapped two of Nantes' American players to help the team prepare for their European Club Cup final against rival Daugava Riga, their third final in four years. Calzonetti and teammate Vincent Schafmeister arrived and transmitted their technical expertise to help problem-shoot eventual confrontations against Semjonova.[57]

"That team was stacked with the best, absolutely all the best players in France," Calzonetti recalled decades later.

> You saw a very professional organization. They were all dressed well, they had the best equipment. They practiced all the time and they were the best players in the country in one spot. They also followed basketball, so they knew who I was—and I certainly knew who they were. So there was some respect.[58]

Given this previous working relationship, it was no surprise that CUC once again called upon Calzonetti when they were in a bind two years later. It was 1976 and they needed someone to coach the team during a three-week tour in Senegal as Sweek was unable to travel. That's how Calzonetti took his first trip to Africa, though it would hardly be his last, and in the process struck up a friendship with Chazalon.

Because Sweek had introduced American-style drills, sets, and practices, it was easy for Calzonetti to step in.[59] "They had a higher education in basketball than any other women's team throughout France," Calzonetti recalled of his CUC players. "How talented they were! . . . They had techniques and skills: dribbling, passing, the right shooting form. You didn't have to explain anything. They knew it right away. They were used to winning, they were used to playing together."

CUC's competition that trip, the Senegalese women's national team, was very good, too. Coached by Bonaventure Carvalho, who studied in Paris at the National Institute for Sport under Michel Rat in the 1960s, Senegal won the African championship in 1974 then repeated the feat in 1977, 1979, 1981, and 1984. "Senegal was highly competitive and organized in the 1970s," Calzonetti recalled for the Basketball Diplomacy in Africa Oral History Project of how the Senegalese Basketball Federation benefitted from cooperation with and funding from its French counterpart.

> The French system was intact in Senegal, and they just went with it. In Senegal, everyone played basketball because they saw that was ticket to get to France to play basketball. And in the period around 1974 or 1975 when the French Federation opened up these *réintegrés*, there was this ton of talent that left Senegal to play in France.[60]

The reigning African champions did not win a single game against CUC during that 1976 trip. Yet, Calzonetti noted, the competition was fierce. "The games were not blowouts," he testified of a point disparity that was only ten or fifteen points maximum.[61]

It was during this trip that Calzonetti struck up a friendship with Chazalon. They discussed at length how to train kids in the game, and Calzonetti explained how growing up, he often attended camps in Los Angeles or New Jersey. Why couldn't something similar be inaugurated in France?[62] These discussions led to a partnership to run one of the country's first big notable basketball camps. It was a recipe that blended the expertise and drive of each partner, and tapped into Calzonetti's network of US coaches, who came over to contribute their knowledge and technical expertise.

It was a trail-blazing move.[63] The first camp was held the summer of 1977, in Istres, north of Marseille on the Étang de Berre, a one-week training camp for 100 French kids who lived basketball from 7.30 a.m. until nearly 6 p.m.[64] By its third summer in 1979, the camp expanded to offer two one-week stages each for girls and boys, and one week for boys and girls aged eleven to eighteen, and featured some of the country's best-known players, like Alain Gilles.[65] One of their first campers to win a Most Valuable Player award was a young Vincent Collet, future Les Bleus coach; later campers included NBA Hall of Famer Tony Parker.[66]

Among the camp's first international interlocutors in 1977 was the Senegalese women's national team. That summer, a thirty-person delegation flew to France for a two-week training camp but also contributed to Chazalon's camp.[67] Team Senegal were not strangers to playing in the *hexagone* to fine-tune their game. In 1970, the Senegalese Basketball Federation wrote to its French counterpart to express interest in attending a training stage at INS. It also invited the French women's and men's teams to Senegal to play as part of their preparations for the 1971 African Championship (today's AfroBasket).[68] These snapshots illustrate how French, American, and African basketball rubbed shoulders throughout this period, fostering numerous cultural, technical, and knowledge exchanges between the players and coaches, regardless of their origin.

Post-Game

Despite CUC's on-court successes, it wasn't easy for the players to marry their sporting careers with regular life. They fought social stereotypes that twenty-something-year-old women should be married rather than playing basketball, that they were homosexuals, or that their height made them unfeminine and were treated more like men.[69] Such sentiments served to spur Riffiod in her doctoral thesis as she worked on her Ph.D. in sociology; she interviewed some sixty female basketball players who played at the national level during the course of her four years of research.[70]

Riffiod left CUC in 1978 after six French championship titles and four EuroLeague finals. Her CUC career was never one composed of racking up the points. Instead, as she pointed out to *L'Équipe Magazine*, "it is perfectly possible to be a good basketball player without scoring lots of points."[71] She won another championship title with Asnières in 1982 then played with Mont-de-Marsan before finishing her career with Saint-Eulalie en Région in 1993. She continued to play for France, serving as Les Tricolores captain from 1976 to 1980. Riffiod remains the fifth most capped national team player ever, women's or men's, with 247 appearances for France, the same number her son, Boris Diaw, also holds.

Her story and that which emanated from CUC illustrates how different types of sports diplomacy helped to invigorate women's basketball from the late 1960s through the 1980s. It was infused with a US vibe, from the people-to-people cultural, technical, and knowledge exchanges of American players and coaches who interacted with their female counterparts as well as through the emulation of an idol, Bill Russell. But the *hexagone*'s hoops were also interwoven with some of its African counterparts, most notably those in Senegal. Although Frenchwomen had much more success internationally in club and continental competition than their male counterparts during this era, similar changes were afoot that helped rebrand and revive the men's game, too.

Notes

1 Joë Jaunay, "L'Équipe de France Feminine: Le Point . . . Après Les Championnats d'Europe," *Basket-Ball*, September 1968.

2 Jaunay.

3 Frédéric Bozo, *French Foreign Policy Since 1945: An Introduction* (Berghahn Books, 2016), loc. 1680.

4 For more, see "*Le Deuxième Sexe (The Second Sex)* (1949) by Simone de Beauvoir | Towards Emancipation?," https://hist259.web.unc.edu/secondsex/; "The achievements and uncertainties of French feminism," *Cairns Dossiers* 2, no. 8 (October 1, 2018): 1; "France's Women's Liberation Movement Turns 50," RFI, August 26, 2020, https://www.rfi.fr/en/france/20200826-french-womens-liberation-movement-turns-50-feminism-mlf-abortion-equality-may-68-metoo.

5 For more on Pierre Mazeaud and the Mazeaud Law, see Lindsay Sarah Krasnoff, *The Making of Les Bleus: Sport in France, 1958–2010* (Lexington Books, 2012), 51–8.

6 Krasnoff, 57–8.

7 Krasnoff, 58.

8 Krasnoff, 70–71; Jonathan Wilson, "The Man Who Took Ajax to New Heights and the Brink of Destruction," *Guardian*, January 8, 2008, sec. Football, https://www.theguardian.com/football/2008/jan/08/europeanfootball.ajax.

9 For more on the early football academies and what the life of a young footballer was like in them, see Krasnoff, 71–8.

10 Jean-Pierre Dusseaulx, Interview with the author, October 16, 2015.

11 The game was first played in the early 1890s by female student-teachers at the Buckingham Grade School, and in 1893 was adopted as a physical activity for women at Smith College. See FFBB, "Le Basket Feminin," *Basket-Ball*, December 1965.

12 L. Prudhomme-Poncet, *Histoire Du Football Féminin Au XXe Siècle*, Collection "Espaces et Temps du Sport" (L'Harmattan, 2003); Pierre Bordieau, *La Domination Masculine* (Seuil, 1998).

13 Mary Lynn Stewart, *For Health and Beauty: Physical Culture for Frenchwomen, 1880s–1930s* (Cambridge University Press, 2001).

14 Some of the earliest included Femina Sports, Academia, Les Sportives, A.S. Strasbourg, Racing Club de France, and Golfer-Club Feminin.

15 FFBB, "Le Basket Feminin."

16 The first national women's team performed at the 1930 World Games.

17 Tancrède Adnot, "L'histoire de l'équipe de France de basket féminine—Episode 2 : Championnes avant l'heure (1929–1939)," *QiBasket*, March 4, 2020, https://www.qibasket.net/2020/03/04/lhistoire-de-lequipe-de-france-de-basket-feminine-episode-2-championnes-avant-lheure-1929-1939/.

18 Paul Geist, "L'Opinion du Manager," *Basket-Ball*, October 27, 1938.

19 Dominique Wendling, "Premier Championnat d'Europe féminin—Leçon à Rome en 1938," *Basket Retro* (blog), January 4, 2022, https://basket-retro.com/2022/01/04/premier-championnat-deurope-feminin-lecon-a-rome-en-1938/.

20 Pascal Legendre, Interview with the author, August 11, 2017.

21 Philippe Cazaban and Daniel Champsaur, "1953, Première Médaille Française," in *Géants: Tout l'histoire du Basket-Ball* (Éditions Chronique, 2015), 126–7.

22 Philippe Cazaban and Daniel Champsaur, "'Jacques Baeyens, Ambassadeur de France au Chili à Son Excellence M. Georges Bidault, Ministre Des Affaires Étrangers, Santiago le 14 Mars 1953,' Reproduced in" (Éditions Chronique, 2015), 127.

23 Cazaban and Champsaur.

24 Jean-Pierre Dusseaulx, "15e Championnat d'Europe de Basket-Ball: Clermont-Fd 1976," *L'Équipe Basket Magazine*, May 1976.

25 Louis Lapeyre, "Élisabeth Riffiod: Une Grande Fille Tout Simple," *L'Équipe Magazine (Basket, Handball)*, January 12, 1971.

26 FFBB, "Stage Féminin de Formation d'entraineurs à l'INS," *Basket-Ball*, October 1963; Sébastien Roumiguie, "Les Clubs de Sport Collectif de Haut Niveau Dans Les Villes Moyennes: Les Exemples de Perpignan et Besançon," in *Les Territoires Du Sport Entre Politiques et Pratiques*, ed. David Giband and Jean-Marc Holz, Études (Perpignan: Presses universitaires de Perpignan, 2013), 49–75, http://books.openedition.org/pupvd/514.

27 For more on this effort, see Lindsay Sarah Krasnoff, "Developing Athletic 'Atomic Armaments': The Role of Sports Medicine in Cold War France, 1958–1992," *Performance Enhancement & Health* 2 (2013): 8–16.

28 Lapeyre.

29 Lapeyre.

30 "Élisabeth Riffiod: 'Je n'ai plus Le Complexe de Ma Taille,'" *L'Équipe Basket Magazine*, n.d.

31 Élisabeth Riffiod-Diaw, Interview with the author, 2016.

32 Lapeyre; FFBB, "Le Basket Feminin."

33 Lapeyre.

34 Riffiod-Diaw.

35 All Élisabeth Riffiod quotes in this chapter, unless specified, from Riffiod-Diaw.

36 Riffiod-Diaw.

37 It was not until 2003, when her son, Boris, played in the NBA Summer League that Riffiod finally met Russell in person. "I cried with emotion when I saw him . . . I never thought that one day I would meet him," she recalled. Riffiod-Diaw.

38 Riffiod-Diaw.

39 ASM Omnisports, "Historique Basket," *ASM Basket* (blog), accessed January 14, 2022, https://www.asm-omnisports.com/basket/historique/.

40 For more, see Julien Hector, "Les Demoiselles de Clermont (1966–1985)," *Basket Retro* (blog), December 14, 2016, https://basket-retro.com/2016/12/14/les-demoiselles-de-clermont-1966-1985/.

41 Philippe Cazaban and Daniel Champsaur, "Le Clermont Université Club et l'Europe," in *Géants: Toute l'histoire du Basket-Ball* (Éditions Chronique, 2015(, 192–5.

42 Philippe Cazaban and Daniel Champsaur, "Jacky Chazalon, La Première Étoile," in *Géants*, 186.

43 *Origin Story: Joan Cronan—IX at 50: The Lady Vols Experience*, 50, accessed October 1, 2022, https://ixat50.buzzsprout.com/1948784/10181748-origin-story-joan-cronan; "L'Amérique Cherche La Femme," *L'Équipe Basket Magazine*, January 1976.

44 "L'Amérique Cherche la Femme."

45 "L'Amérique Cherche la Femme."

46 Dusseaulx, "15e Championnat d'Europe de Basket-Ball: Clermont-Fd 1976."

47 Dusseaulx.

48 Jacques Marchand, "Le Relais Passé Aux Femmes . . .," *L'Équipe Basket Magazine*, May 1976.

49 Fédération Française de Basket-Ball (FFBB), "Historique Des Matches," n.d., http://www.ffbb.com/edf/historique-des-matches.

50 Paul Bonnetain, "Bill Sweek a Rendu La Santé aux Demoiselles de Clermont," *L'Équipe Basket Magazine*, January 1977.

51 Bonnetain.

52 Philippe Cazaban and Daniel Champsaur, "Les Demoiselles de Clermont," in *Géants*, 167.

53 "Le C.U.C. et . . . Les Autres," *L'Équipe Basket Magazine*, January 1976.

54 Carmine Calzonetti, Interview with the author, September 18, 2020.

55 Calzonetti.

56 He taught English classes at the local university when he wasn't practicing. Guillaume Paquereau, "[ITW] Carmine Calzonetti 'A Nantes, j'ai joué pieds nus,'" *Basket Retro* (blog), February 23, 2022, https://basket-retro.com/2022/02/23/itw-carmine-calzonetti-a-nantes-jai-joue-pieds-nus/.

57 "Les Féminines Du Clermont U.C.: Troisième Finale En Quatre Ans," *Basket Hebdo*, April 5, 1974, No. 2 edition.

58 All Carmine Calzonetti quotes this chapter, unless specified, from Calzonetti, Interview with the author.

59 Calzonetti.

60 Carmine Calzonetti and Kenny Grant, Carmine Calzonetti and Kenny Grant Transcript, May 14, 2020, 2–3, Basketball Diplomacy in Africa: An Oral History from SEED Project to the Basketball Africa League (BAL), https://eprints.soas.ac.uk/32908/.

61 Calzonetti, Interview with the author.

62 Paquereau, "[ITW] Carmine Calzonetti 'A Nantes, j'ai joué pieds nus !'"

63 George Eddy, Interview with the author, September 30, 2021.

64 Paquereau, "[ITW] Carmine Calzonetti 'A Nantes, j'ai joué pieds nus !'"

65 "École de Basket Jacky Chazalon Stages Été 79," *Basket-Ball*, February 1, 1979; "L'école de Basket de Jacky Chazalon," *Association Française Des Entraîneurs de Basket-Ball*, April 1, 1979.

66 Calzonetti, Interview with the author.

67 Calzonetti and Grant, Carmine Calzonetti and Kenny Grant Transcript, 16.

68 FFBB, "Relations Internationales," *Basket-Ball*, April 1, 1971.

69 Hélène Riviere, "Un Mariage Difficile: Être Championne et Femme," *Basket-Ball*, May 1, 1982.

70 Riviere.

71 Jean-Pierre Dusseaulx, "Élizabeth Riffiod: Un Volcan En Sommeil," *L'Équipe Basket Magazine*, April 1975.

4

Triangulating Foundations, 1968–84

New York-born Art Kenney was twenty-two in fall 1968 when he arrived in Le Mans to play for its local team, Sporting Club Moderne (SCM, also known colloquially in the basketball world as Le Mans). The towering six-foot-eight-and-one-half-inch power forward originally cut his teeth on-court alongside Lew Alcindor (later Kareem Abdul-Jabbar) at Power Memorial High School, then at Fairfield University in Connecticut, where he became the team's top rebounder, accumulating nearly 500 rebounds across sixty-nine games.[1] Following graduation, Kenney signed with Jim McGregor, an agent who took teams of NCAA alumni to play around the world in exhibition matches; players were often signed by local clubs, thus the McGregor tours were effectively a marketing tactic to display basketballers' abilities to prospective teams.[2] It was through McGregor that Kenney ended up in Le Mans, beginning a new chapter for the storied club. He was one of the first Americans to play after a June 1968 rule change allowed each team to field two foreign players.

Kenney quickly found that the American game was oceans apart from its French sister, starting with the rules. For example, there wasn't a back-court game, thus players on the offense were limited to playing in the forecourt. The lanes were wider. The gyms were unheated and sported thin plexiglass backboards. Moreover, the style of game was different, too. "It was a little more helter-skelter because you had a shot clock, so you had to get the shot up in thirty seconds at the time," Kenney recalled.[3]

For several seasons, Kenney hooped in Le Mans (1968–70, 1973–5) and in the process imparted some of his New York basketball style to French teammates. During his second season, SCM's elevated game snagged third place in the Nationale 1 standings, earning a berth in the Coupe d'Europe. Despite playing in Italy for several seasons, Kenney returned to Le Mans in 1973, for, according to the press, he preferred the French-style "bourgeois" basketball over the glitzier, popular class Italian version.[4] But for Kenney, the return was due to the community that surrounded the club, from then-president Bernard Gasnal and his wife to Le Mans mainstay Christian Baltzer and SCM teammates.

Kenney was representative of a new openness towards transatlantic players to improve the game, the start of an era that began to transform the French game. The June 1968 rule change launched a new phenomenon: the basketball migrant. Prior to 1968, there were Americans who played basketball in France, but they did not go to France specifically to do so, as longtime basketball journalist Jean-Pierre Dusseaulx noted.[5] They were there and discovered that the French played the game. After 1968, foreigners were enticed to go to France specifically to play basketball, which strengthened the game.

Players like Kenney could help teams win, but the newer mindset was more expansive. Teams were willing to entertain American coaches, and several of the US players who found their way to French hardcourts also took up coaching posts. There was even discussion in 1967 of an American head coach for Les Tricolores, although it never materialized.[6] Still, US players and coaches deeply imprinted French basketball after 1968 and, despite the criticisms of an "American colonization," transmitted their cultural, knowledge, and especially technical know-how to counterparts throughout the *métropole*'s hardcourts.

Scouting Report

Despite *détente*, the eased tensions between the two nuclear superpowers, the Cold War sports arena was hot. Increasingly, battles occurred in the pool, on the pitch, on the hardcourt as countries worldwide harnessed the soft power of sports to relay the superiority of their ideology, culture, or legitimize their independence within the international community. Technological advances like satellite broadcasting and color television helped infuse new potency to images, whether still or in motion, of athletic "wins." Sports mega events like the Olympics took on new importance as platforms for more than just sporting prowess.

The 1968 Summer Games crystalized how individuals, not just states, could tap into the symbolism and global attention that the sports arena offered. When US sprinters John Carlos and Tommie Smith gave a black-gloved Black Power salute on the podium that October alongside Australian Peter Norman, who sported his own pro-human rights protest, the world took note. Athletes of all ages the world over were inspired by these symbolic acts that infused politics into the Olympic arena in new ways. It wasn't all peaceful protest. In a far more horrifying fashion, the Palestinian Liberation Organization (PLO)'s massacre of Israeli athletes at the 1972 Munich Games also grabbed global attention for their cause. Moreover, hosting events were increasingly ways for countries to communicate to the world, such as how West Germany staged the 1972 Olympics and 1974 FIFA World Cup to present a revived, postwar face to the world.

Basketball was squarely within the Cold War sports battleground. The 1972 Olympic basketball final in which the USSR walked away with gold after a highly controversial final minute of play, remains deeply disputed by US officials and players; Team USA still refuses some fifty years later to accept the contested award. The game was used in other, non-ideological ways. The rise of basketball in Africa in the early post-colonial period was one way for newly independent nations to announce themselves on the international stage. FIBA Africa and its continental championships were ways for African countries to foster national identity while wins cultivated pride in national teams. By 1968 the Senegalese men's team was a top contender. They claimed the African Championship four times during this era (1968, 1972, 1978, 1980), were three-time runners up (1970, 1974, 1975), and bronze winners in 1983.

Between 1968 and 1984, basketball grew worldwide, and a new cohort of countries entered the elite ranks of international play. Within men's Olympic and FIBA World Cup competition, US–USSR dominance was challenged by the rise of Yugoslavia thanks to the sport's popularity and use in the Balkans post-1945. The game grew more competitive, even the French men's team, albeit very gradually.

As a result, three key transformations helped revive the men's game. First, the most immediately impactful evolution was the infusion of players, especially from the United States, the Antilles, and francophone Africa. The resultant cosmopolitan melting pot on the *métropole*'s hardcourts provided an instant lift that energized basketball's tempo, aerodynamics, and adherents, most notably in the game's traditional outposts in the medium- and smaller-sized cities. These players engaged in daily acts of informal sports diplomacy with French teammates and each other as they shared their home cultures, basketball, tactics, and techniques. These exchanges also benefited basketball migrants, some of who became naturalized French citizens, for they learned about the country and surrounding communities.

These organic exchanges helped the seeds for basketball's revival to sprout and grow. They also illustrate the power of the individual in informal people-to-people sports diplomacy, which is why this chapter focuses mostly on three different types of basketball migration: from the Antilles, from the United States, and from France to Africa.

Antillean players

Players from the French Antilles followed the jet stream across the Atlantic to the *métropole* and breathed new life into the game. The Antilles, part of France's overseas empire since the 1600s, finally passed from colony to department standing on March 19, 1946. Despite the new status as integral albeit overseas parts of France, the Antilles (Martinique, Guadeloupe, Guiana) remained a forgotten space for many on the mainland for the transition from colony to department did not bring about true equality.[7]

Another aspect of inequality was economic. The republic did not fully invest in or develop Antillean economies, which meant that by the mid-twentieth century, high unemployment rates and weak industry presented real problems for everyday citizens on the islands. Instead, the government encouraged emigration to the mainland as well as birth control policies.[8] The older ideal of assimilation was contested as strikes, protests, and other public illustrations of discontent rippled through the region.[9]

But at the same time, sport was ever more used as a social tool within the French Caribbean. The islands' traditional games were replaced by sport in the nineteenth century.[10] By the *fin-de-siècle*, elites on Martinique and Guadeloupe enjoyed yachting, tennis, motor sports, but introduction of mandatory military service for Antillean males starting in 1913 prodded the government to incorporate physical education in the islands' schools, just as throughout the *métropole*. Prior to 1960, the government in Paris did not invest in sports or their promotion across the Antilles; this changed after 1960, as local populations embraced sports as one way to express belonging to the republican community geographically far away.[11]

American players

The largest pipeline of talent into French leagues was from the United States. Top clubs favored US players to flesh out their rosters, as *Le Monde* noted in November 1968.[12] Part of this was due to the international dominance of Team USA in international competition; at that summer's Olympic Games in Mexico City, the United States won the basketball tournament's gold medal for the seventh consecutive time. On the one hand, *Le Monde* reasoned, US players elevated leagues to their strongest level of play since the Nationale 1's 1949 creation. During the 1968–9 season, only ASVEL Lyon-Villeurbanne fielded a roster uniquely of Frenchmen, while every other club employed at least one foreign player. For *Le Monde*, "the arrival of these Americans might give a new elan and make French basketball exit its semi-lethargy. Already this season, the game rhythm is more rapid." But this had far more consequential implications. "National Technical Director Joë Jauney intends to 'use' the Americans to perfect the national team game."[13]

Some of the newly arrived Americans weren't terribly impressed, reported *The New York Times*. "French basketball is still played with such Gallic individualism," without much perceived dedication to the craft or its fundamentals.[14] As one observed of French counterparts, "when tired, they stop . . . just give up. We have only three practices a week for a total of five hours. You know how many showed up last week? We didn't even have enough guys for a scrimmage."[15]

The issue of professionalism complicated things for technically, basketball remained an amateur or semi-professional endeavor. Yet, as *The New York Times* pointed out, many players were on the payroll of team-owning companies, municipalities, or were paid under the table to maintain the aura of amateur status. For small

TABLE 4.1 *US player salary-earning opportunities in Nationale 1, 1969, 1980*[17]

Year	Monthly Salary (Francs)	Monthly Salary USD	Inflation adjusted to 2022
1969		$500.00	$4,035
1980	8,000–20,000		$3,602–$9,010

clubs, paying to have one or two American players on the team could cost 50–90 percent of their budget; by 1980, that could translate into 10–40 percent of the overall budget for one of the country's elite clubs, according to *Le Monde*.[16]

Despite recognition that US players could bolster team performances and results, there remained a prejudice towards Caucasian Americans. As one US agent confided to *Le Monde*, "80% of clubs want to have a white player who is more than six-foot-five and capable of winning any match single-handed, no matter how tough!"[18] Still, there was an ever-increasing number of African Americans who began to play in France.

Part of the reason why so many young American men migrated to France, and Western Europe, was that there were limited opportunities to play after college. By the late 1960s, there were two professional basketball leagues in the United States: the NBA and the American Basketball Association (ABA), which from 1967 until 1976 was known for a glitzy show-time type of game that featured three-point shots, slam dunks, and some of the country's best talent.[19] When the ABA ceased play in 1976, four of its teams merged into the NBA, which added talent like Julius Erving and new game options, like the three-point shot, but which further reduced the number of professional team roster spots. Thus ever-more young American men turned to Europe as rule changes offered new opportunities to play abroad.

By the early 1970s, the impact of this American influx riveted the game. As Dusseaulx wrote in 1972, foreign players had already rendered the on-court show "regenerated and attractive," which drew in more fans. "[T]hese Americans ... carry out actions of a superior dimension for France," Dusseaulx admitted. Yet,

The Americans often fall into a forceful individualism which is not always good for the performance of the team. But the spectators are not so attached to this problem since only the spectacle interests them, the Americans cultivate this penchant perfectly.[20]

African players

A third wave of players who migrated to the French mainland in this era and began to leave their mark on the game were from the former empire in Africa. The Fourth Republic's constitution created the French Union in 1946 and provided Union citizenship to its members. In a rapidly evolving post-1945 world, that was not enough, and political destabilization spread in the 1950s. Charles de Gaulle's return to power in 1958 established the Franco-African Community out of the Union's former African members, a blueprint for eventual decolonization while maintaining French influence. Following widespread declarations of independence from Community members in 1960, Paris continued to wield influence, a policy of *Françafrique* that shaped the immediate post-colonial era.[21]

This impacted sport. The January 3, 1973 law that allowed Africans born prior to 1960 in what was formerly the empire to obtain French nationality is often referred to, among sports circles, as the *loi des réintegrés*. Designed to facilitate movement of labor, this had a direct impact on the sports world, and the basketball one, for such players no longer counted towards a team's two-foreign-player maximum. The first *réintégré* in basketball was Togo's Firmin Onissah, who played for ASPTT Nice then earned twelve caps with the French national team to prepare for and contest the 1973 European Championship.[22] Since then, generations of African players, male and female, have migrated to the French mainland to play basketball, which infused new talent and *élan* into the game.

But it wasn't just a one-way flow of talent, and it wasn't just among players. Since 1960, France has maintained basketball ties with several African countries through technical and knowledge exchanges with African coaches, technicians, and officials. Regardless of where players or coaches hailed from, their amalgamation on the *hexagone*'s hardcourts directly benefited the game. According to Carmine Calzonetti, a former American player and coach in France, expansion of who played strengthened the game. "The level just got better and better, and more athletic," he said. "When I first started, French basketball was predominantly a white man's game. By the end of it, it was a multi-diverse group of people that played and came from all over the place."[23]

Against this context, the experiences of three basketballers illustrates how these evolutions played out on-the-ground. The informal sports diplomacy of their exchanges demonstrated the importance of individuals in helping to build the basketball empire.

The (Original) Beard

Jacques Cachemire, one of the "shot kings" of the 1970s, grew up in the transatlantic crosswinds of Guadeloupe and, thanks to the defensive stylings of one of his idols, Bill Russell, helped elevate French basketball. Born February 27, 1947, in Point-à-Pitre, Cachemire grew up in an era of change. "The Antilles entered into a new social era, and one could say a sportive one," he said.[24] There were not yet the big public works sports structures that later helped make the Antilles, Guadeloupe in particular, into a noted *creuset* of athletes. But, as previously noted, sports were a way to assimilate into the republican fabric of citizenship.

Cachemire grew up in the Rue Raspail Chemin-Neuf quartier, a neighborhood close to the Darboussier sugar factory. The grandson of a slave, Cachemire grew up poor: his father died in an accident when Jacques was a young boy, so his mother baked cakes to sell on the beach to scrape together a livelihood. It was difficult, but sports helped. "It allowed us to ignore the misery that surrounded us and to have a physical approach that was fun because it made us compete," Cachemire recalled. Instead, the daily tasks of housework and survival became a game. "[It was] a competition when we went to fetch water from the fountain, a competition to go shopping, a competition to fetch fruit," he told *Basket Retro*.[25]

An American institution that provided aid in developing countries was located nearby across from a basketball court. The institute sought to engage with locals through cultural endeavors like its library that provided access to books, an unaffordable luxury in the Cachemire household. They also provided a glass of milk, cheese, and American cookies to locals who visited. One day, Cachemire discovered a book about Russell, which neatly dovetailed with some of the movies about US basketball that the center screened in the evenings to attract neighborhood youth, "to ensure that we discovered the good side of America."

From that moment on, Cachemire was smitten. "I always dreamed to play like Bill Russell," he said and later, for much of his career, he sported a beard in homage to the legendary Celtic. Through the American center, Cachemire met basketball coach Edouard Lamy, who offered to train and teach the fifteen-year-old. He had no shoes and played barefoot at first. "I had nothing, but I enjoyed discovering basketball." As a debutant to the game "I was terrible," he confided. "I loved to make rebounds, I loved the fans, I loved the work of a center. Finally, my life unknowingly returned towards American basketball."

Cachemire worked hard to overcome his basketball illiteracy. He joined the club Solidarité Scolaire, he finessed his skills, and decided to become a basketball player, even though at the time there was no professional league in France. His team contested and won the Guadeloupe Cup, but Cachemire spent his free time hanging out with *les gens de la rue*, something his team manager, and his mother, worried could be a bad influence.

In 1967, he left for the *métropole* to begin his military service, a fresh start. He was stationed in Rouen, Normandy, and was tasked to put his sports skills and height into action. He played with AL Montivilliers, rapidly came to the attention of federation technicians, and so impressed officials that he was asked to join the military basketball team, which competed at the World Military Championships in Moscow. France placed fifth and were invited to remain to train in the Soviet Union. Upon return to the *hexagone* in 1968, Cachemire joined Stade Auto Lyonnais, where he played with two Americans, Dick Smith and Bill Yeager. From Smith, the young Frenchman learned how to play outside and discovered mid-range basketball.

Cachemire signed with Antibes in 1969 and embarked upon an illustrious decade-long career with the club that set a new tone on hardcourts. Alongside Henry Phil and Dan Rodriguez, the trio wove a rapid, aerodynamic, defensive game that remains a trademark of the French to this day. They won the championship the following spring playing an exciting type of basketball that, according to Cachemire, made people eager to watch and developed an identity for men's basketball. At the time, he noted, the Clermont Université

FIGURE 4.1 *Jacques Cachemire with Antibes. Credit: Musée du Basket.*

Club (CUC) women's team was the media star of the basketball world. "People were talking about basketball being a women's game," he said. But through Antibes, Cachemire believed, "they discovered men's basketball also has its brand image and that basketball in the end was more vicious than some people thought."

His professional career flourished. Dusseaulx wrote in 1971 that the young Guadeloupian "possesses the qualities to become one of the biggest French basketball players of all time."[26] Cachemire was driven by his dedication to the game, Dusseaulx noted, and proved his ability to rebound.[27] In 1979 Cachemire signed with Tours, where he finished his playing career in 1984, then began to coach, first at Tours (1983–4), then Lourdes (1987–92), and Toulouse (1993–4).

It was an era in which ever-more American players arrived. One day, US coach and agent Jim McGregor joked with Cachemire that he could no longer place American players on the Frenchman's team for "you're better than some Americans, you're killing my business." Although US players took spots that young French may have coveted, Cachemire noted they added to the game. "They covered all the places that the French players could not do," he said. "Inside spaces and places to score baskets," he acknowledged of how Americans were coveted interior players and scorers.

Cachemire made his mark at the international level over fifteen years and 250 games *en bleu*. He earned his first selection in September 1969 at a friendly against Spain. Les Tricolores at the time were mired in the ongoing basketball crisis, relegated to play in Group C of the European Championship. "They had lost everything," Cachemire recalled of the era. But he and the team began to create a new dynamic and with it, he thought, a new hope for French basketball: that they could play their way back into the top tier of elite European competition.

One of the problems was that there was a steady rotation into and out of the national team. "If I had to make a team with all the players who [played for Team France], one would have had half of the French league," he observed. Part of the turnover was due to players returning to their studies, especially as parents knew there wasn't much of a future in basketball; others weren't interested in continuing with the national team because there was no financial compensation; also, the federation remained mired in amateurism, not favoring financial reimbursement to entice players to give up their time. The lack of consistency, Cachemire thought, translated into a lack of consistent chemistry.

Cachemire's generation began to turn the tables. Not only did they begin to return improved results on the court, but more players remained with the national team for longer spans of time. He wanted to contribute and remained to mentor younger cohorts and communicated a belief that France could win. His last game *en bleu* was at the 1985 European Championship, where the team placed fifth, a considerable improvement.

Dusseaulx, a close friend, noted that Cachemire was an asset to France in numerous ways. "[He] is an example for all of his teammates," the journalist wrote in 1981.[28] He was also proud to represent France. "He fought for France," Dusseaulx recalled decades later. "When he heard 'La Marseillaise,' he trembled. I saw him tremble, he didn't stop, he adored it." Yet, for all his dedication to the national team, Cachemire always felt more Guadeloupian than French.[29]

Being such a high-profile player had its downsides. Cachemire experienced racism and discrimination in a range of different ways. It was a phenomenon he didn't encounter during his first year on the mainland with the military or upon leaving to play with Montivilliers, where he lived with his coach, André Collet. The then nineteen-year-old enjoyed family life with the Collets, including with their five-year-old son Vincent, the future Team France head coach. "He was 'my basketball baby' when I arrived in France," Cachemire later noted of Vincent.[30]

"[André] welcomed me like a son," he recalled. "Nobody pointed out to me that my color wasn't that [traditionally] found on the mainland." But things were different with the military team. Cachemire unknowingly replaced another player, and teammates were upset. Three of his new colleagues, all Caucasian, took it out on the man from Guadeloupe. "They said I was starting to bother them and to go back to my hometown in the boondocks," he recalled dumbfoundedly of his first confrontation with this phenomenon.

It was not the last time he was singled out. Bigotry once again reared its head when Cachemire was at Tours during the 1983–4 season. He recalled:

We had results that bothered everyone because it was my first year as a coach and some people didn't think the team could have had results with a n*** in charge who hadn't trained as a coach but who, in the end, was pulling off a strange bet.

Certain club officials organized a putsch to oust Cachemire. In the midst of a match, an assistant was dispatched to insult Cachemire, and the coach fought back, knocking the guy out. "Even after 30 years, the color of my skin was the element that bothered some people," he lamented. Cachemire later coached Toulouse where, in the early 1990s, the team played in the lower divisions. "I had more physical problems due to the color of my skin when we went to these small towns than at the national level," he recalled.

Cachemire left Toulouse, and the mainland, in 1993 for Mauritius, where for three years he helped develop basketball at the behest of the country's Ministry of Youth and Sport. As National Technical Director, Cachemire transmitted his hoops culture, techniques, and knowledge to the island's best young basketballers, some who later led the national team in the 2000s.[31] "It's a very nice story, but very sad, too," Cachemire recalled decades later of his career. "It was at the end of my career that I suffered more from racism because society is changing, people who thought it was the fault of the Blacks if things were going badly. We discovered a rise in hatred and distrust."

Mr. Steady

While Cachemire dazzled and delighted at Antibes, a new basketball contender rose to national prominence in Le Mans thanks to men like Bill Cain, who embodied the sports diplomacy that helped reshape Gallic basketball. The White Plains, New York native nurtured a desire to see the world from his earliest days, and basketball was a way to do so. Born February 8, 1948, Cain's hoop dreams were sparked by the books he read in his local library, which served as a portal to the larger world. He began playing the game more seriously during high school and was recruited to play at Iowa State University. When Cain arrived on campus in Ames for his freshman year in fall 1966, the Vietnam War was in full swing, beginning to generate public backlash, and there was growing student support for the Civil Rights Movement.

The six-foot-six New Yorker, known on-court as "Mr. Steady," crafted an ISU Hall of Fame career while maintaining his grades and scholarship. Following the Black Power salute by sprinters Tommie Smith and John Carlos at the 1968 Olympic Games, Cain added the identifier "student protester" to his CV by writing bimonthly columns for the *Iowa State Daily* (*ISD*) student newspaper. Known as "Cain's Scrutiny," the basketballer unpacked his ideas and observations about race relations, patriotism, what it meant to be an American, and more through the 1968–9 school year.[32]

In June 1970, Cain was drafted by the Portland Trailblazers for their debut NBA season. Cut from tryouts, Cain returned to Ames to finish his degree before he embarked on an adventure playing overseas. Following one season in Belgium (1971–2), Cain played three years for Vichy (1972–5) before signing with Le Mans in 1975 as a twenty-five-year-old.

The small city situated halfway between Paris and Rennes served as a bridge between the Ile-de-France capital region and Brittany in the west, as well as between French basketball and its American counterpart. Better known for its legendary auto-racing circuit and the annual 24 Hours of Le Mans, basketball was long integral to the region's DNA. The club was founded in 1938 by the head of Comptoirs Modernes, a food market and later, supermarket enterprise, but at first consisted of only a football team. The basketball section was created in 1940 by the founders' wives and the following year was relaunched as Sporting Club Moderne (SCM).[33] Over time, it was fertile ground for basketball diplomacy as club officials were willing to embrace generations of US coaches and players, which in turn reinforced Le Mans' hoops heritage and contributions to the country's budding basketball empire.

Basketball in Le Mans grew in the postwar era. Families regularly attended home games and, once the team began to win, pride and identity. This fostered community, and was also simultaneously formed among the players. In a pre-professional era, they held jobs off-court with Comptoirs Modernes. The arrangement worked to the club's advantage, for teammates not only played together on-court but also worked together side-by-side. This cultivated an environment of close friendship that translated into team chemistry, a sense of camaraderie passed down for generations.[34]

SCM's ascent in the basketball rungs was led in many ways by Christian Baltzer, known as "the red wire" for his long esteemed career with the club.[35] Born in the Alsatian city of Mulhouse July 5, 1936, the first part of Baltzer's career was synonymous with the region's reigning basketball club, Association Sportive Mulhouse, where he played from 1948 until 1961. At the same time, Baltzer embarked on a storied career with the national team, winning bronze at the 1959 European Championship. Then in summer 1961, he signed with SCM and embarked on a decades-long adventure as player, player-coach, coach, then later club president. Under Baltzer's tenure as player-coach from 1964 until 1971, the club began to integrate its first American players. Le Mans' opening game of the 1968–9 season featured the team's first two US-born players, Kenney and Clarence Denzer, and laid the groundwork for generations of Franco-American ties around basketball, including Cain.

By 1975, little had changed since Kenney first arrived. Cain found that basketball and everything that surrounded it remained vastly different from the United States. "France was really lacking in equipment," he recalled. "Some gyms were linoleum, some were Astroturf. You did everything possible not to fall down because when you got up you'd have no more skin."[36]

Yet, he enjoyed the adventure and decided to remain. Certainly, life in France held allure for a man who as a kid admired Wilt Chamberlain and his legendary season with the Harlem Globetrotters, including their time in the *hexagone*. Learning and adopting to a new culture was also highly appealing, and soon it had him thinking about the longer term. "Picking up the language, maybe making a career out of it being in France," Cain said, "that idea going through my head of cultural change: why not?" It wasn't for the money for he did not make much of it at the time. But then there was also love. He met a Frenchwoman and after they married in 1975 he obtained citizenship.

For nearly a decade, Cain helped put SCM on the record books and served as a basketball ambassador. As a naturalized Frenchman, he no longer counted towards a team's limit on foreign players. Moreover, he embodied the republican model that anyone can become French if they assimilate into the public sphere, such as speaking French. Yet, he continued to diplomatically referee conversations about the United States with teammates. As he recalled, "When I arrived in France, there was the fight against discrimination and Vietnam, which was one of the things we discussed in the locker rooms when I was in Vichy or Le Mans. But that wasn't the daily conversation." After he obtained French citizenship, Cain continued to represent and communicate about the United States to his French teammates and vice versa about France to his American teammates.[37]

Cain felt accepted by locals but believed his US passport facilitated the welcome. "Even though they look at you as an American, of course you're black or white," he said. "But you're an American ... I think it was the passport, but I never felt any discrimination, or if I felt there was a place where there was subtle racism, I tried to avoid it." The community may have identified him first by his American nationality, not by the color of his skin as was too often the case back in the United States. But there was also Cain's identification as a basketball player, one who helped the team improve and win, which likely also isolated him from discrimination.

While the embrace of US-born players in Le Mans can be read several ways, it's undeniable that Cain and others helped provide the club with a certain edge through the technical and knowledge exchange, sports diplomacy, he brought with him. According to Baltzer, Cain played a vital role at Le Mans. "He was one of the best American players in France," the former president said. "He was a good player who was well integrated."[38] Cain may have become a naturalized Frenchman, but his hoops training was thoroughly American and over the years he modeled a US-style of game. Importantly, Cain helped impart a US-style mentality towards approaching the game, from work habits to taking the act of playing more seriously and keeping teammates in line.

Le Mans' Franco-American basketball diplomacy was furthered though a series of coaching hires following Baltzer's retirement that, since 1974, has helped imbue its culture with a transatlantic bounce. First, there was Bob Andrews (1974–7), then the club signed Bill Sweek, a former UCLA standout who made his name coaching CUC and Élisabeth Riffiod to their 1977 French championship. The melding of different basketball styles paid dividends when Le Mans swept to their first-ever national championship in 1978. The city celebrated vicariously with a parade that took the players six hours to traverse the route from the town center to City Hall. "When I got there, my hands were swollen," Cain recalled of all the hands he shook that day. "I couldn't believe there were so many people from throughout the Sarthe. It was amazing."

Such anecdotes shed light on the impact of individuals in seeding basketball diplomacy and how this know-how benefited Le Mans. The team clinched the national championship in May 1979, its first-ever back-to-back title, and three-peated the feat at the end of the 1981–2 season with a roster that included veteran Cain, as well as rookie Vincent Collet.

It was an auspicious beginning for Collet, who later coached Le Mans before his reign as head coach of Les Bleus. Born in 1963 in Normandy, Collet grew up around basketball. His parents were both fans of the game, and the family lodged a young Cachemire. Collet's love for basketball thus began at an early age, spending weekends in gyms with his parents soaking in the game.

Despite this early love and exposure, Collet fell hard and fast for the NBA after watching his first televised game, the May 16, 1980 NBA Final. That evening, Magic Johnson scored forty-two points, fifteen rebounds, and had seven assists for a Los Angeles win over the Philadelphia 76ers. "I was at home," Collet recalled of the match. "After that, I went to play basketball for three hours, I was like crazy."

FIGURE 4.2 *Le Mans, 1982 with Bill Cain (#15) and Vincent Collet (#13). Credit: Musée du Basket.*

For Collet, winning the national championship during his rookie season was special, and the efforts of his teammates helped to ensure that his heart remained forever with the club.[39] He arrived in Le Mans as a young eighteen-year-old, but was quickly taken under the watchful wings of his older colleagues, including Cain, who not only helped him adjust to life on-court but also off-court. "Le Mans was very special," Collet later recalled.

Time-Out

The influx of foreign players helped basketball rebound. If in June 1969 the federation counted 143,708 licensed male and female players, seven years later that number increased to 240,433.[40] But the basketball crisis continued, broken only by CUC and the female Tricolores' 1970 silver European Championship finish. For those responsible for the men's national team, the failure to qualify yet again for an Olympiad was a frustration. As Jacques Marchand editorialized in *L'Équipe Basket Magazine* in May 1976, "everyone comes to bicker over the setbacks of the French team. Everyone rejects the responsibility."[41]

This was part of the reason why French clubs were so open to recruiting Americans, as well as why naturalized Frenchmen born and raised in the United States were tolerated on the national team: because they were tall players who had the ability and dexterity to be nimble on-court.[42] This was ultimately a good thing for the game. As *Le Monde* noted, "the Americans have helped to raise the level of French basketball and, over the past two years, of the French team which last season welcomed three players of American origin" in the forms of Bob Riley, Cain, and George Brosterhous.[43] For National Technical Director and historian Gérard Bosc, "they showed us how to play basketball in an entirely different way . . . they strongly modified our basketball culture."[44]

Yet, the national team's inability to fare well in international competition persisted. It was of increased concern not just to basketball authorities, but to the republic's sports officials, too. In September 1976, a special meeting was held at INSEP to discuss how to improve basketball's fate.[45] In the aftermath, an increased emphasis on youth detection and development was instituted, aided by new provisions in the 1975 Mazeaud Law. One result was the implementation of Horizon 80, programs designed to prepare promising elite youth male and female players for qualification at and competition in the 1980 Moscow Summer Games. Another was the creation of sport-études for basketball, basketball-centric sections within the national school system that enabled interested boys and girls to have increased exposure and time to play basketball within the established scholastic day. Still, these were medium- and longer-term solutions. While ultimately the country's youth development system would bear fruit, in the 1970s it was still in its infancy. That's why the story of how one of the cultivators of the country's future youth development system honed his craft in Africa provides insight into a different type of sports diplomacy.

The Educator

One of the alumni of Paris Université Club's (PUC) 1962 US visit was national team player Michel Rat, who in the 1970s embarked on a new adventure far beyond the Parisian-centric nucleus of his career as player, educator, and coach. Born in Auvers-sur-Oise to the northwest of the capital on March 16, 1937, Rat trained at the country's elite sports school, today known as INSEP, and in 1961 obtained his degree in physical education. From 1957 until 1970, he played with PUC, later served as its captain, and served eighty-one caps *en bleu* from 1959 until 1968. He worked as a physical education teacher, then trainer at INSEP, which is where Rat first began to deepen the exchanges with African players and coaches begun during his time with PUC.

As described in Chapter 1, PUC was open to external basketball influences. From its welcome of French-African players like Roger Antoine (Mali) and Samba Sow (Senegal) to its international travel, this orientation was a natural extension of PUC's ethos that basketball was an education tool. This mentality reflected the game's original 1890s focus upon mind, body, and spirit. The PUC-honed outlook deeply implemented itself in Rat's consciousness.

In 1970, Rat was appointed Director of the Institute de Formation des Professeurs d'Éducation Physique in Antananarivo, Madagascar. He was part of a wave of French technicians and teachers sent to the former empire to help develop home-grown sports institutions and executives. For three years, Rat worked to train coaches but also, in cooperation with one of the university biology teachers, created a basketball team for students. The boys' team were the 1972 Madagascan championship finalists; the girls' team, coached by his then-wife, was also one of the best in the country.

The experience was a way to learn about the country's diverse society, its role in the growing global economy, its national security significance for France. "We learned all that," Rat said of his time coaching in Madagascar. "It placed it in a much broader context of globalization. I experienced it through sport. Inevitably, sport is part of a whole. We learn that way, too."[46]

From 1973 until 1978, Rat and his family were stationed in Senegal, where he was a professor and trainer at the Senegalese National Institute of Sport. Just as he had in Madagascar, in Senegal Rat also worked with female and male university players, and maintained contact with former students as they rose in their careers as basketball officials and tacticians. "We made sure to help, we cooperated," he said of the relationship with local players.

Rat's approach to coaching and education, whether in Madagascar, Senegal, or back in France, remained the same: to impart values, not just basketball tactics or techniques. It was inscribed as part of his time with PUC. "I was instilled with *republican* values," he said.

> But at the same time, as a civil servant [working with] students, I had a professional morality, particularly in the idea of values: the values of the Republic and of secularism and respect for people in their dignity, in their culture.

These were the values he tried to transmit.

But Rat also learned much during this time about sociology, cultural problems, and acculturation. "Living it on a daily basis for eight years is entirely different from reading about [these things] in a book or studying it," he said. "To be in contact is extremely rich, especially since we were in contact with and had strong ties with the teams, with our students, and some of the managers."

In 1978, Rat returned to the *métropole*, where he worked as a professor at the University of Caen (1978–82) before taking a series of posts with the French Basketball Federation (FFBB) stationed at INSEP. At the same time, he continued to work and grow his ties to Africa. He worked in partnership with FIBA Africa to train African

ENTRETIEN AVEC...

ENTRETIEN AVEC...

MICHEL RAT : "Tout pour les jeunes"

Après Yvan Mainini, nous « recevons » ce mois-ci, Michel Rat, entraîneur de l'équipe de France cadets qui vient d'obtenir sa qualification pour le championnat d'Europe qui se disputera au mois d'août prochain en Bulgarie.

B.B. *Michel Rat, pouvez-vous vous présenter à nos lecteurs ?*

M.R. Je suis né le 16 mars 1937 à Auvers-sur-Oise, marié et père de quatre enfants (deux garçons et deux filles). Je m'occupe des cadets depuis 1981 après avoir suivi une filière relativement mouvementée dans la mesure où j'ai toujours beaucoup voyagé.

B.B. *Parlez-nous de votre carrière... ?*

M.R. J'ai fait l'essentiel de ma carrière de joueur au PUC de 1957 à 1970 au poste de meneur de jeu et porté 85 fois le maillot tricolore. Au sein de cette formation évoluaient des garçons comme Beugnot, Monclar ou encore Baltzer. C'était une grande équipe qui connut d'énormes satisfactions comme cette troisième place au championnat d'Europe d'Istambul en 1959 et la quatrième deux ans plus tard à Belgrade. Un autre souvenir, mais à titre personnel, demeure la proposition du Réal Madrid pour m'engager comme joueur ou cette sélection en équipe d'Europe que je dus refuser pour cause d'examens.

Tout en jouant, j'entraînais la formation féminine puciste, alors championne de France. Et puis à la fin de ma carrière active, je suis parti outre-mer et devenu directeur de l'Institut d'éducation physique à Tananarive (Madagascar). Après trois années, c'est-à-dire en 1973, je me suis dirigé vers le Sénégal afin de m'occuper de la formation des enseignants. En 1978 je revenais en France dans la région parisienne puis à Caen. Et en 1981, Pierre Dao me contacte pour m'occuper des jeunes. J'accepte avec plaisir et depuis je m'intéresse aux cadets.

B.B. *N'est-ce pas un peu frustrant de s'occuper d'une formation de jeunes ?*

M.R. Oui et non. Oui, parce que je ressens une certaine désaffection des médias voire de certains dirigeants à l'égard des jeunes. Jamais les projecteurs ne se braquent vers eux et cela me semble un tort. Il faut promouvoir ce basket aussi.

Et non, car le basket des jeunes demeure très important pour le sport d'élite. Au niveau du travail, il se renouvelle constamment puisque nous insistons sur la formation.

B.B. *Comment travaillez-vous ?*

M.R. Je suis pour faire des équipes d'encadrement car je ne conçois pas le travail en solitaire. Nous formons un groupe avec bien sûr définition des responsabilités dès le départ. Ainsi ici, nous comptons sur trois C.T.D. qui travaillent sur observations en cours et après le match. A mon avis ce genre d'action dynamise le corps des C.T.D.

B.B. *Quelles sont les différences entre le jeu des cadets et celui des séniors ?*

M.R. Nous retrouvons plusieurs similitudes dans le jeu mais avec moins de maturité, plus d'erreurs au niveau du tir ou des passes. De plus les cadets n'emploient pas les mêmes systèmes de jeu. Je suis pour un basket de mobilité chez les jeunes.

B.B. *Et les grands ?*

M.R. Vaste problème ! Car la formation des grands gabarits reste longue et délicate. Chez les jeunes en général, les différentes équipes se servent des petits et utilisent mal les grands. Aussi en sélection, ils ont bien du mal à s'exprimer. Et puis nous retrouvons toujours un décalage. Ainsi Plantier qui progresse de jour en jour ne possède que deux ans de basket derrière lui. Il est impossible qu'il sache tout faire tout de suite. Prenez le cas de Butter. Nous pouvons le considérer comme

une révélation tardive au niveau de la performance. Pourtant il a été détecté voici de nombreuses années. Pour apprendre, les joueurs doivent jouer et non pas faire banquette. Voilà pourquoi, personnellement, je suis pour une réforme en profondeur des championnats de jeunes.

B.B. *Qu'attendez-vous du championnat d'Europe 1985 ?*

M.R. Nous partons avec des ambitions relativement modestes ou plutôt réalistes à savoir une place dans les dix premiers. Nous manquons de cohésion, mais tout dépendra du tirage au sort. On ne sait jamais. Je crois qu'il ne faut pas se baser sur ces trois journées de compétition à Alençon. Les garçons n'ont pas joué sur leur valeur habituelle. Nous sommes en fin de trimestre, et la plupart apparaissent saturés. Ceci dit, l'essentiel restait la qualification. Nous demeurons sur une dixième place en 1981 avec Garnier, Servolle, Occansey et une septième en 1983 avec Schmitt. Hughes Occansey, Fedi et Popo.

B.B. *Que vous apporte votre fonction ?*

M.R. Sur le plan professionnel, entraîner des cadets m'apporte un renouvellement continuel et une remise en question. Il faut entraîner, avoir quelques notions de pédagogie. Ce n'est jamais la même chose. Sur le plan personnel, le contact des jeunes m'enrichit. Je comprends mieux mes enfants.

B.B. *Pour terminer comment voyez-vous l'avenir ?*

M.R. Je ne sais pas. J'aime beaucoup ce travail mais que vont donner les nouvelles mesures gouvernementales au niveau du professorat de sport ? Personnellement je souhaite passer l'agrégation du professorat E.P.S. et continuer à œuvrer dans le mouvement sportif.

François-Dominique BRECHER.

FIGURE 4.3 *Interview with Michel Rat. Credit: Musée du Basket.*

coaches, notably in Senegal, Madagascar, Cote d'Ivoire, and Niger, among other countries. It was part of the FFBB's larger politic to maintain and strengthen ties with their African counterparts as discussed in Chapter 13.

Despite this background, Rat didn't always have the easiest of relations with his African colleagues. "It was ambiguous," he later recalled of his role, one that was mired in duality. "There are both convergences and then also rejections ... I was an agent of cooperation. I was the *toubab*, the white guy who comes here ... We weren't there only to pillage and take all that they had [talent-wise]. There were also contributions."[47]

Post-Game

The new era of basketball, forged in the heady years after 1968, increasingly featured Antillean, American, and African players whose talent aided and augmented the game. The informal sports diplomacy of players from the Antilles, perhaps better thought of as a flow of internal exchange given the islands' status as *départements*, was crucial and there's a direct line from Cachemire's Russell-esque style of play to 1980s and 1990s legends Patrick Cham and Jim Bilba. Yet, although there was an increased number of Antillean players, it was not until the 1980s that the basketball world became more serious about implementing a strong detection and development program in the islands.[48]

Players from francophone Africa also exerted influence and helped transform the *hexagone*'s game. As Carmine Calzonetti later recalled to *Basket Retro*, "France advanced with French-Africans," in the 1970s.[49] And of course, part of the changed dimension was attributable to the American "colonization" of French hardcourts.

But there were two other significant transformations that occurred "under the hood," less visible than the players, so often the primary face of the game, but equally as important. Coaching and developing coaches became more of a focus, and several players, French, American, or otherwise, transitioned into a player-coach role before they took over full coaching responsibilities. According to broadcast journalist George Eddy, the US coaches in France in the 1970s and 1980s proved invaluable sources for revitalizing the country's basketball.[50]

Second, youth detection and development grew in importance after the Mazeaud Law created INSEP in 1975 and sport-study sections within schools in the late 1970s began to offer more kids the opportunity to play basketball in congruence with their academic studies. While the FFBB was particularly focused on the provision of federal training opportunities for young women, as the previous chapter notes, it was not until the 1983–4 academic year that its efforts to formulate an elite youth basketball pipeline for girls and boys materialized. At its helm was Rat, who imparted the basketball lessons he learned through his sports diplomacy experiences in the United States and Africa to subsequent generations of aspiring basketballers.

Notes

1   "Stags In Italy: Art Kenney Makes Mark in Milan," Fairfield University Athletics, accessed January 17, 2021, https://fairfieldstags.com/news/ 2017/8/7/mens-basketball-stags-in-italy-art-kenney-makes-mark-in-milan.

2   In his own way, McGregor spread US-style basketball by facilitating people-to-people cultural and technical exchanges around the game through his young players, more than 600 of them from 1967 through 1977. Pascal Legendre, "Art Kenney, l'un des Pionniers du Basket Américain en France (1) | Basket Europe," *Basket Europe*, November 7, 2019, sec. Jeep® ÉLITE, https://www.basketeurope.com/livenews- fr/482835/art-kenney-lun-des-pionniers-du-basket-americain-en-france-1/.

3   Arthur Kenney, Interview with the author, April 9, 2015.

4   Dominique Lapeyre, "Nouvelles Étoiles US," *L'Équipe Basket Magazine*, November 1973, 22.

5   Jean-Pierre Dusseaulx, Interview with the author, October 16, 2015.

6   Thierry Bretagne, "Des Paroles . . . aux Resultats," *L'Équipe Basket Magazine*, December 1976.

7   Françoise Vergès, "Overseas France: A Vestige of the Republican Colonial Utopia?," in Nicolas Bancel, Pascal Blanchard, and Dominic Thomas (eds.), *The Colonial Legacy in France: Fracture, Rupture, and Apartheid* (Indiana University Press, 2017), 166.

8   Vergès.

9   Jacques Dumont, "La Quete de l'égalité aux Antilles: La Départementalisation et Les Manifestiations des Annés 1950," *Le Mouvement Social*, no. 230 (March 2010): 80.

10 Jérome Pruneau, Jacques Dumont, and Nicolas Célimène, "Voiles Traditionnelles aux Antilles Françaises: 'Sportivisatoin' et Patrimonialisation," *Ethnologie Française* T36, no. 3 Iles Réelles (September 2006): 520.

11 Jacques Dumont, "Sport, Culture et Assimilation dans Les Antilles Françaises, des Colonies aux Départements d'outre-Mer," *Caribbean Studies* 35, no. 1 (June 2007): 87.

12 Dominique Laury, "Quinze Américains dans le Championnat National Peuvent Aider les Joueurs Français à Progresser," *Le Monde*, November 12, 1968.

13 Laury.

14 Lloyd Garrison, "2 Imported Americans Find Basketball in France Is Highly Individualistic," *The New York Times*, January 19, 1969.

15 Garrison.

16 Rémy Dessarts, "Le Commerce des Basketteurs Américains," *Le Monde*, September 29, 1980; INSEE, "Convertisseur Franc-Euro," https://www.insee.fr/fr/information/2417794.

17 Garrison, "2 Imported Americans Find Basketball in France Is Highly Individualistic"; Alioth Finance, "$500 in 1969 → 2022 | Inflation Calculator.," Official Inflation Data, n.d., https://www.officialdata.org/us/inflation/1969?amount=500; Dessarts; INSEE, "Convertisseur Franc-Euro."

18 Dessarts.

19 "The ABA Is Long Gone, but It Remains the Soul of the NBA," *Washington Post*, accessed November 10, 2022, https://www.washingtonpost.com/graphics/sports/nba-aba-merger/.

20 Jean-Pierre Dusseaulx, *Cinq Majeur: Gilles, Staelens, Bonato, Gasnal, Fields* (Solar Editeur, 1972), 225.

21 For more see Patrick Boucheron and Steephane Gerson, *France in the World: A New Global History* (Other Press, 2019); Yvan Gastaut et al., "Immigration: From Métèques to Foreigners," in *The Colonial Legacy in France: Fracture, Rupture, and Apartheid* (Indiana University Press, 2017), 209–19.

22 Dominique Wendling, "[Portrait] Roger Antoine a ouvert la voie," *Basket Retro* (blog), January 14, 2021, https://basket-retro.com/2021/01/14/portrait-roger-antoine-a-ouvert-la-voie/; Fédération Française de Basket-Ball (FFBB), "Historique des Matches," n.d., http://www.ffbb.com/edf/historique-des-matches.

23 Carmine Calzonetti, Interview with the author, September 18, 2020.

24 All Jacques Cachemire quotes in this chapter, unless specified, from Jacques Cachemire, Interview with the author, 2015.

25 Cachemire; Guillaume Paquereau, "[ITW] Jacques Cachemire : 'Le jour où je me casse la jambe contre Roanne, il y avait des scouts NBA dans la salle,'" *Basket Retro* (blog), May 31, 2022, https://basket-retro.com/2022/05/31/itw-jacques-cachemire-le-jour-ou-je-me-casse-la-jambe-contre-roanne-il-y-avait-des-scouts-nba-dans-la-salle/.

26 Jean-Pierre Dusseaulx, *Les Dessus du Panier: Les Clubs Qui Font la Gloire du Basket Français* (Solar Editeur, 1971), 41.

27 Dusseaulx, *Les Dessus du Panier*, 41.

28 Jean-Pierre Dusseaulx, "Cachemire Toujours Prête," *L'Equipe*, May 27, 1981.

29 Dusseaulx, Interview with the author.

30 "On Ne Peut Pas Être Éternel," FFBB, http://www.ffbb.com/ffbb/ne-peut-pas-etre-eternel.

31 BonZour, "Andy Tanner: Le Sens du Partage," lexpress.mu, April 30, 2017, https://lexpress.mu/article/305882/andy-tanner-sens-partage; "On Ne Peut Pas Être Éternel"; Cachemire, Interview with the author.

32 Lindsay Sarah Krasnoff, "Bill Cain's 'Scrutiny' and His Transformation into an Athlete Ambassador in French Professional Basketball," in *Sport and Protest in the Black Atlantic*, ed. Brian McGowen and Michael Gennaro (Routledge, 2022), 170–90.

33 "Histoire du Mans-Sarthe Basket et du Sporting Club Moderne," Le Mans Sarthe Basket, https://www.msb.fr/index.php/club/historique.

34 Vincent Collet, Interview with the author, September 26, 2016.

35 Pascal Legendre and David Piolé, *MSB: 20 Ans d'émotions* (Éditions Libra Diffusio, 2013), 39.

36 All Bill Cain quotes in this chapter, unless specified, from Bill Cain, Interview with the author, October 20, 2014; Bill Cain, Interview with the author, February 1, 2015.

37 Nicolas Batum, Katia Foucade-Hoard, and Bill Cain, Sport à l'épreuve du racisme?, Webinar, US Embassy France, September 9, 2020, https://www.facebook.com/130504556373/videos/1048410902284325.

38 Christian Baltzer, Interview with the author, April 10, 2015.

39 Collet, Interview with the author.

40 Gérard Bosc, *Une Histoire du Basket Français . . . Tome II: 1966–90* (Paris: Presses du Louvre, 2002), 20, 61.

41 Jacques Marchand, "Le Relais Passé aux Femmes . . .," *L'Équipe Basket Magazine*, May 1976.

42 Dessarts.

43 Dessarts.

44 Gérard Bosc, Interview with the author, October 26, 2014.

45 Bosc, Gérard, *Une Histoire du Basket Français . . . Tome II: 1966–90*, 66–75.

46 All Michel Rat quotes in this chapter, unless specified, from Michel Rat, Interview with the author, June 29, 2015; Michel Rat, Interview with the author, September 24, 2021.

47 Rat, Interview with the author, June 29, 2015.

48 Bosc, Interview with the author.

49 Guillaume Paquereau, "[ITW] Carmine Calzonetti 'A Nantes, j'ai joué pieds nus !,'" *Basket Retro* (blog), February 23, 2022, https://basket-retro.com/2022/02/23/itw-carmine-calzonetti-a-nantes-jai-joue-pieds-nus/.

50 George Eddy, Interview with the author, September 30, 2021.

5

New Waves, 1984–92

The 1984 Summer Games opened with an elaborate show that celebrated the American culture of entertainment, from Hollywood and Broadway to the popular music of Irene Cara and Michael Jackson. The cultural festivities gave way to the parade of nations, and for the first time since 1960, the French men's basketball team, by now known as Les Bleus, were among the Olympic delegation. The team consisted of homegrown players, including Patrick Cham, who left his own important fingerprints on the game back home. His teammate Hervé Dubuisson became the first European-trained player to sign an NBA contract when he was recruited to play the post-Olympic NBA Summer League with the New Jersey Nets. A few weeks later, twenty-two-year-old French protégé Paoline Ekambi arrived at Marist College in Poughkeepsie, New York, the first French woman to play NCAA Division 1 basketball and part of the first generation of Les Bleues to represent a diverse, postcolonial France enriched by its immigration history.

While these foundational steps were not mainstream conversation back home, the basketball world became more attuned to its American cousin thanks to the diffusion of NBA broadcasts on the new private French television network Canal+. The station, founded in 1984, used a paid subscription model, a first for the country, to broadcast content that centered on movies and sports entertainment. Its offerings included NBA matches, but it was not until Franco-American George Eddy proposed to Canal+ that he announce their NBA games that a pivotal foundation fell into place. When Eddy called his first NBA game for the station in January 1985, he brought the excitement and vocabulary of the league's courts directly into living-rooms in a heavily

American-accented French. In doing so, Eddy influenced generations, helped whet youths' appetite for US-style ball, and began a career as *the* voice of the NBA in France.

The ways that Cham, Ekambi, and Eddy engaged in informal sports diplomacy through people-to-people cultural, technical, and knowledge exchanges helped build a stronger French game. They built upon what the pioneers of the 1950s and 1960s established, but also left their own distinct imprints as they passed on to France-based teammates what they learned from US players, coaches, or, in Eddy's case, his own know-how, helping to enrich and elevate the game.

Scouting Report

The mid-1980s was a time of transformative change. François Mitterrand won the 1981 presidential elections, the first time in the post-1945 era that the Socialist Party held the Elysée Palace, and by 1984 the new government's policies were fully underway. A committed Atlanticist, Mitterrand took a firmer stance toward Moscow than his predecessors as a new hardening of East–West relations followed the Soviet invasion of Afghanistan.[1] He built closer working relationships with Washington and London and kindled personal ties with US President Ronald Reagan. But while Franco-American relations were close, Mitterrand maintained a Gaullist emphasis on independence from Washington and ensured the country's nuclear arsenal.[2]

Elsewhere, longstanding interests and policies reinforced Paris's ability to serve as an influential player. Despite complicated postcolonial ties with Africa, it remained a power in the region and continued to cultivate sports ties to maintain an influential orb.[3] The Quai d'Orsay's Middle East policies also maintained an active French footprint. In 1982, France deployed to Lebanon after Israel crossed the border as part of a multinational peacekeeping force alongside troops from the United States and Italy. While this bolstered the Palestinian Liberation Organization (PLO) of Yasser Arafat, Mitterrand strengthened French–Israeli ties to ensure that France was a more viable player in the Middle East and world politics.[4]

Thus, under Mitterrand, the Fifth Republic didn't need to use sports in quite the same way as previous eras. Under Charles de

Gaulle, sporting successes could illustrate the country's revival and rejuvenation following decades of war and decolonization, as well as demonstrate independence from Washington and Moscow; that French athletes were unable to deliver medals, titles, or "wins" during the 1960s sports crisis rendered this desire moot.[5] Instead, the return of some degrees of sporting success by 1984 helped broadcast images of a new equilibrium.

The government also began to liberalize the economy in 1984. The move was in recognition that the administration's early policies towards state-run businesses did not produce results. As a result, several industries began to privatize, including television. The three public television stations, originally built upon the government's notion that the technology served a public education purpose, now had direct competition in the acquisition of sports broadcasting rights.[6] Canal+ made football central to its sports offerings. It broadcast its first live sports event on November 9, 1984, a football match between FC Nantes and AC Monaco.[7] It also showcased boxing, American Football (NFL), and the NBA, whose rights Canal+ purchased that fall.

The Mitterrand government's liberalization extended to the sports world. In July 1984, the Avice Law was adopted, slackening of the strings of state control over elite sports systems. Previously, the 1975 Mazeaud Law committed government resources to detecting, training, and sustaining high level athletes so that they could optimally perform at elite competitions; recast the national sports school, the National Institute for Sport, Excellence, and Performance (INSEP), to groom the country's most promising youth athletes; and sought to inscribe sports as part of the national culture. Nine years later, the Avice Law situated sports as part of public health and sought to open up sports practice to a broader spectrum of citizens of all backgrounds by transferring some of the power held by national sports federations to the government. Yet, at the same time, it also embraced a more US-oriented attitude toward financing the sports system, encouraging private enterprises to sponsor elite sportspeople, while also fundraising through the national sports lottery, implemented a year earlier.[8]

Sports-wise, 1984 seemed to mark a new era for the country. Early that summer, France hosted the UEFA European Championship for the first time since 1960. Les Bleus, led by the fabled *carré magique* of midfield magician Michel Platini, Jean Tigana, Alain

Giresse, and Luis Fernandez, clinched the title.[9] A few weeks later, a different constellation of French players won the Olympic tournament at the Los Angeles Games. Following close on the heels of the team's fourth-place finish at the 1982 World Cup, it appeared that French football was finally producing thanks to the youth training programs implemented by the French Football Federation (FFF) throughout the 1970s.[10]

The Platini generation reinforced how football was enriched by the country's cosmopolitan demographic base as players with roots in Africa and the Antilles helped France to its UEFA and Olympic titles.[11] It was an important consideration for domestically, the country grappled with a rise of the far-right wing and its emblematic political party, the Front National (FN), as well as increased racism, all of which focused public anxiety on the issue of immigration and who belonged in the republic. Even as the country's economic situation improved in the 1980s, the FN continued to infuse political conversation with its inflammatory rhetoric and ideas. The 1983 youth mobilization for equal rights and to counter the FN led to the creation of SOS Racisme, dedicated to fight discrimination and push for greater civil rights. Sports could foster a sense of belonging, both on the field, as well as by rallying the republic's citizens around its elite athletes given improved performances.

Football portended a French return to sporting results, but basketball also appeared to be on the rebound, too. Les Bleus qualified for the Summer Games in 1984, which reflected the years of work put into ameliorating performance and training a new generation of players who could compete against some of the world's best sides.[12] Although the 1983 creation of the Centre Fédéral de Basket-Ball (CFBB) at INSEP was not yet a factor in national team results, the next generation was inspired by Les Bleus who contested the Los Angeles Games.[13]

The Olympic return also reflected the impact of the "American colonization" of French hardcourts after 1968. Homegrown basketballers schooled in the US-style, tactics, techniques, and game plays that US players and coaches brought with them to the *métropole* featured on the 1984 roster. Team France confronted their US counterparts in their first official Olympic competition that summer and suffered a demoralizing 120–62 defeat. In fact, Les Bleus won just one of their six Olympic matches, a 102–78 victory over Egypt in their last competition of the tournament, finishing in eleventh place. But the experience of being in basketball's homeland proved to be influential, particularly for one player who, molded by the transatlantic hoops forces at play, marked the game and helped craft subsequent generations in the country's emergent basketball empire as a coach and official.

The Watchdog

Patrick Cham etched his place on the hardcourt most fulsomely in the 1980s, while his legacy as a coach first at INSEP and later at INSEP's Guadeloupe outpost continues into the 2020s. The small forward served as an official ambassador of France as part of the national team and later, a French Basketball Federation (FFBB) official, but it was the informal sports diplomacy of people-to-people cultural, technical, and knowledge exchanges with US teammates and coaches on and around the court throughout his career that helped elevate his game, that of players he coached, and that of the national team.

Born May 18, 1959, Cham grew up in Saint-Claude, Guadeloupe, where he played basketball on a court near his house.[14] The Antilles were (and remain) unique for, while they are integral parts of France, they are influenced by their geographical proximity to the United States, and in sports this meant that basketball was prevalent.[15] But when Cham was a kid, there was a distinct absence of diverse coaches. "There were only Guadeloupean coaches and players," he recalled. "It was very local and very insular."[16]

Even his idol was a fellow Guadeloupean, Jacques Cachemire, one of the country's best all-time players. Cachemire was the first Antillean player to mark the French game, one of the country's leading scorers in the 1970s, but originally honed his craft by mimicking the styles, techniques, and shooting of his own idol, legendary Boston Celtics player-coach Bill Russell.[17] Cachemire was "a reference, an example," Cham said, and passed along his Russell-infused strain of the game.

Cham went to the *métropole* in fall 1976 to play with Stade Français Paris. It was the sixteen-year-old's first time in the capital and his first time on the mainland. But as a recent arrival, he observed with keen eyes the sport's relatively unimportant place within popular culture. "When I arrived, basketball was a very provincial sport," he said of how it was popular in medium and small-sized towns, the sport's traditional popular bases.

For the next ten years, Cham fine-tuned his game with Stade Français. The storied club's basketball section was founded in 1920 and while it enjoyed national success in the 1920s, was relegated to the second division (then known as Nationale 2) for much of the twentieth century. N2 Champion in 1963, the club brought Cham in as part of its rebuilding process and won its second N2 title in 1979. Three years later, it united Cham with Hervé Dubuisson, already one of the best players of the era, under US head coach Mike Perry. Together, they helped stimulate basketball interest in the capitol. As Cham recalled, "Paris had a real infatuation with basketball, but it was still a sport of the medium-sized cities." While the men's team attracted the public's attention, it was the women's side that shone most brightly, as six-time champions between 1980 and 1987, and Coupe de France victors in 1982, 1983, and 1985.[18]

Cham was known for his physical, athletic game, hard work, and a reputation for being a watchdog.[19] For George Eddy, the voice of the NBA on Canal+ but also one of Cham's Stade Français coaches during the 1985–6 season, the Guadeloupe native was "an excellent defensive stopper-type player."[20] Cham acknowledged the role that playing with US teammates had to ameliorate basketball. "They raised the level of the game, because they made it more athletic," he said.

The team's head coach that season, Kenny Grant, cited the increasingly athletic style as a reason behind the country's basketball revival in international competitions, including a return to the Olympics. "I felt that the French league was by far, the most athletic league," he said.

> I coached in Italy and Italy was a coach's game. They're playing chess. It wasn't that way in France. It was a player's game. You know, there were loosely formed offensive schemes that the players were going to decide to finish, which ended up adjusting them well for their [eventual] time in the NBA, because that was the same . . . that was similar in France. The players could go off on their own. It could be interpreted by some as a lack of discipline, but it wasn't. They were able to be very successful with very good one-against-one players.[21]

For Cham, players like himself from the Antilles helped inject this new athleticism onto hardcourts.

We had this profile that looked like American players. Because we were athletic, we were tall too. We had a profile that looked like the American player on a physical level. At the basketball level, the Americans had a much bigger basketball culture than ours, because it was already part of their education. Basketball in France is a sport that is practiced in society on a voluntary basis [whereas] in the United States, it is a program that is in schools.

It wasn't just that Antillean players had a certain profile. The region produced basketball players, as well as footballers, handball players, and other athletes due to its Caribbean location. "The weather is always good, so we play sports outside at any time when we were young," Cham explained. But it also became a source of solid basketballers because the FFBB started to focus their youth

FIGURE 5.1 *Les Bleus, European Basketball Championship, 1983.* *Credit: Musée du Basket. Cham, bottom row, third from left.*

detection and training efforts on the Antilles. The more up-tempo style of the mainland game flowed to Guadeloupe and Martinique as coaches began to transmit this technical and game know-how, as well as new tactics, to the islands. Overall, as Cham assessed, the influx of US players and coaches "enabled the growth of French basketball players, but also for Guadeloupean basketball, too."

At the 1984 LA Games, Cham, Dubuisson and their teammates soaked in US basketball even as their on-court performances were psychologically demoralizing. For all, it was their first shot at living the Olympic dream.[22] But while Les Bleus were increasingly known for their on-court athleticism and defense, they were not playing at the same level as the US team, which featured recent University of North Carolina graduate Michael Jordan.

"There was such a gap between French and American basketball at that time," Cham explained to *Basket-Retro*. "We were impressed. There was such a level of play that it was hard to express yourself. It's a great memory as a sportsman."[23] His best friend, Dubuisson, did not return to France with the team after the Games. Instead, he traveled to the New Jersey Nets' summer training camp in Princeton, New Jersey, and after a series of performances that put his games *en bleu* to shame, Dubuission became the first Frenchman and first European-trained player to sign an NBA contract when the Nets hired him to play under their colors in the NBA Summer League.

The Olympic experience underscored the need to invest more in elite preparation, as well as in youth formation, while Dubuisson's American adventure illustrated that a French kid could play in the NBA. To prepare the next generation to be better basketballers, it was necessary to attract more youths to the game. While basketball began to enjoy a revival in how kids viewed the game, it was still necessary to gain greater mediatization.

At the time, there was little basketball on television. Then, as now, basketball remained at a disadvantage as it was not readily accessible to the broad population through free publicly televised games. A small basketball-centric press existed; the 1982 founding of *Maxi Basket* provided a periodical specifically dedicated to the game. But with just 16,000 copies sold for its inaugural September 1982 issue, the magazine and the sport remained a specialist's endeavor among the media landscape.[24]

Drawing more kids into the game was dependent on national team results. As Cham relayed to *Basket-Ball*:

To be more mediatized, we need for the French team to win matches. For the French team to win matches, it's necessary to give them adversaries at their level in every way possible. We cannot win against the United States? Play against Luxembourg ... It's necessary to meet teams that we can fight.[25]

At the start of the 1984–5 season, there were 498,871 licensed basketball players, an increase from 449,680 in 1980.[26] But clearly, work was needed to appeal to a new generation of potential players.

For Cham, playing alongside US teammates or being coached by US coaches in France were his main connection to American basketball. It wasn't until Canal+ began to broadcast NBA matches that he began to encounter that style of the game.[27] Equally, if not more important, it was telecasts of NBA games on Canal+ that began to enable kids around the *hexagone* to want to emulate the stars they saw weekly on television. But the NBA was not—yet—a crucial reference point for elite French talent; instead by the mid-1980s it was the NCAA that was aspirational.

The Pioneer

While Cham lit up courts with Stade Français Paris in the 1980s, a rising young star with the club's winning women's section created the opportunity to live her own American Dream. Paoline Ekambi was the first Frenchwoman to play NCAA D1 basketball in 1984. The experiences gained during her two years with Marist College helped her to become a better player, attributes she passed down to subsequent generations of young women who, like her, set off in increasing numbers to play basketball in the NCAA and, eventually, the WNBA.

The lifelong Parisian was born May 14, 1962, into a multicultural family that breathed sports. Her father was a former professional footballer from Cameroon, her maternal grandmother from Poland, and her maternal grandfather from Catalonia, reflecting France's rich immigration history. At home, the family was well versed in football, boxing, and track and field. She grew up on the exploits of Muhammad Ali and Joe Frazier, and looked up to the former as a role model.

As a kid, she played football with her friends and her four brothers but stumbled into basketball as an abnormally tall thirteen-year-old. Measuring then five-foot-six and reedy thin, Ekambi was diagnosed with the early beginnings of scoliosis.[28] One of her doctors recommended that she try basketball, volleyball, or swimming to help treat her back.[29] The decision for Ekambi was rather simple: one of her girlfriends played basketball with Sainte-Geneviève-des-Bois in the southern Parisian suburbs, so Ekambi also enrolled.

She was a novice in every sense of the word. "I knew nothing about the sport," Ekambi recalled, "nothing about its French or American actors or of its history." But she quickly took to the discipline and rapidly became one of the region's more promising young players. A few months later, basketball National Technical Director Joë Jaunay, the same man who brought Élisabeth Riffiod into what is today INSEP and molded her into one of her generation's great players, recruited Ekambi to INSEP tryouts.

It was an exclusive invitation given only to the country's best young players. Despite her late start in the game, Ekambi passed the physical aptitude and mental tests, and integrated into INSEP's basketball section in September 1977. "I didn't really know how to play," she recalled, "I couldn't even shoot."[30] But she had charisma and character, a pluckiness honed from the *quartiers populairs*, which appealed to Jaunay, an official who believed that a more diverse mix of players could help produce better on-court results. He was thus in the process of remaking the national women's team to be more diverse, inclusive, and taller. "The previous generations, aside from Élisabeth Riffiod and Dominique Leray, were much shorter," she noted.

This basketball section at INSEP was the early precursor to the Federal Basketball Center formalized for the 1983–4 school year. It enabled Ekambi and her teammates to continue their academic study while training with the country's best young basketball players. On the weekends, most girls played with their home clubs for INSEP had not yet created a team that played in the French championship.

While difficult for a teenager to leave home to study, sleep, and practice at INSEP, it was a good arrangement for the Ekambis. "The fact that I was in a club reassured my parents because I was with other girls," she said.

My parents were of the old school mentality, which still exists today, because when I turned thirteen, my parents thought that I couldn't have the same rights to leave the house as my brothers, who could return during school break at 8 p.m., and for me it was 6 p.m. That I didn't like at all.

The ability to all but leave home also came at a critical juncture for Ekambi, who thrived at INSEP.[31]

The school's basketball program enabled its players to engage in informal sports diplomacy in different ways. It encouraged people-to-people cultural, technical, and knowledge exchanges between its young protégés and the US coaches brought in to run clinics, upskill the teenagers, and impart their version of the game's science. "There was already all of that falling into place with the players," Ekambi said of this transatlantic basketball exchange by the late 1970s. "I remember an American coach who came with an American player to explain what we were looking for in the perfection of the shot."

It also introduced Ekambi to women's basketball in the United States through an organized tour of the country. Ekambi and her teammates played a series of games against US teams in Kansas City, Kansas, Kansas City, Missouri, and Tennessee. "We took a beating," Ekambi recalled of how the French fared against their American counterparts. But just as for the players of Paris Université Club, the first French team to play in the United States in 1956, the overall experience was inspirational and instructive. "They were extremely strong, but it motivated me," Ekambi said of her American competition. So did the strength and prowess of the Black American players, with who she was able to identify, a rarity among elite French female players at the time.

Ekambi graduated and left INSEP at age seventeen. She signed a contract with Stade Français Paris, her first elite-level club, and was also selected for the senior national team for the first time. Her debut game *en bleu* on March 27, 1980 was the first time since Sokéla Mangoumbel took the court in 1938 that Les Bleues fielded a player with Black African heritage.[32] The national team, surprisingly, provided Ekambi with another steppingstone to her American dream. At a training camp in Aix-en-Provence, the French met their US counterparts for just the second time on French soil; Team USA beat Les Bleues, 81–80, in a Marseille-based friendly, but the encounter offered Ekambi the opportunity to meet several American players who encouraged her to investigate playing with an NCAA D1 basketball program.[33]

The idea intrigued, but the seventeen-year-old was not ready for the adventure. "I was young, I was in my cocoon," she recalled. "I also saw that we expected a lot more from the foreign players [or players with foreign experience] in the French championship. I wasn't mentally or technically ready to be in that position."

She continued to play with Stade Français but the idea of playing in the United States took root. "I liked the atmosphere, I liked the spirit, the music, the way of training," she explained of what she observed during her tour with INSEP. "I had the impression that [players] were freer to release energies, to give our all" in the US game.

A few years later, Ekambi was ready to realize her dream. She turned to Stade Français' men's head coach Mike Perry for advice. Perry, after two years helming the team, was set to return to the United States to coach Marist College's men's basketball team.[34] He advised her to also go to Marist, as they recruited European players for both men's and women's teams and thought it might be an easier fit than a program with only US players. He also played up the cosmopolitan nature of the New York City metropolitan region, which included Poughkeepsie, arguing that it was likely to be less of a cultural shock for the Parisienne. Convinced, she obtained a scholarship but was only eligible to play two years.

Ekambi thus arrived on campus for fall 1984 in what proved to be the most influential informal sports diplomacy experience of her career. It was a learning experience in every sense. First, it was about learning how to navigate a different culture in a foreign language. It helped that she took six years of English classes during school but learning English in a classroom and speaking it with teammates were two different things. Ekambi was not prepared for the slang she encountered on campus, such as "yo!" and "what's up?"

Moreover, she encountered stereotypes about who does, and does not, play basketball. Tall, svelte, known as Madame Fashion amongst her Les Bleues teammates for her *à la mode* clothing and just-so makeup, she appeared as an enigma to students and her new teammates. But Ekambi oozed confidence and redoubled her desire to show them that she could play and succeed. "I carried France within me," she said. "I also carried within me my dream [of playing in the United States]. I carried all of this within me. I felt I was like an ambassador."

FIGURE 5.2 *The October 31, 1981 cover of* L'Équipe Magazine *featuring Paoline Ekambi. Credit*: L'Équipe Magazine.

The actual basketball was different, too, for the European and American games differed in rules and approach. The mental level and athleticism were on a new level for Ekambi, especially as gamedays were not nearly as arduous as preparations. "Training sessions in the NCAA were much more difficult than matches," she noted. Marist practiced for two hours a day, the maximum allowed under NCAA regulations; with Stade Français she was used to two or three training sessions a day. Yet, the physicality and emotional tenacity required to compete among the Red Foxes was harder in intensity. "It was two hours at 200% investment," she told *Basket-Retro*.[35]

Ekambi rapidly integrated with her new team and began the season as a starter. She was motivated by many factors, including the desire to show Americans that Frenchwomen knew how to play the game.[36] She mastered the smaller-sized basketball used by the NCAA, played hard to match the competition, was named to Metro Atlantic Athletic Conference's First Team, and excelled on court.[37]

Throughout her two-year US dream, Ekambi learned much. She absorbed crucial lessons about mental discipline and leadership, specifically that to help the team overall, she had to up her individual game. She also internalized that leaders are exemplary and accountable to the team. "American college really reinforced my technicality, basketball, and vision of the game," she reflected.

She also came into direct contact with racism in the United States. In France, as a mixed-race woman, she encountered certain stereotypes. "At the time, we were considered bastards," she recalled of opinion makers' attitudes, and sometimes in games she would hear insidious remarks from the stands: "the first word was 'dirty n****ss.'" But at Marist, she found the racism much more upfront. For example, her white teammates sat together in the front of the team bus listening to California-style music while her Black teammates sat at the back of the bus listening to hip hop. When Ekambi asked her coach about the startling divide, she was told she was lucky; the previous season the team had two buses—one for each group. So the player with numerous nicknames, including Frog Legs, Snails, String Beans, French Fries, and Air France, started to sit in the middle of the bus. She progressed to taking turns sitting with the two groups, before she eventually brought them together.

Ekambi returned to France and resumed her club and national team careers after her two years of basketball eligibility ended. She wrote her name into the record books: vice champion of France with Stade Français Versailles 1988–9,[38] with Racing Club de France 1991–2, and with SCAB Clermont-Ferrand 63; Miss Europe of Basketball at the 1989 European Championship; vice champion of Europe in 1993; bronze medal at the 1991 Mediterranean Games; and for twenty years was the second most-capped player for Les Bleues with 254 games to her name.

Ekambi's US experience was crucial in developing her physical game and helping to make her the leader she became known for on-court in the French championship and with the national team.[39] These traits she helped pass along to other teammates in France over the years, just as other players with overseas experience helped enrich and elevate the French game. Ekambi traces a direct line between her own experience and that of subsequent young players she mentored, including the first Frenchwoman to complete four years of NCAA D1 basketball (University of Washington Huskies captain Katia Foucade-Hoard) and to play in the WNBA (Isabelle Fijalkowski). "Our championship was multicultural and stronger [because of] the cultural exchanges," Ekambi said of the Eastern Europeans, Americans, and Africans who played in and contributed to the French game. "It still enriches French performance."

Half-Time

By the mid-1980s, French basketball began to encounter its American cousin in new ways. It wasn't just the novelty of French players going to the United States to play in the NCAA; after 1984 it was French citizens watching the top US league, the NBA, on their televisions.

The NBA was in the midst of a much-needed renaissance. When the league's new Commissioner, David Stern, took over from his predecessor on February 1, 1984, he inherited a beleaguered product. Teams worked to overcome the 1970s fiscal insolvency that threatened to shutter the enterprise but were still disadvantaged by a tarnished public image. That it was composed primarily of Black American players in a US society still to overcome its racist past likely did not help to endear the NBA to certain spheres of influence within the United States.

The league received a lifeline when Magic Johnson and Larry Bird were drafted by the Los Angeles Lakers and Boston Celtics, respectively, in 1979. The two storied clubs created a decade-long rivalry that injected new vivacity and relevance to the NBA, as did attempts, notably by the Lakers, to create a "showtime" entertainment atmosphere. The June 1984 draft class, which included future stars Michael Jordan, Charles Barkley, and University of Houston Nigerian ace Hakeem Olajuwon, gave birth to a new NBA.[40] But a domestic renaissance alone was not enough.

Part of Stern's vision was to build the league's global profile, for he was intrigued by the sport overseas. "My interest in international basketball became intense after I joined the NBA [in 1978] because I was very much suddenly aware that there's a game beyond our borders," Stern recalled.[41] His first NBA game in Europe was in August 1984 when the Phoenix Suns and New Jersey Nets played a series of games in Italy and Israel.

The prospect of developing an NBA market in Europe intrigued the Commissioner. "We really believed that the most advanced basketball at the time in terms of the quality of play was in Italy of all places," he said, pointing to the number of higher profile US players in the Italian league. "That's the year in which I grew up as a professional lawyer and leading executive, and focused more on Italy." France was, he admitted, "not on my radar."

One of the initial focal points was to make NBA broadcasts available to overseas television stations. "I think the television [played] an important part of it," Stern said of the league's initial global growth in the 1980s. "People were beginning to see American players, the games, their lifestyle, their fashion and the fact that they were becoming celebrities in their own country. And international celebrities have a way of driving interest in the sport."

The league's global growth was about far more than just TV access. Stern pointed to how league executives made it easier for overseas reporters to interview players and obtain information about games to enhance broadcasts in their home languages. "People take for granted the speed of information these days, but back in the day, it was very clunky, so to speak. We didn't deliver games by satellite. We delivered them by cycling tapes around."

The Voice of the NBA

If the NBA's popularity in France grew through its diffusion on Canal+, it was George Eddy, who as the voice of the NBA in France did much to transmit US culture and basketball know-how to viewers. Born in 1956 to a French mother and American father, Eddy grew up in Winter Park, Florida, in a family that were active civil rights supporters. After graduation from the University of Florida-Gainesville in 1977 with a degree in criminology and several journalism courses, Eddy went to France.[42]

As the second Franco-American player to evolve in the country's top division, Eddy embarked on a decades-long career in the game. First at Bagnolet, just north of Paris, then at Chalons-sur-Marne and Racing Paris Basket, Eddy balanced a player's career while he coached and taught kids. While the US players were all paid, French basketball was still not fully professionalized. Some like Eddy held jobs on the side, but it was increasingly clear that the sport needed to move towards full professionalization to survive and compete.

Eddy was excited to learn of Canal+'s acquisition of NBA broadcast rights in 1984 and was one of the first to subscribe. After he watched the channel's first NBA matches, he began to sense an opportunity. "I said to myself: 'I speak French, I know the NBA by heart, I live in Paris,'" Eddy recalled in his 2019 autobiography.[43] So the twenty-five-year-old submitted his CV to Canal+ and proposed that he serve as a consultant for their NBA coverage. He pointed out how the existing commentators weren't basketball specialists and were thus covering a sport outside of their area of expertise. Eddy, on the other hand, grew up with the league and, as an American, knew the personalities, team backgrounds, and more. Canal+ decided to make the gamble.

In January 1985, Eddy voiced his first NBA match for the station, a matchup of Larry Bird's Boston Celtics against the New York Knicks.[44] Due to the limitations of the era's technology, they were not broadcast live; instead, there was often a delay of seven to ten days from gameday until it was beamed into French living rooms. But the colorful formula of Eddy's knowledge, excitement, and infusion of US lingo with the product broadcast on television was a hit and helped translate the NBA for generations. As he wrote in his autobiography,

As an NBA enthusiast, I used the expressions of the great commentators, with a vocabulary that is now my trademark. "Slam dunk," "Coast to coast," "Alley-oop" and "Money time" are now part of the French language! I am quite proud to have imported a language that the media and young people have appropriated.[45]

In doing so, Eddy engaged in a form of informal sports diplomacy, communicating, representing, and negotiating the basketball culture and passion of his homeland with his new compatriots. Later generations recalled how he excited them to the game when they were kids. For Vincent Collet, who as a young professional played against Eddy in the early 1980s before embarking on a highly successful coaching career, the Franco-American had a marked impact on how people, kids especially, viewed the NBA. "He brought something from States," Collet attested.

George was fantastic, and he brought a lot of things to French basketball, more than most people think. He had both cultures, and he made the French spectators understand US basketball. He was the best ambassador, and he sold US basketball very well. And it changed the mentality for young people and the way they were able to play basketball, step by step with what they saw on television, that helped our basketball to come closer to US basketball.[46]

Other basketball stakeholders agreed. For journalist and *Maxi Basket* founder Pascal Legendre, Eddy played an important role. "He is one of the fundamental people in French basketball," he said.[47] For former player, coach, and NCAA announcer for French television Johan Rat, Eddy helped kids dream of one day playing in the NBA. "We were open on a mediatic aspect to America early on with games shown on television, NBA games with George Eddy," he said. "So many kids like me, who were born in the 1970s got affiliated with the NBA very young."[48]

While the NBA stoked interest in basketball more generally, not everyone was happy with the development. There were fears within the FFBB and French leagues that the NBA would serve to "vampirize" the domestic game—to suck it dry. The NBA was, after all, a competitor, and many began following the NBA, not

FIGURE 5.3 *George Eddy. Credit: Getty Images.*

French basketball. This was true especially among young adults. As Cham recalled, "kids knew all the names of the NBA stars without knowing the name of a French basketball star." Thus the NBA had no direct contact with the FFBB until after 1990.[49] According to basketball historian and former National Technical Director Gérard Bosc, "[Stern] had polite relationships, but he didn't try to change anything in the relationship [with the FFBB]. He didn't try to impose the NBA style in Europe. He won on his own."[50]

For his part, Eddy viewed the role of US coaches as perhaps even more instrumental in revitalizing French basketball than the NBA initially. They brought different principles of the game, as well as set plays, something that the French game lacked when Eddy first arrived in 1977, but which certain coaches, including Kenny Grant, helped implement. They also brought a US attitude towards professionalism and the on-court quality of play, helping elevate the French product. "Those American coaches and those American players really helped the French players become better," Eddy said.

For some, the NBA served as a gateway to the game, for most French people, it was US coaches and players who had the greatest impact elevating interest in basketball. "They were in direct contact with the population," Bosc explained. "Not everyone could watch [NBA on basketball]. In the Parisian region, people watched TV with American basketball. In the provinces, they couldn't. But they had American players who played [locally]." Either way, the cultural exchanges that occurred in and around basketball helped to bring French players, coaches, viewers, and others closer to the US game.

Post-Game

As the decade progressed, basketball continued to evolve. Critically, the game finally shed its semi-professional status and fully professionalized in 1987. Players were paid wages that were not contingent upon holding a side job with the club's sponsoring company or patron, and they no longer had to balance multiple jobs at the same time, like Eddy did.

The advantage of professionalization was that it formalized youth development academies, which were now required for every club in the country's top division. Just like their football counterparts, the basketball youth academies sought to provide opportunity for promising young players to specialize their hoops training while continuing their scholastic education.

At the same time, the FFBB built out its federal training structures. It created regional training centers for those who were not good enough to develop at the CFBB at INSEP but who the federation wished to keep in the system. It also instituted *pôles espoirs*, feeders designed to help promising boys and girls aged thirteen through fifteen to develop their skills in hopes of being good enough to be recruited to INSEP afterwards. The federation's new structure sought to create a pyramid to feed the best young talent into INSEP, and it was this system in which its future NBA, WNBA, and NCAA players began to matriculate. Legendre noted the impact that such systems, as described in Chapter 12, had. "We started to close the gap we had with Spain, Italy, Yugoslavia, the USSR," he said. "We were very late [to this type of youth training]."

Professionalization also made the French championship more attractive to overseas players, notably Africans. Previously, many of the African basketballers who dribbled on French hardcourts did so while pursuing their university studies (like Roger Antoine) or as a side passion in the early years of their careers. But as a paid endeavor, new waves of players crossed the Mediterranean for the *métropole*, notably those from sub-Saharan Africa. They, too, helped to shape the game in different ways. Many of them fell in love, married, had children, and lived in France. Others, returned home (to Senegal), but remained an influence in their French children's lives.

For Grant, the improvement in French basketball in the 1980s wasn't purely a coincidence, but the amalgamation of the immigration and migration patterns already at play. "The French had a very multicultural society with people from Guadeloupe, Martinique, the réintegrés from Senegal and Africa," he said. "I think that had a great effect on basketball, maybe more than other sports." This helped a French strength: its on-court athleticism.

If you compare with the Yugoslavian game, where shooting was the main thing and a big strength, in France, using their athletic ability was what was important, not just having it. They were able to use it defensively, full court, pressing, things like that.

Fast breaking, going to the basket on people, blocking shots. It was a much more similar game to the NBA than the other countries.

Thus, basketball's professionalization had a much wider impact than merely alleviating labor concerns over wages. It helped reinforce a wider system of infrastructure, from leagues to coaches' training, and youth development. It took time for these efforts to realize basketball results, but the process began to groom the next generation of young talent, the very kids who grew up to play in some of the world's elite leagues, a French response to the growing globalization of the game.

Notes

1 Frédéric Bozo, *French Foreign Policy Since 1945: An Introduction* (Berghahn Books, 2016).

2 As Frédéric Bozo (ibid.) argues, French–American relations were at their closest point since 1962.

3 Pascal Charitas, "A More Flexible Domination: Franco-African Sport Diplomacy during Decolonization, 1945–1966," in *Diplomatic Games: Sport, Statecraft, and International Relations since 1945*, ed. Heather L. Dichter and Andrew L. Johns (University of Kentucky Press, n.d.); Pascal Charitas and David-Claude Kemo-Keimbou, "The United States of America and the Francophone African Countries at the International Olympic Committee: Sports Aid, a Barometer of American Imperialism? (1952–1963)," *Journal of Sport History*, 40, no. 1 (2013): 69–91.

4 For more on Mitterrand's foreign policies, see Bozo; Dominique David, "Independence and Interdependence: Foreign Policy Over Mitterrand's Two Presidential Terms," in *The Mitterrand Years: Legacy and Evaluation* (New York: St. Martin's Press, 1998), 112–29.

5 Lindsay Sarah Krasnoff, *The Making of Les Bleus: Sport in France, 1958–2010* (Lexington Books, 2012).

6 M. F. Lévy and E. Cohen, *La Télévision Dans La République: Les Années 50* (Complexe, 1999), https://books.google.fr/books?id=2w1h43bOsZMC.

7 Bernard Poisuil, *Canal+: L'aventure Du Sport* (Éditoria, 1996).

8 For greater details on the Avice Law and Edwige Avice, the Minister of Youth and Sport, see Chapter 4 in Krasnoff, *The Making of Les Bleus.*

9 For more on the *carré magiques* that helped Les Bleus to success in the 1980s, see Bruno Colombari, "Les carrés magiques (1): Tigana, Fernandez, Giresse, Platini—Chroniques bleues," accessed October 2, 2021, https://www.chroniquesbleues.fr/Les-carres-magiques.

10 For more on France's sports crisis of the 1960s, as well as the FFF's youth development programs launched after 1972, see Krasnoff, *The Making of Les Bleus.*

11 Laurent Dubois, *Soccer Empire: The World Cup and the Future of France* (University of California Press, 2010); Krasnoff, *The Making of Les Bleus.*

12 The team missed qualification for the 1980 Moscow Games after a two-point loss to Czechoslovakia at the Olympic Qualifying Tournament that May in Switzerland. Despite not qualifying, the FFBB joined the US boycott of the Games that summer, and instead sent the men's and women's team to China for a two-week basketball tour. For more on the 1980 China trip and the history of Franco-Sino basketball diplomacy see Lindsay Sarah Krasnoff, "Rétro 1966 et 1980 Les Bleus En Chine: Basket, Propagand, et Diplomatie," *Basket Le Mag*, September 2019.

13 The CFBB was a program that enabled the country's best youth boys and girls to train at the highest level while continuing their scholastic studies, and is covered in the previous chapter.

14 Laurent Rullier, "ITW Patrick Cham—Partie 1 : 'France-USA aux JO 1984, mon grand souvenir de sportif,'" *Basket Retro* (blog), December 13, 2016, https://basket-retro.com/2016/12/13/itw-patrick-cham-partie-1-france-usa-aux-jo-1984-mon-grand-souvenir-de-sportif/.

15 Three different generations of Antilean basketball players interviewed from 2015 through 2021 specifically pointed to this attribute, independent of each other. Jacques Cachemire, Interview with the author, 2015; Patrick Cham, Interview with the author, July 17, 2015; Sandrine Gruda, Interview with the author, September 30, 2021.

16 All Patrick Cham quotes in this chapter, unless specified, from Cham, Interview with the author.

17 Six-foot-two center Max-Joseph Noël from Martinique was the first Antilean player to suit up for the national team in 1964 and 1965. Pascal Legendre, "Roger Antoine, Pionnier du 'Black Power' dans le Basket Français," *BasketEurope*, October 7, 2016, http://www. basketbeurope.com/livenews-fr/ffbb/edf-homme/3816. . ./roger-antoine-pionnier-du-black-power-dans-le-basket-francais/.

18 Stade Français Basket, "Histoire—Basket," accessed October 2, 2021, https://stadefrancais.com/basket/section/histoire/.

19 Antooine Abolivier, "Souvenirs d'Euro: Patrick Cham : 'Nous sentions que le fossé se réduisait mais on arrivait pas encore à concrétiser,'" *Basket Retro* (blog), September 1, 2017, https://basket-retro.com/2017/09/01/souvenirs-deuro-patrick-cham-nous-sentions-que-le-fosse-se-reduisait-mais-on-arrivait-pas-encore-a-concretiser/; Rullier, "ITW Patrick Cham—Partie 1."

20 All George Eddy quotes in this chapter, unless specified, from George Eddy, Interview with the author, October 7, 2016; George Eddy, Interview with the author, March 26, 2015; George Eddy, Interview with the author, September 30, 2021.

21 All Kenny Grant quotes in this chapter, unless specified, from Kenny Grant, Interview with the author, August 26, 2020.

22 Cham's teammate, Jacques Monclar, carried on a family tradition; his father, Robert, completed for the national team three times at the Olympic Games, including in 1960. Antoine Grotteria, "ITW Jacques Monclar: 'Les JO 1984, cela reste toujours une plaie béante,'" *BeBasket*, July 23, 2021, https://www.bebasket.fr/championnat-equipe-de-france/itw-jacques-monclar----les-jo-1984--cela-reste-toujours-une-plaie-beante-.html.

23 Rullier, "ITW Patrick Cham—Partie 1."

24 *Maxi Basket* sales figures provided by its founder, Pascal Lelgendre. Pascal Legendre, Interview with the author, August 11, 2017.

25 Jean-Pierre Dusseaulx, "La Renaissance de Patrick Cham," *Basket-Ball*, March 1993, 8.

26 Gérard Bosc, *Une Histoire Du Basket Français . . . Tome 3, 1990–2000* (Presses du Louvre, 2002), 151.

27 "ITW Patrick Cham—Partie 2 : 'Perpétuer la formation des joueurs en France,'" *Basket Retro* (blog), December 16, 2016, https://basket-retro.com/2016/12/16/itw-patrick-cham-partie-2-perpetuer-la-formation-des-joueurs-en-france/.

28 Ekambi would continue to grow until she reached six-foot-one. Paoline Ekambi, Interview with the author, September 20, 2021.

29 Ekambi.

30 All Paoline Ekambi quotes in this chapter, unless specified, from Ekambi.

31 Ekambi was the victim of incest as a fourteen-year old; basketball was thus more than a passion, at the time it was a way out. For more see Liliane Trévisan, "Paoline Ekambi: 'Ta mère le sait, la famille le sait et

personne ne bouge,'" *L'Équipe*, February 3, 2021; "Paoline Ekambi, victime d'inceste : 'Le sport permet de se reconstruire,'" *TV5MONDE*, March 29, 2021, https://information.tv5monde.com/video/paoline-ekambi-victime-d-inceste-le-sport-permet-de-se-reconstruire.

32 Dominique Wendling, "[Portrait] Roger Antoine a ouvert la voie," *Basket Retro* (blog), January 14, 2021, https://basket-retro.com/2021/01/14/portrait-roger-antoine-a-ouvert-la-voie/.

33 FFBB, "26/04/1980 à Marseille (France)Etats-Unis b France 81-80 (43-40)," accessed October 3, 2021, http://web32.ffbb.com/historique_edf/index.php?refer=match&param=243; Ekambi, Interview with the author.

34 Perry recruited another French player, Rudy Bourgarel, to the Red Foxes program. Bourgarel was immortalized on film in the movie *Coming to America*, in which the Eddy Murphy character attends one of Marist's playoff games. He is also known as the father of Utah Jazz and three-time NBA Defensive Player of the Year Rudy Gobert, who played a critical role winning France's 2020 Tokyo Olympic silver medal.

35 Gary Storck, "ITW Paoline Ekambi—Part 1 : 'Chaque titre nous marque. On travaille dur pour les obtenir,'" *Basket Retro* (blog), December 17, 2014, https://basket-retro.com/2014/12/17/itw-paoline-ekambi-part-1-chaque-titre-nous-marque-on-travaille-dur-pour-les-obtenir/.

36 Storck.

37 As of March 2021, Ekambi remains among the Marist Red Foxes' top ten all-time rebounders, with an average 6.7 rebounds per game. "1984, Paoline Ekambi ou la première française à jouer en NCAA !," *Basket Retro* (blog), January 21, 2021, https://basket-retro.com/2021/01/21/1984-paoline-ekambi-ou-la-premiere-francaise-a-jouer-en-ncaa/; Marist College Athletics Department, "2021 Marist WBB MAAC Championship Notes," March 2021, https://s3.amazonaws.com/sidearm.sites/marist.sidearmsports.com/documents/2021/3/9/2021_Marist_WBB_MAAC_Championship_Notes.pdf.

38 At Stade Français Versailles, she was coached and influenced by Henry Fields, one of the first US players to make a mark on the game. "I was young and listened to him with a lot of respect and stars in my eyes," she recalled. Paoline Ekambi, Interview with the author, September 20, 2021.

39 Yannick Souvre, "Équipe de France Le Reveil!," *Basket-Ball*, June 1991.

40 Filip Bondy, *Tip Off: How the 1984 NBA Draft Changed Basketball Forever* (Da Capo Press, 2007).

41 All David Stern quotes in this chapter, unless specified, from David Stern, Interview with the author, interview by Lindsay Sarah Krasnoff, Telephone, March 17, 2016.

42 George Eddy, *Mon Histoire avec la NBA* (Talent Sport, 2019), 23.

43 Eddy, 13.

44 Eddy, 15.

45 Eddy, 18.

46 All Vincent Collet quotes in this chapter, unless specified, from Collet, Interview with the author.

47 All Pascal Legendre quotes in this chapter, unless specified, from Legendre, Interview with the author.

48 Johan Rat, Interview with the author, September 24, 2021.

49 Gérard Bosc, Interview with the author, October 26, 2014.

50 All Gérard Bosc quotes in this chapter, unless specified, from Gérard Bosc, Interview with the author, October 26, 2014.

6

From Dream Team to Sydney, 1992–2000

At midnight July 18, 1992, members of the US men's basketball team arrived in Nice *en route* to Monaco for their pre-Olympic preparation.[1] That year's Summer Games were the first time that professional players could compete in an Olympic basketball tournament, the result of an April 1989 FIBA decision, one fully supported by then NBA Commissioner David Stern.[2] That's how some of the league's biggest stars, including Magic Johnson, Michael Jordan, Larry Bird, Scottie Pippin, and Charles Barkley, assembled to form the first US Dream Team, a legendary squad that contested the Barcelona Games.

For six days that July, the team's Monegasque training camp provided a luxe break with some basketball involved for good measure. The respite in Monaco was Stern's idea. "It was well located. Frankly, I wanted our players to have a good time," he later recalled. "We could get a sell-out crowd in a relatively small arena. . .you were in the center of it all."[3] Beyond daily practice, the team played a July 21 exhibition game against Les Bleus, landing a 111–71 finish in front of a sold-out crowd of 3,500.[4] The Americans, reportedly exhausted from Monte Carlo life, fell behind twice in the first half.[5] The French, proud of playing against the NBA's very best, were dazzled. Georges Adams, the twenty-five-year-old Papeete-born French wing, scored fifteen points during the match, a feat he would regale teammates with for years to come.[6] The following day, the famed Dream Team scrimmage occurred, a tune-up before the Games, one that Jordan remembered as the "greatest game I've ever played in."[7]

The Americans' presence permeated the principality. Gilles Noghès, future Ambassador of Monaco to the United States, found himself driving behind the team bus one day with his fourteen-year-old son and American nephew, incredulous that their idols were so close at hand. They followed the bus, Noghès recalled. "The boys were waving madly and trying to catch their attention." It was fortuitous for, when the driver got lost, Noghès offered directional assistance. "Members of the team came out of the bus and started taking pictures of the magnificent view of the sea from the Corniche. [The boys] were overjoyed to have this opportunity to ask them for photographs and autographs." As for the players, Noghès mused that they were amused by the reception.[8]

The 1992 Dream Team helped globalize the NBA and its star players' appeal, irrecoverably growing the game as kids dreamed to "Be like Mike [Jordan]" and other US players they saw on television. In Barcelona, they dazzled with an 8–0 record. They crushed countries with some of the strongest basketball traditions outside of North America, like Angola and Lithuania. The United States cruised to the gold medal after defeating Croatia 117–85, the closest margin of any of their Olympic matches.[9]

Kids in France were tantalized by what they saw on television. Previously, access to NBA games was limited to those whose families could afford the Canal+ subscription or a video cassette recorder to watch tapes of NBA matches. But the Olympics, including the basketball tournament, were broadcast on national (i.e., free-to-air) television and thus widely accessible.

Kids were awestruck by the American superstars. As NBA Hall of Famer Tony Parker recalled, the Dream Team was so influential in turning him into a player that, "in 1992, I decided to change sports."[10] Just two weeks later, France won the FIBA European Championship for Junior Men, held in Hungary on August 16–23; this rising generation included basketballers who eight summers later helped France to a 75–85 loss against the United States at the 2000 Sydney Games' gold medal match.

The Dream Team was pivotal for the future of French basketball, but other sparks throughout the 1990s helped shore up the game. From the surge of registered basketball players in organized clubs and the grassroots playground game to refining youth detection and development pipelines, the era was one of growth and revival. But also, critically, the continued basketball-centric cultural, technical, and knowledge exchanges between Frenchwomen and men in the United States and their American counterparts in France provided basketball models of success, including in the NBA and WNBA. French kids could now see it to dream it, and, as of 1997, had the blueprints to make their hoop dreams realities.

Scouting Report

In some ways, the NBA-inspired global hoops reorientation reflected larger events at work reshaping the international political arena. Dissolution of the Soviet Union after 1991 effectively ended the Cold War and left the United States as the sole superpower while the 1990 reunification of Germany and growing disintegration of Yugoslavia further recast European and global affairs.

In this cauldron, the Fifth Republic sought to reaffirm its place in the rapidly realigning international order. Foreign policy under François Mitterrand (1981–95) then Jacques Chirac (1995–2002), remained activist, working across multilateral organizations in the realms of peacekeeping, humanitarian assistance, and diplomatic endeavors. Paris focused on strengthening its leadership of European integration and in 1992 entered the Economic and Monetary Union (EMU), the pathway towards one European currency. The following year the Treaty of Maastricht went into effect, providing for more comprehensive alignment via the European Union.[11] Throughout the decade, the Quai d'Orsay worked with its European and NATO allies as violence and ethnic cleansing inflamed the Balkan peninsula.

Paris also worked in greater concert with Washington. Although Mitterrand forged a strong relationship with US President Ronald Reagan, personally courting the American president, the 1990s were an era of greater transatlantic cooperation. France was part of the US-led coalition to free Kuwait from Iraqi rule in 1991, and eight years later its air force participated in the bombing of Belgrade.

The end of the Cold War also impacted France's longstanding focus on Africa. New pro-democracy movements induced Paris to support the shift from one-party to multi-party democracies, even as it continued to support authoritarian leaders, established stronger relations with the continent's anglophone and lusophone countries, and increased development aid to francophone Africa to counter that of the United States.[12] Tragically, the Elysée Palace stood by as the Hutu regime in Rwanda, in which it had invested considerable support, unleashed a 100-day campaign of ethnic genocide against the Tutsis in 1994.

Domestic affairs were also in flux as the Chirac administration grappled with a host of competing issues. There was increased uncertainty about the future in the face of economic stagnation and high unemployment. The return of cyclical anti-American sentiment was fueled by fears of an Americanization of French culture. Farmer José Bové's 1999 destruction of a McDonald's in Millau capped a new era of globalization begun with the 1992 opening of Disneyland Paris, one led by US multinational companies and thus perceived by some to feed this threat.[13] The NBA was part of this equation, notably its global star Michael Jordan who was a perceived part of the "new global capitalism" forged by US cultural influences.[14]

Fears of a generation addicted to Big Macs, Air Jordan sneakers, and MTV fed into a certain sense of anxiety as youth once again became a focal point. What was different from previous eras' concern that kids were being led astray by the rise of an American-inflected global culture was that this time it was intimately connected with the complexities of coming to terms with France's Vichy and colonial past. Chirac's 1995 apology for the country's deportation of Jews during World War II began a national rethink of the republican narrative over its colonial past, notably vis-à-vis Algeria. It took nearly twenty more years before a French president apologized for treatment of the *harkis* and torture of anti-colonial advocates during the Algerian War. But these debates, coinciding with the issue of how to assimilate a postcolonial population and the role of France in an increasingly globally Internet-connected world, reframed the question of national identity.[15]

This fueled the continued rise of the far right, and the spread of its toxic blend of nationalism, racism, and xenophobia. Jean-Marie Le Pen, longtime head of the Front National, won 15 percent of the first-round presidential vote in 1995, a record for post-1945 French politics.[16] His brand of nativist fearmongering bled into sports, when in 1996 he infamously noted of the country's national football team, "it's a bit artificial to bring players from abroad and call it the French team."[17]

The reality was that the football Les Bleus, as the celebrated 1998 FIFA World Cup victors, represented a modern amalgamation of late twentieth-century French people. By 1999, 23 percent of the population had family roots in another country, meaning that at least one parent or grandparent was born abroad. Although France was historically an immigrant destination, concerns over the more recent generations who often were not of the Caucasian Christian-Judeo tradition caused further anxiety. The 1993 Pasqua Laws, which sought to cut off immigration, were a reaction to these fears and added fuel to social unrest, notably in the *banlieues* which bubbled up throughout the decade.[18]

There were growing concerns over youths in the often racialized *banlieues* and their basketball courts.[19] Many, regardless of their family's socioeconomic or immigrant backgrounds, emulated the urban inner-city culture that the NBA symbolized by the 1990s. The fashion, the sneakers, the lifestyle of basketball was accompanied by hip-hop and rap, whether in English or French, which took root a decade earlier but now transformed into a more mainstream and professionalized showbusiness.[20] Both genres were increasingly integral to the identity of being a basketballer in France, for that, too, was a construct in flux during this period.

The Dream Team further revived basketball's popularity and image. It allowed the NBA to build upon the foundations laid by Jordan's famous September 1990 exhibition at Paris's Geo André stadium, longtime home of Stade Français. Everyone who was anyone in the Parisian basketball world was there, including Johan Rat, whose father, Michel, was a player, coach, and then director of youth development at the Federal Basketball Center (CFBB). "The gym was about to explode at the time," Johan recalled. "There were so many people there, more than the organizers expected, because Jordan was already a myth in France. Everybody loved Jordan."[21] In 1991, the McDonald's Open tournament showcased the LA Lakers, which furthered appetite for the NBA ahead of the league's first preseason game on French soil in October 1994, when the Charlotte Hornets and Golden State Warriors met on the parquets at Bercy Arena.

But it wasn't just the American league that stoked renewed interest in the game. So, too, did the success of professional clubs at the elite European level. In April 1993, CSP Limoges nabbed the first European Champions' Cup title by a French team, building on its third-place finish during the 1989–90 season, and went on to contested the Final Four in 1995. The higher-level success of both NBA as well as domestic French leagues provided numerous reference points for hoops-obsessed youths, who consumed it through publications like *Maxi Basket* and *5 Majeur*, the game's go-to guides. On television, while interest in watching NBA games increased, domestic appetite for its home game declined. By September 1997, Canal+ dropped its coverage of domestic professional National Basketball League (LNB) games due to an insufficient audience.[22]

All of this helped the French Basketball Federation's (FFBB) efforts to increase the number of people, especially youths, who played the game. In June 1992, there were 385,952 licensed basketball players, an increase of 8.7 percent from the previous season.[23] Overall numbers were up year over year for boys and girls, despite a dip at the end of the decade; some attributed this to the spike in football's popularity following the 1998 World Cup while others pointed to the inability of the French game to retain interest years after the Dream Team's phenomenal feats.[24]

But there was a growing divide between the game as played in formal organized clubs and its unorganized grassroots counterpart, playground basketball. A phenomenon that began in the 1980s as playgrounds began to install basketball hoops and kids flocked to the makeshift courts, by the early 1990s playground basketball exploded onto the scene. Vitally, it was popular not just in Paris, but around other urban areas across the country. While oftentimes complementary to the organized game, boys and girls could and did enjoy and participate in both, playground ball developed its own

TABLE 6.1 *Fluctuation of basketball licenses*[25]

Year	Number of licenses
1990	352,000
1993	432,000
1994	454,000
1999	422,000
2000	437,000

culture, style, and reference points. It was a basketball intimately associated with its American cousin, one integrally tied to rap, hip-hop, sneaker culture, and fashion, and thus one often in the firestorm of cultural conversations about race, immigration, and youths in the *banlieues*.[26] As *Le Monde* pointed out, Limoges' European Club championship in April 1993 exhibited a stylistic game that eschewed the flashier basketball of the playgrounds and the NBA.[27]

The formal club vs playground basketball divide was also shorthand for the difference between the provinces and its urban counterpart.[28] While it's tempting to reduce this to a Caucasian versus immigrant dynamic, the reality was far more complex. Kids of all backgrounds played the game in the provinces as well as in the cities. But the urban–rural schism in basketball can be viewed more through the types of development and formats of the clubs themselves. There was a divergence between the kinds of kids that basketball officials recruited into the country's elite development programs and those who were overlooked but whose talent manifested itself when given the opportunity to thrive in the United States.

The schism between formal and informal, urban and provinces, Caucasian and immigrant basketball weren't the only issues that confronted the domestic game. There were continued tensions over the number of foreign players on teams, backhand for growing concerns about an over-Americanization of the game. Each team was limited to two foreign players, but many continued to field naturalized Frenchmen. Such players came from all over Europe, Africa, and the Americas, even though Americans were a clear majority of naturalized players. Critics argued that using naturalized players took opportunities away from younger French players to gain experience and thus to improve.[29] These issues were further fueled by the December 1995 Bosman Ruling, which provided for freedom of labor movement within the European Union's football establishment, effectively mandating that European Union players no longer be counted as a team's foreign player allotment. This had repercussions for basketball which, through the European Court's 2000 Lehtonen ruling, effectively did the same.[30]

For some, the continued influx of American basketball, players and the NBA style that so many kids sought to emulate, was a good thing. They argued that it helped to make the home game more competitive. But not everyone agreed, and critics noted how the

French press glorified the American-style game over its homegrown one. For former National Technical Director Gérard Bosc,

> This press, run by enthusiastic journalists, is fascinated by the game from across the Atlantic, the formulas (playoff), the glitter and the power of the NBA. It sells dreams, insists on the US model, and encourages French basketball to be inspired by its operation. . .little by little, basketball will pass for an illegible sport which does not correspond to the aspirations of our society, and will become the standard bearer of an invasive culture with which the general French public will find it difficult to identify.[31]

Yet there were several bright spots. In February 1998, the first professional women's basketball league was founded. The Feminine Basketball League (LFB), ushered in a new era and provided greater structure and support for high-level clubs. It also benefitted from the 1998 FIBA decision to liberalize circulation of players around the world, thus leading to a new era of player migration in the professional game.

The LFB built upon the rebound of Les Bleues in European competition. The team won EuroBasket silver at Italy 1993, placed eleventh in 1995, and failed to qualify in 1997. Then the team returned to EuroBasket 1999 with vigor; held in Poland, Les Bleues narrowly lost to the home team 56–59 in the gold medal match.[32] That performance assured their first-ever qualification for the 2000 Olympic Games. It was reinforced by the reemergence of French clubs in elite European competition, notably Bourges, which won the women's EuroLeague title in 1997 and 1998. Collectively, this rebirth translated into optimism and confidence heading into the twenty-first century. "French women's basketball deserves to come out of its anonymity," proclaimed *Le Monde*.[33] Les Bleues did exactly that after they parlayed their Sydney experience into the 2001 EuroBasket title, with a 73–68 victory over Russia.[34]

The men's national team also enjoyed stronger results. Les Bleus did not qualify for the 1994 or 1998 FIBA World Cups, or the 1996 Olympic Games. While they continued to achieve middling EuroBasket results, things were different in 1999 when France hosted the biannual championship. That summer, the longer-term evolutions in the game coalesced. Notably, the youth detection and training system continuously improved upon since the 1980s, combined with the maturation of a new generation of players, led to significantly better results. The team was inspired by the FIFA World Cup champions, but several players had already enjoyed success as the 1992 European Junior champions. Les Bleus coach Jean-Pierre de Vincenzi sought out advice from his football counterpart, Aimé Jacquet, in the quest to learn from football's success on home soil.[35] That wasn't the only comparison between the two teams; the press made ready note of how the basketball team, like the football one, was also ethnically diverse. "Half of the French basketball team is black or mixed," *Le Monde* noted. "Originally from the West Indies (Jim Bilba, Stéphane Risacher, Alain Digbeu), Guyana (Tariq Abdul-Wahad), Texas (Ronnie Smith) or even Senegal (Moustapha Sonko), these Blues offer a mosaic as diverse as that of Zidane, Thuram and company."[36] Les Bleus lost its semifinal against Spain 63–80, as well as the match for third place, a 62–74 defeat to FR Yugoslavia. But the tournament was a stepping stone.

In September 2000, both teams made an historic voyage to Sydney, the first time that the men's and women's teams qualified for the same Olympiad. Les Bleus surprised themselves and the world when they contested the gold medal match against the United States, while the women, knocked out in the quarterfinals by South Korea 59-68, placed fifth in the final standings. The improved performances of both teams by the late 1990s and at Sydney was the byproduct of the game's continued evolutions, but also the informal people-to-people cultural and technical basketball exchanges that began to flourish in the years after the Dream Team put the NBA on the global, and French, map.

A Magical US Dream

Katia Foucade, one of the players in the nexus of this change, was a harbinger of what was to come. Born in Paris May 9, 1971, to parents who migrated from Martinique, Foucade grew up in the capital enjoying basketball on different levels. As a player, she first played organized ball with storied side Paris Université Club (PUC). At the same time, Foucade also played playground basketball. "That's where I had fun, that's where I dreamed of going to the United States," Foucade recalled. "[Our] basketball culture was happening in the street, just like in the United States."[37]

It was on courts around the city that she first met George Eddy, who brought the NBA-style game to French living rooms as a commentator for Canal+ broadcasts. These courts were also where Foucade and her friends, boys and girls alike, tried to imitate what they saw during Eddy's broadcasts. At the time, Canal+ subscriptions were fairly exclusive as they were expensive, but Foucade's mother understood how much her daughter loved the game and subscribed. The future point guard began to watch Eddy and the NBA in the middle of the night to feed her passion. Foucade and her friends also consumed the game through *Maxi Basket*, which was their key reference for all things basketball related.

Part of the appeal was to replicate NBA-style fashions. "It was cool to wear the same gear as the [NBA] players," Foucade recalled. "It was cool to act as if we were Americans because we played on the playgrounds." They tried to dress in styles they saw on US television, spoke English, or at least the phrases they picked up from following the game, and listened to American music, specifically, hip-hop. As she noted,

> Basketball was more than just the game; it was a culture we belonged to. It was ours, with our codes, and it became very trendy. Those of us who played in clubs, we brought this culture to the club teams we played on.

Yet, if going to the United States was a dream that more boys and girls fantasized about, it was still not viewed as an attainable one. "We thought it was impossible," Foucade noted, even as she and her cohort recognized that playing at the game's highest levels meant playing in the sport's homeland. "That's why we welcomed American culture with open arms."

Gone were the days when kids viewed basketball as a sport of the elderly or elites; it was now a sport of the rising generation. The culture was increasingly fed by the sneaker-sponsored tours that sent NBA players to Europe, including France, a phenomenon that grew in the 1990s. Michael Jordan first visited France as a young Nike signee in August 1985; Foucade was privileged enough to be in a gym that Jordan visited that trip. "No one really knew who he was," she said of the forty-person crowd that day. "But that's how we got connected with American basketball, because the players came to Paris."

Foucade was recruited into the country's elite youth training system. She spent the 1986–7 academic year at INSEP, part of an elite group who practiced on campus during the week while continuing their studies; on the weekends they returned home to play with their clubs. But in 1987, the CFBB decided to pause their program to retool and reconfigure it to better meet scholastic and sports-oriented training needs; it did not reopen for young players until the 1988–9 school year.

Meanwhile, Foucade joined the sport-study section (now a *pôle espoirs*) at Lycée Henri-Martin at St. Quentin (1987–8) a destination for top youth talent nearly 100 miles north of Paris established by Bertrand Gamess.[38] The coach, enamored of US-style basketball, proved a lasting influence on Foucade's game and onwards trajectory. Acknowledged as one of the early leaders of girls' basketball in the region, he organized a trip to Seattle for his team to play in a high school tournament.[39] There, Foucade caught the attention of University of Washington Coach Chris Gobrecht, who subsequently recruited her to play and offered a scholarship after she finished high school.[40]

Foucade arrived on campus in fall 1991, intent on making the most out of her American dream. She was inspired by Paoline Ekambi, the first French woman to play basketball in the United States. "She was everything I dreamed of: a great basketball player, determined, who did what she wanted to do and I thought that was very empowering," Foucade recalled decades later. It was Ekambi who gave her younger Les Bleues teammate advice on how to make the most out of her forthcoming US experience. "She told me, 'I heard you are going to the University of Washington. You're going to love your experience. Just go for it and stay as long as you can,'" Foucade said. "I listened to her advice."

The Huskies' freshman was ready and discovered "an extraordinary country."[41] Thanks to spending Christmas breaks in New York with her mother, Foucade was familiar with the United States. However, university was an entirely different experience. Although she knew English, Foucade rapidly found that speaking the language and communicating every day was vastly different from the "marshmallow language" she and her friends spoke on Parisian basketball courts. Overcoming the language barrier was her most difficult, and immediate, challenge. But language immersion facilitated mastery of English. "I had great teammates who helped me, and who laughed with me while making fun of my accent," she said. "They were very kind, so I never felt laughed at."

There were other discoveries. Foucade learned about US basketball and its culture, floored by the attention given to the women's game. The Huskies played in front of a full house, were well loved by fans, and were treated well by the media. "It was unbelievable to me," she recalled of the press attention given to their seasons. "That would never have happened period for women's basketball, regardless of how great you can be, [even today] they still barely talk about the national team." It helped that, aside from the national championship-winning football team, they were the school's most successful team on campus.

Foucade also found that being French on campus was "magical." Her peers were intrigued to learn that she was a Parisienne and relayed how much they liked or admired her hometown. "I'm always so proud to be French everywhere I go," she said. "I was a French ambassador, but I was also an ambassador for my culture, because I'm French, I was born in Paris, but I'm Black."

Foucade challenged US students' assumptions of who was French. "It was always surprising to them," she recalled.

> It was very intriguing to a lot of people. A lot of times I had conversations talking about our history, talking about colonization, and how that connected to French culture. Martinique, it's the Caribbean, but we are still French. . .To actually learn it at school is one thing, but to actually speak about people from different parts of the world is different because you can talk about your own experience. It's only one perspective, but it broadens people's view of what French culture was like.

Such people-to-people exchanges illustrate how, through basketball, Foucade was able to communicate, represent, and negotiate US perceptions about France, its culture, history, and people. She also helped Huskies' fans understand that she could be French, Black, and a basketball player.

But the issue of racism was entirely different from back home. Growing up in Paris, Foucade was aware of the racial and social disparities for Black French versus their Caucasian colleagues. "It was softer than in the United States, but it still existed," she noted in a 2020 US Embassy France webinar.[42] But the United States was entirely different.

> I was surprised by how color was so important. Yet, it was incredible that my color wasn't important because I wasn't American. I was French and the simple fact of being French and Black nullified my skin color, people only saw my nationality.[43]

Foucade thus claims that she did not experience discrimination based on the color of her skin during her years in Seattle. "My color wasn't important in the eyes of my interlocutors. What they retained was that of my origins as a Frenchwoman."[44]

It's a notable point, for she arrived on the West Coast in the middle of the Rodney King incidents. In March 1991, King was brutally beaten by Los Angeles police after resisting arrest; the violence against an unarmed African American was caught on film for the entire world to see. The police officers' acquittal after trial in April 1992 touched off three days of violent rioting around the city and touched off renewed waves of racial discrimination and biases in the United States.

Such tensions were new to Foucade for although police brutality against minorities occurred back home, "it was much less mediatized." In the days that followed, the Huskies' locker room spoke of the LA riots, of the ways the police acted inhumanely towards King, of the differences between police and public perceptions of race between France and the United States, and more. There was no disagreement amongst Foucade and her teammates as they all viewed the events as unjust. "It was very nice to be able to discuss the reasons and above all find solutions so that it does not happen again," she said of that bonding experience.[45]

The cultural exchange Foucade lived enriched her understanding of both the United States and France, as well as their basketball cultures. On the court, she solidified this notion. The three-time co-captain led the team in assists for her sophomore, junior, and senior seasons, and remains inscribed in the Huskies' record book for all-time leading assists in an individual game as well as all-time career leaders in assists as of December 2021.[46] She acknowledged that playing in the NCAA was tough and unlike the French leagues, yet her time at INSEP prepared her for the challenge.

To play college basketball, you have to be extreme. You have to be tough. When I went to college, I had that mental toughness. . .to go to INSEP you have to be extremely tough. . .and being able to push forward, being able to push through the pain of practice was different from regular French basketball practice. But it was very similar to what we did at INSEP.

Number 24 was already advanced basketball-wise, thanks to the French development system, and started all of her games with the Huskies. But aside from on-court maturity, Foucade brought another trait honed back home: the unselfishness of team play, something generations of French (and European) players are known for. "I love to play and put people in the right spot, I like to be a leader," Foucade said. "But I don't have to be the one making the last shot. The US players, they love to score, they love to be in the light. I knew my role, so I was a great added piece to my team because I knew that I could bring the light to them, and I was very happy doing so."

Foucade also learned from her college career, notably the US mentality of hope and a player's mental toughness that anyone can win. "It doesn't matter when the ball goes up in the air. Anyone is as good as anyone else, even if on paper it shows that the other team is better," she said of how on-court play dictated who was best, not a club record or single player.

This mentality, that her team could win regardless of their opponent, was something Foucade contributed to her later French clubs, as well as to the national team. She first played with the senior side on May 6, 1991, and throughout her NCAA career juggled Les Bleues service during summertime competitions. The double duty paid dividends: Foucade won silver at the June 1993 EuroBasket tournament alongside Ekambi, the team's first podium finish since the team of Élisabeth Riffiod and Jacky Chazalon in 1970. Foucade also featured for Team France at the 1994 FIBA World Cup in Australia, Les Bleues' first appearance at that tournament since 1979.

National team service was different from playing with the Huskies. To begin with, Foucade was not a starter; she was a bench player. Although there were tensions among the staff ("they didn't care much for the players who went to the States to come back with the American mentality"), Foucade understood her role with Les

FIGURE 6.1 *University of Washington Huskies co-captain Katia Focuade. Credit: University of Washington.*

Bleues: to be a great teammate, a key element for a national team that she learned while living her American dream.

A third aspect that Foucade contributed to Les Bleues was the work ethic of her NCAA experience. "I showed that we can work hard, we can be in the gym all the time and work on our craft,"

Foucade said of how she contributed to the French team's successes. "It wasn't something that people did at the time in France, but in a very humble way, I had an impact."

French Women Can Hoop

Another Frenchwoman joined the NCAA D1 basketball ranks during Foucade's senior year, her longtime Les Bleues teammate Isabelle Fijalkowski. The six-foot-five center played the 1994–5 season with the University of Colorado Buffaloes. But unlike Foucade, Fijalkowski did not grow up dreaming of playing basketball in the United States. Instead, her path passed through the provinces, notably through the storied center of women's basketball, Clermont-Ferrand.

Fijalkowski was born in that city on May 23, 1972, to parents who emigrated from Poland. The town was well known for one of its women's basketball teams, Clermont Université Club (CUC), which throughout the decade accumulated a litany of titles and accolades with stars like Chazalon, Riffiod, and Irène Guidotti. Despite this heritage, Fijalkowski wasn't a basketball fan growing up; it was not something that her parents followed. They nonetheless encouraged her to start playing the game as she was so tall. Nine-year-old Fijalkowski began to play with a local team in Cébazat, next to Clermont; she excelled and soon advanced to play with a larger club.[47]

At the time, the other storied women's basketball club in town was AS Montferrand (ASM). One ingredient for its successful revival after 1975 was its youth academy. Among the first of its kind for French women's basketball, ASM's academy focused on providing its young players with structured training and academic tutoring while students completed high school.[48] As such, players from different parts of the country matriculated at the academy and lived in club-provided lodging.

Twelve-year-old Fijalkowski matriculated in ASM's academy. She lived at home but, starting at age fourteen, trained with the boarded players twice a day.[49] Her high school was near the training facility, which enabled her to train during the school lunchtime (12 p.m.–2 p.m.), bypassing the cafeteria for the gymnasium before returning to school, and again in the evening. "It was not organized, but it was possible to do," she recalled of how she and her fellow teammates were self-starters. "We organized it."[50]

Throughout this time, she read *Maxi Basket* but didn't watch the NBA as her parents did not subscribe to Canal+. Instead, she watched domestic league games, followed the men's and women's competitions, and was inspired by regional legends like Édith Tavert, Christine Rougerie (CUC), and Cathy Malfois (ASM).

Fijalkowski first played with ASM's senior team as a sixteen-year-old and after finishing her *baccalaureate* seized the opportunity to gain experience with the national team. That's where, thanks to her fellow Les Bleues teammates Ekambi and Yannick Souvré, who relayed their NCAA experiences, Fijalkowski began to think of playing in the United States as a way to ameliorate her basketball.[51] She made inquiries and found that legendary University of Tennessee coach Pat Summitt was intrigued, but did not have scholarships left to offer; so the Lady Vols coach called her counterpart at Colorado, Ceal Barry, and encouraged her to take the young Frenchwoman. The Buffaloes sent a coach to France to watch one of Fijalkowski's games, then made an offer: full scholarship to play for one year.

Fijalkowski arrived in Boulder to begin her senior year in fall 1994. It was not just a basketball adventure, but a genuine cultural shock. "The Americans didn't have any idea of the difference between life in the United States and France, they left me as if I was a student who came from another state," she recalled to *Basket Le Mag*.[52] She had a difficult time integrating. For starters, there was a language barrier: although she spoke Polish and French and learned some English in high school, Fijalkowski did not speak the sort of English used in everyday parlance by her peers. She also didn't know how to register for classes as the university bureaucracy was vastly different from its French counterpart.

The language of basketball was the same, however, and Fijalkowski found her footing on-court and with her teammates. That season, Fijalkowski helped her team shine as the Buffs compiled one of their best results. They tallied a 30–3 overall record, with a clean Big Eight sheet of 14–0.[53] On December 28, 1994, Fijalkowski played the Huskies, squaring off against Foucade and fellow Frenchwoman Laure Savasta as Colorado squeaked out a 55–51 win.[54] The Buffs made a deep run in the March NCAA tournament, and were ranked No. 2 by the Associated Press Top 25 poll, a program best. In the first several rounds, the team showed their mettle, notching victories over Holy Cross, Southwest Missouri State, and George Washington. They faced off against Georgia in the Elite Eight, a game in which Fijalkowski played a decisive role, arguably her best in the NCAA, garnering thirty-five points, nine rebounds, and four assists.[55] But Colorado fell to Georgia 79–82.[56] "It was a huge disappointment, we were very near our dream," Fijalkowski recalled for *Made in France* of the deflation she felt.[57]

Still, her NCAA experience strengthened her game. "You develop your mind through very hard physical preparation," she noted. "The physical aspect is very difficult." Training sessions were hard, and Fijalkowski found herself pushed to her limits alongside her teammates; if someone messed up, they would have to redo a given exercise all together.

> We knew that we would find ourselves in very difficult situations at the end of a match, where we couldn't listen to our body but had to listen to our head because we know we can do it. . .these are things that I had not known. In France, we did not dare to go so far.

She also learned how Americans, or at least the team at Colorado, framed their sports objectives. "In France, one doesn't say 'we want to be Champions of France.' You can be the French champion and not say that you want to be the champion. In the United States, you work always with very elevated objectives," she said. The team-orientated attitude she learned with the Buffaloes aided in meeting this objective, which for the 1994–5 season was to reach the NCAA Final Four as a gift for Coach Barry ahead of her fortieth birthday.[58]

Notably, Fijalkowski observed how entire coaching staffs throughout the NCAA at the time were composed of female coaches, something not really seen back home. "That confirmed to me, even if I already knew it, that competence doesn't have a gender," she recalled for *Made in France*. "One could be a woman and a super coach."[59]

While Fijalkowski learned these aspects from her NCAA experience, she contributed to the team, too. She played against adults since age sixteen, and thus brought those lessons, as well as a hard work ethic, into the equation. Former *Boulder Daily Camera* reporter Greg Johnson recalled that the French center had impressive post moves, as well as a "shooting touch."[60] The Buffaloes appreciated what their French teammate contributed. "They saw that I could help them as a team because there weren't any other players with my profile, thus they were delighted," she said.

After Colorado, Fijalkowski returned to France. She played two seasons with Bourges during which she won two French championships and the EuroLeague title in 1997. But opportunity in the United States once again knocked when in February 1997 the Frenchwoman was selected second by the Cleveland Rockers in the WNBA Draft. The league, colloquially referred to at times as the W, began play that year with eight teams. Officials wanted to include international players, and when Coach Barry was asked whether or not Fijalkowski could adapt to the competition, she answered affirmatively.[61] "I was drafted because I had played one year with Colorado, so people knew me from having played there," Fijalkowski said.

> It was an adventure because it wasn't sure to work, because it had never worked previously with predecessors. I was part of this adventure and I'm very content to have been able to play in a professional championship. . .I adored being part of it.

In Cleveland, Fijalkowski continued her US experience. She lived downtown and found it much easier to insert herself into American life this second time around.[62] Alongside her teammates, which included Lynette Woodard, the first woman to play for the Harlem Globetrotters, and Czech guard and 1992 Olympian Eva Nemcová, Fijalkowski enjoyed that first WNBA season. The team played in front of crowds that averaged 10,000 spectators in NBA stadiums, which gave heft and symbolism to the nascent league.[63]

The French center was part of the starting five and quickly proved herself to be an offensive weapon, becoming the Rockers' leading scorer. She averaged 11.9 points per game in her first season, but accounted for 23.4 percent of the team's overall points scored. The team went 15–13 but did not make the playoffs, squelched by the New York Liberty in overtime of their last game of the season.[64]

In their second season, the Rockers made the playoffs as Eastern Conference champions after defeating the Liberty 70–64 in their final match. But they were knocked out of the semifinals by the Phoenix Mercury. Despite that disappointment, Fijalkowski notched an average 13.7 points per game that season, 25.6 percent of the team's overall points.[65]

Throughout her WNBA career, Fijalkowski sought to show that French women could play the game.

> I wanted to show that we play basketball. We can bring things and that in France, we know how to play basketball. We are taught to play basketball. At the time, we did not yet have great European results, but I wanted to show that in Europe, basketball also counts and that we can be different, but bring complementary things.

She was known for her teamwork and trying to find solutions in tough situations. But after two seasons, she stopped, for the constant playing cycle of club, national team, WNBA took a toll

With the W, Fijalkowski learned greater aggressiveness on-court. While she wasn't a fan of the US focus on individualism in the game, she found that she learned to take responsibility and develop greater aggressiveness. The upbeat rhythm of the W game was also a new style to learn. "It permitted me to get better because it was a very high level," she said.

> Playing against the players who were on the American team, so it was complicated. But it also gave me confidence because I could play eye to eye. . . .It also allowed French basketball, when you come back to the national teams, to raise that level of confidence.

These cultural and technical exchanges enriched Fijalkowski's game and she helped lead Les Bleues in their 2000 Olympic qualifying games, a key goal. "That allowed us to dream, and to take charge of our destiny," she told *Basket Le Mag*.[66] France opened the tournament on a high note with wins in their first four matches. They lost their last pool phase game to Australia 62–69, then fell to South Korea 59–68 in the quarterfinals; that experience left many disillusioned and psychologically marked.[67] Yet, France still placed the highest of any European team at the Games, a result aided by having players with experience in some of the world's best basketball leagues.[68]

Fijalkowski and her teammates returned twelve months later to win the 2001 EuroBasket tournament on home soil, a historic first for any French basketball team. Les Bleues posted a clean tourney

FIGURE 6.2 *Isabelle Fijalkowski with the French national team at the 2000 Sydney Olympics. Credit: Getty Images.*

sheet, unbeaten by any of their opponents. Then, in the gold medal match, France won over Russia 73–68, coached by Vadim Kapranov, the man who helmed one of the dominant French sides of the era, Bourges. Her coach, Alain Jardel, noted how the team was stocked with high-quality players who helped make the difference, including Fijalkowski. "Isabelle Fijalkowski, if she was American, could play with the USA without problem," he said of her on-court abilities.[69]

"The First Guy's Going to Catch the Bullets"

Fijalkowski predated the first Frenchman to hit US professional parquets by just a few months. Tariq Abdul-Wahad, né Olivier Saint-Jean, suited up for the Sacramento Kings in October 1997 and went on to make history over a decade-long NBA career that included stints with Denver, Orlando, and Dallas. Abdul-Wahad, like Fijalkowski, found his way to the professional game in the

United States through the springboard of an NCAA career, first at the University of Michigan then at San Jose State.

But unlike Fijalkowski, Abdul-Wahad had a very different outlook toward French basketball. Overlooked as a young player by a system that still prized height, in some ways his story presaged the way that later stand-out talent was bypassed at tender ages by the CFBB, like three-time NBA Defensive Player of the Year Rudy Gobert. Moreover, it's ironic that Abdul-Wahad proved to be the first Frenchman to excel in the NCAA and play in the NBA given his often terse relations with French basketball officials over claims of racism and discrimination. But his story illustrates how cultural exchanges through sports helped improve the French game and set it on the precipice of breaking through after 2000.

Born November 3, 1974, in Maisons-Alfort, a southeastern suburb of Paris, Abdul-Wahad was from the outset influenced by his mother. George Goudet, a native of Cayenne, French Guiana, migrated to the *métropole* and ran track and field until she discovered basketball at age twenty-one.[70] Known for her speed running the floor, she nabbed rebounds and put up a fierce defense to compensate for the lack of technical hoops skills. But she enjoyed the game and played with a semi-professional team, Stade Français Versailles, alongside notable players Guidotti and future Naismith Memorial Basketball Hall of Famer, American forward Denise Curry.

Thus, throughout Abdul-Wahad's childhood, he was courtside at his mother's games and practices, raised in the bosom of the women's game. "I grew up on Denise Curry," he said. "I'd sit [in the stands] watching this lady that looks like Larry Bird, and she's just cooking everybody." These "hardnosed winners" were his introduction to, and whetted his appetite for, the game. "I'm going to the game to watch the show, and the show was Denise Curry. That's where the show was at," Abdul-Wahad recalled.[71]

But they also introduced him to how serious a life in basketball could be, above and beyond a recreational activity.

When your mom tells you, "I'm going to Novosibirsk on Wednesday," I mean, my mom is going to go play basketball in Siberia for the European [women's] Championship [Cup]? It's a serious thing. It helped me understand very early that basketball was serious, and if you wanted to be good, you had to work hard.[72]

Abdul-Wahad was not immune to the men's game. He came of age in an era during which Limoges dominated domestic, and by the late 1980s and early 1990s, elite European competition.[73] Yet, he looked unquestionably to US hoops culture for his inspiration and influence. Thanks to family friends in the United States, Abdul-Wahad got his hands on videotapes of NCAA and NBA games, which he watched over and over. This proved to be pivotal. "When we put that tape on, our minds were blown," he said. As a fourteen-year-old, he watched videotape of the 1983 University of Houston team that featured Hakeem Olajuwon and was inspired to play college basketball in the United States.[74] The NBA was also influential. Although he looked up to Johnson, Bird, and Thomas, it was Jordan—notably 1989's "Come Fly With Me"—that captivated the young basketballer. "That tape, it stayed in the VCR," he said, "it didn't even come out. I watched this on the loop."

Against this backdrop, Abdul-Wahad evolved as a young player. He first learned the game from his mother, who used to beat him playing one-on-one, and she was one of his hardest critics.[75] He started to play organized ball with Versailles Basket Club, wore Number 15, his mother's number, and was eventually selected to represent the Ile-de-France region with the team from Yvelines.[76] But he was also part of the playground basketball culture, where he met Foucade, and played at the Bir Hakim courts under the metro in Paris's fifteenth arrondissement as his father coached football nearby.[77]

Abdul-Wahad was overlooked by recruiters for INSEP. It wasn't that he was in the wrong place at the wrong time; good friend David Lesmond was recruited and spent the 1990–1 academic year at the CFBB.[78] Instead, Abdul-Wahad maintained that he did not fit the profile of the era's INSEP recruits: he wasn't as tall as some, despite his athleticism, and was from the playground game, not the basketball of the provinces like Pau and Limoges. "In France, there wasn't a formation for guys like me," he explained to *Basket Infos*. "It's: 'Black, you jump, you run fast, you jump high, go inside, take rebounds while the others, the shooters, the guys that we will train technically to become high level players do what they have to do.'"[79]

Instead, Abdul-Wahad entered the youth academy at Evreux. There, he attended training sessions with the club, earned a small weekly salary for his efforts as stipulated by FFBB regulations, followed his studies at Lycée Saint-François-de-Sales, and boarded with a local family.[80] At the time, not every club's basketball academy functioned the same; at Tours, another program Abdul-Wahad was recruited for, young players lived in apartments provided by the club.[81] But perhaps his biggest learning experience at Evreux was from the team's two American players, Darren Queen and Michael Hackett. At their sides, he learned their style of the game and English.

A break came when he traveled with the French Junior team to Germany to play a European Championship qualifying game. There, Abdul-Wahad caught the eye of an NBA scout, and received an exclusive invitation to attend the Academic Betterment and Career Development (ABCD) camp in California, renown as a fertile recruiting ground for NCAA programs. At camp, he had a tough time playing against Americans, physically out maneuvered and boxed out.[82] But he impressed and began to receive recruiting packages and phone calls from US colleges and universities; the University of Michigan ultimately won him over.

His arrival in Ann Arbor for the fall 1993 semester was the realization of a dream. Although he knew English, the version spoken around campus and in the gym was different from what he expected.[83] So he sat in his dorm room watching CNN to learn English, but also enrolled in English as a Second Language (ESL) classes for his first two semesters.[84]

It was also the overture of an entirely different lived experience of basketball. To be orientated toward the United States and its hoops culture was one thing; it was different to live the dream in Michigan's Crisler Center. Especially playing at home against rival Duke University in front of some 13,000 fans whose noisy cheering drowned out all else. "That's a whole other thing," Abdul-Wahad said of the experience of not being able to hear himself think due to the noise levels in the arena.

> I had no idea what the level of madness that big universities such as Michigan could offer when it comes to sport. It was shocking to me—I was shell shocked. That game against Duke at home, when it gets tight in the second half and you feel the fans going crazy, there's a point where the decibel levels, where your brain can't function properly any longer. I was like, "This is hot. This is almost too much!"

It was an induction into the place and rhythm of sport in US culture, one that played a big role within the university and college system, unlike back home. But it was also a red flag for the young player. He earned playing time as a freshman in a program that was the national vice-champion the previous season, a record subsequently vacated due to NCAA sanctions.[85] Abdul-Wahad played again his sophomore season, including when the team returned to the tournament the following year.[86]

But Michigan wasn't the best fit. "I was not that good of a basketball player," he said, something he attributed to not being taught properly due to being overlooked by the French system. He recognized that he needed to learn. "Even though my experience as a student and athlete at Michigan was out of this world," he said, "Michigan is not an environment where you learn to play. Michigan is an environment where you go to win national championships."[87] Thus, at the start of his sophomore year, the nineteen-year-old Frenchman told his coach that he wanted to transfer.

Abdul-Wahad sought out a smaller school where he could learn the fundamentals of the game. He selected San Jose State, which the previous season accrued a 4–23 record but where the coaching staff could help him learn basketball fundamentals.[88] Abdul-Wahad thought SJS authorities viewed him as a "Martian" for having left Michigan for their program, especially as there were no scholarships on offer.[89] Instead, he forged his way, working at a restaurant to make ends meet financially, an effort he was proud of. "My adventure in America wasn't sweet," he said of balancing classes, work, and training. "I didn't go for the easy thing, the flash thing. I went there to learn the game, like an apprentice looking for a master."

For a player who claimed he didn't know how to play the game extraordinarily well, Abdul-Wahad had great success and immediate impact with San Jose State. His first year, he helped the Spartans to a 13–17 overall season, going 9–9 in the Big West Conference and winning the conference title. The team made its first NCAA tournament appearance in sixteen years (it lost to Kentucky in the first round 72–110), while he tallied up an average 17.2 points and 6.3 rebounds per game.[90] Abdul-Wahad became known as one of the Big West Conference's best players.[91] "The Flying Frenchman" also garnered a reputation as a defensive specialist.[92]

The following season lacked the same limelight. Although the Spartans posted a 13–14 season, going 5 for 12 in its new Western Athletic Conference, it did not make a postseason appearance. But Abdul-Wahad's personal game improved, putting up an average 23.8 points and 8.8 rebounds per game.[93] That season he inscribed himself in the San Jose State record book as a single-season all-time scorer (No. 4 with 619 points across 26 games), field goals made (No. 4 with 225), free throws made (No. 7 with 143), and remains the program's tenth all-time career leader in free throws made (260 across just 51 games) and earned all-conference first team honors both seasons.[94]

Being French in the NCAA was an adventure, even more so a Black Frenchman. Whether in Ann Arbor or San Jose, Abdul-Wahad's French identity followed him, while people complimented him on his accent and good English. He thus taught his teammates and classmates about France's history of colonization and migration in informal discussions, for people were often incredulous that Black people lived in France. "You have to explain, you have to give this history lesson, this history overview about once a week," he recalled of schooling his friends about the size and impact of the African diaspora around the world.

The conversation was a bit of a surprise for Abdul-Wahad, who grew up with all sorts of references to Black Americans. "Our identity came through African American experience, even though the Caribbean experience is completely different," he recalled. "Yet, [African Americans] don't even know that they lead the way." He was familiar with Prince, Michael Jackson, Eddie Murphy, but not some of their cultural reference points. "I had a million questions," Abdul-Wahad said and peppered Michigan teammate Ray Jackson with questions about Texas barbeque and cookouts.

Abdul-Wahad claimed he never encountered overt racism during his university career. While he credited part of that to the fact that he attended school in two very liberal bastions, Ann Arbor and San Jose, he also pointed to the fact that as a basketballer, especially within the NCAA ecosystem, he was part of the privileged. France was a different case.

He declared for the NBA Draft in 1997 and was selected eleventh by the Sacramento Kings, thrilled to be greeted by NBA Commissioner David Stern in French.[95] It was more than ironic that the player shunned by his country's elite basketball systems, who was vocal about it needing to diversify, but who was also raised in the heart of the French basketball family, was the Fifth Republic's first player to play professionally in the NBA.[96] "I exposed them in their hypocrisy," Abdul-Wahad said of his public critiques of French officials. "Maybe I pressed the button that made them go, 'Yeah, maybe we need to start recruiting the Boris Diaws, the Ronny Turiafs, the Tony Parkers.'"

NBA teams were aware that France produced sound players but being its first Frenchman was akin to fighting an uphill battle. "The first guy's going to catch the bullets," he said of the experience. But he was ready and soaked it all in, even as he fought for playing time during his first year. "I gained experience and I'm stronger mentally," he told *Le Monde* in April 1998. "You learn an enormous amount when you play against and with the best players in the world."[97]

He became known as a role player in a league that at the time played an intense, physical defensive game. The Frenchman was

FIGURE 6.3 *Tariq Abdul-Wahad, the first Frenchman to play a regular season NBA game, with the Sacramento Kings. Credit: Getty Images.*

incredulous when he guarded Kobe Bryant, played against Scottie Pippen, or was crossed by Allan Iverson. It was humbling. "Playing with your heroes or against your heroes, it's your dream, it's the best thing ever," he confided to *Le Monde* of being among peers, the best in the world.[98]

For FFBB President Yvan Mainini, Abdul-Wahad was an inspiring example. "Seeing some of our youngsters at the gates of the NBA is quite rewarding," he said. "It's proof that we know how to detect and train top-level players."[99] Yet, Abdul-Wahad was not a product of the INSEP system that Mainini referenced. He was overlooked and instead took ambition into his own hands to leave for the NCAA. This was not always met with enthusiasm back home, although the press begrudgingly acknowledged that Abdul-Wahad's accomplishments provided a blueprint. According to *Le Monde,*

> The insolent success of Tariq Abdul-Wahad paved the way for the wildest dreams, to the point that today there are around thirty young French players, aged seventeen to twenty-one, in universities and in American colleges, the best antechambers to the NBA.[100]

This terse dissonance was fed by Abdul-Wahad's clashes with the press and some within the basketball world. "I said what no one wanted to hear, and I did what no one had the courage to do, really, to be honest," he said of calling out perceived racism and discrimination. "When I come back to France to play, it never goes well. Some of it is my fault," Abdul-Wahad said, "but some of it is the environment."

Despite this, he returned home to play with Les Bleus when called for national team service. He didn't do it for patriotic reasons, even though his father served in the air force.[101] Instead, he did it because he wanted to continue playing with his childhood friends, and also jumped at the chance to play organized ball during the NBA off-season to maintain conditioning and stay on top of his game.

Coming from the NBA, French basketball now appeared a different world. "They didn't know what's being done at the highest level," he said. "There's a true disconnect between the level of the player and the level of the coaching." From July 1998 through June

1999, he played twenty-one friendly games with Les Bleus as they prepared to host that summer's EuroBasket tournament, averaging double-digit points most games.

For a time, it seemed like a truce was in effect. Abdul-Wahad notched twenty-four points in France's 71–67 opening match win over Macedonia. He continued to contribute offensively, including eleven points in Les Bleus' 74–69 win over Slovenia, which secured passage to the quarterfinals. However, the team fell to Spain in the semifinal 63–70, while Abdul-Wahad was injured, eliminated from the third-place match.

Although he rehabbed and recovered, playing the 1999–2000 season with the Orlando Magic, Abdul-Wahad continued to have tenuous relations with the FFBB. On May 9, 2000, he accused some of the federation's officials of discrimination because he was a Black kid who hailed from the suburbs; yet, at the time, the national team captain was Jim Bilba, a Black Frenchman from Guadeloupe.[102] Abdul-Wahad was recalled again in 2003 to help Les Bleus' EuroBasket campaign, but the terseness continued. While he trailblazed a path into the NBA, his transatlantic basketball experience didn't foment a revolution of players in the French pipeline, perhaps because he was considered by some officials and journalists as basketball's *enfant terrible*. Instead, the flourishing pipeline would come thanks to Abdul-Wahad's 2003 Les Bleus teammates Parker, Diaw, and Turiaf.

Coalescing Two Basketball Worlds

As Abdul-Wahad began his US dream in the NCAA, another player embarked on a transatlantic career that illustrated a different way that informal Franco-American sports diplomacy began to positively impact French successes. Born in Ithaca, New York, in September 1970, Crawford Palmer was raised in the Washington, D.C.-centric mid-Atlantic basketball corridor that fed some of the dominant 1980s US college teams, including Georgetown University and the University of Virginia. He began to play basketball, enjoyed it, and found the game served as an outlet for a pent-up aggressiveness; as a kid far taller than everyone else, it was constantly drummed into Palmer to be nice, to be gentle, and to be careful not to hurt people.[103]

Palmer was recruited by Virginia but opted for Duke, where he arrived on campus for fall 1988. A role player with the Blue Devils' basketball dynasty, he played in three consecutive NCAA Final Fours and won the 1991 NCAA Championship alongside teammates Christian Laettner and Grant Hill. But in May 1991, Palmer transferred to Dartmouth College so that he could devote more attention to the "student" part of the "student-athlete" equation.[104] He redshirted one year, during which he focused on his studies, then played the 1992–3 season with the Big Green. Despite playing in the Ivy League, he was invited to compete at that April's Portsmouth Invitational Tournament, a four-day tournament in Portsmouth, Virginia, considered the first of the NBA's pre-draft camps. The competition was an opportunity for players from smaller schools to compete in front of scouts and agents from the NBA and professional leagues in Europe.[105] Although his older brother, Walter, relayed PIT exposure into a springboard to the 1990 NBA Draft, where he was selected by the Utah Jazz (thirty-third), Crawford did not. Instead, he returned to Hanover, New Hampshire to complete his undergraduate degree, then spent July working out in the hopes that an opportunity to play basketball would materialize.

The phone finally rang with an offer to play in Fos-sur-Mer, France. At the time, Palmer was excited about playing in Europe for he had previously experienced a world of cultural adventure and travel through basketball. "I was open to pretty much anything," he recalled, "and I needed a job."[106] Fos-sur-Mer was not known as a hotbed of basketball. But it had an international bent via Franco-American head coach Gino Prybella, who coached at St. Joseph's University in Philadelphia and who had a friend friendly with Palmer's Big Green coach, Dave Faucher. Fos was allowed to hire one US player, as they advanced into the Nationale Masculine 2 division, and they needed a traditional big man to flesh out the squad; Palmer fit the bill.[107]

Palmer flew into Marseille's Marignane Airport that August, the scrub brush of the surrounding countryside clashing with the surrounding chemical and oil refineries forever etched into memory. There were key differences between the basketball land he left and the one he was to call home. The gym was far smaller than expected and only seated around 500 people, but at least had a parquet floor; many of the "away" games were played on rubber-coated cement (Taraflex) or harder interior courts.[108]

Prybella helped Palmer adjust and eased the way for his new recruit. But Palmer did the hard work. "You had to score twenty and get ten rebounds a game or you weren't doing your job," he recalled. "It was a very small time and a lot of pressure," but he loved the environment.[109] Palmer was initially confronted with a language barrier, so cultural exchanges were limited, but as he learned French, he was able to learn from and also impart about the United States, its culture, and its basketball with his teammates.

After three seasons, Palmer moved on to Bourg-en-Bresse in eastern France, which played in ProB, the country's second division, then finally into the ProA with ASVEL, where he spent the 1997-8 and 1998-9 seasons. He played three seasons in Spain before returning to France and SIG Strasbourg (ProA), where he finished his professional career (2002-6). Throughout, Palmer continued to focus on the aspects he learned in the United States: giving it his all, hard work, attention to detail, and being a student of the game and opponents to improve every day, and at a certain point, to maintain a high level of basketball ability. "I think that would be something that few French players had encountered in quite the same way," he noted, while also pointing out that this is no longer the case in the 2020s.

> The thing I learned [in the United States] that transferred to my career in France was my being willing to play tough and hard and set screens to get rebounds and not have to score. It came completely naturally, so that was my mentality and it transferred well.

Palmer's career was aided by French citizenship, which he obtained two years after marrying former international Sandrine Chiotti in 1995. Thanks to the Bosman ruling, he was able to play in Spain as a European but had to wait until 2000 for his FIBA eligibility as a Frenchman to materialize. Thus, Palmer was officially eligible to join Les Bleus for the team's pre-Olympic camp. "I worked hard all summer," Palmer recalled of his efforts, which paid off when FIBA cleared his naturalization paperwork.

For the Ithaca-born basketballer, the 2000 Sydney Games were a meeting of his two basketball selves. Many, including within the FFBB, were apprehensive that the 2000 Olympic team not repeat the same mistakes as the 1984 team, which was still, nearly two decades later, remembered for an unprofessional approach towards the Games. It helped that 1984 Les Bleus alumni Patrick Cham was the team's press attaché, a role he held since 1998, and was with the team for its one-month-long pre-Olympic training camp and the Sydney Games.[110] He was thus able to impart some of his own lessons learned, particularly how the Games were entirely different from EuroBasket.[111]

Palmer recalled the anxious undercurrent just beneath the surface that summer. "We talked about [LA84]. We were made aware of the importance, not only of playing and trying to play well, but also acting right, to represent the country." Still, most people were not expecting the team to do much, let alone to do exceedingly well.

Les Bleus had an uneven start to the Olympic competition. They won their opening match against New Zealand 76–50, then lost to Lithuania 81–63. They were victorious over China 82–70, but beaten by Italy 67–57. France then played the United States in the final game of group play on September 25 to a 94–106 defeat, but their overall record was enough to push them through into the quarterfinal playoffs. A 68–63 win over Canada set up France's semifinal match against Australia, a 76–52 victory that Palmer considered one of the emotional highlights of his overall basketball career. But Les Bleus then had to turn around and play the United States in the tournament's gold medal match.

Much like its 1948 Olympic counterpart, the 2000 men's basketball final was a David versus Goliath matchup, with the US team heavily favored. Yet, many of the international public, including in France and the French team, had the impression that Team USA was arrogant.[112] "The Americans had throughout the Games a form of arrogance," recalled one of France's pivotal players, Cyril Julian. "They put themselves on the outskirts of the village, in a hotel. It always poses a problem when part of a delegation thinks it is superior and does not participate in the life of an Olympic village."[113]

The match itself was like a dream. France was nervous and had difficulty at first getting into the game. The players were "paralyzed by the fear of shooting and would rather make one more pass than take responsibility for going to the basket," *La Croix* noted.[114] For a while it appeared that the French were overly impressed by the physicality of the US team.

But contrary to expectations, the game was not a blow-out. Going into the half, France trailed the Americans by fourteen points. Then, something clicked during halftime. When the Yanks accelerated the pace in the second half, Les Bleus proved they could hang tough. "We saw that they were afraid," Palmer recalled for *Basket Le Mag*.[115]

France bounced back, played as a team, and came within four points of the Americans just minutes before the final buzzer. "We held on, and we managed to make them doubt," Palmer told the magazine.[116] The United States prevailed 85–75, but as France captain Jim Bilba noted,

> Despite our low shooting percentage (40%), we made them doubt until the last minutes. It is this note that we will keep forever. I am proud of all my teammates. We showed the Americans that European basketball had evolved. . .we have proven that with heart we can move mountains. It's a big step in the history of French basketball.[117]

The French press was wowed. "They held up well to a dream formation that had only the name, a team of stars made in the NBA, more arrogant than dominating," commented *Le Monde*.[118] "A magnificent Olympic campaign for a team that no one saw at this level," observed *La Croix*.[119]

FIGURE 6.4 *Crawford Palmer (third from right) and France men's team at the Sydney 2000 Olympics. Credit: Getty Images.*

The game was a special triumph for Palmer. He delighted in singing both the French and US national anthems during the basketball medal ceremony on October 1. "I was in a special niche in that game that made it special," he said. He also enjoyed mixing it up with some of his friends on Team USA, including his friend since high school Alonzo Mourning, and Vin Baker. He enjoyed being around Americans, even though it was a little odd to play against them.[120]

It was an extraordinary time. It was the realization of the generation who won the 1992 European Junior Championship, the crystallization of the youth detection and formation structures put in place in the 1980s, and the maturation of a generation schooled on playground basketball and its strong US influences. French results were also aided by Palmer's American outlook and mentality, which brought a will to succeed, confidence, positive attitude, and the winning mentality.[121]

Post-Game

The basketball world revolutionized between the 1992 to the 2000 Olympic basketball tournaments. Although the original US Dream Team helped globalize the appeal of the NBA and its bevy of stars, including Jordan, its larger impact in France was to stimulate greater interest in the game as more youths dreamed to "Be Like Mike." Basketball was able to convert this interest into results eight years later thanks to several aspects put into place in the 1980s, namely youth development and detection programs at INSEP and increasingly in the professional clubs, as the next section details. Importantly, the rise of playground basketball provided a third, albeit informal, pipeline for the development of young talent—one that remained overlooked until the new century.

Yet, none of French basketball's successes by the early 2000s would have been possible without the continued transatlantic influences fomented by informal sports diplomacy. Playing in the NCAA's top division provided valuable experience for players who then helped enrich their Les Bleus and Les Bleues teams with US lessons learned, notably related to mental toughness, the confidence to win, and physical preparation. The arrival of Fijalkowski and Abdul-Wahad in the WNBA and NBA in 1997, respectively, demonstrated that French players were good enough to compete in the world's top professional leagues. These players were the product of France's immigration history and complicated colonial legacy, but later, after 2000, the French-African pillar was strengthened in new ways.

Notes

1 S.I. Staff, "Jack McCallum: Dream Team Scrimmage Greatest Game Nobody Ever Saw," *Sports Illustrated*, July 24, 2012, https://www.si.com/more-sports/2012/07/24/usa-basketball-game-nobody-saw.

2 All David Stern quotes in this chapter, unless specified, from David Stern, Interview with the author, interview by Lindsay Sarah Krasnoff, telephone, March 17, 2016.

3 Stern.

4 The arena was sold-out within fifteen minutes of tickets going on sale. Staff.

5 Staff.

6 Crawford Palmer to Lindsay Sarah Krasnoff, "Email to the Author," January 25, 2016.

7 Micah Adams, "The Dream Team Scrimmage in Monte Carlo," ESPN.com, July 22, 2017, https://www.espn.com/blog/statsinfo/post/_/id/133080/the-scrimmage-in-monte-carlo; Staff.

8 Gilles Noghès, "Email to the Author," May 11, 2016.

9 USA Basketball, "Games of the XXVth Olympiad—1992," September 14, 2012, https://www.usab.com/history/national-team-mens/games-of-the-xxvth-olympiad-1992.aspx.

10 Daniel Champsaur and Philippe Cazaban, "1992–2014 Du Rêve Aux Médailles," in *Géants: Toute l'histoire du Basket-Ball* (Éditions Chronique, 2015), 261.

11 The euro went into effect on January 1, 1999.

12 Abdurrahim Sıradağ, "Understanding French Foreign and Security Policy towards Africa: Pragmatism or Altruism," *Afro Eurasian Studies Journal* 3, no. 1 (Spring 2014): 111–12.

13 Wayne Northcutt, "José Bové vs. McDonald's: The Making of a National Hero in the French Anti-Globalization Movement[1]," *Proceedings of the Western Society for French History*, 31 (2003), http://hdl.handle.net/2027/spo.0642292.0031.020.

14 Walter LaFeber, *Michael Jordan and the New Global Capitalism* (W.W. Norton, 1999).

15 Tyler Stovall, *Transnational France: The Modern History of a Universal Nation* (Taylor & Francis, 2015), 444.

16 James G. Shields, "Le Pen and the Progression of the Far-Right Vote in France," *French Politics and Society*, 13, no. 2 (1995): 21–39.

17 For more on this issue, see Christopher Clarey, "WORLD CUP '98; France Hoping for Title at End of the Rainbow," *The New York Times*, July 7, 1998, sec. Sports, https://www.nytimes.com/1998/07/07/sports/world-cup-98-france-hoping-for-title-at-end-of-the-rainbow.html; June Thomas, "Les Bleus et Les Noirs," Slate, April 26, 2002, https://slate.com/news-and-politics/2002/04/le-pen-vs-les-bleus.html.

18 Fabien Jobard, "An Overview of French Riots: 1981–2004," in *Rioting in the UK and France* (Willan, 2009).

19 Cathal Kilcline, *Sport and Society in Global France : Nations, Migrations, Corporations* (Liverpool: Liverpool University Press, 2019).

20 Rap became officially recognized by 1991. For more on the history and evolution of hip-hop and rap in France, see Karim Hammou, *Une Histoire du Rap en France* (La Découverte, 2014); Rebecca Fisher, Emma Kaplan, and Elena Kim, "Une Chronologie Sonique de Hip-Hop Français," Francophone Hip-Hop (blog), n.d., http://sites.duke.edu/globalfrance/francophone-hip-hop/chronologie-de-hip-hop-francais/.

21 Johan Rat, Interview with the author, September 24, 2021.

22 Gérard Bosc, *Une Histoire du Basket Français. . .Tome 3, 1990–2000* (Presses du Louvre, 2002), 89.

23 Two years later, there were 454,729 licensed players. Bosc, 21, 49.

24 Alain Mercier, "Un Sport Qui a du Mal: Réussier Sa Percé Populaire," *Le Monde*, June 22, 1999.

25 Bosc, 142.

26 Jean Jacques Bozonnet, "Le Limoges CSP Champion d'Europe des Clubs: La Culture Basket. Du Stade à La Rue. Les Jeunes des Banlieues Plébiscitent un Sport Magnifié Jeudi à Athènes par les Joueurs de Limoges," *Le Monde*, April 17, 1993; Yann Descamps and Ismaël Vacheron, "Où le ghetto (se) joue. Playground, basket-ball et culture afro-américaine," *Géographie et cultures*, no. 88 (December 1, 2013): 169–89, https://doi.org/10.4000/gc.3088; David Sudre, Helene Joncheray, and Antoine Lech, "'Let Go of Your Ball, This Is Not the NBA!': The Influence of Hip-Hop Ball on Institutional Basketball

Around Paris (France): Cultural Antagonisms and Difficult Cohabitation," *Journal of Sport and Social Issues* 43, no. 3 (2019): 147–66.

27 Bozonnet.

28 Loic Artiaga and Fabien Archambault, *Double Jeu : Histoire Du Basket-Ball Entre France et Amériques* (Paris: Vuibart, 2007).

29 Since 1988, FIBA mandated that clubs could only play two foreign players plus two players who had obtained citizenship three years or more previously. Benedicte.

30 "PRESS RELEASE No 30/00 Judgment of the Court of Justice in Case C-176/96 : RULES PREVENTING PROFESSIONAL SPORTSMEN FROM TAKING PART IN COMPETITIONS IF THEY HAVE BEEN TRANSFERRED AFTER A SPECIFIED DATE MAY CONSTITUTE AN OBSTACLE TO FREEDOM OF MOVEMENT FOR WORKERS" (Court of Justice of the European Union, April 13, 2000), https://curia.europa.eu/en/actu/communiques/cp00/aff/cp0030en.htm.

31 Bosc, 139.

32 "La Pologne bat la France (59–56) en finale du championnat d'Europe féminin," *Le Monde* (1944–2000), June 8, 1999, sec. Aujourd'hui-Sports.

33 "La Pologne bat la France (59-56) en finale du championnat d'Europe féminin."

34 FFBB, "Historique Des Matches FFBB," FFBB History Database, accessed June 29, 2020, http://www.ffbb.com/edf/historique-des-matches.

35 Fréderic Potet, "Les Bleus d'Aimé Jacquet Inspirent les Basketteurs Français," *Le Monde*, June 29, 1999.

36 Potet.

37 All Katia Foucade-Hoard quotes in this chapter, unless specified, from Foucade-Hoard, Katia, Interview with the author, November 1, 2021.

38 Fanny Martin and Vincent Janssen, "Le Basket-Ball Picard & Son Creuset de Talents: 25 Ans de Formation au Pôle Espoirs Picardie" (La Commission Patrimoine picarde, Ligue de Picardie de Basketball, November 2014), 11.

39 Martin and Janssen, 9–13.

40 Foucade left Saint Quentin to finish her last two years of high school while playing with Villerbanne, near Lyon. Foucade-Hoard, Katia, Interview with the author.

41 Foucade-Hoard,

42 Foucade-Hoard,

43 Foucade-Hoard,

44 Foucade-Hoard,

45 Foucade-Hoard,

46 University of Washington Athletics, "History: University of Washington 2006–07 Women's Basketball Media Guide," November 2006, https://washington_ftp.sidearmsports.com/old_site/pdf/w-baskbl/wash-wb-history07.pdf.

47 Benjamin Henry, *Made in France: Ces Français à l'assaut u Rêve Américain* (Hugo Sport, 2021), 20.

48 Isabelle Fijalkowski, Interview with the author, interview by Lindsay Sarah Krasnoff, October 4, 2021.

49 Fijalkowski; Henry, 20.

50 All Isabelle Fijalkowski quotes in this chapter, unless specified, from Fijalkowski, Interview with the author.

51 Souvré played at Fresno State for the 1989–90 season, the second Frenchwoman to play NCAA basketball. Guillaume Paquereau, "1989–1990 : La Saison NCAA de Yannick Souvré," Basket Retro (blog), January 13, 2022, https://basket-retro.com/2022/01/13/1989-1990-la-saison-ncaa-de-yannick-souvre/.

52 Yann Casseville, "Moi, Je. . .Isabelle Fijalkowski," *Basket Le Mag*, November 2021.

53 "Colorado Women's Basketball History/Records," University of Colorado Athletics, 109, accessed January 14, 2022, https://cubuffs.com/documents/2020/12/29/7.pdf?id=20461.

54 University of Colorado Athletics, "Women's Basketball vs Washington on 12/28/1994—Box Score," University of Colorado Athletics, December 28, 1994, https://cubuffs.com/sports/womens-basketball/stats/1994-95/washington/boxscore/5735.

55 "Magical Season: A Reporter Remembers 1994–95 CU Women's Team," University of Colorado Athletics, accessed January 14, 2022, https://cubuffs.com/news/2020/2/15/womens-basketball-magical-season-a-reporter-remembers-1994-95-cu-womens-team.aspx.

56 University of Colorado Athletics, "Colorado Women's Basketball NCAA History," University of Colorado Athletics, 211 https://cubuffs.com/documents/2020/12/29/8.pdf?id=20462.

57 Henry, 26.

58 Fijalkowski; "Magical Season."

59 Henry, 26.

60 "Magical Season."

61 Henry, 27.

62 Henry, 27.

63 Henry, 27.

64 Case Western Reserve University, "CLEVELAND ROCKERS," in Encyclopedia of Cleveland History | Case Western Reserve University, May 11, 2018, https://case.edu/ech/articles/c/cleveland-rockers.

65 WNBA, "Isabelle Fijalkowski Career Stats," WNBA Stats, https://stats.wnba.com/player/100089/.

66 Casseville, "Moi, Je. . .Isabelle Fijalkowski," 60.

67 Yann Casseville, "Eurobasket 2001: 12 Filles en Or," *Basket Le Mag*, March 2021.

68 IOC, "Basketball. Official Report of the XXVII Olympiad—Results.," Olympic Official Reports Collection, LA84 Digital Library, accessed March 14, 2022, https://digital.la84.org/digital/collection/p17103coll8/id/49173/rec/5.

69 Casseville.

70 She played under her then-married name, George Saint-Jean. Tariq Abdul-Wahad, Interview with the author, January 21, 2022.

71 All Tariq Abdul-Wahad quotes in this chapter, unless specified, from Abdul-Wahad, Interview with the author.

72 Stade Français Versailles and Dinamo Novosibirsk both contested the FIBA Women's European Basketball Cup in the 1980s.

73 The storied club won EuroLeague (1992–3), claimed third place in the 1989–90 season, and contested the Final Four three times (1990, 1993, 1995).

74 Ian Thomsen and International Herald Tribune, "For French Teen, a Chance to Play in Webber-Land," *The New York Times*, August 5, 1993.

75 Ian Thomsen and International Herald Tribune,

76 "Tariq Abdul-Wahad, à Jamais Premier (les débuts en France)," Basket USA (blog), accessed January 21, 2022, https://www.basketusa.com/dossiers/histoire/54699/tariq-abdul-wahad-a-jamais-premier-1ere-partie/.

77 "Tariq Abdul-Wahad, à Jamais Premier (les débuts en France),"

78 "Tariq Abdul-Wahad, à Jamais Premier (les débuts en France)" ; FFBB, "Media Guide: Pole France Basketball Yvan Mainini 2020–2021" (FFBB, 2020), 86.

79 Christophe Brouet, "Tariq Abdul-Wahad : 'T'arrives en Équipe de France et t'es Coaché par un Prof de Sport. . .Mais Comment?!,'" Basket Infos (blog), accessed January 21, 2022, https://basket-infos.com/2020/10/29/tariq-abdul-wahad-tarrives-en-equipe-de-france-et-tes-coache-par-un-prof-de-sport-mais-comment/.

80 He received 400 francs (approx. 60,97 euros) weekly. "Tariq Abdul-Wahad, à jamais premier (les débuts en France)," Basket USA (blog), accessed January 21, 2022, https://www.basketusa.com/dossiers/histoire/54699/tariq-abdul-wahad-a-jamais-premier-1ere-partie/.

81 "Tariq Abdul-Wahad, à Jamais Premier (les Débuts en France)."

82 Thomsen and Tribune, "For French Teen, a Chance to Play in Webber-Land."

83 Thomsen and Tribune; Abdul-Wahad, Interview with the author.

84 Abdul-Wahad, Interview with the author.

85 University of Michigan Bentley Historical Library, "University of Michigan—Men's Basketball," University of Michigan Athletics History, July 18, 2018, https://bentley.umich.edu/athdept/baskmen/baskmen.htm.

86 University of Michigan Athletics, "Michigan Men's Basketball Records: NCAA Tournament (PDF)," University of Michigan Athletics, 20, accessed February 7, 2022, https://mgoblue.com/documents/2017/3/20/bkm_ncaa_tournament.pdf.

87 Abdul-Wahad, Interview with the author.

88 Abdul-Wahad converted to Islam and officially changed his name from Saint-Jean to Abdul-Wahad while at SJU.

89 "Tariq Abdul-Wahad, à jamais premier (les années NCAA)," Basket USA (blog), accessed January 21, 2022, https://www.basketusa.com/dossiers/histoire/54761/tariq-abdul-wahad-a-jamais-premier-les-annees-ncaa/.

90 San Jose State University Athletics, "San Jose Spartans Men's Basketball 2021–22 Record Book," 109.

91 Curtis, "Saint-Jean's Winding Way to San Jose."

92 "Tariq Abdul-Wahad Returns to San Jose as Coach," ExNBA (blog), January 7, 2013, https://exnba.com/articles-news/tariq-abdul-wahad-returns-to-san-jose-as-coach/.

93 San Jose State University Athletics, "San Jose Spartans Men's Basketball 2021–22 Record Book," 110.

94 San Jose State University Athletics, 20–3.

95 "Tariq Abdul-Wahad, à jamais premier (les années NCAA)."

96 In addition to his mother's playing and coaching career, Abdul-Wahad's family doctor was the FFBB Vice President while then-head coach of the men's national team, Jean-Pierre de Vincenzi, regularly dined at the family home to discuss basketball with Georges. Tariq Abdul-Wahad, Interview with the author, January 21, 2022.

97 Paul Miquel, "Ma Première Saison en NBA Est Un Échec," *Le Monde*, April 9, 1998.

98 Abdul-Wahad, Interview with the author.

99 Fréderic Potet, "Les Français Disputent l'Euro Basket Mais Rêvent de l'Amérique," *Le Monde*, June 22, 1999.

100 Potet.

101 Brouet, "Tariq Abdul-Wahad."

102 Eric Collier, "Le Propos de Tariq Abdul-Wahad Choquent Le Basket Français: L'encadrement de l'équipe Nationale Dement Les Accusations de Racisme," *Le Monde*, May 12, 2000, https://www.lemonde.fr/archives/article/2000/05/12/les-propos-de-tariq-abdul-wahad-choquent-le-basket-francais_3618661_1819218.html.

103 Crawford Palmer, Interview with the author, interview by Lindsay Sarah Krasnoff, December 8, 2021.

104 "Duke's Palmer Transfers to Dartmouth," News & Record (Greensboro, N.C.), May 17, 1991, https://greensboro.com/dukes-palmer-transfers-to-dartmouth/article_23e75b33-0e12-57f7-b647-559eaba2a302.html.

105 "Pro Scouts to Judge Players' Skills," *Daily Press*, April 7, 1993, https://www.dailypress.com/news/dp-xpm-19930407-1993-04-07-9304070348-story.html.

106 The center had already experienced European basketball through a 1987 summer high school exchange program in Greece shortly after Hellas' June 14 European Championship victory over the Soviet Union, as well as a 1989 summer program in Leningrad through Duke Universities' Russian Studies department. Crawford Palmer to Lindsay Sarah Krasnoff, "Email to the Author," January 25, 2016.

107 N2 was then France's third-division professional league.

108 Palmer to Krasnoff; Palmer, Interview with the author.

109 All Crawford Palmer quotes in this chapter, unless specified, from Palmer, Interview with the author.

110 Claude Hességé, "Les Artisans d'une Médaille," *L'Humanité*, September 29, 2000.

111 Yann Casseville, "Le Première Match NBA En France," *Basket Le Mag*, January 2020, 37 edition.

112 Champsaur and Cazaban, "1992–2014 Du Rêve Aux Médailles," 282.

113 Yann Casseville, "Sydney 2000: Le Grand Récit," *Basket Le Mag*, May 2020.

114 Yves Pitette, "La France dans le Haut du Panier," *La Croix*, October 2, 2000.

115 Casseville, "Sydney 2000."

116 Crawford Palmer, "'Ma grand-mère était traumatisée par le fait que je vienne en France,'" *Basket Le Mag*, May 2019.

117 David Reyrat, "Bilba : 'Un Grand Pas Pour Le Basket Français ,'" *Le Figaro*, October 2, 2000.

118 Collier, "L'équipe de France s'approche de Son Rêve Américain."

119 Pitette, "La France dans le Haut du Panier."

120 Palmer, "'Ma grand-mère était traumatisée par le fait que je vienne en France.'"

121 de Vincenzi.

PART TWO

French in the USA

Global Scouting Report

Part Two centers upon the transatlantic stories of some of France's legendary twenty-first-century basketballers who embody the basketball empire in its geographical and cultural senses. Snapshots of their early influences bring the game's regional stimuli into better focus, while windows into their youth formation highlights the systems that developed in response to the game's global growth and evolution. Learning how they communicated, represented, and negotiated to colleagues, coaches, and fans about a twenty-first-century global France, its culture, and its hoops scene is instructive. The insights players provided about their US experiences denotes the types of informal sports diplomacy at work through cultural, technical, and knowledge exchanges. It's a different role than their more formal Team France representation examined in Chapter 15, although the two are complimentary.

The story of being French in the NBA, WNBA, and NCAA did not occur in a bubble. Larger international and domestic concerns of the last two decades set the background context for the next several chapters. These broad contours inform the basketball empire's evolution, although it's too recent to adequately analyze and place the players' stories into greater historical perspective.

Les Bleues' successful campaign for the European title began just three days after the September 11, 2001, terrorist attacks on US soil. "We are all Americans," editorialized *Le Monde* two days later in solidarity while France contributed troops to NATO's war in Afghanistan, retaliation for the Taliban-led attack. The United States and France cooperated on the larger Global War on Terror but Paris opposed the 2003 Washington-led invasion of Iraq. The resultant acrimony was one of the tersest points in the transatlantic relationship in decades. Relations rebounded but the September 2021 discord over the Australia–United Kingdom–United States security partnership (AUKUS) highlighted the importance of cultural and people-to-people ties beyond the diplomatic, military, and economic relationship.

During this time, France worked to diversify its relationship with different parts of Africa. Senegal remained a special partner, but the Quai d'Orsay courted ties with non-francophone countries like Nigeria and Angola while it sought to reset relations with francophone continental counterparts. In 2021, President Emmanuel Macron inaugurated a new era of relations with Rwanda when he officially acknowledged France's "overwhelming responsibility" in that country's 1994 genocide.[1] When the Malian government requested French military intervention to help counter-terrorist groups in 2013, troops were warmly welcomed; however, relations between the two soured by their February 2022 withdrawal.[2]

Against this backdrop, globalization progressed apace. The Internet made the world smaller as it interconnected societies in real time. The emergence of social media platforms and blogs, the development of Web 2.0, further stitched people together and promoted a new form of global community. The growth of international travel thanks to a new class of no-frills bargain airlines enabled more people to experience the wider world than before, further compounding the sense of global citizenship. Yet, increasingly, disinformation and misinformation, combined with media illiteracy, posed challenges worldwide.

The Great Recession that began in the United States in 2007 spread across the world's interconnected financial, banking, and trade hubs. The economic downturn exacerbated social tensions, as did the increased influx of refugees and asylum seekers to Europe. The Arab Spring of 2011, a series of popular anti-government uprisings, further destabilized the international community. In some countries, such as Tunisia, Egypt, Libya, and Bahrain, it led to regime change; in others it forced governments to address economic stagnation, while in Syria a brutal civil war erupted. The resultant waves of refugees, asylum seekers, and those forced to escape the impacts of a warming planet's climate change by 2015 posed a vast migration crisis in Europe. These larger socioeconomic pressures fed anxiety, fueled xenophobia, and provided greater opportunity for the growth of far-right-wing and far-left-wing political parties in

France, the United States, and elsewhere. Outbreak of the global COVID-19 pandemic in early 2020 further destabilized sociopolitical and economic equations.

Domestically, France contended with several issues. Stronger economic growth of the late 1990s and early 2000s gave way to stagnation after 2005; while France felt the impact of the Great Recession, the country remained relatively stable economically. But not for all citizens. Lack of socioeconomic opportunities for some, especially those in the *banlieues* who were subject to myriad types of discrimination and police heavy-handedness, fueled three weeks of urban riots across the country in 2005. The government promised policy changes, but there was minimal relief to what Prime Minister Manuel Valls described in 2015 as remaining a state of "territorial, social, and ethnic apartheid."[3] Although a continued reexamination and acknowledgement of France's colonial past continues to force a reconfiguration of a twenty-first-century identity and shared history, it has not alleviated the situation. Nor did the terrorist attacks of 2015–16, which while they provided moments of national unification, did little to ease discrimination.

The bitter social divide was seized upon by the far-right Front National (FN) and used to their benefit. Party leader Jean-Marie Le Pen gained enough votes to contest the second round of the 2002 French presidential election but then floundered; in 2011, his daughter Marine took over party leadership and rebuilt the FN to again contest the second round of the 2017 and 2022 presidential elections. She did so on an anti-globalization, anti-immigration, xenophobic platform while presenting a less acrimonious visage that helped normalize the party beyond its cosmetic 2018 rebranding into the National Rally.

Somewhat similar trends were at work within the United States. The election of Barack Obama, the first Black American president, gave great hope for the future of the country socially, as well as economically, as his administration worked to mitigate the Great Recession. Yet, it reopened the floodgates of racism which, aided by free speech and anonymity of the Internet and social media, normalized once-taboo public behavior. The lack of socioeconomic recovery and upward mobility for many outside the coastal tech and finance hubs helped fuel the far right, including the Tea Party faction of the Republican Party.

The sports world was not immune to any of these developments. One of the November 2015 terrorist attacks symbolically targeted the France–Germany football friendly at Paris's Stade de France, while another occurred in European Championship host city Nice the following July. The French sports world helped bring their fellow citizens together in the immediate aftermath in numerous ways. Meanwhile, the 2016 election of Donald Trump as President of the United States punctured the fallacy of a separation between US sport and politics.

Ever-more athletes used their platforms in political and social advocacy measures. While some supported the president, far many more spoke out in favor of greater human and civil rights issues, particularly those within the NBA and WNBA which emerged as the most progressive professional sports leagues on earth. Even basketball players whose home countries did not have the same historical culture of sports activism increasingly took on greater advocacy roles.

Sports diplomacy of different stripes thus gained greater import after 2000. The more traditional form of the genre that involved official state representatives, such as diplomats or elite athletes, grew as recognition of its use as a soft power cultivation tool came into greater focus. The US Department of States launched what is today the Sports Diplomacy Division in the aftermath of the September 11th attacks and has since focused its efforts on using sports as a programmatic tool through sports exchanges, sports envoys, sports visitors, and sports-related grant-making efforts. The government of France, on the other hand, took a different approach. In 2013, it launched its sports diplomacy policy pegged to three pillars: increasing French influence in sport, setting sport as a priority for the Ministry of Foreign Affairs, and positioning sport as part of economic diplomacy.

But as the global sports industry grew, including increased sports migration, the types of informal sports diplomacy engaged in by non-state actors proliferated. That is to say, the role of citizen diplomacy became more prevalent within the context of global sports as international colleagues worked together in unprecedented in-person proximity and digital interconnectivity. They organically communicated, represented, and negotiated about their home countries, ideals, and sports as part of the natural cultural, technical, or knowledge exchange that occurs to foster successful teamwork. This was particularly true within the NBA and WNBA, the two US professional leagues with the greatest number of international players or players who play abroad during the off-season.

Notes

1 Laure Broulard and Pierre Lepidi, "Warming Relations between France and Rwanda, One Year after Emmanuel Macron's Visit in Kigali," *Le Monde.Fr*, May 29, 2022, https://www.lemonde.fr/en/le-monde-africa/article/2022/05/29/warming-relations-between-france-and-rwanda-one-year-after-emmanuel-macron-s-visit-in-kigali_5984938_124.html.

2 La France au Mali [@FranceauMali], "[THREAD] 1)La France est intervenue au Mali entre 2013 et 2022 pour luter contre les groupes terroristes, à la demande des autorités maliennes," Tweet, Twitter, August 17, 2022, https://twitter.com/FranceauMali/status/1559986029456756736; Annie Risemberg, "Mali Accuses France of Supporting Islamist Militants," VOA, https://www.voanews.com/a/mali-accuses-france-of-supporting-islamist-militants-/6706877.html.

3 Manuel Valls, "Manuel Valls évoque 'un apartheid territorial, social, ethnique' en France," *Le Monde.fr*, January 20, 2015, https://www.lemonde.fr/politique/article/2015/01/20/pour-manuel-valls-il-existe-un-apartheid-territorial-social-ethnique-en-france_4559714_823448.html.

7

Renaissance Man Boris Diaw

Two months before the French teams sparked Olympic basketball dreams anew in Sydney, a younger cohort of players arrived in Zadar, Croatia, to contest the biennial 2000 European Championship for Junior Men (today's U18 Championship Men). France won the 1992 edition, snagged silver in 1996, and placed tenth two years later. The 2000 tourney was the chance to change course, helped by the chemistry of a tight-knit team.

France's July 14 opening match, a dominant 83–33 win over Bulgaria, set the tone. Les Bleuets won three more group-stage games before they lost to Croatia 59–67 in an off-beat game remembered for a Ronny Turiaf dunk that shattered the backboard glass. France rebounded to win its quarterfinal against Latvia 59–53 and semifinal against Greece 71–57.

The final again pitted France against the host. The arena's capacity of 4,500 was exceeded as hometown fans flocked to cheer on Croatia. "The public was ready," Boris Diaw said of the throngs that squeezed into the gym to create a hot, tense atmosphere to watch him and the French play.[1] His close friend, teammate Turiaf, recalled, "I feared for my life, I feared for the lives of my father and mother in the stands."[2] The teams traded baskets throughout the match, French prodigy Tony Parker fouled out of the game with four minutes left, and two overtime periods ensued to break the tie. With France down one point in the last four seconds of second overtime, Turiaf made a critical basket to put Les Bleuets ahead by one, 65–64. Croatia's attempt to answer with a last-minute basket failed as France burst onto the court in euphoric celebration of their gold medal.

Continental victory had a tantalizing taste, one that drove the team leaders. The resultant confidence the title conferred changed French basketball as subsequent generations approached competitions to win gold. As one longtime journalist noted, "it's really this team that evolved the mentality."[3] Parker, upon rewatching that championship final, noted, "it's where the fire was created."[4] The trio of Parker, Diaw, and Turiaf fueled their fire through friendship forged at INSEP, the national sports school.[5] They were also close friends with two other teammates, Mickael Piétrus and Yakhouba Diawara; within five years, all five cracked the NBA and provided blueprints for French basketball's revival.

One of them, Diaw, served as a particular guiding force. Although he wasn't the ultimate scorer like Parker, Diaw, scion of the country's basketball family and product of its post-1960s sports revitalization, helped build cultural cachet through informal sports diplomacy as this "Frenchiest dude in the NBA" became a fan favorite and NBA Champion.[6] Importantly, his career inspired and contributed to building the next generation back home, in the NBA, and in Africa, providing snapshots of the basketball empire at work.

Return of the Prodigal Son

Two years earlier, Diaw arrived on the INSEP campus for his first year at the Federal Basketball Center (CFBB), the successor program of the one that trained his mother some thirty years earlier. It was *la réntrée*, back-to-school season of 1998, and the country was still energized by the national football team, which hosted and won the FIFA World Cup earlier that summer. For the elite teenaged sportswomen and men at INSEP, it was a heady environment full of new possibility that they, too, could one day win it all and achieve their sporting dreams.

Surprisingly for some, Diaw's dreams at the time didn't include playing in the NBA. Born April 16, 1982, in Cormeilles-en-Parisis, some twelve miles northwest of Paris, Diaw grew up in southwestern France as his mother's career transitioned. Élisabeth Riffiod-Diaw met Senegalese-born high jumper Issa Diaw during the 1970s when they trained at what is today INSEP; although they never married, they had two sons, Martin and Boris. When Issa returned to Senegal, the blonde-haired blue-eyed Riffiod-Diaw remained in France and raised the boys. In spring 1983, she took an offer with Mont-de-Marsan and moved the family to the Nouvelle Aquitaine region; often Boris tagged along to her practices and games.

"I was born into it," Diaw said of how basketball played in the background during his childhood as he grew up in the heart of the women's game. "I was over there on the court pretty much my whole childhood."[7] In 1989, Riffiod-Diaw was nominated to teach at the University of Bordeaux and the family decamped to one of the city's southwestern suburbs, Gradignan, closer to campus.[8]

Thus began Diaw's formative years in Bordeaux, the southwestern pocket of the country with a strong basketball culture. Although football dominated, both rugby and basketball enjoyed robust followings thanks to the religious geography of France. The region was traditionally more Protestant-leaning and basketball was a sport originally associated with the Protestant-affiliated YMCA. The game's country-wide spread through Catholic patronages in the 1920s and 1930s also left an imprint, notably in the region's clubs rooted in that tradition, like Pau-Orthez. Yet, others including Diaw, pointed out that basketball was far easier to organize than other, larger team sports in a region with a lower population density.

Although Riffiod-Diaw was one of the country's preeminent players, she never steered her sons to the game, but the game was still played around the house. Diaw described himself as a hyperactive kid and invested his energies productively in sports. He was curious and tried rugby, fencing, volleyball, handball, judo, and enjoyed them all. But he always returned to basketball. "I just loved it because of my mom playing," he said. "I did try a lot of things, but always came back to basketball." The 1992 US Dream Team figured prominently in his love of the game. "A lot of kids watched that," Diaw said of that summer's Olympic basketball blitz that inspired generations. "I was like, 'Oh, yes! I want to do basketball.'"

He sought out and found numerous ways to hoop for "in Bordeaux, they have a good culture of basketball." He recognized the excitement that playground basketball provided. "It was the simplicity of being able to start a hoop [game] and you could play anywhere," he said of the genre's appeal. "You could just go with a couple of friends and play two-on-two...that's why you saw playgrounds popping up a little bit everywhere all around France."

On the Saige playground courts of Pessac, the southwestern Bordeaux suburb where the University of Bordeaux Montaigne resides, Diaw honed a different appreciation of the game. He began to play against older players, including Cameroonian-born coach Vincent Mbassi, who arrived in Bordeaux to pursue his university studies but quickly developed a passion for the game. Mbassi and other African-born students formed a group, the Black Stars, and played an NBA-inflected streetball style and enjoyed "wild, endless games" against neighborhood kids like Diaw all day long during the summer.[9]

Diaw debuted in his first organized club, US Talence, at ten years old. Four years later, he entered the sport-étude at Mont-de-Marsan, then trained at Les Jeunes de Saint Augustin (JSA) Bordeaux, a club founded in 1938 that dominated the basketball scene, in the evenings.[10] At fifteen years old Diaw entered the Regional Physical Education and Sports Center (CREPS) at Toulouse where he could pursue both his academic and basketball training in one location. He boarded on campus during the week and returned home on the weekends. "Some parents don't want you to leave home," he said of how attending the special program wasn't for everyone. But it was something that acculturated him to focus both his academic and basketball studies.

His CREPS basketball coach Daniel Gendron was one of the first to recognize that Diaw had talent and could go far in basketball, if he wanted.[11] The problem was, at the time, Diaw had one objective: to play in the Nationale Masculine 1, the country's third division.[12] Diaw had plenty of basketball influences, and one of his idols was Magic Johnson for the Los Angeles Lakers' polyvalence.[13] But Diaw's basketball ambitions were not yet about contesting the American championship.

That changed when Diaw was recruited by INSEP. "You don't go through a process, really," he said. "They call you." Thus at sixteen, Diaw landed on the same campus that, for his mother decades earlier, was "the most beautiful years of my life."[14]

It was the start of the 1998–9 academic year and some of the new arrivals had to adjust. Diaw no longer returned home at the weekends; instead, he spent three months at a time at INSEP before a return to Bordeaux. "You would go away for a long time," he said, "and some guys got homesick."

One of those homesick players was soon to be one of Diaw's close friends, Turiaf. For the future NBA and European champion, who was born and raised in Martinique, it was the first time living away from home and in the far less sunny climate of the mainland. "I remember Ronny missing his island," Diaw recalled. "He was very homesick in the first couple of months." But Diaw didn't have that same sort of homesickness. "Wherever I ended up, I always made the most out of it, it was cool."

Élisabeth's son rapidly adjusted to life at INSEP. From the get-go, he and Turiaf formed a close friendship with Parker, who lived across the hall. They practiced together, ate together, and studied together. But they also learned from each other. Parker, whose father Tony Parker Sr. was an American basketball player, was credited with bringing a US-style drive, winning mentality, and optimism.[15] This left an impression on Diaw. "The American mindset of the winning culture, the 'we can do it,' and 'we can be the best,' and the work to do so, I've seen that from [Parker] when we were at INSEP. He was already saying, 'Yes, I'm going to be in the NBA one day and have a great career,'" Diaw recalled. "We French, we're usually shy about expressing or putting ourselves out there like that. Yes, he had the mindset." It was a revelation and illustrated the subtle yet impactful ways that cultural exchange can fuel new dreams and influence the sporting scene.

The teens would hop the No. 112 bus from campus to the metro for their forays into the capital. But they didn't have lots of leisure time. Diaw and his teammates woke up at 7 a.m. and hit the campus canteen for breakfast before reporting to school at 8 a.m. Classes recessed at 11 a.m. so that the basketball players could hit midday practice, from 11.15 a.m. until 1 p.m., before a one-hour lunch and afternoon classes from 2 p.m. until 4.30 p.m. or 5 p.m. Diaw would grab a snack then head to a two-hour practice, then eat dinner. The day didn't end there. "You've still got to do homework for a couple of hours after dinner," he said, at which teachers were available to help on an as-needed basis. The boys only had an hour of leisure time before bed, usually from 10 p.m. until 11 p.m., only to rise and begin the cycle all over again the next day.

Saturdays were match days, and the team piled into buses to travel to away matches. "Sometimes, we had a seven-hour drive to go somewhere," Diaw recalled. Moreover, because the CFBB boys' section competed in Nationale Masculine 1, they competed against teams largely composed of adults, not fellow teenagers. They didn't always win, but their season record did not matter; the team was never promoted or relegated. Sundays were typically spent traveling back to INSEP from wherever the away match was, but if the games were at home then it was a rare day off. "That's when we went to the movies, or we'd go into Paris," Diaw explained.

The entire operation was funded by the government and the FFBB. Students did not have to pay to attend INSEP or for their equipment and gear.[16] The CFBB was overseen by federation officials, themselves longtime stalwarts of the country's basketball family who were influenced by their earlier transatlantic basketball exposure. The senior boys' team was coached by Lucien Legrand and their assistant coach was Patrick Cham, one of the game's 1980s stars. "Very laid back, cool guy," Diaw recalled of Cham's relaxed demeanor. "It's good for the players to have somebody like that, close to the players, to joke around with us." While the younger generation wasn't as aware of Cham's on-court accomplishments, they appreciated his expertise and experience.

Michel Rat, who helped found INSEP's basketball section in 1983, was also a constant presence. The former international and coach served as a bridge, connecting the younger generations with the country's larger basketball family. "He's keeping hold of the values of basketball and team spirit, why basketball was valued as a smart game, as a team sport, as putting the team in front of individuals and stuff like that," Diaw said of how Rat transmitted his hoops culture and knowledge, one influenced by his American experiences and teammates at Paris Université Club, as well as his time in Africa, to new generations at INSEP. "He was definitely there to keep those values around, to help the players grow athletically on the court, but also [to grow] as good people."

After Diaw's second year at INSEP, he, Turiaf, and Parker won European Championship for Junior Men then separated to follow their unique pathways. Parker had already begun his professional career with Paris Basket Racing in 1999 and continued with the club until he was drafted in 2001 by the San Antonio Spurs, a first-round twenty-eighth-place pick. The nineteen-year-old rapidly found his way into Coach Gregg Popovich's starting lineup and embarked on a highly decorated Hall of Fame worthy eighteen-season NBA career, seventeen of which were with the Spurs. As part of San Antonio's core crew, one that is credited with helping to further internationalize the league, Parker engaged daily in informal

FIGURE 7.1 *The boys' Juniors team at the Federal Basketball Center (CFBB), INSEP, with Michel Rat (bottom row, far right), Boris Diaw (bottom row, #13), Ronny Turiaf (top row, #9), and Patrick Cham (top row, second from right), circa 1999–2000. Credit: Musée du Basket.*

sports diplomacy with teammates and helped impart a little French flair to NBA hardcourts.[17]

Turiaf returned to INSEP to finish his studies then matriculated at Gonzaga University, where he crafted a sterling NCAA Division 1 career. In 2005, he was named West Coast Conference player of the year and was later inducted into the WCC's Hall of Honor.[18] Drafted by the Los Angeles Lakers in 2005, for nearly a decade Turiaf impacted NBA hardcourts, teammates, and fans, and in 2012 won the NBA Championship with the Miami Heat.

Diaw embarked on a professional career in 2001 with storied club Élan-Béarnais Pau-Lacq-Orthez. Known colloquially as Pau, the famed club's basketball section was founded in 1931 and rose to national and international success in the 1980s. The club continued to dominate France's professional rungs, reclaiming the national titles in 1992, 1996, 1998, and 1999. In 2001, with Diaw, the team again won the French championship, a symbolic cap to Diaw's first pro season.

Into the NBA

The June 26, 2003, NBA Draft was unusual in several ways. First, the number one draft prospect was an eighteen-year-old named LeBron James, reputed to be one of the league's strongest prodigies in a decade.[19] Second, it was a very international affair with sixteen players of the first fifty picks from overseas. Third, for the first time ever, three of these were Frenchmen: Diaw (twenty-first), his Pau teammate Mickael Piétrus (eleventh), and Paccelis Morlende (fiftieth).[20] Interestingly, neither Diaw nor Piétrus were in New York as Pau in the midst of the national championship race. Thus, when Diaw was selected in the first round by the Atlanta Hawks, he did not shake the hand of league Commissioner David Stern like so many other players before and since. Instead, he followed the proceedings from his computer.[21] Diaw first learned he was selected from Parker.[22] Two days later, Diaw and Piétrus helped Pau win their eighth French championship title with a 74–66 victory over Villeurbanne.

Diaw understood that he had to prove himself to the Hawks franchise and the league. "The objective is the same as when I arrived at Pau: to show people that they have reason to believe in me," he told *L'Équipe*.[23] But, thanks to his friendship with Parker, he had some idea of what to expect. When Parker went to the NBA, he didn't forget his friends back home. Parker and Diaw regularly spoke twice a week, and Diaw spent Christmases in Texas around the dinner table with Parker, Popovich and Spurs legend-in-the-making Tim Duncan.[24] Through these cultural and knowledge exchanges, Diaw gained greater understanding of what it took to succeed in the NBA.

Eleven days before draft, the Spurs won the NBA Championship. For Parker, it was the realization of a dream first begun years ago. But it was much bigger than just one young man's dreams; Parker winning the NBA Championship was a historic moment for French basketball and ushered in a new era.[25] Thanks to Parker's megawatt success in the NBA, kids in France began to dream of being like him and pursuing their own hoops dreams, which started to change the tenor of the game back home.

Following the Draft, twenty-one-year-old Diaw played Summer League for the Hawks in Boston, alongside a rookie cohort that included James.[26] Riffiod-Diaw flew to the United States for the occasion where she also met her idol, Boston Celtics legend Bill Russell. "I cried with emotion when I saw Bill Russell," she recalled of the dual-thrill experience. "I never thought that I could one day see him."[27]

French in the NBA

On September 18, 2003, Diaw moved to Atlanta to embark on his NBA career after a frenzied summer.[28] Within the previous three months he was drafted by the Hawks, won the French championship, played NBA Summer League, and helped Les Bleus to fourth place at that summer's EuroBasket tournament. Life for an NBA rookie wasn't much slower, but Diaw had a relatively easy time with the transition from France to the United States.

Adapting to a new country and the NBA was and remains complicated and complex for international players, no matter from where they come. But thanks to Diaw's previous visits to San Antonio, the US experience wasn't entirely alien.[29] It helped that his mother was on hand to help him settle in, although at first he lived out of two boxes and an inflatable bed.[30] Diaw delved into life in Atlanta. He visited Martin Luther King Jr.'s home, church, and tomb, and reveled in the city's history and culture.[31] He was impressed by how big everything was and struck by how different groups self-segregated within their living communities, something different from France.[32]

The food, however, was a different story. Diaw missed French food, especially good cheeses and breads. "That's what I miss the most," he confided more than a decade later while still playing in the United States. He also missed seeing his friends, but many of them crossed the Atlantic to visit, so that adjustment was less onerous.

In a league in which nearly three-quarters of the labor force self-identifies as Black and with a name that most Americans wouldn't identify as French, Diaw didn't stand out. "I blend in pretty easily," he said and did "not really" experience discrimination in the United States based on his color. That isn't to say that he didn't escape discrimination back home based on the color of his skin. "You have some when you talk about going out, racial profiling and stuff like that," he explained.

When I was in France, when I'd go out to a club, they'd tell you it's members only, that is the way they put it. So sometimes, yes, you don't get inside nightclubs. Once you become more or less famous, doors open and things become different. We used to get shielded from that in sports, specifically in basketball because there is a lot more of a racial mix in basketball.

But in his experience within the sports world, especially the basketball world in France, there was no racial profiling. "If you're good, you're going to play, [the color of your skin] doesn't matter." Within the basketball world in the United States, he fit in, although he admitted "the French accent, they recognize right away."

There were other cultural differences that Diaw experienced. For starters, the mentality of the game in the United States, and particularly in the NBA, was different than what he was used to back home. The lingo was also different, too. "Here, the players don't say 'swish' after a basket," he confessed to *L'Équipe*. "The word used is 'money.'"[33]

Expectations about a player's role on a team were also different and haunted Diaw throughout his early NBA career. Yet, it all began with great promise. Hawks head coach Terry Stotts played several years in France's top division just before full professionalization occurred, first at Voiron then Roanne. Of his new French draftee, Stotts told *L'Équipe*, "he's a very intelligent player who possesses very solid game fundamentals. There isn't an ounce of egoism in him, and his polyvalence makes him the player that we need on this team."[34]

By December 2003, Diaw was part of the Hawks' starting five.[35] For the next two seasons, he learned the ropes, but increasingly his style of game was called into question. He wasn't a high-scoring player, nor was he terribly flashy despite his obvious athleticism. In Diaw's first two seasons with Atlanta, he averaged less than twenty-two minutes of playing time and 4.6 points, 3.5 rebounds, and 2.4 assists per game. Instead, he focused on fundamentals and teamwork.

Still, questions over his abilities and fit in the NBA lurked in the background. "Since I was eight years old, I've lived with the word 'potential' attached to my name," he confessed to *L'Équipe*.[36] His mother tuned into many of his games, rising early to catch the action live but with the television on mute so that she wouldn't be able to hear commentators' criticisms of Diaw. "I cannot put up with that level of torture at that hour," she told *The New York Times*.[37]

Diaw was traded to Phoenix where, from 2005 until 2008, his career underwent a renaissance. The Suns were known for their seven-seconds-or-less fast-break offense, and Diaw, although a bench player, fit in. For Suns coach Mike D'Antoni, the Frenchman's polyvalence was a big asset.[38] It all paid off and in Diaw's first year, he averaged 35.5 minutes per game, 13.3 points, 6.9 rebounds, and 6.2 assists.[39] He won the league's Most Improved Player award in 2006, then signed a $45 million contract extension.[40] It was, finally, recognition of his on-court abilities.

He was traded to what is today's Charlotte Hornets in 2008, where he spent four seasons while one of his early basketball references, Michael Jordan, played an increased role with the organization. The NBA legend, who purchased a minority ownership stake in 2006 and served as the team's general manager, became the majority club owner in 2010. For Diaw, it was surreal. "That first year, it was really bizarre for me to shake his hand," Diaw recounted to *La Nouvelle République Dimanche* of interacting with Jordan. "[Then] it becomes commonplace. Plus, he lives above me. He did two training sessions with us this year and he's still in the game."[41] In this way, Diaw engaged in a form of technical exchange with the basketball legend.

During the 2011 NBA lockout, Diaw, like many of his compatriots, returned home and played with a ProA team; in this case, JSA Bordeaux. Not only was it the club that he played with as a teenager, but by this time he was an investor and served in its executive leadership, first as Vice President, then in 2010, as President. Returning to play ProA during the lockout was "an act of citizenship," he told *Sud Ouest*. "We have a duty to promote our basketball."[42]

When the NBA resumed operations, NBA players headed back to the United States, but Diaw wasn't sold on a career for the *longue durée*. "I decided to terminate my contract before its end in Charlotte," he told *L'Équipe*. He was swayed by the idea of playing with the Spurs and Parker as it had an air of familiarity, but the prospect of playing for Popovich enticed him most.

On March 2, 2012, Team France coach Vincent Collet and Patrick Beesley, then head of the CFBB, flew to San Antonio to visit with Parker. They arrived at the designated rendezvous place, a wine bar, but instead of their all-star they found his NBA coach expectantly awaiting their arrival. Popovich explained that Parker and Diaw knew they were all speaking, then ordered a bottle of Puligny-Montrachet over which he, Collet, and Beesley swapped notes on basketball and the two players in question. "It was an exceptional moment," Collet confided to *L'Équipe*.[43] Ten days later, Diaw was signed to the Spurs.

The San Antonio experience was special for Diaw. He played with Parker, the first time they did so as professionals, and lived with his friend for a while, too.[44] They were also joined for the 2012–13 and part of the following season by another Frenchman, Nando de Colo. In Popovich, Diaw found a coach who recognized what he brought to the team and respected those contributions.[45] "The certitude that I would be in the hands of a coach who understood and appreciated my qualities," won the day, Diaw told *L'Équipe*. "It was a breath of fresh air to go there, with basketball and a philosophy adapted to my vision. In this sense, Pop breathed new life into my career."[46]

Popovich was important for Parker, too. Not only did he give Number 9 his first real break in the NBA, but he also helped Parker realize his best performance. As Collet told *L'Équipe*,

> [E]ven if [Parker] was a strong prospect when he left in 2001, [he] progressed in an incredible way in San Antonio. Gregg Popovich polished the diamond, made Tony the exceptional player that he became. When you know afterwards what Tony did for the French team, French basketball owes [Popovich] a lot.[47]

In these small ways, the informal technical, cultural, and knowledge exchanged within and among the Spurs, particularly vis-à-vis their esteemed coach, helped refine Parker and Diaw's games. Another example of the technical exchange that occurred between the Spurs and the French national team comes from Collet. The French coach acknowledged how he integrated some of the Spurs' systems into Les Bleus' plays. As he told *L'Équipe* in 2022:

> We took over some Spurs systems, it's true, and we still do. This allowed players to find landmarks more easily, to be comfortable. I had noticed that in these systems, Tony Parker found many solutions. And then, Boris had played there, Nando De Colo too. . .Tony's career gave Spurs basketball an attractiveness in

France. This basketball, this family spirit, this desire to do things together—not the best shared virtue in the NBA—have rubbed off on French basketball.[48]

An argument could be made for how playing together in the NBA cemented the ability of Les Bleus captain Diaw to mesh with his team general, Parker, at the 2013 EuroBasket tournament, which resulted in a championship title, the country's first. But the chemistry gelled on court, too, for the Spurs. The team lost the NBA Championship to the Miami Heat in 2013 only to roar back and win it all in 2014. Game Five of the 2014 NBA Finals was a breakout for Diaw and illustrated how, after eleven years in the league, the thirty-two-year-old could be a "Finals momentum-changer."[49]

The Frenchiest Dude in the NBA

For Diaw, he and other European players brought the European basketball philosophy with them to the NBA, one more team-spirit based than what many US programs focused on at the time. "It's very much from what you learn on the court as young players," he said of a system that acculturates all players to touch the ball, shoot, and screen for each other. That playing philosophy may not be as flashy as the kind that scores thirty-five points a game or plays one-on-one to win for the team. But "sometimes, I think that's what coaches are looking for, that player that can do those team things on the court because they've been doing that for years."

This impressed American colleagues. Basketball Hall of Famer Grant Hill noted that Diaw was one of his preferred teammates when they played together in Phoenix. "He is polyvalent, can do anything, especially the things that don't show up on the stat sheet," he explained to *L'Équipe*. "He is an altruistic, intelligent player."[50] Over the years he's won fans around the basketball industry. Diaw earned the nickname "teatime" from LaMarcus Aldridge for how casual and breezy he made playing appear.[51] NBA Hall of Famer Bill Walton remarked that Diaw "reminded him of Beethoven," and that his game "flows like Liszt on the piano."[52] He also impressed fans, according to *GQ* in 2016, who admired his passion for travel, space documentaries, and passion to discover countries through their food and basketball (like the Philippines).[53]

Diaw influenced others in the NBA during and after his career. In 2016, he signed with the Utah Jazz where he helped ease the way for fellow Frenchman Rudy Gobert, who had toiled in Salt Lake City since the franchise drafted him in 2013. Although the elder statesman was kept to a maximum playing time of 15–20 minutes per game, he served as a mentor in other ways.[54] Diaw helped Gobert become more comfortable and helped the younger Frenchman with his game; Gobert emerged a year later as a Defensive Player of the Year contender.[55]

The following season, Diaw returned home and played for Levallois Metropolitans in ProA, now known as Levallois-Boulogne Metropolitans 92, but he still impacted the NBA. He played elder statesman for fellow Bordeaux native Elie Okobo, who was drafted by the Phoenix Suns (thirty-first) in 2018. As a kid, Okobo watched replays of Spurs games and was awed by Parker's moves.[56] But he also admired Diaw, and the two have known each other since the former was a seven-year-old (Diaw played pick-up basketball with Okobo's father).[57] Diaw helped Okobo in his transition from France to the NBA. Some of the advice that Okobo received from Diaw early in his NBA tenure included to remain humble and focus on utilization of his game IQ.[58]

Diaw's career continues to inspire NBA players, even after his September 2018 retirement from playing professionally. During the 2022 NBA Finals, Golden State's Draymond Green admitted how he studied Diaw's approach as a way to fine-tune his own game. "There was definitely some guys that I took things away from, and over the course of my career I still continue to watch and try to take things away from those guys," the American said.

> I studied Boris Diaw so much early in my career and just how he moved the ball and how he used DHOs [Dribble Hand Offs]. More so than a specific action, how he out thought the opponent. It was very special to me.[59]

A Sports Diplomat

Diaw tried to serve as a form of ambassador of France during his NBA years. "When I talk about wine, I'm an ambassador of France and of Bordeaux, my region," he explained. "[I'm] definitely always an ambassador of French culture in that way as far as food and wine, these kinds of things." This is in part why he and other French players tried to stay out of the tabloids. "There is stuff that we know is going to bring a lot of attention, and we are not necessarily looking for that," he said. Instead, the desire is "to be very low-key in general, don't try to overdo it, and over asserting ourselves." That's how a culture evolved in which Diaw and other international players would have dinner or go see movies together when on the road.

The NBA Champion also champions basketball in Africa. His father was not a constant presence, thus as a kid Diaw did not spend much time in Senegal and didn't visit the country until he was around twenty.[60] "I have two roots, but I don't pretend to know two cultures. If my double origin gives me a somewhat different look, I am the fruit of the Southwest," he told *Sud Ouest*.[61]

Yet, despite this complicated relationship, Diaw invested in Senegalese basketball. In 2005 he led his first basketball camp in the country. That same year, he founded Babac'ards, a foundation that organized these camps regularly. Babac'ards joined forces with SEED Academy on a girls' school in 2015 through which girls could train and develop their basketball skills while finishing their academic studies. The program was founded on SEED's existent program for boys, and enrolled twenty girls per year. For Diaw, the partnership with SEED was a continuation of his decade-long work in Senegal, working through basketball to encourage the next generation. "I am excited to utilize the power of sport to help change lives, especially for girls who traditionally lack educational and athletic opportunities," he told FIBA.[62]

In July 2015, Diaw traveled to Johannesburg, South Africa, to participate in the first NBA Africa Game. He competed for Team Africa in a nod to his Senegalese roots alongside fellow Frenchman Nicolas Batum (father, Richard, was from Cameroon) and coached by Popovich. The game, held in conjunction with that year's Basketball Without Borders Africa camp, was one of the first high-octane displays of how the NBA's investment in Africa, which dated to 1993, started to pay off. For these efforts and others, Diaw was awarded with the Naismith Basketball Hall of Fame's Mannie Jackson—Basketball's Human Spirit Award in 2018.[63]

But it was at a 2017 U16 African Championship in Mauritius where Diaw saw first-hand the promise of basketball in Africa. He was impressed by the level of competition at that tournament, notably of the Malian team, which sealed victory with a 76–65 win over Egypt.[64] Two years later, he watched Mali play the FIBA U19 World Cup, a tournament run that was ended by the United States in the final 93–79.[65] Following that performance, Diaw told FIBA, "Mali's performance at the FIBA U19 Basketball World Cup 2019 is the proof that Africa has the capacity to win at the international level." But, he emphasized, there was a critical need to focus on multidimensional development programs that encompassed both training and education.[66]

Diaw left a mark on the NBA, just as his American experiences imprinted the man himself. He played his last game *en bleu* on July 2, 2018, the 247th time he suited up as a player for France, the exact same number of times his mother did during her career with the national team. General Manager of the men's national team since then, Diaw continues to influence the basketball empire. He serves as the key lynchpin between the federation and its players in the NBA, facilitating and negotiating the delicate balance between summers off and national team duty, a role once held by Les Bleus' 2000 Olympic silver medalist Crawford Palmer. According to Palmer, it involves "dealing with the [NBA] franchises of being that liaison, of building that bridge to help convince them that French basketball was serious, that the guys would be well taken care of, that they'd be in a professional situation."[67] That's critical for success of the national teams each summer.

After retiring from professional and national team service, Diaw continued to invest in and give back to African basketball. In January 2020, he spent a week in Côte d'Ivoire with the Forces françaises en Côte d'Ivoire (he joined the French Navy as a citizen reservist in 2018), but still found time to lead a basketball workshop with Ivorian youth in Yogougon and, alongside football legend Didier Drogba (who spent his childhood in Colombes, France), attended the opening ceremony of a sports center.[68]

His story illustrates the internationalization of the NBA. A product of France's youth development system, a response to the greater globalization of the game, Diaw's experiences helped build the country's soft power and cultural cachet through his on- and off-court exploits. His ability to communicate, represent, and negotiate about France (and the NBA) through a variety of cultural, technical, and knowledge experience provides insight as to how the basketball empire is built and sustained.

Notes

1 *Les Enfants de Zadar—L'Équipe Explore*, Web (L'Equipe Explore, 2015), https://www.lequipe.fr/explore/wf6-les-enfants-de-zadar-video/.

2 *Les Enfants de Zadar.*

3 *Les Enfants de Zadar.*

4 *Les Enfants de Zadar.*

5 See Chapter 12 for greater details on the youth formation system and its evolution.

6 Alex Wong, "Boris Diaw, the Frenchiest Dude in the NBA, Is Down to Go to Mars," *GQ*, October 27, 2016, https://www.gq.com/story/boris-diaw-interview.

7 All Boris Diaw quotes in this chapter, unless specified, from Boris Diaw, Interview with the author, February 26, 2017.

8 Rémi Monnier, "L'enfant de La Balle," *Sud Ouest*, March 29, 2006.

9 "Interview de Vincent Mbassi, Fondateur de Kameet Basketball—Sapsnshoes," June 20, 2017, http://sapsnshoes.com/interview-de-vincent-mbassi.

10 Monnier.

11 Monnier.

12 Diaw, Interview with the author; Monnier, "L'enfant de La Balle."

13 Jean-Julien Ezvan, "Diaw-Riffiod, l'artiste Altruiste de La NBA," *Le Figaro*, October 31, 2005.

14 Monnier; Alexandre Carlier, "INSEP: The School of French Champions," *FIBA Assist Magazine*, 2005.

15 Jean-Pierre de Vincenzi, Interview with the author, September 22, 2016.

16 During Diaw's INSEP years, Adidas was the official sponsor of the federation. In later years, it was NIKE. Jordan Brand has been the official brand of the FFBB since November 2017. Boris Diaw, Interview with the author, February 26, 2017.

17 For more, see Joel Gunderson, *The (Inter) National Basketball Association: How the NBA Ushered in a New Era of Basketball and Went Global* (Sports Publishing, 2020); Tony Parker, *Tony Parker: Beyond All of My Dreams* (Triumph Books, 2020).

18 Jim Meehan, "Former Gonzaga Great Ronny Turiaf Gets WCC Hall of Honor Call," *The Spokesman-Review*, January 31, 2018, https://www.spokesman.com/stories/2018/jan/31/former-gonzaga-great-ronny-turiaf-gets-wcc-hall-on/.

19 "Ils Vont Changer de Pau," *L'Équipe*, June 28, 2003.

20 Paccelis Morlende was traded to the Seattle SuperSonics but never was signed or played with an NBA team.

21 Maxime Cazenave, "Boris Diaw: 'La Formation Française Est Appréciée en NBA,'" *Vox Stadium* (blog), February 8, 2015.

22 François Bontoux, "NBA-Diaw: 'Quand J'ai Dit à Tony Que Je le Battrai, Il a Rigolé,'" *AFP*, June 27, 2003.

23 Bontoux.

24 Bertrand-Régis Louvet, "Les Copains de Parker Se Souviennent," *Le Parisien*, June 16, 2003.

25 "Diaw: 'Tony a Montré la Voie,'" *L'Équipe*, May 31, 2003.

26 "NBA-Atlanta: Débuts 'très Satisfants' pour Diaw-Riffiod," *AFP*, July 15, 2003; Chad Finn, "The Story of LeBron James and the 2003 Boston Summer League," Boston.com, July 27, 2018, https://www.boston.com/sports/nba/2018/07/27/lebron-james-2003-boston-summer-league/.

27 Élisabeth Riffiod-Diaw, Interview with the author, 2016.

28 "Diaw à La Conquête d'Atlanta," *L'Équipe*, October 28, 2003.

29 Diaw, Interview with the author.

30 "Diaw à La Conquête d'Atlanta."

31 Christophe Lucet, "La Gazelle de Phoenix," *Sud Ouest*, September 3, 2006.

32 Lucet.

33 "Diaw à La Conquête d'Atlanta."

34 Lucet.

35 "Boris Diaw Est Désormais Solidement Installé dans le Cinq de Depart des Atlanta Hawks," *L'Équipe*, December 11, 2003.

36 "Diaw à La Conquête d'Atlanta."

37 Robbins, "Thanks for Everything, Mom (the Jumper, Too)."

38 Jean-Julien Ezvan, "Boris Diaw, Si Près Des Étoiles," *Le Figaro*, September 26, 2005.

39 NBA, "Stats: Boris Diaw," NBA, n.d., https://www.nba.com/stats/player/2564/career/.

40 Robbins, "Thanks for Everything, Mom (the Jumper, Too)."

41 Pierre-Yves Croix, "Boris Joue les Boss," *La Nouvelle République Dimanche*, November 13, 2011, sec. S.

42 Christian Seguin, "Le Retour du Fils Prodigue," *Sud Ouest*, November 27, 2011.

43 Yann Ohnona, "NBA: 'Le basket français lui doit tant' Déclarent Vincent Collet et Boris Diaw à propos de Gregg Popovich," *L'Équipe*, March 12, 2022, https://www.lequipe.fr/Basket/Article/Nba-le-basket-francais-lui-doit-tant-declarent-vincent-collet-et-boris-diaw-a-propos-de-gregg-popovich/1321720.

44 Rodriguez.

45 Marc Stein, "Boris Diaw's Unlikely Arch of Triumph," ESPN.Com, June 15, 2014, https://www.espn.com/nba/playoffs/2014/story/_/id/11084748/boris-diaw-dishes-san-antonio-spurs.

46 Ohnona, "NBA."

47 Ohnona, "NBA."

48 Ohnona, "NBA."

49 Stein.

50 Yann Ohnona, "Diaw Les a Convertis," *L'Equipe*, June 8, 2014.

51 Jeremy Woo, "Boris Diaw Earns 'teatime' Nickname, Casually Scores 20 vs. Rockets," *Sports Illustrated*, January 2, 2016, https://www.si.com/nba/2016/01/03/san-antonio-spurs-boris-diaw-lamarcus-aldridge-tea-time-highlights.

52 James Herbert, "Bill Walton on Boris Diaw: 'His Game Flows like Liszt on the Piano,'" CBSSports.Com, November 13, 2014, https://www.cbssports.com/nba/news/bill-walton-on-boris-diaw-his-game-flows-like-liszt-on-the-piano/.

53 Wong, "Boris Diaw, the Frenchiest Dude in the NBA, Is Down to Go to Mars."

54 Pierre Francoual, "The Boris Diaw Situation, Explained," Courtside Diaries (blog), September 21, 2017, http://www.courtsidediaries.com/the-boris-diaw-situation-explained/.

55 Kareem Copeland, "Lean on Me: International NBA Players Supporting Each Other," The Associated Press, February 21, 2017, https://apnews.com/article/dd7477c04e6f46679810a8cb31747491.

56 Gina Mizell, "Young Frenchie: Elie Okobo's Orientation Includes Lessons from Childhood Idol Tony Parker," *The Athletic*, January 19, 2019, https://theathletic.com/775900/2019/01/19/young-frenchie-elie-okobos-orientation-includes-lessons-from-childhood-idol-tony-parker/.

57 Sean Gale, "The French Connection: Boris Diaw & Elie Okobo Catch Up with Suns Fans on Valley Chatz, Brought to You by Firstbank, This Sunday," Phoenix Suns, May 8, 2020, https://www.nba.com/suns/french-connection-boris-diaw-elie-okobo-catch-suns-fans-valley-chatz-brought-you-firstbank-sunday.

58 Haboob, "Diaw Razzes Okobo on French Pickup Game, Drake Music Video Appearance," Arizona Sports 98.7FM (blog), May 10, 2020, https://arizonasports.com/story/2299220/boris-diaw-razzes-elie-okobo-drake-music-video/.

59 "Draymond Green: 'Studying Boris Diaw's Game Was Very Special to Me,'" basketnews.com, accessed June 15, 2022, https://basketnews.com/news-173469-draymond-green-studying-boris-diaws-game-was-very-special-to-me.html.

60 Willy Le Devin, "Boris Diaw. Panier, Piano," *Libération*, October 7, 2013.

61 Seguin.

62 "Boris Diaw and SEED Project to Launch Girls Academy in Senegal," FIBA.basketball, February 3, 2015, https://www.fiba.basketball/news/boris-diaw-and-seed-project-to-launch-girls-academy-in-senegal.

63 Jeff Garcia, "Ex-Spur Boris Diaw Receives 2018 Basketball's Human Spirit Award," WOAI, July 19, 2018, https://news4sanantonio.com/sports/ex-spur-boris-diaw-receives-2018-basketballs-human-spirit-award.

64 "Final Standings of the FIBA U16 African Championship 2017," FIBA.basketball, n.d., https://www.fiba.basketball/africa/u16/2017/groups.

65 "Final Standings of the FIBA U19 Basketball World Cup 2019," FIBA.basketball, accessed August 15, 2022, https://www.fiba.basketball/world/u19/2019/groups.

66 "Diaw Shares Valuable Advice on the Progress of Basketball in Africa," FIBA.basketball, January 29, 2020, https://www.fiba.basketball/news/diaw-shares-valuable-advice-on-the-progress-of-basketball-in-africa.

67 Crawford Palmer, Interview with the author, interview by Lindsay Sarah Krasnoff, December 8, 2021.

68 "Forces Françaises en Côte-d'Ivoire: Une Semaine d'immersion Pour le Champion NBA Boris Diaw," *Connection Ivoirienne* (blog), February 14, 2020, https://www.connectionivoirienne.net/2020/02/14/forces-francaises-en-cote-divoire-une-semaine-dimmersion-pour-le-champion-nba-boris-diaw/.

8

Transatlantic Champion Sandrine Gruda

The 2001 WNBA Championship was one for the books. Contested by the Los Angeles Sparkles (today, the Sparks) and the Charlotte Sting, both debutants to the WNBA Finals, the West Coast city swept its East Coast competitor with two straight wins, 75–66 (Aug. 30) and 82–54 (Sept. 1). The two-game series proved that the fledgling league provided space for more than one team to dominate. Founded in the aftermath of the Atlanta-hosted Summer Games, the W, as the league is colloquially known, played its first season in 1997. But its first four Finals were dominated by the Houston Comets, and thus raised the question of how competitive other teams could be.

Los Angles held the answer that summer. Its star Lisa Leslie was the W's first-ever player to win regular season, All-Star, and Finals Most Valuable Player (MVP) accolades, and in the two-game sweep led in playoff scoring, averaging 22.3 points per game, and rebounding, 12.3 per game. A University of Southern California standout, Leslie crafted an elite Hall of Fame career during her twelve seasons in the WNBA, one of its early stars and founding ambassadors. She was also part of the US team that snagged the 1996 gold medal at the Atlanta Olympic Games, a feat she repeated three more times with Team USA. The ambidextrous Compton, California native approached her game with the mentality of "somebody's got to be the best, so why not me?" and reset expectations about female basketballers.[1]

This competitor's mentality drew a fourteen-year-old budding *basketteuse* an ocean away to Leslie as her inspiration. Sandrine

Gruda had just arrived on the French mainland to embark upon her dream of being a professional player when her hoops idol won it all with Los Angeles. Little did this young woman from Martinique dream that one day, she, too, would win a WNBA Championship with the same team and befriend the American star. In the process, Gruda became part of the W's global evolution and made history in her own right thanks to hard work and the informal cultural, technical, and knowledge exchanges facilitated by basketball diplomacy.

Growing Up Gruda

Gruda was born June 25, 1987, in Cannes, where her father played professionally, but the family soon moved back to Martinique. Her father inherited a tract of farmland, which he worked, and also served as mayor of Fort-de-France but maintained a place in the game as a coach.[2] The island, long at the center of transatlantic crosswinds, was a blend of cultural influences: French, American, and Creole cultures. As Gruda explained, "for me, as a French island, it is French culture, it is Caribbean culture, and American influence."[3]

There was also a blend of sports culture, too. Martinique's population historically used sport and physical education to assimilate into an ideal of citizenship that dates to the colonial era of the late nineteenth century. The island's colored middle class drove this desire to assimilate, and education in all of its different forms, including sportive, was a means to do so.[4] Basketball was part of this equation.

As a kid, Gruda tried several sports, from track and field and gymnastics to dance and archery, but nothing compared to her passion for basketball.[5] Certainly, her choice was influenced in part by her proximity to the game. Her father, Ulysse, played in the *métropole* in the 1970s and 1980s. He was also a former French international who played seven games *en bleu* in 1980 alongside two of the Nationale Masculine 1 (N1) "shot kings" of the 1970s, Bill Cain and Jacques Cachemire, and rising star Hervé Dubuisson.

Basketball was in Gruda's DNA but the passion she brought to the game was entirely her own making. As a six-year-old, she began playing organized team basketball and rapidly progressed; she was eventually recruited into the island's *pôle espoir* basketball section, located at Trinité on Martinique's northeastern shores.[6] But Gruda also played across the island in Forte de France with Golden Lion Basketball, one of the elite Antillean clubs, where she first met former French international Saint Ange Vebobe. As a young teenager, Gruda's height was something she was painfully self-conscious about as people made fun of her appearance.[7] Basketball was a saving grace.

Yet, as a kid, she didn't have any French basketball role models. Instead, it was Leslie that sparked Gruda's interest. "I saw the way she shined in the WNBA," the Frenchwoman recalled. Playing in the US professional women's league thus drove her childhood ambitions. "I first dreamed of the WNBA before dreaming of the French national team because Lisa Leslie was in it," she confided. "When I went to France, I naturally integrated into the French national team. I became a professional, but I only had one idea in my head: to be a WNBA player."

Hungry for the Dream

Fourteen-year-old Gruda left sunny Martinique for the colder climes but better basketball opportunities of the *métropole*, driven by her objective of becoming a professional player.[8] For the 2001–2 academic year, she lived, studied, and trained with the Pôle France cadette at the Regional Physical Education and Sports Center (CREPS) at Toulouse in the southwest.[9]

The homesickness was real because the climate, culture, and environment was entirely unlike anything she previously experienced. "It was very different to leave Martinique for France," she said of the many ways she was forced to adapt, which also included food and mores/way of life. Moreover, the language was not quite the same, either; at home, French and Creole were spoken but, on the mainland, one spoke French and *verlan* (slang). Gruda was willing to sacrifice and adapt in her quest to become a professional player, but it wasn't easy.[10] She became depressed and desperately wanted to return home. Her grandmother, however, convinced her to remain and finish what she began.[11]

Gruda was scouted by the head of the Federal Basketball Center (CFBB) girls' section during one of her matches playing with the

GuyMarGua girls' selection, the best girls from French Guiana, Martinique, and Guadeloupe, who was impressed by the teen's abilities and drive.[12] That's how Gruda was recruited by, passed entrance tryouts for, and matriculated at INSEP, the CFBB's home at the famed sports school, in September 2003.

On campus in Paris's Bois de Vincennes, Gruda and thirteen other girls lived, trained, studied, and ate together with some of the country's other top young sports talent. Minors lived in one building, those of legal age in another as the two were not allowed to live together. But they all attended academic classes in the same school buildings on campus, shared the same library, study spaces, canteen, and training facilities.

Congregating some of the best young female basketball players together provided unparalleled athletic development opportunities, a distinct advantage for Gruda. "Among the girls, the level was very good, very high, thus you could easily confront the best players and thus elevate your level of game," she said. Moreover, the constant challenge made her, and her teammates, better players. "If you do not play [someone who is better], then you get in a comfort zone and you don't progress as rapidly." That first year, Gruda and her teammates finished third in the fourteen-team Nationale Féminine 1, which at the time was France's second basketball division (today it is known as the Ligue Féminine 2).[13]

INSEP provided a good balance and setup for Gruda. "It was very good conditions to allow me to grow," she said. There weren't many other options available for girls at the time. Unlike the men's side, which since the mid-1980s mandated that all professional teams in the top division run and maintain accredited youth academies, there were far fewer academies for girls. The main option was the CFBB, Gruda explained. And that made all the difference in terms of the level of play the INSEP girls' team engaged in. "The level of play you compete against on the weekend is elevated," one rung below the country's top professional league.

Unlike some of her classmates, Gruda didn't head into Paris during her limited free time for shopping or to walk around. Instead, she remained on campus and worked on her game. "I was really focused, concentrated on my objective," she later recalled. The occasional free weekend was spent with family, but aside from basketball, Gruda didn't have many other hobbies. By her second year, she had just one objective: to join one of the country's best teams. "I worked more than the others, I worked even on Sundays, thus I rarely went out," she said.

It was a work ethic reinforced by living, studying, and training at the country's Olympic training ground, an ethos perpetuated each time elite athletes visited for pre-competition preparations or to inspire the younger generations. Younger generations like Gruda. To jumpstart the school year, that September (2003), one of INSEP's most famous alumni returned to campus with his NBA Championship-winning teammates to encourage and spark the next generation. Tony Parker and the San Antonio Spurs, who were in Paris to play a pre-season match against the Memphis Grizzlies, detoured to the hallowed sports school. Then INSEP director Lucien Legrand confided to *FIBA Assist Magazine* that the special visit "makes people realize that [Parker] worked really hard here to get there, just like Boris Diaw. . .they are competitors who didn't balk at the task ahead."[14]

In fall 2005, Gruda left INSEP and signed with Valenciennes, seven years after the creation of the Ligue Féminine de Basket (LFB), the country's top women's league. Founded in 1998 to regularize the elite division of women's basketball, the LFB paved the way for professionalization.[15] When Gruda debuted for Valenciennes that October, she competed for the first time against a WNBA player, for she faced off against Mourenx's US player, Tamika Whitmore, a Memphis University stand-out who clocked several seasons with the New York Liberty and the Los Angeles Sparks before that 2005 match in Paris' Coubertin arena.[16]

Gruda played two seasons with Valenciennes, and in September 2007 signed with Russian club Ekaterinburg, where for nearly a decade she fine-tuned her game, won eight Russian championship titles, and two EuroLeague titles (2013, 2016). There was a lot of informal sports diplomacy in Russia, for the team and league featured international players and coaches, including Americans who played during the W's off-season to earn a livelihood. Many of her teammates were American, and Gruda became friendly with several of them. Her time with Ekaterinburg also provided the chance to work on her English, a language she spoke poorly when she first arrived but had mastered within just a few months.[17] Thus the sorts of cultural, technical, and knowledge exchange engaged with and by her teammates helped prime Gruda for her eventual US dream.

French in the WNBA

It was a dream Gruda finally realized on May 27, 2008, when she debuted with the Connecticut Sun. Selected thirteenth in the 2007 WNBA Draft, Gruda played nearly fourteen minutes and notched two points although the Sun lost 46–75 to the Indiana Fever.[18] "For me, the United States, it is the American dream," she said of her arrival State-side. But at twenty-years-old, she didn't have a driver's license, which is so often the key to freedom of movement in the United States. Thus, her first year living her American dream was spent studying to pass her driver's exam. Fortunately, her teammates helped her adapt, explaining the culture, some of the American mannerisms, and showing her around town.

Gruda also was introduced to the American style of practicing basketball, which necessitated polishing up her English. "When your back is against the wall, when you don't have the choice, you learn very quickly," she recalled.

Beyond basketball and the basics of life in the northeast, Gruda also learned how Americans viewed her homeland. "France is respected in the United States and thus so is French culture," she said. But she pointed out that the French culture known in the United States was that of the aristocrats.

> That's how the French are perceived in the USA, as I am such a respectful person, when you saw me functioning, immediately, it was Sandrine, the delicate, the aristocrat. They didn't ask specific questions about the culture. . .they were very curious to know what Martinique was like. I think the Caribbean, with its turquoise waters, instills a lot of dreams.

This perception wasn't entirely the fault of Americans. Gruda pointed out that the absence of an ingrained sports culture in France—or respect for sporting cultures—was part of the problem. Traditionally, culture was thought to be about the arts, about literature, about museums so that was associated as being its "cultural" export. Sport doesn't have a primary place within this context, she noted, thanks to political biases. Yet, she noted the inherent irony,

> We are the country that does a lot for basketball, but at the same time that has failed to ensure that sport is really part of the

culture, because sport is not necessarily part of French culture...we do a lot for basketball with Quai 54, the only street basketball competition in Europe, [sponsored by] Jordan. We have everything we need for sport or even basketball to become the Top 3 sports in France, but French culture does not allow it.

Gruda did not experience any discrimination in the United States based on her ethnicity, at least that she was aware of. But she admitted that many Black Americans didn't know that Black French people existed. "Thus, I think they didn't think that I could be French," she said. Her mere presence on the team, and explanations of how Martinique was French, provided educative lessons for her US teammates and served as informal acts of sports diplomacy.

Gruda returned to Connecticut in July 2009, albeit a bit tardy thanks to her work with the national team (with whom she won the European title). Although Sun coach Mike Thibault received criticism for holding a roster spot for her, it was a decision he did not think twice about. "[Gruda] is one of the best young centers in the world," he told the Associated Press. "We weren't waiting for our ninth man."[19] Thibault's decision was vindicated during the European champion's first match back with the Sun, in which she scored twenty-three points, at that point, her WNBA career high.[20]

As Sun blogger Jim Fuller observed, the Frenchwoman was far more confident during her sophomore season. "Not only is Gruda further along as a player than she was a year ago but watching an interview (in English) of Gruda after the EuroBasket semifinals, I barely recognized Gruda's confident, easy-going persona," he wrote. "It was a stark contrast to the shy, reserved way she carried herself around the media with the Sun."[21] Part of Gruda's progress was credited to the work of US coach Marianne Stanley, an assistant coach with Ekaterinburg.[22] It was progress fully displayed and acknowledged throughout the W, too. Gruda was the WNBA Eastern Conference Player of the Week for the week of August 17–23, 2009, the first in her North American career. She led the team in rebounding (6.3) and was second in scoring (13.5 points) that season.

The 2009 and 2010 FIBA Player of the Year again returned to the W, but her third season did not dazzle in the same way. She averaged fewer minutes, but on July 14, 2010, she helped lead the

Sun to victory over the Indiana Fever 77–68, which kept Connecticut's playoff hopes alive. The constant grind of effectively playing year-round was not easy, and Gruda sat out the 2011, 2012, and 2013 WNBA seasons to focus on national team obligations; she helped France to a silver medal at the London Summer Games, and a silver (2013) and bronze (2011) at EuroBasket.

In March 2014, Gruda was traded to the Los Angeles Sparks, the squad with whom her basketball idol Lisa Leslie won two championship titles. The city was far larger than those she played in previously. But one that Gruda found agreeable. "The people like sport, they respect basketball. To say that one is a professional player impresses because they measure the work behind it," she told *Sud Ouest*.[23] In a town of celebrities, Gruda initially wanted to take her photo with actors whose shows she watched, an idea rapidly abandoned as the novelty of living in the land of celebrities wore off.[24]

Her role with the Sparks was very different than with the Sun or her other teams in Europe. The team already had a richness of talented players, but for Gruda, the attraction of Los Angles was that they were playing for a championship title—and had a real shot at it.[25] That season, LA lost the conference semifinals, but the taste of being so close to the W's finals tantalized.

After the season ended, the French and US national teams played a friendly exhibition match that September in Paris. Gruda helped France top the United States 76–72, with twenty-six points and fifteen rebounds. It was the first time that Team USA lost since 2011. The Americans, to their credit, knew not to underestimate France. As US Coach Geno Auriemma told the Associated Press,

> It's not easy to beat a really good team on their home floor if you don't shoot the ball well. . .when we got into a little bit of a lull, France and Sandrine (Gruda) especially, they just made shots. They deserved to win tonight. No question about that.[26]

Gruda sat out the 2015 WNBA season in order to prepare for and play in that summer's EuroBasket tournament, but 2016 was a whirlwind that realized many objectives. She began the year with Ekaterinburg and claimed the national Russian title, then rejoined Les Bleues for their fourth-place Olympic campaign in Brazil. Following the Games, Gruda spent a few days at home in Martinique then flew to Los Angeles to rejoin the Sparks.

Her 2016 W season, albeit truncated, proved the realization of a dream and conferred a new lesson. When the Sparks tipped off their WNBA Finals series against the Minnesota Lynx, Gruda made history as the second Frenchwoman ever to contest the feat.[27] On Thursday October 20, 2016, the Sparks fought off the Minnesota Lynx in a nail-biting Game 5 77–76 to claim the champion's crown (Sparks won the series 3–2). Although Los Angeles led as the game entered its last three minutes 71–63, Minnesota dug deep to tie the score at 73–73. The Sparks hung tight for the win thanks to a Candice Parker basket with three seconds left. It was LA's third title in its history, and first since 2002; it was also a testament to the franchise's turnaround under Magic Johnson, who became the team owner in 2014.

Gruda didn't have a standout game or playoff series against the Lynx but seemed unphased.[28] "I wasn't used like I would be in Europe or with the French team," she told Agence France Presse. "That isn't something that I control, it's a coach's choice, and I respect their choice, I accept the positive, and the positive is the title."[29]

But the woman known as "The Drine Machine" was beyond thrilled. "It is everyone's dream, of any American, to win this title," she said.

> The fact that I, a European, a French, won it, it was "wow!" It was just beautiful. Then, in the conditions in which I won it, for me, it was unique. I am a major player in almost all the teams where I go. I am a leading player. And in that group, I was not a leading player. I had to adapt and find a way to be able to contribute, to help the group without necessarily being able to give minutes of play, because I did not control my playing time, I hardly played and yet, it was one of the best experiences of my life.

Instead, she was happy to play her role on the bench, serving akin to a mini-coach by sharing what she noticed on court. It was an entirely different role and experience, but an instructive one. "I discover[ed] that I have a faculty of analysis, I can help someone in the moment. And I didn't know that before," she reflected. "I learned a lot, I discovered myself at that time, so for me, it's wonderful. I was really happy for this title, without ulterior motive, without feeling of frustration."

The Sports Diplomacy Connection/ Evolving the Game

Gruda was long known for her mental tenacity and leadership, the ability to step up and take control at clutch moments. "She has this capacity to be decisive in the moments that count," Isabelle Fijalkowski told *Basket Le Mag* of Les Bleues' all-time highest scorer, an accomplishment Gruda attained on June 5, 2021, when her thirteen points against Sweden helped France to a 71–51 victory.[30]

In many ways, Gruda was a good fit in the WNBA, for the American mentality she found in the league corresponded perfectly with her own outlook and desire to work to attain her objectives. "I am a very ambitious woman," she noted. She's also very optimistic, focused on the positive aspects, something she found far more commonplace in the United States and her fellow colleagues in the WNBA. "In the United States, everyone dreams of greatness, and me, I've always been like that, [that mentality] suited me." She thus felt quite at home in the United States.

It was an illuminating realization and thanks to her time in the WNBA, helped in other ways. First, it reinforced her mentality and outlook towards realizing her objectives. "That is the first thing," she said of the experience. "It reinforced my idea that at some point, in order to succeed, you have to be ambitious, you have to think positive. Then work. I had a strong taste for work and I work a lot." It was an affirmation that she took with her back to Europe. Moreover, it reinforced that she was not abnormal in this sports work outlook and ethic. As she explained,

> When I was young in France, I was seen as a UFO, an extraterrestrial whereas when I arrived in the United States, it was normal, because you can't learn something if you don't practice more. . .So, that made me feel even better. It somehow validated my way of thinking and approaching my practice of basketball.

Her game also benefitted from the technical exchanges incubated by the W. Among them were tips and tricks that helped her become a better player. "The positioning of elbows, arms, body, things like that, to be able to negotiate my one-on-one better," she explained. Moreover, playing with some of the world's best players in its elite championship provided the ability to grow, just as her time at INSEP with some of France's best young female players did.

For Valérie Garnier, who coached Gruda on the national team from 2013 to 2021, the Martiniquais is the example of a true athlete. "One can see the difference when she isn't there like in the last Euro," Garnier told *Le Télégramme* in 2018. "She evolved with the greatest players and is now one of the leaders [of the national team] with Endy (Myem) et Diandra (Tchatchouang)," the coach underlined.[31]

The WNBA gave French basketball players like Gruda a chance to polish their know-how and knowledge by playing professionally among the world's best. But they also took away a better understanding of teamwork, of how together as a team they can win.

> The fact that the French players are going to the WNBA, they will be more experienced. We can think that they are stronger. When they return to France, to the French team or to their French club, they will inevitably bring more to their team and therefore raise the level of the team.

For Gruda, being an ambassador or sports diplomat of sorts has a variety of different levels, a more nuanced understanding. She noted the special role that she holds as one of her country's elite athletes. "You have a reputation which makes you immediately an ambassador," she said. She didn't feel like she was an informal ambassador for France when she first entered the WNBA as she was so young, just twenty years old. But she accepted that playing professionally abroad for nearly her entire career provided another layer for consideration. "When you are an expatriate, you are immediately a representative, an ambassador of your country" she said. "It's like that. As a result, I was [an informal ambassador] without necessarily wanting it."

But she very much identifies as being a diplomat and elder stateswoman communicating, representing, and negotiating betwixt and between the different generations on her teams. After seventeen years playing at the game's elite level, it's a role that she's naturally suited for, whether it's with Les Bleues or her professional clubs. As

FIGURE 8.1 *Sandrine Gruda, 2016 WNBA Champion. Credit: Getty Images.*

she explained, "I have seen many things in the countries I have visited. Basketball was appreciated, was welcomed by the public. I tried to give to the France team, because I don't play in France." As this book went to press, Gruda continued to dominate courts and began to leave her mark in other ways, by handing down some of her lessons learned to younger teammates on the national team. "I am transmitting my knowledge, my counsel," she said. "I also tried to always be able to put the player forward with her needs...I always try to get the maximum, to be able to give the maximum also to the players."

It is this transmission of *savoir-faire*, in addition to her on-court feats, that Gruda is known for. In many ways, her WNBA experience taught her how to do so. "[Winning the championship in 2016] allows me to talk to anyone, because I lived it. I've been through this," she explained. And younger teammates are receptive. Iliana Rupert, speaking upon her 2021 WNBA draft selection by the Las Vegas Aces, noted the ways Gruda inspired and transmitted the knowledge accrued during her career. "It's been a longtime since there was a Frenchwoman who could be drafted this high, so it's exhilarating," Rupert told *Le Maine Libre* in 2021.[32] For the then-nineteen-year-old, who grew up on the NBA then followed the WNBA's Breanna Stewart, Gruda served as a reference point. "[S]he succeeded in doing it all for six years and she won a WNBA title in 2016, that makes you envious!" Ruppert said. "That shows that it's possible to have such a dense career."[33] The young player, who herself trained at INSEP from 2015 to 2018, won the 2022 WNBA Championship with the Aces, becoming the second Frenchwoman to attain the feat.

Tony Parker, speaking as president of ASVEL, noted the valuable role and impact that Gruda continues to play upon signing the thirty-five-year-old to a three-year contact in June 2022. "She has become over the years a player emblematic of the French team. It's a model of work and determination. She has won it all but is always thirsty for victories and titles. Her return to Lyon will permit the group to gain in experience and leadership."[34] Gruda's story illustrates how French players helped broaden and diversify the WNBA, and how her US experiences enriched her game. A product of France's youth development system, a French response to the game's globalization, Gruda's career helped build the basketball empire's soft power reserves through the different types of sports diplomacy she engaged in on- and off-court.

Notes

1 Naya Samuel, "Lisa Leslie Is Never Scared," *Sports Illustrated*, October 28, 2021, https://www.si.com/wnba/2021/10/28/lisa-leslie-los-angeles-sparks-100-influential-black-women-in-sports.

2 Yann Casseville, "Moi, Je. . .Sandrine Gruda," *Basket Le Mag*, April 2020.

3 All Sandrine Gruda quotes this chapter, unless specified, from Sandrine Gruda, Interview with the author, September 30, 2021.

4 Jacques Dumont, *Sport et Formation de La Jeunesse à La Martinique: Le Temps des Pionniers (Fin XIXe Siècle-Années 1960)* (L'Harmattan, 2006), 14.

5 "2005–2006—Les débuts professionnels de Sandrine Gruda," *Basket Retro* (blog), December 16, 2020, https://basket-retro.com/2020/12/16/2005-2006-les-debuts-professionnels-de-sandrine-gruda/.

6 The *Pôle Espoir* was where some of the region's most promising youth players trained under the supervision of French Basketball Federation-credentialed officials. For more on the system, see Chapter 12.

7 *Women in Basketball | Sandrine Gruda Portrait*, 2022, https://www.youtube.com/watch?v=Qs7fvQ28yIk.

8 Yann Casseville, "Sandrine Gruda: Parcours d'excellence," *Basket Le Mag*, June 2021, 13.

9 "2005–2006—Les Débuts Professionnels de Sandrine Gruda."

10 Gruda, Interview with the author.

11 *Women in Basketball | Sandrine Gruda Portrait*.

12 "2005–2006—Les Débuts Professionnels de Sandrine Gruda."

13 FFBB, "Media Guide: Pole France Basketball Yvan Mainini 2020–2021" (FFBB, 2020), 42.

14 Alexandre Carlier, "INSEP: The School of French Champions," *FIBA Assist Magazine*, 2005, 12–13.

15 Four years later, under the presidency of Jean-Pierre Siutat, the LFB expanded from eleven to twelve teams; for the 2005–6 season, the field expanded to fourteen sides. "2005–2006—Les Débuts Professionnels de Sandrine Gruda."

16 "2005–2006—Les Débuts Professionnels de Sandrine Gruda."

17 Gruda, Interview with the author.

18 WNBA, "Sandrine Gruda Official WNBA Stats," WNBA Stats, accessed August 25, 2022, https://stats.wnba.com/player/201058/boxscores-traditional/?Season=2009&SeasonType=Regular%20Season.

19 "Gruda, Phillips Help Sun to Overtime Win," Associated Press, July 6, 2009.

20 "Gruda, Phillips Help Sun to Overtime Win,"

21 Jim Fuller, "Gruda Joins Sun," *Elm City to Eagleville* (blog), July 4, 2009.

22 Fuller.

23 Cédric Soca, "Le Rêve Américain de Dumerc et Gruda," *Sud Ouest*, September 9, 2014, sec. Sports.

24 Soca.

25 Casseville.

26 "France Shocks US Women 76–72 in Exhibition Game," Associated Press, September 21, 2014.

27 The first was Edwige Lawson whose San Antonio team lost to the Detroit Shock in 2008 (they were swept, 3–0).

28 "Sandrine Gruda, Première Française Championne WNBA," *LeFigaro. Fr*, October 21, 2016.

29 "France: Sandrine Gruda, Intérieure Tournée Vers l'extérieur," AFP, October 25, 2016.

30 Casseville, 13; "Sandrine Gruda Meilleure Marqueuse de l'Histoire" (FFBB, June 5, 2021).

31 Luc Besson, "Gruda. L'ADN de La Gagne," *Le Télégramme*, February 14, 2018.

32 Alexis de Azevedo, "Le Rêve Américain d'Iliana Rupert," *Le Maine Libre*, June 19, 21AD, sec. Sport 72.

33 Azevedo.

34 Christophe Remise, "Basket: Gruda, Une Légende à ASVEL," *Le Figaro.Fr*, June 17, 2022.

9

"We Did It!" Nicolas Batum and Marine Johannès

Boris Diaw and the Phoenix Suns contested the April 2008 Western Conference Playoffs against Tony Parker and the San Antonio Spurs, a gritty series that demonstrated international players' value-add. Parker shone in the third match, notching forty-one points in another San Antonio win, but Diaw rallied his team for a comeback Game Four victory on April 27 105–86, with twenty points, ten rebounds, and eight assists. Although the Spurs wrapped up the series in five matches, it inspired kids half a world away.

One of those kids was nineteen-year-old Nicolas Batum, a professional player in Le Mans who hoped to follow in Diaw and Parker's footsteps in that June's NBA Draft. The Normandy native eagerly awaited his shot in the spotlight but as the big day neared, his odds were thrown to the wind. Physical tests following a workout with the Toronto Raptors uncovered a potential heart ailment; when compounded with his father's premature death, NBA teams were overly cautious to take on the young player. Cleared by medical teams, Batum was drafted in the first round by the Houston Rockets, then rapidly traded to the Portland Trail Blazers, a small city like Le Mans.

Another kid who followed Parker's 2008 odyssey was Marine Johannès, a thirteen-year-old from Batum's hometown, Lisieux. The aspiring basketballer, part of USO Mondeville's youth academy, already demonstrated promise and early pizzazz on court. But due to the lack of mediatization of the WNBA in France at the time, she followed the exploits of NBA players, including fellow French artists like Parker and, eventually, Batum.

The player who eventually would become like a "basketball big brother" to Johannès began his NBA career with a bang. He cracked Portland's starting lineup in early November 2008, four games into his rookie season.[1] It helped that during his first games Batum was able to visit and interact with Parker when the Spurs visited Portland on October 31, then Diaw when the Blazers traveled to Phoenix for a game the next night.[2]

In many ways since those heady early days of the 2008–9 season, Batum has replicated the advice he received as a rookie from fellow Frenchmen and passed along the knowledge to others. He's thus served as a bridge between generations of French players in the NBA and Les Bleus. He's helped popularize the league, connected the NBA to viewers and consumers in France and Africa, but also played an important role helping Johannès towards the WNBA.

These two players from Lisieux chased their hoops dreams to play in the NBA and WNBA, helping to broaden and diversify the leagues. Both are products of France's youth academy system and while the men's and women's systems are separate, players interact with and thus inform and enrich each other. Importantly, their stories illuminate the importance of the basketball empire's knowledge exchange, the ways that the NBA and WNBA's global successes are increasingly finessed by how players hand down lessons learned from one cohort to the next, and how this in turn informs French basketball. As a result, players like Batum and Johannès contribute to building cultural cachet as their abilities, durability, and artistry are recognized in the United States and beyond.

Growing Up Batum

Batum was born with a basketball in his hands, but arguably was molded by the numerous sports diplomacy influences that surrounded and shaped him growing up. The oldest child of Richard and Sylvie Charrière-Batum was born December 14, 1988, in Lisieux, a small Normandy town in the Calvados, better known for its apple brandy than for breeding basketballers. Richard was born in Eseka, near the Cameroonian capital of Yaoundé, but arrived in France as a ten-year-old and was assimilated into the republic's fabric.[3] In 1981, he started to play competative basketball, including the 1987–8 season with Pont L'Évêque, then signed with Proville, a small club in the Nord-Pas-de-Calais. A versatile player able to shoot as well as he intimidated, Richard notched an average fourteen points per game during his last season and helped lift Proville to a fourth-place finish at the end of the 1990–1 season.[4]

Then disaster struck. Richard died on-court of a ruptured aneurysm at the free-throw line during Proville's September 23, 1991, game at Autun. In the stands, his wife was in tears while infant daughter Pauline and two-year-old Nicolas watched in horror as the television cameras descended to record the moment.[5] It was a profound shock.

Life continued and Nicolas became accustomed to his new normal. Growing up, he played football, had a poster of Zinédine Zidane in his bedroom, and was blissfully happy when France won the 1998 FIFA World Cup.[6] Like many young boys, he dreamed of being a footballer, even as he started to pick up basketball. His mother was an influential force in the eventual choice between the two disciplines. "She didn't want to go see my game outside under the rain and get cold," Batum later recalled of the decision to pursue basketball more fully.[7]

Five-year-old Batum started playing organized basketball with nearby Pont-L'Évêque, his father's old team which, since the 1970s, built a reputation for training young players. Once Nicolas began practice in earnest, he was drawn to the game. "It was a natural fit for me," Batum explained. "I think it's the most spectacular game, the most exciting game in the world."[8] He learned and expanded his basketball reference points. He began to watch "NBA Action," a weekly television show that rounded up the top NBA action and fueled his thirst for the game. "That makes us dream," he said of the impact sports broadcasting had. "I wanted to be part of it. I wanted to be a big star like the guys on TV."

The budding basketballer preferred Scottie Pippen for the Chicago legend's ability to complement Michael Jordan on-court and pull out plays to help the team win.[9] As a kid, Batum tried to replicate moves like Jordan's signature one-footed jump shot shooting with his left hand.[10] He later admired French players who forged careers in the NBA, like Mickaël Gelabale, and reinforced his basketball education by reading *5 Majeur*, *Mondial Basket*, and *Basket News*.[11] He also discovered Team France.

In 1999, France hosted the European Basketball Championship, EuroBasket, which drew a new generation of kids to the national team. Batum followed Les Bleus' successes that summer and the following year when they battled the United States for the gold medal in the Sydney Olympics. Batum watched these feats at home on television and realized that he, too, wanted to play for France one day.[12]

Batum continued to improve upon his basketball basics and honed his craft, though he had difficulty being the only mixed-race kid in the area. "I was different, I was the only Black person that people saw, especially at school," he recalled in a 2020 US Embassy France webinar.[13]

> I got to know it very early on and that's what also helped shape me for later, when I was able to face it, especially in basketball while traveling in other countries, and especially before in the United States, because I know that maybe, I had a difference when I got there, even if I could face it I still managed well and I was never touched by it deeply because I always knew how to get over that no matter what.[14]

When Batum began to dominate on-court with his skills, parents complained that he cheated and wanted him taken off of the court. His mother occasionally got into fights with parents in the stands who wanted her son removed from the game.[15]

It helped that Batum met another young player, Camille Eleka, with whom he could relate. Eleka's mother, a Caucasian woman, married his father, a basketball player from the Republic of Congo (Brazzaville), and together they made a home in her native Normandy. Eleka, like most other boys, played football but was drawn to basketball after watching an NBA game featuring Jordan. "When I saw Jordan and the NBA players, I wanted to play basketball," he recalled.[16]

At first, the two played on rival teams, the only boys of color on each side. But that lone fact drew them to each other. "When we met, we were curious [about each other] and began to know each other," Eleka said.[17] He and Batum began to speak and build a friendship that further blossomed when they played together with the Pôle Espoirs at Caen Basket Calvados (CBC) as well as at the regional sport-étude, where they were in the same school class.

In 2001, Batum matriculated in the youth academy at Le Mans-Sarthe Basket Club (MSB) to elevate his game. "I knew I could become somebody because [of] that culture and tradition [at Le Mans]," he said. It was a crucial decision, for the academy's outlook, as well as the personalities in and around it, paved the way for Batum to blossom. One of those was MSB's president Christian Baltzer, the second was the professional team head coach Vincent Collet, and the third, Philippe Desnos.

The Durtal native was synonymous with MSB's youth academy, a young coaching prodigy who trained as a gym teacher. Desnos passed his coaching exams early and embarked on a career split between coaching and playing; he suited up for two games with Le Mans during its championship 1981–2 season and played alongside Bill Cain and Collet. But his true calling was as a coach, organizer, and motivator, which is why in 1989 MSB leadership tasked him with building the club's academy.

The youth formation center at Le Mans is akin to a small basketball-oriented boarding school. Roughly twelve students at a time, aged between fifteen to nineteen years old, live, eat, and study under Desnos' supervision, and attend classes at the local high school located next door. MSB's objective was to help its young students complete their all-around education, scholastic, sportive, and otherwise.[18] "It's not just basketball, basketball, basketball, and then the rest," Desnos said. "We're also noted on our scholastic results and the good education and good behavior of our young people. The reputation of Le Mans is recognized as much by its academic and educational results as by sports results." This reputation of education, academics, and basketball appealed to Batum's mother, who thought that Desnos and the tight-knit MSB community would serve as a good substitute father figure for her young son.[19]

But it meant sacrifice, for Batum didn't live the life of a normal teenager. Between the school year living and training in Le Mans to summertime work with the national teams, there was little time for much else. "You maybe have 10 days to be a kid," Batum told the *Charlotte Observer*.[20] His mother later admitted to *Le Monde* that her son had a difficult time when he first entered the center at Le Mans as he was so young.[21] It was the first time that he was separated from his tight-knit family.

When Batum began his apprenticeship with MSB, he was a tall and gifted player, but very thin and thus a little gangly. He was rapidly christened "Bambi" for his perceived fragility and reserve but impressed with his talent. "We quickly understood that, without doubt, Nicolas was a particular player," Desnos recalled. Despite his reediness, Batum had a powerful shot. As a fourteen- and fifteen-year-old, he demonstrated an evolving basketball intellect, facilitating plays for and helping his teammates on-court. "He lit up the game," said Desnos. It was not obvious in 2002 that MSB had a future NBA player on their hands, but it was clear that they had a different kind of player. Batum grew into his height, developed a longer wingspan and continued to learn his craft. By the third year, Desnos recalled, they knew that Batum was an exceptional player ready for the next step: to go pro. The move put a hard stop on Batum's scholastic studies; he was about to enter his last year of school, just shy of sitting for the *baccalaureate*, but could not train and play with the professional team while remaining in school for eight hours a day.

Thus, at age sixteen, Batum started to play with the professional team under head coach Collet, who took the teenager under his wing.[22] It was the start of a long collaborative relationship, in which Collet helped mold his first "basketball son." He built his young protégé's confidence, a key contribution to Batum's development, as did playing with older, more experienced players, many of them Americans who introduced their youngest teammate to another style of ball. "The American people bring that athletic esthetic of the game, that craziness of the game," Batum recalled of those early years. "That's what I learned from them. Because I practiced every day against Kenny Gregory, that helped me to understand what the NBA game, American basketball, was going to be." It was an example of how informal basketball diplomacy in Le Mans, here the technical exchanges on-court, helped improve Batum's game.

In 2007, Batum initially filed for the NBA draft. It was the first of the "one and done" era in which recruits had to be either nineteen years old or one year removed from high school. The controversial rule was implemented by the league to encourage slightly older, more mature recruits, but forced US teenagers to sign with an NCAA program or go play a year overseas. Opponents argued that it unfairly advantaged elite young European talent like Batum who, given the continent's different school and development systems, often already played professionally by their late teenaged years and thus were not subject to the rule. Although he was a highly anticipated candidate, Batum withdrew his candidacy after counsel from his mother and Collet. Instead, he remained in France to finesse his skills while Collet handed him the keys to the 2007–8 team.[23] "That was big time for me," Batum later told FIBA.[24]

After he was drafted in 2008, Batum had the chance to live his NBA dream. But he had to prove himself to an American audience that remained skeptical of French players as, with the exception of Parker, they tended not to be the scene-stealing high scoring stars that US audiences and media thought of as markers of excellence. Batum also had to defend his abilities in a new league that played a more antagonistic game than back home. Collet acknowledged that his nineteen-year-old protégé may not have been as physically aggressive as US counterparts but remained confident that his enormous basketball IQ would counteract this weakness.[25]

Batman in the NBA

The transition from Le Mans to Portland, both relatively smaller cities, was a good fit. Once it became clear that he was headed to Oregon, Batum started learning more about his future home. "We prepared for a lot of rain," he recalled as everyone told him it rained a lot. Some parts of the adjustment were more difficult. Batum initially missed the food from home. But one new discovery was a US-style breakfast, replete with eggs and bacon, a change from his more usual cereal, croissant, or *pain au chocolat*.[26]

Overall, however, Batum found it easy to integrate into the local community and he was welcomed with open arms.[27] He understood English because at Le Mans, Collet always spoke in English so that the American players could fully understand him.[28] But at times there was a little language barrier. It helped that Batum was in contact with other French in the NBA, particularly Mickaël Piétrus, who offered advice and suggestions for how to acculturate and succeed in the North American league.[29]

Batum experienced US culture first-hand living and playing in the NBA, but he also engaged in informal sports diplomacy when he explained about his homeland, its culture, and its basketball. Portland fans were naturally curious about their new rookie. "They ask me lots of questions about France," he said of fans and noted how they tried to include a few words in his native tongue.[30]

Teammates and players around the league also asked about France, wanting to know more, especially about Paris, where many of them traveled during the summer.[31] Basketball helped facilitate the transition, and with Portland Batum found an organization that believed in him, just as in Le Mans. That confidence helped.

Batum broke into the Trail Blazers' big five and eventually started seventy-six games during his first season.[32] The team made the playoffs, Portland's first postseason appearance in five years. Over the following several seasons, he notched up an impressive constancy on the court, fully owning his nickname, Batman. He also continued to serve as a bridge between his homeland and the United States, subtly lobbying teammates and other NBA colleagues about the beauty and excitement of France, its geography, and culture, while participating in local Portland-area youth outreach initiatives with francophone and anglophone communities.

During the 2011 NBA lockout, Batum returned home and played with Nancy in ProA. Like other NBA players who flocked to France during this unusual year, it was hoped their presence would help spur greater interest in the game, both from consumers and media as well as potential future players. For the players, their temporary dislocation was another opportunity to let the game shine while also serving as informal ambassadors for the North American league. It was highly likely that in building team chemistry, players like Batum shared some of their US experiences, thus engaging in different types of cultural, technical, and knowledge exchange with teammates in the LNB.

Batum's return to North American courts continued his on-court ebullience. On December 16, 2012, he notched a rare 5x5, when a player tallies at least five in the five key statistics groups: points, rebounds, assists, steals, and blocks. Only seven players before him had accomplished the feat.[33] Batum also became one of the players most frequently on-court, averaging 38.5 minutes per game during the 2012–13 season.[34] Portland took note, and in summer 2012 negotiated a $45 million, four-year contract for their Frenchman.

After a draining 2013–14 campaign and a postseason truncated by the Spurs, Batum opted in once again for national team duty at that summer's FIBA World Cup.[35] The tournament was Batum's big breakout for he stepped into a new role as the team's clutch playmaker; he led Les Bleus to the bronze medal and was named to FIBA's All-Tournament team. This led the Charlotte Hornets to sign the twenty-six-year-old in 2015, a fit that held promise for head coach Steve Clifford understood Batum's game as a generalist, a playmaker who worked to provide opportunities for teammates, not the guy who racked up twenty-five points per game. As Batum stressed to the *Charlotte Observer*, "it's not all about numbers. It's also about defense. If you don't play defense, you've got a problem."[36]

That first season with the Hornets was one of Batum's best to date. He averaged 14.9 points, 6.1 rebounds, and 5.8 assists over seventy games, building a reputation as a key league swingman.[37]As Charlotte General Manager Richard Cho noted, Batum enhanced the team with his team-oriented style of play. "He helps our other players play better," he said. "He's such a great teammate and is unselfish. Probably sometimes too unselfish. But that's also what makes him a very good player."[38]

Charlotte was so impressed that they signed their Frenchman to one of the franchise's biggest contracts the following summer, a $120 million five-year deal.[39] The move made Batum one of the highest paid French athletes and was named to Forbes' 2018 World's Highest-Paid Athletes list.[40] As a result, he took care to articulate to French audiences the ins and outs of the supersized NBA contract, a feat perhaps necessary given France's difficult relationship with capitalism, especially within the professional sports realm.

Batman's triumph, however, was fleeting. Although he gained Parker as a teammate in October 2018 when the veteran signed with Charlotte, the first time that the duo played together professionally, things on-court rapidly soured. When James Borrego took over as head coach in 2018, the new team vision didn't leave much room for Batum's style of team play; the focus instead was offensive support for Kemba Walker.[41] Being the highest paid player on Charlotte's roster without being its most prolific scorer rapidly became a liability.

Yet, there were bright spots. Despite the negative fan feedback about being an overpaid has-been, Batum remained professional, a trait his teammates appreciated.[42] Moreover, his time with team owner Michael Jordan proved beneficial in numerous ways. First, Batum left adidas and signed with Jordan Brand, Jordan's namesake NIKE division. As part of the Jumpman empire, Batum helped to translate Jordan's NBA cultural sensibilities, from shoes to fashion, to French audiences. He also had the opportunity for at-length exchanges with the basketball legend, including after a 2019 Jordan Brand seminar in Monaco.[43]

Second, Batum was part of the NBA's first-ever regular season match held in France when he and the Hornets tipped off against the Milwaukee Bucks. The January 2020 week spent in and around the City of Light was one of constant sports diplomacy as Batum showed his teammates around town, including classic tourist sites like the Eiffel Tower, took them to restaurants, and introduced them to French and Parisian basketball. It was a high point for Batum that season: he was the French team captain, a position Les Bleus coach Collet (at the reins since 2009) conferred to his first "basketball son" once longtime captain Diaw retired from national team service on July 2, 2018. As such, he was welcomed like a rock star by the crowds at AccorArena.

When the Los Angeles Clippers signed Batum on December 2, 2020, few expected the six-foot-eight veteran to have much left to give. Except Batman himself, whose career renaissance since then has once again polished his star. His on-court individual performances improved and his polyvalence expanded to focus on defending against centers, something his earlier game wasn't really known for. As a result, he's proved pivotal to the Clippers' fortunes, an integral component of their 2021 and 2022 playoff runs. But his team impact and basketball intelligence has become far more mediatized and acknowledged by the coaching staff. For assistant coach Dan Craig, "he's one of my favorite players I've had a chance to coach."[44] Teammates also appreciate Batum's abilities and qualities. As guard Reggie Jackson noted of the French "glueguy,"

> That's somebody you want to be like, that's somebody you look to, that's somebody who's a great vet, that's somebody who you follow when you have the chance and he'll take you further and further in your career. . .his talent is unmatched.[45]

This team-first attitude created a supportive public that formed a "Batum Battalion." Coined by a Clippers podcast in support of the newly acquired Frenchman's impact on the team, the battalion rapidly went from phrase to fan club as individuals, most of them not French, embraced the team's new "glueguy." In doing so, they

FIGURE 9.1 *Nicolas Batum. Credit: Getty Images.*

learned a bit more about France, its flag and symbols, some of its words such as *magnifique victoire*, and more.[46] Batum was surprised by the acknowledgment but admitted it helped make his welcome to the West Coast even warmer.[47] The team, too, embraced the Batum Battalion, and sold tee-shirts with the phrase emblazoned on the front, and more. When they bought a Paris airport advertisement in support of Batum ahead of the Tokyo Olympic Games signed the Batum Battalion, the Clippers very consciously communicated, negotiated, and represented about the US and its basketball culture to passers-by.[48]

Batum linked his NBA longevity to his ability to adapt and change his game. "[I've] been like four or five different players since," he told the *Los Angeles Times* of his durability. "That's the thing I'm pretty proud of, is I always find a way to change my game to stay."[49] There are likely linkages to this ability and the fact that back home, players are trained to play all positions, not just one post.

As part of the twenty-first-century European influx, Batum helped impact the league. He attributed the rise of French players in the NBA and WNBA to two key components. First, he pointed to the country's youth development structures and how it teaches the technicalities of the game. "I think the way they teach us the game, they make us understand how to play basketball," he said.[50]

But he also pointed to the importance of how players like himself and others inspire the next generation of kids to play and dream of making it to the NBA and WNBA. Each year the country's hoops stars return home to run workshops and basketball camps. "Now, when I go home and I do a camp, there's young kids who say, 'I want to be in the NBA like you,' and they mean it, they really mean it," Batum relayed. Alongside Parker and Diaw, Batum is credited with making it possible for other generations of French players in the NBA.

These knowledge exchanges helped subsequent generations of French players acclimate to and put in performances in the United States, but they've also helped stimulate hoop dreams in the homelands of their parents or grandparents. For Batum, this has come in phases. Despite his father's roots, Batum did not visit family in Cameroon until age thirteen, although he later acknowledged that at that age, it was difficult to fully understand how his African heritage factored in.[51]

But a 2012 return was pivotal. During a four-day stay, he visited kids in a small village outside the capital and met with teenaged girls who, because one or both of their parents were dead, raised their siblings. "I was just shocked," he said, "they couldn't even go to school because they had to work."[52] The experience left an imprint, and he established a foundation to help young mothers and orphans.

It also put into greater perspective his relationship with his father's homeland. One night, his uncles took him to a local bar where villagers congregated to catch his games at 4 a.m. local time to cheer him on. "I couldn't believe it. They were supporting me all this time" he told NBC Sports.[53] "Seeing my roots has done me a lot of good," he told reporters. "Everyone knows I'm French, but I'm lucky to have a second culture."[54]

Subsequently, Batum's understating of his African heritage and his French identity has become more fine-tuned. In 2015, he proudly represented Team Africa for the NBA's Africa Game, the first game played by a professional US sports league on African soil. Three summers later, the 2018 FIFA World Cup win by France and the subsequent anglophone world discussion of the French team being Africa's team provided the opportunity for Batum to be more outspoken. The conversation, sparked by South African-born US-based comedian Trevor Noah, rapidly made its way outside its origins in Noah's "The Daily Show" broadcast to international dimensions. The French Ambassador to the United States at the time, Gérard Araud, was one of the most outspoken voices who took Noah and the American-centric discourse to task in the emphasis that all but one of the French national team were French, born, raised, and trained.

Batum took to Twitter to express the nuances involved and his frustration at those who conflated French and non-French understandings of identity. "Sorry for my language but for all those who're saying 'congrats Africa for the World Cup' go 'check' yourself (I'm too kind I want to say way worse but some kids might read this)," he wrote. He pointed out how he consistently represented, communicated, and negotiated about France in FIBA competition and in the NBA.

> Yes my dad and my last name are from Cameroon but I was born, raise [sic], educated, taught basketball in France. Proud to be FRENCH. I'm playing for the youth in France who want to be like us and make the country proud. And I'm proud of that and proud of our 2018 world champ! Vive la France.[55]

In response to online comments, Batum clarified that he did not forget his cultural heritage or family origins, of which he was proud.[56] He pointed out that his father's family remained in Cameroon, as well as the work his foundation does in country to promote maternal health and early childhood development.[57] In December 2022, he reflected further on the connections between French basketball and its African cousin. "It's huge," he said and noted his family heritage. "I'm proud of it. I know I'm French, I play for the French team, but we never forget my roots and my family on the African side."[58]

In these ways, Batum has engaged in various types of sports diplomacy. As a result, particularly through knowledge exchange, he serves as a bridge, building relationships between different basketball generations in France, the United States, and Africa.

Growing Up Johannès

As Batum's career progressed, he became ever-more vested in helping the next generation of basketballers back home, including fellow Lisieux native Marine Johannès. The player known as the French Steph Curry arrived in the WNBA in 2019, and while she has only played two seasons in the United States, due to the COVID-19 pandemic and national team commitments, she's already tapped into sports diplomacy, inspiring others along the way.

Born January 21, 1995, Johannès grew up playing a variety of sports, but gravitated towards basketball. For Lisieux, a small town of some 6,000 to 7,000 people that bucked the nationwide trend of football domination, basketball was given primacy of place. But eight-year-old Johannès' first introduction to the discipline came thanks to tagging along to one of her sister's basketball practices. "In fact, it was me who was trained," she recalled of that formative experience. She's been a basketball convert ever since and began playing with Pont-l'Évêque.[59] It was the same club where Batum first honed his hoops skills and he had the opportunity to watch her unvarnished talent early on. "She was already crazy on the court," he later recalled of watching the young Johannès at their shared formative club.[60]

Johannès dreamed to one day go to the United States and play basketball. It was an objective sparked by watching and following Tony Parker's career, for the lack of mediatization of the WNBA in France at the time made the league difficult to follow. Instead, she sought out DVDs of NBA games for inspiration, including those of Michael Jordan and Kobe Bryant, although she also adored Jason Williams. As she grew older, her basketball influences transitioned to focus more on Steph Curry.[61]

While Pont L'Évêque helped develop her skills, Johannès understood that realizing her dream required more than once-a-week practices (Wednesdays) and games (Sundays). So, in 2007 she matriculated into the USO Mondeville youth academy in Caen, forty minutes away from her family home. The club, known for developing female players since its academy's 1998 foundation, is where she lived and trained for several years while finishing her studies at the nearby Lycée Victor Hugo. Classes began at 8 a.m. followed by a midday training session, then more school and an evening practice.

Thanks to the academy system, Johannès began to integrate with Mondeville's senior team, which played in the Ligue Féminine de Basket (LFB), the country's top pro league. In 2011, she played her first professional match, notched seven more the following season, and finally played a full season's worth of twenty-six matches in 2013–14. Johannès continued to learn the ropes with Mondeville, then played three seasons with Bourges (2016–19) where she helped the team win the French championship (2018) and three French Cups. In EuroLeague competition with Bourges, she was named Most Entertaining Player and Best Guard (2018–19).[62]

Throughout it all, Johannès kept in touch with Batum, who grew into a type of basketball big brother. He encouraged her at every turn and tried to help her when he could. While they previously discussed possibly playing in the W, when the opportunity arose to play with the New York Liberty, Johannès didn't ask Batum any questions. "She was really excited," he recalled."[63]

French in the WNBA

In July 2019, Johannès became the thirteenth French player to contest the WNBA. Her first season was a bit difficult as she joined the New York Liberty halfway through the season, once her French club season was over. The constant routine, without a rest period, wasn't the easiest and confronts many players who split their time between the W and the professional leagues in Europe.

It helped that the Liberty had an air of familiarity. She knew two of its players: Bria Hartley, a French-American who she played with on Les Bleues, and Nayo Raincock-Ekunwe, who she played with at Bourges. Knowing that two former teammates would be there to ease the transition helped with her decision to make the transatlantic jump. "In a new country, a new league, a new culture, *voilà*, I didn't want to be 'alone,'" she explained. "Each time I had questions, they were there." This knowledge exchange helped pave her way, as did her ongoing conversations with Batum.

It also helped that the Liberty were based in New York, a city Johannès enjoyed. She visited the Statue of Liberty and Times Square, all of the places depicted in films about the United States. When she wasn't too tired from practices and games, Johannès explored the city and its restaurant scene. But she still missed her family, friends, and the food back home.

Johannès quickly discovered how the basketball cultures and games between France and the United States differed. The transition into the W's game was difficult. "It's more physical, and it is much faster," she said. "You have to be ready from the get-go." But there was also the variance in approaches towards playing. "In France, we are cultivated to always think of others," she explained of how in the W she had to try to think more about being herself on the court. As a result, her role with the Liberty was different from back home, or even with the French team, where she admitted she had more on-court responsibilities.

The 2022 season was Johannès' sophomore stint in the W, one that proved how much her game progressed since her rookie US experience. She averaged 10 points, 3.4 assists, and 1.7 rebounds per game, and helped the Liberty to the postseason. Although New York lost to Chicago in the three-game Eastern Conference playoffs, Johannès' performances were impactful and impressed US fans. One blogger noted how her "on-court sorcery" was a key ingredient to the Liberty's success.[64] Another enthused, "though she came off

FIGURE 9.2 *Marine Johannès. Credit: Getty Images.*

the bench, make no mistake, Marine Johannès is a starter in this league. . .[she] scores in flurries that bring energy to the Liberty when needed."[65]

For Batum, "the odds of having two players who end up in the NBA, the WNBA, and also on the French national team is zero." His and Johannès' career trajectories were so rare. "But we did it!"[66]

The two have thrived thanks to the transatlantic influences of their basketball experiences. They've helped build the country's soft power cultural cachet through their different types of sports diplomacy exchanges. But the Batum-Johannès story also illuminates the vital ways that the basketball diplomacy framework, notably its knowledge exchange, strengthened the basketball empire and how the pipeline is enriched from one cohort to the next. For Batum, it's about the next generation. "We inspire the young kids. That's what we want to do, to inspire those young kids so they can do the same stuff after us," he said.[67] Which is why the NBA and WNBA's French accent continued to grow and thrive thanks to two basketballers from Normandy.

Notes

1 Associated Press, "Okur, Boozer Solid as Jazz Beat Blazers to Stay Unbeaten," ESPN.com, November 6, 2008, https://www.espn.com/nba/preview?gameId=281105026.

2 "2008–9 Portland Trail Blazers Schedule and Results," Basketball-Reference.com, accessed December 10, 2020, https://www.basketball-reference.com/teams/POR/2009_games.html.

3 Nicolas Batum [@nicolas88batum], "Mon père est arrivé en France il avait 10 ans. Ce pays l'a adopté, l'a éduqué, l'a aidé à grandir. Je suis né ici d'une mère française blanche, mon père est mort sur un terrain j'avais 2 ans et il voulait que je suive ses pas. Il est camerounais et fier de mon parcours en EDF! https://t.co/Th5tC1qS9F," Tweet, *Twitter*, July 17, 2018, https://twitter.com/nicolas88batum/status/1019341243795542018.

4 "Le 2 juin, Proville rendra hommage à Richard Batum à travers une grande," *Ouest-France*, May 4, 2011, Cambrai MaVille.com edition, https://cambrai.maville.com/actu/actudet_-basket-ball-le-2&160;juin-proville-rendra-hommage-&224;-richard-batum-&224;-travers-une-grande-f&234;te_34536-1785538_actu.Htm.

5   Ian Thomsen, "For Selfless Nicolas Batum, Priorities and Roles Have Changed on and off the Basketball Court | NBA.Com," NBA, January 24, 2017, https://www.nba.com/news/hornets-nicolas-batum-its-about-team-over-stats-and-bigger-picture.

6   Batum later admitted that he nearly cried after Zidane was ejected from the 2006 World Cup final after headbutting Italian defender Marco Materazzi. Matt Calkins, "Basketball Wasn't Always Blazers' Players' Passion," *The Columbian*, March 12, 2012.

7   Lindsay Sarah Krasnoff, "French Basketball, from Cain to Batum," *The New Yorker*, May 15, 2015, https://www.newyorker.com/sports/sporting-scene/french-basketball-from-cain-to-batum.

8   All Nicolas Batum quotes this chapter, unless specified, from Nicolas Batum, Interview with Nicolas Batum, February 4, 2015.

9   Rick Bonnell, "Hornets' Nic Batum 'got Lost a Little Bit.' Will Finding His Way Back Quiet Critics?," *Charlotte Observer*, January 27, 2019.

10 Damien Dole, "Nicolas Batum: 'Golden State a Révolutionné La NBA,'" *Liberation*, June 2, 2016.

11 Ray Richardson, "Timberwolves' Gelabale Has a Fan in French Countryman Batum," TwinCities.Com, February 4, 2013.

12 Batum, Interview with Nicolas Batum, February 4, 2015.

13 Nicolas Batum, Katia Foucade-Hoard, and Bill Cain, Sport à l'épreuve du Racisme? Webinar, US Embassy France, September 9, 2020, https://www.facebook.com/130504556373/videos/1048410902284325.

14 Batum, Foucade-Hoard, and Cain.

15 Batum, Interview with Nicolas Batum, February 4, 2015.

16 Camille Eleka, Interview with the author, April 15, 2015.

17 Eleka.

18 Philippe Desnos, Interview with the author, April 18, 2017.

19 Desnos.

20 Rick Bonnell, "How Hornets Forward Nic Batum Faced His Father's Death and His Own Fear of Dying Young," *Charlotte Observer*, January 21, 2020, https://www.charlotteobserver.com/sports/charlotte-hornets/article239440933.html.

21 Romain Brunet, "Le Basketteur Nicolas Batum, un Leader en Devenir," *Le Monde*, September 19, 2011.

22 Brunet.

23 "Et Bambi Est Devenu Batman...," *L'Est Républicain*, October 14, 2001.

24 "Batum Says Collet Is the Right Coach for France" (FIBA.com, October 27, 2016).

25 Vincent Collet, Interview with the author, September 26, 2016.

26 Batum, Interview with Nicolas Batum, February 4, 2015.

27 Batum.

28 Collet, Interview with the author.

29 "NBA-Nicolas Batum: 'Un Début de Saison Au-Delà de Mes Attentes,'" AFP, January 8, 2009.

30 "NBA-Nicolas Batum."

31 Batum, Interview with Nicolas Batum, February 4, 2015.

32 Thomas Berjoan, *American Dream: L'épopée des Français en NBA* (Solar Editions, 2016), 73.

33 Leandro Fernández, "How Rare Is a 5x5? Portland Trail Blazers Centre Jusuf Nurkic Joins an Exclusive Club with a Performance for the Ages," January 2, 2019, https://ca.nba.com/news/jusuf-nurkic-trail-blazers-5x5-olajuwon-kirilenko-draymond-green-anthony-davis/1pge8q036e6551bp4q9djn8ill.

34 Berjoan, 73.

35 Batum played a career-high 82 regular season matches, plus 11 playoff games. Joe Freeman, "Trail Blazers' Nicolas Batum Will Play for France This Summer, but Vows to Get Plenty of Rest," *The Oregonian*, March 10, 2015.

36 Bonnell.

37 Quinton Pierr-Wash, "Renaissance Man: Inside the Many Worlds of Nicolas Batum," NBA.Com, February 6, 2017.

38 "Pas Qu'une Histoire d'a(r)Gent" (Comsport, February 4, 2017).

39 Bonnell.

40 "The World's Highest-Paid Athletes Earnings 2018 Nicolas Batum," *Forbes*, accessed January 9, 2021, https://www.forbes.com/profile/nicolas-batum/.

41 Bonnell.

42 Bonnell.

43 Le10Sport.com, "NBA : Batum lâche une anecdote sur Michael Jordan," Le10Sport, accessed December 2, 2022, https://le10sport.com/basket/nba/nba-batum-lache-une-anecdote-sur-michael-jordan-611145.

44 Andrew Greif, "Ultimate Glue Guy: How Clippers' Nicolas Batum Keeps Growing His Defensive Repertoire," *Los Angeles Times*,

March 8, 2022, sec. Clippers, https://www.latimes.com/sports/clippers/story/2022-03-08/clippers-nicolas-batum-improving-defense.

45 Andrew Greif [@AndrewGreif], "Reggie Jackson Got Emotional Describing Nico Batum's Influence. He Answer Ran 774 Words Long. 'We Know Each Guy Is Going to Pick Each Other up. . .and Him Being Here Last Year, He Definitely Helped Change That for Us. In Our Locker Room He Helped Ingratiate That.' Https://T.Co/Bf94zczja6," Tweet, Twitter, January 23, 2022, https://twitter.com/AndrewGreif/status/1485374766949314563.

46 "Santa Ana Man Rooting for Clippers Championship with the 'Batum Battalion,'" accessed December 2, 2022, https://spectrumnews1.com/ca/orange-county/sports/2021/06/24/santa-ana-man-rooting-for-clippers-championship-with-the--batum-battalion-.

47 LA Clippers [@LAClippers], "One Time for the Batum Battalion. Https://T.Co/Z9AYF9gKe8," Tweet, Twitter, July 1, 2021, https://twitter.com/LAClippers/status/1410703304334606339.

48 Farbod Esnaashari [@Farbod_E], "Nicolas Batum Found a Batum Battalion Sign in the Paris Airport! @lockedonclips Https://T.Co/UClfvs9BgV," Tweet, Twitter, July 14, 2021, https://twitter.com/Farbod_E/status/1415402377700528130.

49 Greif, "Ultimate Glue Guy."

50 Nicolas Batum, Interview with Nicolas Batum, July 31, 2019.

51 Stéphanie Trouillard, "NICOLAS BATUM—PROVILLE BASKET," Proville Basket (blog), August 14, 2019, https://proville-basket-officiel.fr/2019/08/14/nicolas-batum/.

52 Chris Haynes, "Batum's Emotional Trip to Africa Gave Him New-Found Perspective on Life," NBC Sports, November 20, 2012, https://www.nbcsports.com/northwest/batums-emotional-trip-africa-gave-him-new-found-perspective-life-0.

53 Haynes.

54 Benjamin Adler, "Les Bleus, Son Rôle à Portland, La Réusisite des Français en NBA. . .Nicolas Batum Se Confie," BasketUSA, April 29, 2015.

55 Nicolas Batum [@nicolas88batum], "https://t.co/sP3IZzpTob," Tweet, Twitter, July 17, 2018, https://twitter.com/nicolas88batum/status/1019284803118608390.

56 Nicolas Batum [@nicolas88batum], "Sans oublier la fierté de nos origines, car elles font partie de nous," Tweet, Twitter, July 17, 2018, https://twitter.com/nicolas88batum/status/1019287679496794112; Nicolas Batum [@nicolas88batum], "Je n'ai rien oublié, mon père est

mort enterré au Cameroun, ma famille est là bas, ma fondation construit des maternités et centres scolaires en Afrique! Je n'en fait juste pas la pub, je le fait car ça doit être fait. https://t.co/rNKb2EBIgF," Tweet, Twitter, July 17, 2018, https://twitter.com/nicolas88batum/status/1019339726493536257.

57 Nicolas Batum [@nicolas88batum], "Je n'ai rien oublié, mon père est mort enterré au Cameroun, ma famille est là bas, ma fondation construit des maternités et centres scolaires en Afrique! Je n'en fait juste pas la pub, je le fait car ça doit être fait. https://t.co/rNKb2EBIgF."

58 Nicolas Batum, Interview for the author, interview by Los Angeles Clippers Communicatons, December 14, 2022.

59 All Marine Johannès quotes in this chapter, unless specified, from Marine Johannès, Interview with the author, July 30, 2019.

60 Lindsay Sarah Krasnoff, "'Crazy on the Court': What the Liberty Have in Marine Johannès, Their French Rookie Who Plays with Flair," The Athletic, August 12, 2019, https://theathletic.com/1128658/2019/08/12/crazy-on-the-court-what-the-liberty-have-in-marine-johannes-their-french-rookie-who-plays-with-flair/.

61 Johannès, Interview with the author.

62 "Incredible Engagement by Fans as They Determine Regular Season Award Winners," FIBA.basketball, accessed December 2, 2022, https://www.fiba.basketball/euroleaguewomen/18-19/news/incredible-engagement-by-fans-as-they-determine-regular-season-award-winners.

63 Batum, Interview with Nicolas Batum, July 31, 2019.

64 Geoff Magliocchetti, "Marine Johannès Serves as Liberty's Humble Magician," Sports Illustrated New York Knicks News, Analysis and More, accessed January 2, 2023, https://www.si.com/nba/knicks/news/new-york-liberty-marine-johannes-wnba-playoffs-french-bench.

65 Jackson Kowalski, "Marina Johannès: Put Some Respect on Her Name," High Post Hoops (blog), August 16, 2022, https://highposthoops.com/2022/08/16/marina-johannes-put-respect-name/.

66 Batum, Interview with Nicolas Batum, July 31, 2019.

67 Batum.

10

Representing Paris: Diandra Tchatchouang and Evan Fournier

"For a basketball player, it's going to the NBA, like Boris. The bigger they are, the more stupid," teased the thirteen-year-old basketballer with curly brown hair, ball clutched to his right-hand side.

"When it's small, it's cute but it doesn't win games," a twenty-three-year-old Boris Diaw responded as he towered over his foil and introduced himself as the two-time ProA champion and NBA player.

"Hello! I'm Evan, double world champion of my bedroom," retorted the kid, Evan Fournier.[1]

Thus began a 2005 commercial to promote basketball to kids. Filmed in Levallois along Paris's northwestern outskirts, the seventy-second spot was part of the larger "C'est quoi ton sport?" campaign produced in partnership with the French Olympic Committee and McDonald's. It illustrated the intergenerational gravity at work and how Les Bleus captain Diaw sought to inspire the next generation. It foreshadowed how a future national team captain would similarly seek to stimulate kids' basketball dreams.

That same fall, across town at INSEP, the country's elite sports school, another Parisian-born-and-grown basketball talent began her first year at the Federal Basketball Center (CFBB).[2] The fourteen-year-old Diandra Tchatchouang, a prodigy trained within the Ile-de-France's elite basketball structures, was excited to finally embark on a key stepping stones to her future career as a professional, driven by her own hoop dreams.

Tchatchouang and Fournier both embodied the capital city's rich basketball traditions, the larger basketball empire, and attended INSEP. Although their careers differed markedly, the cultural exchanges of their US experiences strengthened their games and ultimately benefitted the national teams, French basketball, the NCAA and NBA, and the African game. Snapshots of how they received, perceived, and navigated the informal sports diplomacy framework is instructive for how the basketball empire is building the global game.

Growing Up [Super] Humains: Diandra Tchatchouang

The playground basketball phenomenon popularized in the 1980s and 1990s provided the spark for one of the country's future elite basketballers to fall in love with the game. On the courts in the northern Parisian suburbs, eight-year-old Tchatchouang and her sister were introduced to basketball by their older cousins. The game they played was so exciting that the following year Tchatchouang asked her parents to enroll her in an organized basketball club. Without that first point of entry to the game, the French game and sports scene more broadly would likely be quite different today.

Throughout her career, Tchatchouang always represented Paris and her home Seine Saint-Denis district, department number 93. Born June 14, 1991, she grew up in the northern Parisian suburb of La Courneuve, a lower-middle-class city. Although her Cameroonian-born parents enrolled her in judo and dance classes, once she had a taste of basketball, she was hooked.

It wasn't just that she had fun playing the game with her friends. Tchatchouang also excelled at it and, from the age of ten, was selected for department and regional competitions. Along the way, one of her coaches explained that for those who were as good as Tchatchouang, there were two possible paths to pursue the game to its highest levels: to progress up the basketball pyramid to train and study either in a professional club's youth academy or at INSEP. "She told me, 'INSEP, it's better,'" Tchatchouang recalled, "so straight away I said, 'I want to go to INSEP, it's the best.'" Just like that, she had an objective.[3]

Her trajectory to INSEP was a more "classic" route. At twelve years old she integrated into the Ile-de-France *pôle espoir*, where she lived, trained, and studied, while she continued to play with her home club, Paris Basket 18, on the weekends. Then she received a call to participate in an entrance test for INSEP, part of a cohort of twenty young women, some of the best fourteen-year-old talents across the country, who tried out for a spot at the prestigious sports school.

She successfully passed, and at INSEP found an entirely different approach to her sporting passion. "It was the culture of elite sport, it was very disciplined," she recalled of how she was surrounded by people whose objectives were explicit: to become professional players. "You're not there to amuse yourself and have a holiday," she explained. "You're there to work, to progress, and to attain your objectives."

It was an outlook and a work ethic that pleased her for the CFBB was a set-up designed to allow its young charges to focus on their goals. It was the same as when Diaw and Sandrine Gruda were there as teenagers a few years earlier: twice-daily training sessions in addition to school and homework time in the evenings. It was also a bonus that the basketball sections could readily mix with other young athletes their age who were similarly training, studying, and living at INSEP. "It was an experience because I met so many others from other sports," Tchatchouang said. "We don't stay locked in our little thing. We try to open up to the world and we also learn how to work on other sports and everything."

Long inspired by her parents, Eugene Tchatchouang and Jeannelte Noganmy, and four siblings, Tchatchouang developed a more basketball-specific admiration for Tamika Catchings. At the time, the All-American University of Tennessee stand-out was three years into her storied WNBA career with the Indiana Fever. "I liked her style of game and I wanted to be a bit the same," the Frenchwoman said. The budding basketballer also watched the Ligue Féminine de Basket-Ball (LFB) rivalry between Bourges and Valenciennes, where Gruda began her professional career in 2005, and followed the NBA, notably LeBron James.

INSEP enabled Tchatchouang to focus on basketball and school, an important consideration for her and her family. She passed her *baccalaureate* exam and decided to go to university in the United States. "In France, it's very complicated" to pursue both sport and higher education at the same time, she said. "When you leave INSEP, [sport] becomes your *métier*. Thus, you cannot say 'I don't want to train today because I have a thesis to write.'" But she also wanted the experience of attending university abroad. "To go to another country, to meet people from another culture, that's hyper-important, it's super-rich to do that," she explained. That's how Tchatchouang arrived on campus at the University of Maryland in College Park, Maryland, for fall semester 2009.

French in the NCAA

"It's truly a period of my life that I will never forget," she recalled of the experience. As an African American studies major, she learned about the US civil rights movement, the culture of athlete activism in the United States, and that athletes could be more than just sports people. It was a revelation. "I could understand that it was legitimate, that it was normal, that it was necessary," she said. The history of US sports activism helped her grow. "Without my American experience, I might have these ideas, but I wouldn't know that it was legitimate to have them," she explained of how the lack of a French heritage of athlete activism made this discovery an "ah-ha" moment. She used to think of herself as just an athlete, but "it was in seeing the grand American champions that I told myself, 'no, it can be about more than just sport.'"

While Tchatchouang developed off-court, she was also there to play basketball. Maryland was a Division 1 NCAA program and an entirely different experience from what she was used to back home. For starters, the team practiced and played in an arena that held some 18,000 people; many professional basketball stadiums in France accommodate just a few thousand fans, the experience was thus akin to being in the largest basketball hall in France, Paris's AccorArena, which holds approximately 16,000. That meant there were thousands of people who turned out for Terrapins games. Moreover, the visibility of basketball was vastly different. Back home, the game struggled for media attention (it still does today), but at Maryland, some of their games were broadcast on ESPN, which made the team and its games broadly accessible across the country.

Her new teammates had all sorts of questions about France and its basketball, which Tchatchouang fielded. But she also had to answer on-court, too. "I had to do two times more than the American" player, she reflected.

> To arrive and take the place of an American, you really need to prove yourself. Only the terrain can give that chance. I think the United States is a great experience but when you go there, you have to know that you're going to have to work ten times harder.

Tchatchouang rapidly proved that Frenchwomen can hoop. During her freshman season (2009–10), despite the difficult transition to a new country, she started all thirty-four of the Terrapins' games and notched double-digit points in more than half of them. At the same time, she worked her defensive skills, with forty-four blocks, which at the time made her the program's No. 3 for all-time freshman blocks.[4] The Terps' Number 24 was also named to the Atlantic Coast Conference (ACC) All-Freshman Team and All-Academic Team.

She played and started thirty-two games in her sophomore season, averaging 8.7 points per game. Then injury struck. Maryland entered the 2011 NCAA women's basketball tournament with high hopes despite being a young team with nary a senior on its roster. Its first-round win over Pennsylvania's Saint Francis 70–48 was firestarted by Tchatchouang, whose first-minute jump shot launched a 13–0 run.[5] The Terapins advanced to the second round, but within the first minutes of the game against Georgetown on March 22, Tchatchouang exited the match with a knee injury. Maryland lost the game 79–57 and their starting forward, who returned home to rehabilitate.[6] It proved to be her last NCAA appearance.

For Tchatchouang, her US experience was beneficial in numerous ways. First, it taught her to have better basketball communication and to speak up during training. Second, it imparted leadership lessons as well as how to support the team. As a result, she reflected, "I learned that, regardless of your place on the team, you have something to bring to the team, whether on the court or off the court." Part of this ethos included ensuring that everyone felt comfortable on the team, "that everyone knows that they have a role that is important, the hierarchical position is irrelevant."

Tchatchouang returned to France where she enrolled in university classes and embarked on an illustrious professional career.[7] Although drafted by the WNBA's San Antonio Silver Stars in 2013, she never played in the league. Instead, she shone in the *hexagone*. Tchatchouang played one season each with Lattes Montpellier and Perpignan before a five-year stint with Bourges. In 2016, she helped Bourges clench the EuroCup title, in addition to the French championship in 2015 and 2018. In 2018, she returned to Lattes Montpellier, where she played until her 2022 retirement.

The lessons learned during her US adventure served her well as captain at Montpellier, where she tried to bring this same leadership, communication, and team inclusion ethos she first absorbed on the Maryland courts. Tchatchouang also credited her overseas experience with how she later formed easy bonds with American players on her French teams. "I know that it's not easy to be a foreigner, I was in their place," she explained. That's why she tried to aid them when she could. "I know what they need, and I can help them as others helped me when I was in the United States."

Throughout her career, Tchatchouang represented, communicated, and negotiated in different ways through basketball. For France, she won the 2007 U16 European Championship then crafted a 107 game career with Les Bleues in which she amassed 535 points, four EuroBasket silver medals (2013, 2015, 2017, 2021), and bronze at the Tokyo Olympics. But she also represented La Courneuve, Paris, and her department, the 93, and fought for kids from her hometown to have greater opportunities. Tchatchouang created Study Hall 93, a nonprofit that creates space for young athletes to do their homework and also practice basketball. She also founded Take Your Shot, a day-long basketball program for young female players from all over the Seine-Saint-Denis region to work on their game while exchanging with women from other domains, not just sports.

For Tchatchouang, part of the motivation was to help others better understand and invest in her hometown. "The 93 is a territory that's not spoken well of in the media," she noted to the FFBB. "Having lived there, I know that a lot of good things are happening there, and that there is a lot of talent, overlooked talent, so the goal is to bring out these talents."[8] But, she emphasized, not every kid will become a basketball player so it was imperative to provide them with the tools to succeed.

That's why, for me, the goal is for everyone to find their own path, for everyone to give themselves the means to reach this path that they have given as a goal. . .it's a way of keeping young people away from bad influences.

In her representation of the 93, and of France, Tchatchouang also represents a modern French identity. Given the family's Cameroonian origins, she often visits her parents' homeland and acknowledges the larger cultural issues involved. "I am African basketball; I am its evolution" she said of how offspring like herself helped feed French basketball. But she also follows African basketball closely. "I have lots of respect for African basketball, for the histories of these girls who leave behind nothing," she said. "I also admire the combativeness they can exude on the court."[9]

Still, Tchatchouang acknowledged to *REVERSE Magazine* that her position as an elite athlete from such an early age meant that she experienced life differently than other Black women in France. "For me, [racism] is present very simply when I see the people who I know struggling ten times more than the average to find a job because of their name with a foreign connotation or to have access

FIGURE 10.1 *Diandra Tchatchouang. Credit: Getty Images.*

to housing."[10] She admitted to the magazine in 2021 that she, personally, had not experienced such discrimination, likely thanks to her privileged position. "In all the towns in which I've stayed, I am welcomed a little 'as a princess' because I'm part of the basketball team," she said.[11]

Yet, despite her work on- and off-court, Tchatchouang thought of herself as less a sports diplomat and more of a spokesperson. "I try to pass messages, to talk about the fights that there are as a sportswoman, as a female athlete, and I try to pass on these messages too," she explained of an approach informed by her US experiences and studies.

One of the issues she's most outspoken about is advocating for sportswomen, especially the challenges that female basketballers still confront in the early 2020s. One of the biggest as this book went to press remained the lack of mediatization of women's basketball, and women's sport more broadly, in French media, notably on television. "Often, I think in these instances, there's the sentiment that boys aren't interested in women's sport and thus won't even give them the possibility to watch women's sport," Tchatchouang mused. "These perceived ideas aren't necessarily real. That's one of the first things I fight. We have to fight for women's basketball to be known."

From her perspective, television was the most important platform. While social media provided a new way for female athletes to engage with audiences directly and generate a certain domestic and global cultural currency, Tchatchouang pointed out that the majority of French public remain informed through television. Including her parents and their generation, who aren't on Instagram. "Television is still what brings everyone together," she noted.

There are other hurdles faced by female basketballers. Motherhood and the issue of whether, or when, to become pregnant was one. So, too, was the constant struggle for the country's elite athletes to gain recognition and respect. When asked by *REVERSE Magazine* editor-in-chief Théophile Haumesser how the public acts when they learn she's one of France's best basketballers, Tchatchouang responded:

It depends on contexts and environments. The classic reaction is astonishment, because it's actually quite rare to rub shoulders with people who make a living from their sport. I'm also a tall Black woman and sometimes you can feel a kind of contempt. In those moments, I never talk about my profession. When I have this feeling, I have no choice but to talk about it. . .it's true that the attitude of the person in front of me can change. They can suddenly become a little more jovial.[12]

Her experience reflected the fact that even in the twenty-first century, while the country produced some of the world's elite sports talent and hosted some of the biggest sporting mega events, France lacked a sporting culture. Within the public, unless they're performing on the major stage, there's a bit of a demeaning attitude towards sports people. Tchatchouang related that when she was a student-athlete in her primary school's sport-study section, some of her teachers perceived them to be less intelligent.[13] But, she told *REVERSE Magazine*, thanks to her US experience, she knows that things can be different. "Culturally, sport—notably basketball or American football—[in the United States] is a religion. That's why there, the athlete is king, here they are only when they win."[14]

Still, Tchatchouang is committed to trailblazing the way forward. "My time in the United States allowed me to have this experience of 'giving back'" she said of her commitment to the next generation. Tchatchouang embodied how French basketball players can be more than just athletes. From running a non-profit and flexing her journalism muscles as a television analyst, guest editor, and producer of the "[Super] Humains" podcast to the Paris 2024 Athletes' Commission, she represents her hometown, France, and the basketball empire in numerous ways.

Growing Up Evan Mehdi Fournier

A young Fournier was in tears on the sidelines in the immediate aftermath of his team's loss when one of his teammates' parents approached and implored him not to be sad. "You tried your best, trying your best is the most important thing," they consoled. Fournier's father overheard and came over to express quite the contrary. "No, it's a disaster, you can't lose, you've got to win!" It was then that the young player understood his parents had a different mentality than most others, a champion's mentality cultivated from competing at the highest levels of sport. This outlook Fournier credits with giving him an edge in crafting a professional basketball career in what is arguably the world's elite championship, the NBA.[15]

The exchange illustrated how, from his early playing days, Fournier's work ethic and mentality were shaped by his parents and their world. Born October 29, 1992, to François and Meriem Fournier, professional judokas who met at INSEP, Evan long called the leafy campus a second home as his father taught at the famed sports school. Thus, Fournier grew up with the country's Olympic champions, an ethos that infiltrated his approach to his love of basketball. "I was just dreaming about being a professional," he said. "Once I started playing basketball, my ambition was to just be as good as I could be, and obviously, to be an NBA star."[16]

He watched "Space Jam," NBA games, and was surrounded by a popular culture in which the NBA was present. It informed his hoop dreams, as did Tony Parker's NBA Championship wins, which helped open the door of possibility. "Unconsciously, I was like, 'Okay, if he can do it, then why not me?'" Fournier reflected of seeing the French legend on television. Opportunities such as filming the 2005 ad with Diaw further fueled his desire.

Fournier officially began his basketball career at INSEP in fall 2007 and immediately felt at home. It helped that as a kid he spent considerable time at INSEP with his parents, thus he knew a lot of the people who worked and trained there. The days were fairly routine as the aspiring basketballers pursued a rigorous scholastic curriculum. But it was one that also emphasized basketball.

"The advantage of being in INSEP is you can practice twice a day with the national coaches," Fournier said. Moreover, because everything was on-site, the players could focus on basketball and school, without having to commute to/from classes. Perhaps the biggest time management issue was accounting for what floor of the dormitory one lived on; for Fournier's first year, it was the third floor. "The best was when we were on the first floor," he said, "you had no excuse to be late." There were pluses and minuses to the program. It wasn't the quickest path to playing professionally, yet, he acknowledged, "only a few guys can play pro when they're eighteen." Even though he left after his second year and did not stay to complete the program, he acknowledged that "INSEP is, in my opinion, a lot better in a lot of stuff."

FIGURE 10.2 *Evan Fournier during his days with the CFBB at INSEP.*
Credit: FFBB/Bellenger.

While at INSEP, he became close with Michel Rat, an ever-present basketball and educative resource since 1983. But the former *bleu* never spoke about his career or accomplishments. "He was really focused on helping the young guys to develop," Fournier recalled of his elder basketball statesman. "He taught us the right play to make or the right way to play basketball. He was more of a teacher than a guy who talked about what he had done."

Moreover, at the time, INSEP had a contract with NIKE, so the US-based sportswear conglomerate regularly sent sneakers to young players on campus, further fusing the basketball-sneaker-hip hop culture that's as intertwined in France as it is in the United States. "NIKE would send us boxes of basketball shoes," Fournier recalled. "It was one of the most exciting things because you never knew what pair you're going to have because it depended on the size. Afterwards, we'd compare the shoes [among each other]. You're fifteen, sixteen, and every time you got something from NIKE you were all excited." The most memorable pair of NIKE sneakers Fournier extracted from the *mélée* was a pair by LeBron James during his second year on campus. "I wore them the whole year," he recalled.

In 2009, Fournier signed with Nanterre for one season, then Poitiers, where he played for two seasons. It was a decision he took for his career, but it wasn't well received in other circles as some federation officials were anxious over his future.[17] Fournier's decision to leave INSEP early meant that he did not study and sit for the *baccalaureate* (*bac*). Normally, the CFBB—and some pro club academies—pride themselves on the high percentage of their student-athletes who sit for and pass their *bac* exams, one of INSEP's strengths. But as Fournier pointed out, today it is difficult to get a job in France without a university degree. For him, the *bac* wasn't the key to life outside of basketball. "Why stay one year just to get my *bac* and waste a year of basketball, when my *bac* is not going to help me at all in my life?" he asked.

He thus embarked upon a professional career aged seventeen. While it was eventually a helpful experience in terms of adjusting to future life in the NBA, it wasn't the easiest of existences. Fournier had to cook for himself, do the laundry, and make his way independently. "That helped me a lot," he said.

> I had to grow faster than most of the guys, and that really helped me because I could carry that into the NBA, even though it's a

different country. I was already used to living by myself, having a budget. I think a lot of guys coming from college kind of struggled with that the first couple of years.

Fournier had a good first season with Poitiers, and the next year entered the 2012 NBA Draft. "I wanted a new challenge," he told EuroSport. Selected twentieth by the Denver Nuggets, he recalled that waiting for his name to be called felt like eons. When he shook Commissioner David Stern's hand, the young draftee was too excited and couldn't fully understand what the American official attempted to convey *en français*.[18]

French in the NBA

Fournier arrived in Denver the day after the Draft and began preparations to play NBA Summer League. But he also had to acclimate to life in Colorado. The Nuggets franchise helped: they gave him a phone, a social security card, assisted with his lodging, car, and everything else that a player needed. That included English. Although he had an English instructor for four hours a week throughout the year prior to the Draft, he acknowledged that studying English was vastly different from living in English twenty-four hours a day.

He rapidly found that life in the NBA could be supersized in numerous ways. Everything was bigger than back home, from the hotels to the beds and televisions and beyond. But it all lived up to his expectations. "The first time I got into the gym, here [in the United States] they are just so much better than what we have in Europe. It was beautiful: the wooden floor, the rims, the facility, the Gatorade, everything." It was also a much more professional approach to the behind-the-scenes preparations and daily ins-and-outs of basketball, such as simply having cups of water ready for the players. Those little things made the difference, he noted. It was a stark change from his time as a pro in France, where he had to bring his own laundry, his own bottle of water.

Life as a rookie in a new country with a foreign culture and language was not easy by a long shot. "You're by yourself in the United States," he told Eurosport. "You're on trips, you're tired. I had no money because my club in France no longer paid me as

I was no longer under contract."[19] The lifestyle of arriving home or to an away city at 1 a.m., then reporting for 9 a.m. practice the next day was grueling. He was homesick, a sentiment that wasn't immediately eased by new teammates who broke out the standard US jokes about French people not showering. "I don't know where that comes from," Fournier said, "but that's something you get every time." He was dubbed "Frenchy," but opponents never ridiculed him for his nationality. On court, it was all about winning.

But the media was a different story. Fournier had to contend with US stereotypes of European players being "soft" and not mentally tough enough. "Stuff like that, we have to fight through," he said. "But it's just part of being a European, it's not just being from France."

It was a bit different from back home where Fournier said he never encountered discrimination because of where he or his family is from. Although his mother was born in Algeria, Fournier acknowledged that between his father's last name and Caucasian background, he was perhaps spared greater scrutiny. As a *métissage*, a mixed player, a term Fournier said is not considered impolite or offensive to use, he found the American relationship to skin color vastly different.

> Here in America, at least from my experience, you're either white or Black, and that's something I don't understand, because at first, they said, "Yeah, Evan Fournier, you are white." And then I said, "No, my mom was born in Africa, so I'm half Algerian," and then they said, "Oh, you're Black!"...most of the time, when you say Africa, [in the United States] they only think about Black Africa, like Senegal, but North Africa, where most of the people are Arabic, they're not necessarily Black. So, when we say, "Yeah, I'm from Africa," they necessarily think about Black people, which is a mistake.

The adjustments impacted Fournier's self-confidence on-court. He played thirty-eight games during his rookie season, including four as a starter. While his second season was an improvement, he appeared in seventy-six games and started four times, he still worked to find his NBA game. Then on June 26, 2014, Fournier was traded to the Orlando Magic, where he began to thrive. The following season, he started thirty-two times for his new team, and while he only played fifty-eight games due to injury, still averaged a career-high 12.0 points per game.[20]

For the next several seasons, the Frenchman was a near-constant starter and grew into France's best shooter in the NBA. In mid-2020, he was traded to the Boston Celtics, then in 2021, to the New York Knicks where on March 23, 2022, he broke the franchise's single-season three-point shot record when he notched his 218th made three-pointer.[21]

In his representation, communication, and negotiation with NBA fans, Fournier strove to serve as an ambassador of the game. And he's keen to help provide a good image of basketball back home, particularly through his career with Les Bleus.[22] Still, Fournier admitted in 2016 that he did not feel like an ambassador of France in the United States during the NBA season. "I represent France somehow because I was born there," he said. "But maybe I'm just focused on doing my own thing and I don't think about being an ambassador. I'm just a basketball player."

Fournier was ambivalent about his role as an ambassador of France in the United States in 2016, but he's been clear in his subsequent mission as a basketball diplomat in Algeria. His middle name, Mehdi, reflected a double culture inherited from his mother, although Evan was primarily exposed to it when he visited his Arabic-speaking maternal grandparents in Marseille.[23]

In the summer of 2017, he went to Algeria for the first time to reconnect with his family's roots and run a basketball camp. The experience inspired a desire to return and help Algerian basketball develop. That camp's MVP, Meriem Saadaoui, won a spot at the NBA's Basketball Without Borders camp in South Africa, where she was scouted and in 2019 offered a scholarship to play at Arizona Western College.[24] Fournier described on an episode of The Basketball Africa League (The BAL) "Hang Time" show how "she looked like I had given her the best news of her life," when he announced the award. They were both emotional and cried. "I never cry, but that time was special," he said.[25]

For Youcef Ouldyassia, a French-Algerian former basketball player, documentary filmmaker, and since 2022 Associate Vice President and Head of Content for The BAL, the story of Fournier and Saadaoui is a good illustration of the power of informal basketball diplomacy.

"She was great," he recalled of Saadaoui the player and how everyone present, including all of the boys at camp, applauded when she won the award.

> For me, that's diplomacy. Because a kid from Algeria, she goes to the States, she does well, she's really well-educated. With that, I'm sure people around her in the States will say, "Maybe we should go check what's going on in Algeria, so maybe there is talent, but not just sports talent, maybe also talent for studies or something like that."[26]

For Saadaoui, it was a dream come true. "It motivated me to work harder, get better, and always be at the top," she shared on "Hang Time." She also noted how that particular camp sparked others in Algeria, for it was the first time any of them saw an NBA player in real life. Another of Fournier's Algerian campers, Adem Djemai, relayed on the show what he learned from the NBA player, and emphasized the technical exchange that was an inherent component of the event. "It helped a lot of Algerian basketball players," he testified. And it was not a one-off relationship. Some former campers like Saadaoui and Djemai continued to exchange with Fournier via text message as late as 2020.[27]

Fournier represented Africa and the NBA in other ways. For example, in 2018 he was tapped to play with Team Africa at the NBA Africa Game in Johannesburg. "It was a proud moment to represent my mother's country, Algeria," he said on "Hang Time." "It's part of my childhood, my upbringing, and who I am today, so representing them was a source of pride for me."[28] And while playing with Orlando in the NBA Bubble in July 2020, he joined Ouldyassia for an edition of The BAL's "Hang Time" video series, designed to promote the new league and introduce it and African basketball to an international audience. Throughout it all, Fournier credits his double culture. "It helps me a lot, to see things differently, you learn to live in different ways," he told Ouldyassia.[29] Even as he was fiercely proud of representing France and playing for the national team.

Fournier helped kids beyond Algeria. Back home in France, he invested in Hoops Factory, a series of indoor basketball spaces that provide regular access and opportunity to help develop the next generation of basketballers. "When I was a kid and I wandered around Paris, I looked for courts, balls," he told *Basket Le Mag* of his hunt to find places to play. "I always said that when I was in the NBA I'd open my twenty-four hours basketball salle in Paris so that all the world could come to practice. . .Today, I am really doing this for the people, I'm not going to win a dime from this."[30]

Despite their different approaches and pathways, both Tchatchouang and Fournier have worked to progress French basketball and its place within French society. They represented not just Paris or France, but the sport at large in numerous ways. It's an objective much more difficult than many may realize in a country that traditionally lacks a sports culture, and one in which football is king. "A lot of our players have great results, even in summer [with the national teams], but during the year they play abroad, in the United States, in the NBA," Tchatchouang said. "That makes them less visible for the French [due to the time zone differential]."

That's why the country's basketball players are perhaps less known than its other star athletes, like those in football, handball, and rugby. Things are starting to change with both national teams' results at the Olympic level. "I think that that puts stars in the eyes of kids," she said. Following the Tokyo 2020 Olympics, which were held in summer 2021 due to the COVID-19 pandemic, there was an increase of kids enrolled in basketball teams, she noted. "They asked their parents to enroll them in basketball because that summer, they were able to enjoy basketball at the Olympics."

The basketball empire and its role evolving the NBA has helped pave the way building the country's cultural cachet through sports diplomacy interactions. But also, too, through the hard metrics of results. "We have NBA champions, we have guys that went to All-Star Games," Fournier said of how the country's players and national teams have inspired since 2000. "Clearly it's different now."

Notes

1 "C'est Quoi Ton Sport Avec Boris Diaw," FFBB sur Dailymotion, 2009, https://www.dailymotion.com/video/x8gv1s.

2 See Chapter 12 for more on the youth development system.

3 All Diandra Tchatchouang quotes in this chapter, unless specified, from Diandra Tchatchouang, Interview with the author, September 26, 2021.

4   "Diandra Tchatchouang—Women's Basketball," University of Maryland Athletics, accessed November 18, 2022, https://umterps. com/sports/womens-basketball/roster/diandra-tchatchouang/4800.

5   "Postgame Notes: 4-Maryland 70, 13-Saint Francis 48," University of Maryland Athletics, 1, https://umterps.com/sports/2011/3/20/ 207271606.aspx.

6   "Maryland Falls to Georgetown, 79-57," University of Maryland Athletics, accessed December 3, 2022, https://umterps.com/sports/ 2011/3/22/207294143.aspx.

7   She took classes at Sciences Po in Paris, which offered coursework via Skype as needed. Yann Casseville, "Sandrine Gruda et Diandra Tchatchouang: Basketteuses. . .et Étudiantes," *Basket Le Mag*, September 2018, 41.

8   "Le 93 dans le cœur," FFBB, n.d., http://www.ffbb.com/equipe-de-france-feminine/le-93-dans-le-coeur.

9   Tchatchouang, Interview with the author.

10 Théophile Haumesser, "Parole à La Rédac' Chef," REVERSE Magazine, March 2021, 9.

11 Haumesser, 9.

12 Haumesser, 7.

13 Haumesser.

14 Haumesser, 8.

15 BAL Hang Time—Episode 5 with Evan Fournier, 2020, https://www. youtube.com/watch?v=hToOTgsZu0E.

16 All Evan Fournier quotes in this chapter, unless specified, from Evan Fournier, Interview with the author, May 11, 2016; Evan Fournier, Interview with the author, part 2, May 19, 2016.

17 Jean-Pierre de Vincenzi, Interview with the author, September 22, 2016.

18 Fournier.

19 Glenn Ceillier, "La Draft, Ce Rite Initiatique Raconté par Evan Fournier," Eurosport, June 25, 2015, https://www.eurosport.fr/ basketball/nba/2014-2015/la-draft-ce-rite-initiatique-raconte-par-fournier_sto4796382/story.shtml.

20 "Broadcasters Bulletin: Nov. 9, 2015" (NBA Media Central, November 9, 2015), https://mediacentral.nba.com/broadcasters-bulletin-nov-9-2015/.

21 NEW YORK KNICKS [@nyknicks], "Grateful. @EvanFourmizz Reflects on Breaking the Knicks' Single-Season Three-Point Record. Https://T.Co/Zu6CzBI8rp," Tweet, Twitter, March 24, 2022, https://

twitter.com/nyknicks/status/1506986692045017100.

22 Fournier.

23 Evan Mehdi FOURNIER: Retour Aux Sources, Algérie 2017, 2017, https://www.youtube.com/watch?v=WsiHdZsysc8&feature=youtu.be.

24 Evan Fournier [@EvanFourmizz], "Pour ceux qui ont vu mon documentaire en Algérie. Sachez que la MVP du camp, Meriem, qui avait donc été invitée à participer au camp NBA BWB, a décroché une bourse d'étude ds une université américaine. Je ne peux mm pas vous expliquer la fierté que je ressens. #YouCanBeNext https://t.co/aWXUxJPlEC," Tweet, Twitter, October 10, 2019, https://twitter.com/EvanFourmizz/status/1182335678828466177.

25 BAL Hang Time—Episode 5 with Evan Fournier.

26 Youcef Ouldyassia, Youcef Ouldyassia Transcript, interview by J. Simon Rofe and Lindsay Sarah Krasnoff, May 14, 2020, Basketball Diplomacy in Africa: An Oral History from SEED Project to the Basketball Africa League (BAL), https://eprints.soas.ac.uk/32959/.

27 BAL Hang Time.

28 BAL Hang Time.

29 BAL Hang Time.

30 Yann Casseville, "Evan Fournier: Je n'ai Jamais de Moments de Toute," *Basket Le Mag*, January 2017.

11

From Cholet to the NBA

What do an Institut Paul Bocuse-trained chef and a three-time NBA Defensive Player of the Year and NBA All Star have in common? A pathway that, from their teenaged years with Cholet Basket Club to their later NBA careers with the Minnesota Timberwolves, proved the importance of the sports diplomacy framework's technical exchanges to forge the French pipeline of basketball talent.

Mickaël Gelabale returned to Cholet in November 2009, the club that prepared him for his first vocation as a professional basketballer, to resume a career interrupted by an anterior cruciate ligament (ACL) tear. The injury occurred during a March 2008 practice with his NBA team, the Seattle SuperSonics, and set in motion Gelabale's path back to the game. Once in France, Gelabale interacted with the kids in Cholet's youth academy, remembering how he, too, was once inspired by and benefitted from such proximity to older players who shared their experiences and transmitted their technical expertise to the rising generation. One of those youths was a seventeen-year-old named Rudy Gobert, then in his second year at the academy. Gobert eventually followed Gelabale into the NBA, first to the Utah Jazz, then to Minnesota (which was also where Gelabale played his last NBA season, 2012–13), accumulating a trophy case of NBA accolades along the way.

The unlikely stories of Gelabale and Gobert provide a deeper understanding of how youth academies strengthen French soft power when their players engage in informal sports diplomacy in the NBA. As they craft careers overseas, these basketballers communicate, represent, and negotiate foreign attitudes, perceptions, and opinions of their home country, culture, and its hoops scene, whether they relish the role or not. The picture that emerges from these two stories is how the youth formation system provides a front-row seat for aspiring professionals to learn the tactics and techniques that later enable their own pro careers, often from the senior team's American players.

Creating a Youth Development Powerhouse

Cholet, located in the Maine-et-Loire department in western France, is an agricultural and industrial hub that over the past half century put itself on the basketball map. Cholet Basket Club (hereafter, Cholet) can trace its roots to 1926 when a local Catholic patronage established a basketball section, but the present-day club was founded in 1975. At that time, club leadership decided to invest in and level up its basketball to ascend into the country's topflight division, the Nationale 1 (N1). That decision changed the equation.

At first, Cholet relied on importation of US technical know-how. For example, they hired Denis Calzonetti, their first US coach, to lead the team for the 1978–9 and 1979–80 seasons, while in 1981 the team welcomed its first American player, James Sarno.[1] Results improved and in 1986 Cholet contested their first season in the N1, followed subsequently by integration into the professional Ligue National de Basket-ball (LNB) in 1987. These moves attracted some of the country's top talent to Cholet. Patrick Cham, one of the national team stalwarts, played the 1988–9 season with the Red and White, as the club is known for its colors.

Cholet then switched gears and invested to develop home-grown players to sustain the professional team. Although the French Basketball Federation (FFBB) mandated that every LNB top division club have a youth academy, Cholet became one of the first to focus upon youth development. The program was directed in its infancy by Jacques Castel, a former physical education teacher, who scouted players and served as liaison to their schools in recognition that academics remained the priority.[2] Constructed around the values of work, solidarity, tenacity, and team spirit, the academy is integral to the club's history, success, identity, and future.[3] But it's also become one of the country's most accomplished academies, designated as one of the best in 1988 by the FFBB.[4]

One of the academy's first and best-known graduates was Jim Bilba, a future team Hall of Famer, Les Bleus captain, and one of the club's earliest links to the Antilles, a pipeline that strengthened over time. Born April 17, 1968, in Point-à-Pitre, Guadeloupe, Bilba grew up playing football but, as a tall sixteen-year-old, he attracted the attention of local scouts who recruited him to basketball. The legend's first club was his hometown's Ban-é-Lot, where he caught the eye of a scout from the Red and White. That's how, in 1986, Bilba made the transatlantic journey to Cholet, the start of a glittering career.

The list of Cholet graduates who rose to the heights of the game and contested US professional hardcourts is impressive. They include future French basketball and FIBA Hall of Famer Antoine Rigeadeau, who played eleven games with the Dallas Mavericks during the 2002–3 season and EuroLeague and Les Bleus star Nando de Colo, who played with the San Antonio Spurs and Toronto Raptors between 2012 and 2014. Other Cholet alumni who graced NBA hardcourts include Gelabale (2006–8, 2012–13), Kévin Séraphin (2010–17), Rodrigue Beaubois (2009–13), and two who as of press time were still active in the league: Gobert (nine years) and Killian Hayes (two years). Although their backgrounds and motivations differed, these young men helped build France's cultural cachet through their informal sports diplomacy exchanges within and around the NBA.

Growing Up Gelabale

Gelabale, who embodies the basketball empire, was the first of Cholet's youth academy alumni to craft an NBA career. His longevity on hardcourts, whether in North America or Europe, has made him an indisputable link between generations even as he makes his preparations for a post-basketball career, thanks to his NBA Player's Union benefits. Born May 22, 1983, in Pointe-Noire, Guadeloupe, a town where basketball was the number one sport, Gelabale grew up surrounded by friends who hooped. Both of his parents worked and stressed the value of getting an education but at school, he dreamed about basketball.[5]

The sport was a family endeavor. Gelabale began to play with his brother and sister, and soon joined his cousins and the rest of the family as they engaged in the game. "We were born to play basketball," he said.[6] He played with club Étoile de l'Ouest, but also sought out opportunities to hoop outside of organized games and practices, all the while inspired by players he observed on different courts. As a result, Gelabale developed a dream to one day play with the island's top basketballers—to be those he saw. Little did he imagine pursuing his love for the game beyond Antillean shores.

"I couldn't see myself leaving Guadeloupe at all," Gelabale confided years later. But an older cousin began to crack open the idea of possibility when he began to gift the youngster with posters of NBA players. Each one was a seed planted; a seed that germinated as Gelabale's collection grew to some thirty posters, including those of Scottie Pippen, Sam Cassell, Gary Payton, and Michael Jordan.

Gelabale sought out every opportunity to practice and play, yet he was initially overlooked by the regional detection system.[7] Selected by former French international Saint-Ange Vébobe to play in a regional tournament for some of the best players from French Guiana, Martinique, and Guadeloupe (known as GuyMarGua), he was finally noticed by local federation officials. Selected to play with a Guadeloupian side in an exhibition in western France at La Roche-sur-Yon against Cholet's academy team, Gelabale caught their attention and set his sights set on the mainland's hoops opportunities.[8]

That's how a sixteen-year-old Gelabale found himself matriculating into the youth academy at Cholet in September 1999, far from home. "I was a bit sad to leave Guadeloupe," he said of leaving his family, friends, and everything he knew more than 4,000 miles away, including the warmth and sunshine.

> When I first arrived at Cholet, as long as I played basketball, everything was fine but apart from basketball at the beginning, those first weeks were really very hard. I didn't know anyone. I had to get used to a new life.

Basketball enabled him to adapt. He and the other academy players lived together in housing provided by the club (they shared two apartments and used a third as communal space). Gelabale attended high school and worked towards a carpentry degree.[9] Team practices were held every day, two hours a day after school. Sometimes practices began at 4.30 p.m. or 5 p.m., sometimes not until 6.30 p.m., depending on when different players finished their classes. Sometimes they watched senior team practices, and every Saturday attended the professional side's games. "We would say, 'One day, I want to be in their place,'" he recalled of how this proximity and access to professionals motivated him and his fellow teenaged apprentices to excel.

During his second year, Gelabale began to train with the professionals, and during the 2002–3 season integrated into the team. While he continued to play with the academy team, his exposure to and experience gained from playing with the senior team helped prepare him for a future career in the field. It's one of the benefits he perceives of the French system. "I think that it gives a bit of experience to youths when they leave France to not arrive in a European country or the United States without having had experience as a professional," he said. "To be a professional [basketball player] is beautiful, but there are also negative sides, too, where you have to adapt to a country or adapt to the language and to teammates."

In 2004, Gelabale signed with Real Madrid's basketball team, one of the best in Europe, and at the end of the season was drafted 48th by the Seattle SuperSonics. Playing in the NBA had not been his dream as a kid. Yet, after years of honing his craft, Gelabale found himself in demand by some of the world's elite basketball leagues. The June 2005 Draft night was one of his best memories. "When I was called, I was truly surprised to be there and that they called me," he laughed. But when NBA Commissioner David Stern handed him the Seattle hat, the twenty-two-year-old Frenchman didn't want to put it on. "I had so much hair," he recalled of fears that the hat might not fit on his head as a result.

It was an unforgettable experience, but Gelabale decided to remain in Europe and continue to play with Madrid. Over the next year, Seattle went to watch him compete in the Liga ACB and continued the conversation to prepare him for life in the NBA. Gelabale joined the SuperSonics for the 2006–7 season but, despite being well prepared by the franchise, he arrived not speaking English.

It was a language he was forced to learn on the fly. At first, he took English classes but between practices and games on-the-road, they were difficult to regularly maintain. His teammates helped him adjust, especially fellow Frenchman Johan Petro, also drafted by

Seattle in 2005, who had one season in the league under his belt. Petro proved an invaluable resource and explained anything Gelabale didn't understand, which is how he began to speak and understand the language better. "I spoke all the time with my teammates about basketball, but to speak about life and other things was much more difficult," Gelabale recalled, a situation common for many of the game's expatriates.

The experience was educational in other ways, notably on the cultural front. Gelabale learned about Seattle, its Space Needle, and observed how that seminal site served a similar function as the Eiffel Tower in Paris: a rallying point of beauty for residents. He was impressed by how big everything was, from buildings to cars to streets, and while he missed his family, they visited, just as they did when he played in Spain.

Gelabale also got used to communicating, representing, and negotiating about modern French identity through his exchanges with teammates and the Seattle public. When asked, he told them he was French Guadeloupean. "We say we're French," he said. "We have a French passport, we never think about that double combination" of identity that is common in the United States, such as Italian-American or Irish-American. "Even when they ask me, I say 'French Caribbean' to distinguish where I come from," he explained. "The difference is that we have to say it to denote that we did not grow up alongside France, but more alongside the United States."

There were other initial adjustment pangs that first season in Seattle. As the *Seattle Times* reported in October 2006, "while he practices with flair and above-the-rim athleticism, he has been subdued in two exhibitions and has looked like a travel-weary twenty-three-year-old who is 6,000 miles from home."[10] By December 26, the outlet noted that he "has become an integral part of the Sonics and one of their most consistent bench players."[11] Three days earlier, the Frenchman notched an NBA career-high nine rebounds against Toronto.[12] Ultimately, Gelabale's first year with the Super Sonics was productive on court, averaging 17.7 minutes of playing time across seventy games.

He returned for a second season and struggled to gain time on court. Then in March 2008 suffered an ACL tear on his right knee. Once healthy, Gelabale spent time in the G-League to play his way back, then signed with Cholet for the 2009–10 season. He spent the next several seasons in Europe, first in France, then Belgium, Russia, Croatia, and Spain before making his way back to the NBA with the Minnesota Timberwolves during the 2012–13 season. Gelabale played a critical role in the Wolves' January 19, 2013, win against the Houston Rockets, a feat remarkable because he only joined the team that morning after signing a ten-day contract to provide greater roster depth. His ability to come off the bench in the fourth quarter and, in conjunction with Chris Johnson (who had also just signed with the team that morning), score twenty-three points was a game changer; Gelabale played the remainder of the season in Minnesota before returning to Europe.[13]

Throughout it all, he likened the NBA to a show. It was a vastly different atmosphere than EuroLeague. Still, Gelabale acknowledged, even with the smaller number of minutes he played in the NBA as compared to EuroLeauge, he wouldn't exchange his US adventures for a minute.[14]

It was a stage on which he communicated, represented, and negotiated with the American public about his homeland. But Gelabale noted in 2017 that ne never thought of himself as an ambassador of France during his time in the NBA. Instead, that

FIGURE 11.1 *Mickaël Gelabale. Credit: Getty Images.*

sense manifested itself when he played for the national team. "I conveyed the *bleu, blanc, rouge* spirit," he said. Gelabale described his role *en bleu* was to serve as a bridge between the established generation of Tony Parker, Boris Diaw, and Florent Piétrus and the younger generation that began to integrate into the team, like a young Nicolas Batum in 2009. "I managed the atmosphere between the two generations," he said.

As this book goes to press, Gelabale remains a presence on French professional parquets. But he's also preparing for a post-playing career as a chef, something he long wanted to do, first influenced by his mother's own cooking.[15] Gelabale spent two summers, the basketball off season, training at the Institute Paul Bocuse, a culinary school near Lyon, to upskill ahead of the day when he will eventually hang up his kicks as a professional player. Until then, he continues to share his technical expertise with the next generation.

Growing Up Gobert

Meanwhile, Rudy Gobert, who as an apprentice with Cholet's youth academy had a front-row seat to the technical exchanges engaged in by Gelabale and the team's pro players, is making his own mark on NBA hardcourts. As he continues to accumulate individual and team honors, Gobert is forced to communicate, represent, and negotiate critical US media and player attitudes about French basketballers and, in the process, provides a blueprint for how to succeed even if others underestimate one's abilities.

Gobert was born June 26, 1992, in the northern French city of Saint Quentin, better known for its architecture than its basketball. His mother, Corinne, was a single mother as his father, basketball player Rudy Bourgarel, returned home to Guadeloupe and was not a proactive presence. Although raised alongside his half-brother and sister, Gobert admitted that it wasn't always easy being a mixed-race kid. "Sometimes in a white family, there were some challenging times," he remarked to Andscape of how some family members originally did not want to visit when he was a baby.[16]

In Saint Quentin, everyone played football for it was readily available wherever two goals could be created, often outside in school yards. That's where Gobert played with his friends, but he also always liked and was attracted to basketball.[17] He read *5 Majeur* and other basketball publications online. "Pretty much all of my information, I got them online," he said.[18] He began to dream of one day playing in the NBA. He got his start in the game in 2003 with JSC Saint Quentin, then played in the departmental club Saint Quentin Basket-Ball for the 2004–5 academic year. He also began to train with the Pôle Espoirs in Amiens, but was not selected into the elite national sports school, INSEP, and was overlooked for the U16 national team.[19] Instead, he was forced to work to prove himself on the court and to federation officials. In 2007 he came to the attention of Cholet, which is how Gobert arrived at the club as a lanky fifteen-year-old that summer. [20]

From 2007 until 2011, Gobert lived, studied, and trained at Cholet's academy in close proximity to the club's professional team. That first season, men such as the American shooting guard/small forward DeRon Hayes (father of future Detroit Pistons' Frenchman Killian Hayes) played for the senior section alongside young academy-developed talent Séraphin, Beaubois, and de Colo. For Gobert, it was invaluable experience. "Basically [we would] just watch the pros," he said of having an up-front seat to what a future career and talent on the court could look like.

It was an influential, informative lesson and way to transmit the older players' technicality and tactics. "We tried to practice [what they observed] every day and tried to get better." It was an experience he likened to that of the football academies. During the 2011–12 season, Gobert integrated into the club's pro side and notched games in ProA, thus he already had some professional experience under his belt by the time he began to prepare for the NBA.

At the May 2013 NBA Draft Combine in Chicago, Gobert impressed with his height and wingspan, assets he later relayed into becoming one of the league's best defensive players. NBA Assistant Vice President and Head of Elite Basketball Chris Ebersole, a French speaker, was in attendance and closely observed Gobert. "He didn't speak a whole lot of English," Ebersole recalled. "But at that point, I was one of the few that he could talk to." It was a small thing, but important given the circumstances, which can be overwhelming for many. As Ebersole explained,

He was far away [from home], he's jet lagged, he doesn't speak the same language—he's trying to learn. Coaches are putting him through drills and he's trying to figure it out on the fly during a process that—the pre-draft process is a high stress one. It's like a big extended job interview with people poking and prodding. And you're out there doing drills and you don't know who anybody is, who these coaches are, but they're yelling at you in a language that's new to you. So, to see Rudy's experience was eye-opening for me.[21]

The next month, Gobert was drafted 27th by the Denver Nuggets then immediately traded to the Utah Jazz. Cholet president Patrick Chinon was on hand to support his young player. "We're really happy for him," he told *Ouest-France* of the academy's fifth player to be recruited into the NBA. "It's a little hard to see the players go away, some should remain a little longer, in my opinion, but we also know what this represents for them and, again, we're so proud."[22]

The twenty-one-year-old had to continually prove himself to the naysayers. He did not play much in his first year, just forty-five games with the Jazz. He spent time in the G-League but used the experience to dig in to regain a roster spot. "I've always had to work harder than everyone and keep my head down," he told Andscape.[23]

In Salt Lake City, Gobert learned the ropes of the NBA and progressed each season. By 2015, he was part of a cadre of the league's big men who proved they could also be highly skilled. As *Grantland* noted, "Gobert has done just enough on offense to unleash his own personal reign of terror on the other end. He is the NBA's Godzilla."[24] When fellow Frenchman and longtime Les Bleus captain Boris Diaw arrived in Salt Lake City for the 2016–17 season, he helped mentor Gobert.

The hard work paid off. Gobert was named the league's 2018 Defensive Player of the Year, an award he reclaimed the following season and again in 2021, one award shy of Dikembe Mutombo and Ben Wallace, who each hold a league record four DPOY awards. He was also named as an NBA All Star for the first time in 2020 (an honor he received again in 2021 and 2022). All of this was recognized by the Jazz, who in 2020 signed their defensive star to a five-year extension worth some $205 million. It made Gobert the highest-paid center in the league.[25] But in 2022 Salt Lake City traded him to the Minnesota Timberwolves, where fellow Cholet graduate Gelabale played his later NBA career.

FIGURE 11.2 *Rudy Gobert. Credit: Getty Images.*

While Gobert acknowledged that the NBA had many international players, making it somewhat easier to fit in, he noted it was more difficult for non-US players. "I think it's harder for international players to make a name," he said, while also pointing out that a foreign player's trajectory depended on his coach.

Despite all of Gobert's work on and off the court, including his Rudy's Kids Foundation, sometimes being French hindered acknowledgement of his accomplishments by US teammates, media, and fans. At least, that's how it appeared to some observers, such as osteopath Fabrice Gautier, who works with Gobert as well as with the French national team. "I think probably that prejudice about French players, there's still a little something there," Gautier observed. "Take a guy like Rudy, a lot of people are shitting on him for all the stuff that he cannot do, but nobody talks about the things that he can do very well."[26]

Gautier pointed to Golden State Warriors defensive specialist Draymond Green, who has long been critical and made fun of the French center. In 2019, the American mocked Gobert's emotions when bypassed for All-Star selection.[27] Then at the Tokyo Olympics,

Green accused the Frenchman of trash talking and being "very mouthy when it comes to [Team USA], but they don't beat us when it matters."[28] The following winter, Green pushed back against media who compared him and Gobert because they were both central defensive pillars for their teams.[29] In a late November 2022 match between the Warriors and the Wolves, Green appeared to laugh on-court as Gobert fell to the floor during a play.[30] As Gautier noted, "they like to make fun of the French."

Gobert reflected on how he's had to constantly fight critics, within the NBA as well as the US press corps. "It's not just Draymond," he told Bleacher Report's Taylor Rooks in March 2022. "It's a lot of guys who try to discredit what I do every night, who I am as a player." But, he noted, it was also a reflection of his basketball abilities. "For me, I will always take that as respect. If I was an average defense player, they wouldn't talk about me, right?"[31]

As a far-from-average defensive player, Gobert is still weaving his NBA story, but does not forget the club that gave him his first opportunity to excel. He serves as an ambassador of Cholet's academy, as well as for the game at large. "I think that a lot of young people now dream about becoming basketball players," he said. "It's also a way to have fun, when you're young and you get a basketball court." Kids back home are inspired by players like Gobert. "But there are more and more players coming up," the pipeline, Gobert said. "I think we're getting respected in the world."

For more than twenty-five years, players from France's basketball pipeline have helped internationalize and globalize the NBA, helping to build their country's cultural cachet through their informal representation, communication, and negotiation around the league. Cholet, a historic incubator of basketball talent, has contributed to this flow thanks to the ways its youth academy facilitated technical exchanges between youth players like Gobert and the adult pros on its senior team, like Gelabale, Hayes, or others. Gelabale was its first youth player to be drafted and play a full season in the North American championship and others have followed in his footsteps. The most recent to do so was the Detroit Pistons' Killian Hayes, who featured in the January 2023 NBA Paris Game, a different way for the basketball empire to flex its muscle.

Notes

1   Denis's brother was Nantes player and occasional coach at Clermont Université Club Carmine Calzonetti. "James Sarno," Cholet Basket, https://www.cholet-basket.com/personne/james-sarno.

2   Gérard Curé, *Cholet Basket* (Hérault Editions, 1988), 98.

3   "Cholet Basket Le Centre de Formation Saison 2007–08" (Cholet Basket, 2007).

4   Curé, 98–9.

5   Yann Casseville, "Moi, Je. . . .Mickael Gélabale.," *Basket Le Mag*, March 2020.

6   All Mickaël Gelabale quotes in this chapter, unless specified, from Mickaël Gelabale, Interview with the author, April 18, 2017.

7   Xavier Collin, "Mickael Gelabale, l'Étoile de l'Ouest: Les Origines et l'arrivée en Métropole," *Le Journal de Saone-et-Loire*, March 30, 2019.

8   Collin.

9   *CAP de menuiserie*. Mickaël Gelabale, Interview with the author, April 18, 2017.

10 Percy Allen, "The Education of Gelabale," *The Seattle Times*, October 20, 2006.

11 Percy Allen, "World of Hoops at His Fingertips," *The Seattle Times*, December 26, 2006.

12 "Mickael Gelabale | Seattle SuperSonics," NBA, n.d., https://www.nba.com/player/101153/mickael-gelabale/.

13 "Top 5 Surprises of the 2012–13 Season," NBA, May 6, 2013, 5, https://www.nba.com/timberwolves/news/top-5-surprises-2012-13-season.

14 Casseville.

15 Yann Soudé, "Passionné de cuisine, le basketteur Mickaël Gelabale prépare sa reconversion," *L'Équipe*, August 5, 2022, https://www.lequipe.fr/Basket/Article/Passionne-de-cuisine-le-basketteur-mickael-gelabale-prepare-sa-reconversion/1346228.

16 Marc J. Spears, "Rudy Gobert on Big Payday: 'I Could Have Never Imagined This,'" *The Undefeated*, December 22, 2020, https://theundefeated.com/features/utah-jazz-rudy-gobert-on-big-payday-i-could-have-never-imagined-this/.

17 Rudy Gobert, Interview with the author, January 20, 2015.

18 All Rudy Gobert quotes in this chapter, unless specified, from Gobert.

19 For more on the Pôle Espoir and INSEP system, the elite youth structures run by the French Basketball Federation, see Chapter 12.

20 "Rudy Gobert," Cholet Basket, n.d., https://www.cholet-basket.com/personne/rudy-gobert.

21 Chris Ebersole, Interview with the author, March 11, 2021.

22 Antoine Bancharel, "Direction Utah Jazz Pour Rudy Gobert," *Ouest-France*, June 29, 2013.

23 Spears.

24 Zach Lowe, "The Rebirth of Big Men: A Breakdown of Old-School Bulk and New-Era Skill," Grantland (blog), 227359, https://grantland.com/the-triangle/the-rebirth-of-big-men-a-breakdown-of-old-school-bulk-and-new-era-skill/.

25 Spears.

26 All Fabrice Gautier quotes in this chapter from Fabrice Gautier, Interview with the author, November 14, 2022.

27 Tristi Rodriguez, "Gobert Breaks Silence on His 'beef' with Draymond," NBC Sports Bay Area, March 20, 2022, https://www.nbcsports.com/bayarea/warriors/jazzs-rudy-gobert-opens-about-draymond-green-beef-first-time.

28 Bleacher Report [@BleacherReport], "Rudy Gobert Responds to Draymond's Comments about the French National Team Full Interview with @taylorrooks Https://Bit.Ly/35519BY Https://T.Co/XULhrarojI," Tweet, Twitter, March 24, 2022, https://twitter.com/BleacherReport/status/1506784691755626502.

29 Rodriguez.

30 Tom Dierberger, "Draymond Appears to Laugh at Gobert after Wolves Turnover," NBC Sports Bay Area, November 28, 2022, https://www.nbcsports.com/bayarea/warriors/draymond-green-appears-laugh-rudy-gobert-timberwolves-after-turnover.

31 Rudy Gobert Talks Beef with Draymond Green and More | Taylor Rooks Interview, 2022, https://www.youtube.com/watch?v=eous_k50F6k.

PART THREE

Going Global

Going Global in the Twenty-First Century

Part Three explores some of the main themes to emerge in the twenty-first century around basketball and the ways it continues to serve as an incubator for cultural, technical, and knowledge exchange. These chapters are informed by conversations with French, US, and African basketball officials, as well as players, to provide an industry insider's reflection of the evolutions at hand. Although not complete or definitive, these snapshots provide a glimpse of how the story at hand plays out on hardcourts and illuminate areas for future research.

What emerges is a sense that the basketball empire at hand serves as a tool in multifaceted ways. It cultivates French soft power through on-court results of Les Bleues and Les Bleus, as well as the work of its players in the world's best leagues and their engagement with fans, colleagues, and the media. The construction and evolution of the country's youth development systems that underpins this cultural cachet occurred in response to the game's globalization: to feed the national teams and maintain French relevancy in FIBA-sanctioned competition as well as in reaction to changing market conditions. Although this was articulated in Part One, its twenty-first-century manifestation is more interesting for France, alongside Australia, has significantly informed the NBA's own youth development programs, the NBA Academy system.

At the same time, the basketball empire empowers francophone basketball more broadly to flex its muscle globally, within and outside of the NBA. The longer-term ways that French and African basketball have "rubbed shoulders" is changing as in the 2010s and

2020s it's increasingly French from the African diaspora, as well as Africans with formative experience in the *hexagone*, who are some of the driving forces in the game's growth. They are doing so at the grass-roots level, as well as within the NBA itself.

These ongoing evolutions circle back to the larger question posed earlier: whose empire is this anyway? Geographically, this story centered around the former French empire, but culturally things are a bit different. The NBA was now part of a lifestyle thanks to the league's television broadcasting and marketing efforts of basketball and all that was associated with it. For former NBA Commissioner David Stern, by the 2000s, "people were beginning to see American players, the games, their lifestyle, their fashion, and the fact that they were celebrities in their own country," he said. "International celebrities have a way of driving interest in sports."[1]

This connection of basketball, celebrity, and cultural cachet is something that Katia Foucade-Hoard, the former University of Washington co-captain and French international, denoted, too. "The culture of celebrity impacted our sport in a way," she said. "But more the culture, which made basketball very trendy."[2] She noted that there remained distinctions between the US and European game. But, "for the basketball lovers, the culture of celebrity really made a big difference because basketball is no longer just a sport, it's a culture."[3]

That helps to explain in part why French football players love American basketball. After the European football season ends, many of the sport's biggest names fly to the United States to watch the NBA Finals. "It's impacted our culture in a sense that it's cool to play basketball, but it hasn't changed the game," she noted. "It didn't change the way the French see basketball. Even if we have an NBA game each year in Paris, it doesn't change how basketball is perceived in French culture as a global culture."[4]

Instead, the strong American accent has dissipated somewhat as the NBA globalized and the WNBA became more diverse. The basketball empire may thus be ever-more about a global one, underpinned by a broader hoops identity, culture, lifestyle, community, and sense of citizenship. That's not to say that national pride is moot; on the hardcourts in Olympic, World Cup, and FIBA continental competition, national rivalries remain strong. But as Team USA has shown its fallibility, notably at the hands of France, a new type of friendly clash is emergent between the United States and its oldest ally as the Summer Olympic cycle of Paris 2024–Los Angeles 2028 swings into high gear ahead of the 250th anniversary of the Franco-American alliance in 2028.

Notes

1 David Stern, Interview with the author, interview by Lindsay Sarah Krasnoff, telephone, March 17, 2016.
2 Foucade-Hoard, Katia, Interview with the author, November 1, 2021.
3 Foucade-Hoard, Katia.
4 Foucade-Hoard, Katia.

12

Youth Pipelines

The names on the courts may be those of France's biggest NBA stars, but a different one has been omnipresent at the Federal Basketball Center (CFBB) since its 1983 inception: Michel Rat. The former French international and alumni of Paris Université Club's (PUC) 1962 trip to the United States spent most of his post-playing career educating young players. After stints in Madagascar and Senegal, he was named the first head coach of the boys' team at the CFBB, located on campus at the country's elite sports school, INSEP. Over the years, Rat served in different capacities, most recently as CFBB president, an eyewitness for basketball's evolutions. "Sport has become part of the economic framework of globalization," he said. "Basketball gives rise to the commodification of sport because there is money in it."[1]

Although this trend began in the late 1960s, its acceleration in the twenty-first century placed new pressures and scrutiny on the French system of youth detection and development. The evolution of professionalization was just one part of the equation. Another was that early successes of French players in the NBA, notably Tony Parker, made the country's youth training centers attractive scouting grounds.

One of the constants over time remains the stated commitment to the larger mission: education of basketballers. But it is education in the larger sense of the word, not a purely scholastic one. "In French, we say: holistic," Rat explained. This means a focus on academics, on basketball fundamentals, on humanistic learning, as illustrated in anecdotes from INSEP and two youth academies in Part Two. But also on the integral whole and the networks that bind. According to Rat,

In a team, the player exists as an individual, but he also exists in the relationships, the interrelationships, the rejections, in the complexity of "the whole and the parts": the individual and the group. The child and the family. We are always in relation, interconnected.

In this way, basketball *formation à la française* can be a tool that forges citizens in the republic's values, ideals, and ethos. Between INSEP and professional clubs' youth academies, it trains French kids from all over the country and thus brings together the different cultures that constitute modern France. It introduces young basketballers from different parts of the *hexagone* to counterparts from French Guinea, Martinique, or Guadeloupe so that a teenager from northern France learns more about the Caribbean culture of her or his teammates. This includes teammates who grew up with double or triple cultural heritages, even as they themselves were born and raised in, and identify as, French, as well as those of the African diaspora, born on the continent but who grew up in France.

In the twenty-first century, basketball *formation à la française* helps build the country's larger cultural cachet through the soft power influence of sports. The last several chapters examined how the products of the system helped to communicate, represent, and negotiate about France to the US basketball world. This chapter looks at how these pipelines remain a response to globalization through a focus on the French sense of education in its broadest sense. This holistic approach also influences the NBA's own youth development programs. Thus *formation à la française* enables French basketball to engage in different types of sports diplomacy that's informing the NBA and WNBA.

A French Response

The system of detecting and developing teenaged basketball talent, *formation à la française*, was fine-tuned during the last quarter of the twentieth century. Born out of Cold War geopolitical concerns, decolonization, a post-1945 desire to project an image of refreshed rejuvenation, and the intertwined sports and youth crises of the 1960s, they have evolved as a French response to globalization. In the aftermath of French sport's "zero hour" at the 1960 Rome Olympics, the identification and training of promising young talent was something that preoccupied the French Basketball Federation (FFBB). Subsequently, basketball systems developed two tracks: a federal elite one run by the FFBB and a private one centered around professional teams.

The elite level centered around INSEP. The federation began new efforts to train the country's most promising teenaged girls in the 1970s and in 1983 implemented the CFBB for both girls and boys to provide both scholastic and basketball education. In the early years, the CFBB welcomed twelve girls and twelve boys each academic year from around the country who returned home on the weekends to play with their clubs. It was a difficult rhythm. "It obviously lacked coherence," Rat said of how the clubs still held the keys to the players, not the CFBB. That's why, since the late 1990s, players remain on campus and compete for the CFBB teams in the country's second (women's) and third (men's) divisions.

The CFBB, also known as the Pôle France, is the peak of the elite pyramid for those aged fifteen to eighteen, but there are lower levels for younger players. Starting in the mid-1980s, the federation worked with the Ministry of Youth and Sport to develop a program for the U14 and U15 levels. First called Elite Level Regional Training Centers (CEHRN), today they are known as Pôle Espoirs, which translates literally into "hope poles," centers for those hopeful to progress into the Pôle France. The Pôle Espoirs allow students to pursue a "triple project" of scholastic, basketball, and personal "education," replete with medical, academic, and adult supervision, while returning home to play with their clubs on the weekends. Today there are thirty-one of these centers throughout the mainland and overseas departments co-financed by the Ministry of Youth and Sport, the FFBB, and the regional basketball leagues; sixteen of these are located within larger state-run elite sports training establishments (Regional Centers of Physical Education and Sports, CREPS).[2]

INSEP itself was originally influenced by the Eastern European state-centric sports training approach, and as it liberalized after 1984, informed by a more American model.[3] But its approach to forming young basketballers remained infused by the ethos cultivated at PUC and transmitted to newer generations through the work of Rat and others. There was also a desire to protect players from the sport's growing capitalistic forces. International scouts took note as the CFBB began to produce players who competed in the NBA and WNBA. In 1999, CFBB educators implemented a new rule that prohibited players from speaking to scouts to stave off impromptu visits and telephone calls to the campus that interrupted training.[4]

But the forces of globalization that began to favor the migration of French players to US leagues also posed problems to the CFBB, namely that players began to leave the system. Sometimes they left the Pôle France early to pursue a professional career in France but increasingly they left the system for opportunities to play in Europe or the United States. "At a time of globalization, it seems logical to me that they would want to progress [in the United States] where the basketball is better," Rat, then-CFBB Director, told *Le Monde* in 1999. "Furthermore, American universities propose a curriculum of excellent quality that the French club academies cannot offer."[5] The Pôle France's ultimate mission is to form well-rounded basketballers who feed the national teams. For those who leave for the NCAA, NBA, WNBA, or EuroLeague, it's difficult to balance national team service with professional careers abroad, particularly under the new FIBA competition windows of November, February, and June which can conflict with those leagues and thus prohibit some players from participation.

The private track developed differently. The mid-1980s professionalization of basketball required that every professional club found and run a youth academy. Once a professional women's basketball league was founded in 1998, all first division pro clubs also had to run an academy. The academies borrowed from the work pioneered by their football counterparts in the 1970s but fine-tuned their points of emphasis for a more basketball-centric audience and objectives.[6]

Known as *centres de formation*, formation centers, these basketball programs have over time matured to provide a key pipeline of talent into the world's elite championships. They are best described as a miniature sports boarding school where players or "apprentices" eat, sleep, study, and train together while continuing their scholastic studies at one of the affiliated nearby schools. On paper, academics are a strong component of the formula, for as the FFBB noted, "the path to a professional career is uncertain."[7] Reality may be different at some academies, where perhaps more emphasis is given to basketball than to scholastic studies. But all academies are regulated by the Ministry of Youth and Sport and FFBB who regularly visit and conduct biennial inspections.[8] Since

January 1, 2021, every four years youth academies must go through reaccreditation with their regional academic rectors to ensure academic compliance and are subject to revocation of accreditation at any time if they fail to meet stipulated criteria or for "any serious reason."[9]

While there are pluses, there are also minuses to both pipelines. For NBA Champion Boris Diaw, an INSEP alumnus, one benefit of the CFBB program is the lack of obligation to a specific club. "You're free," he said. "If you signed a contract as a sixteen-year-old player, you're pretty much locked in for seven years, you don't have the freedom of moving, of going somewhere else."[10] Moreover, the competition is greater at INSEP. "You play with the best potential around you," he said. "You have a lot of great players, and the more that great players are together, the more you improve." Playing against grown men, "makes you grow up pretty quick too, as far as the toughness of the game and all that," Diaw noted. Lastly, he pointed to the academic setup at INSEP, of the small classes of ten to fourteen students maximum, as another beneficial ingredient to the federal program. "It makes it a lot easier to learn, to interact with the teacher than if you go to a public school of forty or forty-five people in a class."

Yet, there are only places for a small number of players in each year's class. Thus the professional club youth academies play an important role in scouting and training a greater number of youths. For longtime Le Mans President Christian Baltzer, this is an important differentiator and a key club contribution. "One can search for youths, and they train with a coach day and night," he said of the supervised conditions.[11]

Another advantage academies enjoy is proximity to the professional team. For journalist Pascal Legendre, this helps in numerous ways. "They are impregnated in American culture because it already exists in French society," he explained. But interactions with the pro team members, especially its American players, allows young French to learn and practice English. There are more substantial benefits, too. These exchanges provide academy players with better understandings of how US players function and play. As Legendre noted, "they [learn] how Americans react, they listen to the same music, they have the same tattoos."[12]

There are other stakeholders in this *formation à la française*, themselves products and builders of the basketball empire, whose

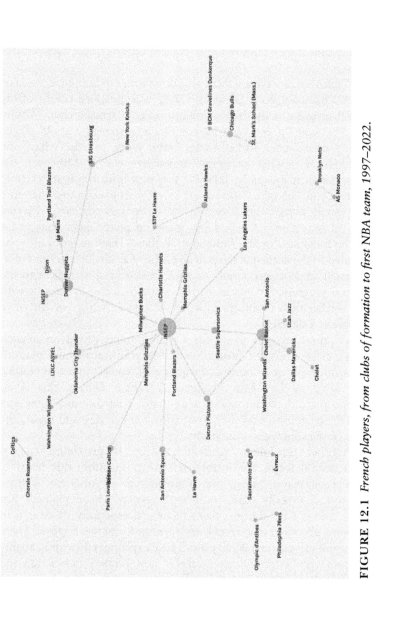

FIGURE 12.1 *French players, from clubs of formation to first NBA team, 1997–2022.*

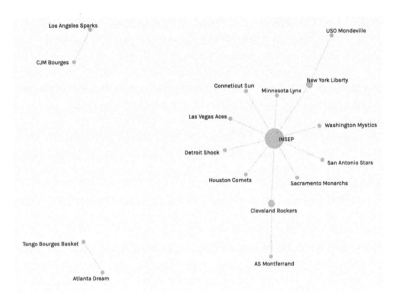

FIGURE 12.2 *French players, from clubs of formation to first WNBA team, 1997–2022*

behind-the-scenes work illustrates the pipelines' focus on holistic education. This is particularly the case in preparing young players for the US market.

The Agent and the French Prince

The sounds of the basketball court have long served as the soundtrack for sports agent Olivier Mazet's life. He grew up in the Parisian suburbs playing the game in the 1980s. His Guadeloupe-born mother first enticed him to the sport when she enrolled him in an organized club program. That's how pre-teenaged Mazet started basketball classes on Wednesday afternoons. "I was really bad," he admitted decades later, "but I liked the speediness of the game, the sensation of the game."[13]

His mother continued to fuel his growing interest in basketball. She brought home magazines *5 Majeur* and *Mondial Basket*, important portals that allowed him to discover Michael Jordan and a world beyond top French clubs Limoges and Pau. At the time,

NBA-style basketball was more of an underground culture for kids in the Parisian suburbs; the growth of playground basketball courts helped ignite greater interest, but it was still tough for the sport to emerge. Yet, Mazet was smitten. He stuck with the game, improved, and played semi-professionally before he pivoted at age twenty-two. Rather than be the focus on the court, he began to shine the spotlight on others. He organized camps for young players so that they could be scouted by, and ideally recruited into, pro club youth academies. In 2005, Mazet obtained his agent's license and began to shine the spotlight on the academies' finished products.

Although he viewed INSEP as the golden standard over the *longue durée*, Mazet argued that the youth academies diversified the system for the larger good. "Before, when you received a call from INSEP, nobody even thought about it, all the French NBA players played for INSEP back in the day," he said. "Before, the best players would go to INSEP," but now that's no longer necessarily the case.

Today, the all-inclusive academy system provides more opportunities for young players to train towards their dreams. As Mazet noted, clubs enjoin a convention with the player's family to ensure their young charge's scholastic as well as basketball education. "That means they will check your grades, they will help you, if you need it, they will give you a private teacher, if you need it," he said. "That was, in my opinion, the first move the teams made in order to be able to build players." Thus, in a way, both pipelines, INSEP and professional club academies, are engaged in a citizen-making project, one as old as the Third Republic's use of education to create Frenchwomen and men.[14]

It isn't simply for altruistic reasons that pro clubs seek out and develop promising young talent. For sponsors, there's allure. "They like the fact that they're giving money to a team that's helping to promote local talent," Mazet said. It's also for the pride, for each time a young player formed by a club's academy is signed to a EuroLeague or NBA team, it bolsters reputation. Then there's the money. "Financially, there is some benefit," he said, particularly of the NBA whose teams pay to acquire French players drafted. In 2018, that payment, known as a buyout, of $675,000 went to the player's French team, financial recognition of how the club trained, developed, and took care of the player. That may not be the largest sum, particularly for clubs in other countries. But, Mazet noted, "for a French team, that's a lot of money because the budget for the highest team [is around] €5 to €6 million euros."

This changed the equation of who sends talent to the NBA. In the 2022 NBA Draft, eleventh pick Ousmane Dieng spent two years at INSEP. Moussa Diabate (forty-third) played high school in the United States then a season with the University of Michigan. Ismael Kamagate (forty-sixth) began at INSEP then transferred to the youth academy of Paris Basketball. Hugo Besson (fifty-eighth) was a product of the youth academy at Elan Chalon, the sixth talent formed by the club to be drafted by the NBA.[15]

There are ripple effects that also impact the WNBA. The 2021 WNBA first-round draft pick, Iliana Rupert, was formed at INSEP and played her first pro year in the United States in 2022, winning the championship with the Las Vegas Aces. But the last French drafted to leave a mark on WNBA hardcourts was New York Liberty's Marine Johannès, who was formed by the academy at USO Mondeville in Caen.

Yet, across both pipelines, the focus remains education at large. This is illustrated in how Mazet helped prepare one of his teenaged clients for the NBA. Frank Ntilikina, born in Ixelles, Belgium, on July 28, 1998, to Rwandan parents, moved three years later to Strasbourg with his mother and brothers. He discovered basketball, began to dream of playing in the NBA, excelled, and as a fifteen-year-old entered the youth academy at SIG Strasbourg.

At the time, Vincent Collet was head coach of the professional team. Collet, the same man who gave a teenaged Nicolas Batum his first break as a professional at Le Mans, was himself a product of the basketball empire: one of his earliest influences was Jacques Cachemire, he was one of the first kids to attend Jacky Chazalon's basketball camp (run in conjunction with Carmine Calzonetti), was impassioned by the 1980 NBA Final, began his professional playing career at Le Mans, and long considered that team's president, Baltzer, and his former teammate from New York Bill Cain as his "basketball fathers."[16] His former Le Mans coach, Kenny Grant, recalled that Collet had many attributes that translated well to developing young talent. "He wasn't a yeller and screamer, he explains to people what they should do and they respect what he's saying," Grant said. "The respect that he has, the knowledge, and what he's telling them is right."[17]

At Strasbourg, Collet rapidly detected special potential in Ntilikina and set about once again to prepare a basketball prodigy for life beyond French hardcourts. He tapped a sixteen-year-old Ntilikina to train with the senior team daily, to push his young protégé in practices and elevate the teenager's game intelligence and defensive understanding to a new level. It was a progression that Mazet thought beneficial. "In terms of improving, it's faster because you're playing against men," he said of the experience. "You're playing against guys who have real high levels of basketball IQ."

This helped prime young French players like Ntilikina for North America. According to Collet, "a young [French] guy at twenty years old that goes to the NBA probably has more basketball IQ than a young US kid at his age. He doesn't have the same aggressiveness, for sure, and very often they suffer in a one-on-one situation. But a basketball understanding seems to be always interesting."[18] In the 2010s, there were often US players who arrived in France and needed to learn more basketball fundamentals. "For me, this is the biggest change," he said. "Some of them are good athletes, they have some talent, and they can make baskets. But some of them, their understanding of the game is very poor."

Collet decided that Ntilikina was ready to start playing full-time with the senior side after his second season practicing with them. For Mazet, it was a move to build Ntilikina's confidence, to provide a high-level challenge and opportunity to run the team as point guard. At first, it was a difficult transition and Ntilikina didn't have immediate success. Then he played with the French team at the European U18 Championship in Turkey over the December 2016 holiday break; while the team placed fourth overall, Ntilikina was the tournament's Most Valuable Player (MVP). The experience and accolades helped shift something for Ntilikina returned to Strasbourg in January 2017 recharged, played more minutes, and was much better on-court.

It became clear that Ntilikina was likely to be drafted by the NBA, so preparations were fast-tracked. "We told him that as soon as he was eighteen years old, we knew that he would go," Mazet recalled. Ntilikina started English classes to gain the ability to communicate with people, including the media.

What we tried to make Frank understand is that he will arrive in a totally different country, with a totally different life. . .[We tried to have him] understand that the NBA is like a big washing machine, and you will have to take care of your time, the way you eat, the way you sleep, and be sure that you will be ready to live your new life because it can be very brutal.

One month after contesting the French finals with Strasbourg, Ntilikina was drafted eighth by the New York Knicks in June 2017, the highest position for a French player to date. It was one of his best memories, but not everyone was happy with the Knicks' selection; LeBron James criticized the franchise for bypassing another player to draft Ntilikina.[19]

Yet, the Frenchman was welcomed to New York in a big way. In October 2017, NIKE unveiled a billboard on the side of a skyscraper near Madison Square Garden that featured the rookie.[20] The player, rapidly dubbed the "French Prince," made good on the hype that first season as he crafted an average 5.9 points, 2.3 rebounds, and 3.2 assists per game. It was a sustained series of performances that impressed US players, even James. "I think he knows how to play the game. That's the best thing, first of all. Very cerebral basketball player," the legend admitted to reporters about Ntilikina's

FIGURE 12.3 *Frank Ntilikina. Credit: Getty Images.*

improvement. "Defensively, he's been good since he probably stepped on a basketball floor."[21]

It helped that the Frenchman had a strong support system to help ease the transition. His mother and brother were regular visitors, Mazet visited for one week each month to help Ntilikina adjust, while Mazet's US-based partner also provided support. "[We tried] to have people around him, and to try to help him, to be family," Mazet said of the agreed-upon approach.

Ntilikina's time in New York soured, however. There was constant turnover within the Knicks organization: during his four years with the club, he had four different coaches and three different executives/team presidents. The crowd and critical media were used to flashier performers who amassed points. That was not Ntilikina's strength. Still, he acknowledged, his NBA experience advanced his overall game, particularly on the mental level. "It made me more involved," he said in 2019 in reflection of how two years in the league left an imprint. That summer, he was reunited with Collet for France's FIBA World Cup campaign. It was a breath of fresh air for Ntilikina, whose "basketball father" helped to re-instill confidence. "[Collet] knew what I was able to potentially do," he said. "He just wanted me to play free minded, being free of leading the team, to play for my teammates and to play like I used to play, so it was good."[22]

It was a bit like the return of the prodigal son. Even if his time with New York wasn't the smoothest, he still learned and progressed. "I think [Collet] saw that I was maybe grown up with all this experience. I think he was surprised in a good way."[23] In September 2021, Ntilikina was traded to the Dallas Mavericks where, as of January 2023, he continues his NBA dream.

"A Culture of High Performance That Permeates"

The products of youth basketball *formation à la française* engage in different types of sports diplomacy that's informing the NBA and WNBA. But less visible is how the systems themselves have influenced how the NBA itself looks to train international talent. When Chris Ebersole, who spent a year in high school living and playing small-town ball in France, began working with NBA

International in 2013, the influx of players from around the world was entrenched and growing. "France has such an established system of basketball, starting with their youth system, and a really comprehensive pyramid sort of system through their clubs, through their federation," he said.[24]

As Associate Vice President and Head of Elite Basketball Operations, Ebersole was involved in how the NBA began to build out its international basketball programs. When work began to design their youth academy system in 2015–16, they looked across the Atlantic. He recalled:

> If you looked at the number of total international players in the NBA, it was a high number, over a hundred players, but the majority of them came from just a few select markets, and one of those was France, one of those was Australia.

The two countries formed one fifth of the international players in the NBA at the time, and had centralized development systems.

The NBA spoke with both federations to better understand their programs and functionality. "With INSEP, some of the things that jumped out to us to try to replicate in other places was the competition level, to have a group of young players play older players and have them learn how to lose, frankly, because that was part of development," Ebersole explained.

> We definitely bookmarked that, it's something we've tried to replicate with our NBA academies, to make sure that we build in the competition, not just to centralize all the best players in one place. But then to also make sure that they learn how to push themselves out of their comfort zones.

There was great appeal in having young basketball players grouped with elite athletes their age, albeit in other sports, as happens at INSEP or the Australian Institute of Sport. Moreover, the two institutions are also the training grounds for their national Olympians and elite athletes, not just their younger aspiring cohorts. "I think that culture of excellence, that culture of high-level competition is contagious," he said. "I think that's a great model."

Those conditions and ethos are what the NBA sought to replicate with its academy in Africa launched in 2017. Located in Saly,

Senegal, at a complex shared with the Diambars football academy, the NBA Academy Africa provides its basketball players their own schedule and staff, but they share spaces with their football counterparts such as weight rooms, cafeteria, and the larger campus. "One of the neat things about the academy in Senegal is that we have built that in," Ebersole noted, something mirrored by the NBA Latin America academy, which in 2021 moved to the La Loma Centro Deportivo multisport complex in San Luis Potosi, Mexico. It isn't just players who benefit from the proximity with other sports, it's the coaches and staff, too. "All those things are beneficial and can only help us think creatively about how to improve our programs," he said.

Another important component that's been incorporated into the NBA academy program is the emphasis on teaching basketball and education in its more holistic sense.[25] The league also looked at the French club professional academy model as a different iteration on educating young players. "The holistic development, life skills, putting together a whole experience that wasn't just show up and play your basketball," was something Ebersole said he and colleagues closely examined. They exchanged with counterparts at the Australian Institute of Sport and football youth academies, too. "That model of having an emphasis on academics, having optionality, I think that's an interesting trend that's going on in Europe in general," he said.

> Looking at that holistic development approach, which is something I think INSEP deserves a lot of credit for inspiring. But I think that's been something that also is a core tenant of what we try to do with the NBA academies.

At the NBA Academy Africa, the interplay of connections between French and francophone African basketball are on display. The NBA organized a trip by French international and NBA Champion with the Milwaukee Bucks (2021) Axel Toupane to their academy in Senegal to share and conduct practices with students. Toupane's father, Jean-Aimé, immigrated to France in 1980 from Kaoluck, Senegal, and built a career within French basketball; he served as head coach of the CFBB boys' juniors team from 2014 to 2021, when he was appointed head coach of Les Bleues. Francophone African coaches are featured as NBA Academy Africa coaches to guide and mold their young charges, like Joe Touomou, a

Cameroonian who hooped at Georgetown before he embarked on an NCAA and NBA coaching and scouting career.

But there are other ties that connect NBA Academy Africa players to counterparts in France: the NBA sent their Africa Academy team to Paris a few years ago for practices and scrimmages against the INSEP team. Ebersole, who was part of that trip, remarked on the benefits of such informal sports diplomacy between the Senegal-based and Paris-based players. "Those exchanges and sharing of ideas and culture, between INSEP and our Academy in Senegal, I think is emblematic of the overall connections between France and the francophone countries in Africa," he said. "Africa has always been in some ways the best known and most celebrated of the Basketball Without Borders camps." The NBA Academy Africa is another way to recognize and shine a spotlight on African basketball, one that was designed by a US-based professional sports league that's become global in its DNA and influenced by basketball *formation à la française*.

France's diverse population and its youth training programs explain why France still dominates the journey of international players into the NBA. According to Kenny Grant, who today works as an agent and thus a first-hand observer of global talent, "they have more athletes, they play in a good league, they have the good *espoirs* system to make sure that no one gets left out," he observed. It has helped that the game practiced on French hardcourts since the 1980s has been more similar to that of the NBA than other countries. It's a strength that is owed to the interwoven generations of informal sports diplomacy between France, the United States, and Africa. As Grant noted,

> The French game was a more athletic game of jumping, running, taking the ball to the basket. Shooting is always part of it, but in France, using their athletic ability as what was important, not just having it. They have been able to use it defensively, full court pressing, fast breaking, going to the basket on people, blocking shots. And I think that's what they're called to do in the NBA.

Notes

1   All Michel Rat quotes in this chapter, unless specified, from Michel Rat, Interview with the author, June 29, 2015; Michel Rat, Interview

with the author, September 24, 2021.

2 "Les Pôles 'Espoirs,'" FFBB, http://www.ffbb.com/ffbb/dtbn/parcours-dexcellence-sportive/les-poles-espoirs.

3 Lindsay Sarah Krasnoff, *The Making of Les Bleus: Sport in France, 1958–2010* (Lexington Books, 2012).

4 Fréderic Potet, "Les Français Disputent l'Euro Basket Mais Rêvent de l'Amérique," *Le Monde*, June 22, 1999.

5 Potet.

6 Krasnoff, *The Making of Les Bleus*.

7 FFBB, "Les Centres de Formation," FFBB, accessed November 23, 2022, http://www.ffbb.com/ffbb/dtbn/parcours-dexcellence-sportive/les-centres-de-formation.

8 Philippe Desnos, Interview with the author, April 18, 2017.

9 FFBB, "Les Centres de Formation," FFBB, http://www.ffbb.com/ffbb/dtbn/parcours-dexcellence-sportive/les-centres-de-formation.

10 All quotes from Boris Diaw in this chatper, unless otherwise stated, are from Boris Diaw, Interview with the author, February 26, 2017.

11 Christian Baltzer, Interview with the author, April 10, 2015.

12 Pascal Legendre, Interview with the author, August 11, 2017.

13 All Olivier Mazet quotes in this chapter are, unless specified, from Olivier Mazet, Interview with the author, March 12, 2018; Olivier Mazet, Interview with the author, March 1, 2018.

14 Eugene Weber, *Peasants into Frenchmen: The Modernization of Rural France, 1870–1914* (Stanford University Press, 1976).

15 "Hugo Besson drafté en NBA," Elan Chalon, June 24, 2022, https://www.elanchalon.com/hugo-besson-drafte-nba/.

16 Vincent Collet, Interview with the author, September 26, 2016.

17 All Kenny Grant quotes in this chapter, unless specified, from Kenny Grant, Interview with the author, August 26, 2020.

18 All Vincent Collet quotes in this chapter, unless specified, from Collet, Interview with the author.

19 *[Grand Format] Rencontre Exclusive Avec Frank Ntilikina*, 2017, https://www.youtube.com/watch?v=u9i-yejblgg; "Knicks Defend Ntilikina after LeBron's Remarks," ESPN.com, November 12, 2017, https://www.espn.com/nba/story/_/id/21391106/new-york-knicks-criticized-lebron-james-selecting-frank-ntilikina.

20 "Nike Features Knicks Rookie G Frank Ntilikina on Billboard Next to Madison Square Garden," October 16, 2017, https://www.

sportsbusinessjournal.com/Daily/Issues/2017/10/16/Marketing-and-Sponsorship/Ntilikina.aspx.

21 Ian Begley, "LeBron James on Knicks Rookie Frank Ntilikina," ESPN.
    com, April 9, 2018, https://www.espn.com/espn/now?now
    Id=21-0775003715407977070-4.

22 Frank Ntilikina, Interview with the author, September 25, 2019.

23 Lindsay Sarah Krasnoff, "How Frank Ntilikina's Summer with France
    Might Have Revived His NBA Career," SBNation.com, November 1,
    2019, https://www.sbnation.com/2019/11/1/20941254/frank-ntilikina-
    knicks.

24 All Chris Ebersole quotes in this chapter, unless otherwise specified,
    are from Chris Ebersole, Interview with the author, March 11, 2021.

25 NBA, "The NBA Academy Africa Opens New Facility in Saly,
    Senegal" (NBA, November 26, 2018), https://pr.nba.com/nba-
    academy-africa-new-facility-senegal/.

13

"Rubbing Shoulders" with African Basketball

Former French Basketball Federation (FFBB) and International Basketball Federation (FIBA) President Yvan Mainini once said, "I've always rubbed shoulders with African basketball," of his playing days gelling with a Comoros-born teammate to his work training African referees and beyond.[1] This phrase "rubbing shoulders" is perhaps apt when thinking about the links between France and francophone African basketball in the decades since independence. The *hexagone*'s role as a basketball breeding ground, from players to culture, is inextricably interconnected to the former empire in Africa, despite the complicated colonial and postcolonial history. Moreover, the rise of African basketball after 1960, particularly the perennial powerhouse of Senegal, has a little French accent. Initially this echoed holdover dynamics of the colonial era. It also reflected the early Fifth Republic's attempt to correct its 1960 Olympic humiliation by cultivation of soft power through technical and knowledge exchanges, such as training African sports executives at France's national sports school in Paris.[2] But today, the script has flipped.

These relationships, no matter how complex, are what set the French basketball market apart and enable it to create cultural cachet through the soft power of sports. They make it distinctive when compared to Australian, Canadian, and European counterparts, the other regions that also serve as pipelines into the NBA and WNBA. They also place the *hexagone* at an interesting intersection between the NBA and its growth in Africa. The advent of the NBA–FIBA Basketball Africa League (BAL), historically significant as the first pan-African professional sports league, draws a solid line under the importance of the African continent for the NBA's enterprises, not just its player pipelines.

With regards to the basketball empire, three flows of people-to-people cultural, technical, and knowledge exchange illustrate how different types of sports diplomacy cross-pollinated basketball. They are built on historic foundations, as illustrated in the case of technical and knowledge exchange between France and Senegal. The first flow centers around players, in which African players infuse French basketball, as examined in Part One, while French NBA players invest in and try to help grow basketball in Africa, as teased out in Part Two. The second focuses on French of the African diaspora, those whose parents, grandparents, or great grandparents immigrated to the *métropole*, are investing in basketball in the land of their family's cultural heritage and helping to grow the game. Third is that of Africans whose first-hand experience in the French system informed their knowledge of the game and are today instrumental to basketball's growth in Africa.

This chapter highlights several snapshots that illustrate these flows of cultural, technical, and knowledge exchange. It is far from comprehensive, and thus invites further study. But in providing a look under the hood for what these interwoven relationships look like, it illuminates the ways that French and African basketball have and continue to rub shoulders, and how the NBA increasingly features into this equation, particularly with regards to The BAL. It also surfaces the question: can such relationships be considered neocolonial when they are undertaken by French sportspeople with African heritage?

The Historic Ties That Bind

A look at how French and Senegalese basketball have historically "rubbed shoulders" provides insights into the ties that bind the two game-wise. It's important to note, however, that this relationship was unique due to Senegal's status during the African colonial era. One of the oldest French holdings in sub-Saharan Africa, since 1887 the inhabitants of Senegal's four communes (Dakar, Gorée, Saint-Louis, Rufisique) enjoyed rights as French citizens. They elected the first Black African to the French National Assembly in 1914,

Blaise Diagne, whose son Raoul played for the French national football team in the 1930s. In contrast, Africans in the rest of France's colonial holdings were subjects until 1946, when creation of the French Union accorded all members citizenship status and French nationality.[3]

Some scholars argue that independence fostered a closer relationship between Paris and Dakar, and that is reflected in the immediate post-independence basketball relationship.[4] Basketball ties between the two in the 1950s and early 1960s focused on knowledge and technical exchange, a formula that later paid dividends as officials trained at what is today France's elite sports school, INSEP, led the sport's growth. Senegalese basketball technicians and coaches then deployed that knowledge to the great benefit of its national teams, which dominated continental competition from the late 1960s through early 1980s.

One illustration of these ties was Claude Constantino, who served in different capacities in African basketball, including President of the FIBA Africa Coaches' Committee. Born in Senegal on December 13, 1938, he started playing at age thirteen and was selected as one of sixty-two players representing French West Africa in a 1953 Paris competition. Constantino's long playing career included representation of Senegal at the 1968 Mexico City Games, the first African team to contest the Olympic basketball tournament; he began to coach the national team in 1971.

But he was also a technician. In the early 1960s, the Senegalese government sent Constantino to INSEP, where he studied under former French international and educator Michel Rat. Upon Constantino's return home in 1963, he co-founded the Senegalese National Technical Detection, the first in Africa designed to train and level-up player skills. His focus on developing youth players very likely employed what he learned in Paris, one example of the technical and knowledge exchange fostered by this "rubbing shoulders" between French and African basketball.[5]

Since the 1970s, French coaches and referees have worked with Senegalese and African counterparts to build knowledge, share technical information, and foster cultural exchange through basketball. They were officials like Mainini, Rat, and Pierre Dao, a former player, coach, and longtime advocate of African basketball who over decades deepened the ties between France, Senegal, and African counterparts.[6]

Then there is the interplay of exchanges fostered by generations of players. There's a long history of African teams traveling to France for training camps and workshops and vice versa, as illustrated with the Senegalese women's team in Chapter Three. In 1992, a French women's team played a tournament in Dakar, where according to *Basket-Ball*, "[basketball] is quite a cult. If you come for basketball, you are welcomed like a Messiah." The country's premier stadium, the 5,000-seat Stade Marius N'Diaye, was considered "the mecca of Senegalese basketball," and, notably, a gift of cooperation from the Chinese government in the 1970s. At the time, the Senegalese National Technical Director was "Busnel" Diagne, named after famed French basketball tactician, coach, and administrator Robert Busnel, "a tireless worker" who in the 1960s "brought his know-how" to the region.[7]

By the early 1990s, Senegalese basketball was a long way from its illustrious continental dominance at the national and club levels of the late 1960s, 1970s, and early 1980s. The reason? Senegalese basketballers, men and women, left to play on the French mainland where more competitive leagues were attractive opportunities, an exodus facilitated by FFBB and FIBA rule changes on player migration and mobility in 1985. According to one Senegalese basketball official in 1992,

> France is the El Dorado for a Senegalese basketballer. Generally, in our time, players came to France after a solid experience in the country. In the teams, we really gave pride of place to training. The leaders were patient, there was a real investment in young people. I have the impression that today, the results take precedence. And that some come to Europe with illusions.[8]

Players Rubbing Shoulders

The flow of African players hooping on French hardcourts gained traction in the 1970s and continues to this day, fostering a variety of exchanges that firm the global game. Previous chapters have provided greater details of what these interplays looked like, but it's a worthwhile reminder that playing professionally in France, and in Europe, wasn't easy for African players competed with Americans and other foreigners for playing time and experience.

Still, the flow of players continues today. By October 2020, when play resumed after the COVID-19 pandemic's first shutdown phase, ten of the top African female players dominated French courts in the Ligue Féminine de Basket-Ball, representing Nigeria, Senegal, Mali, Cote d'Ivoire, and Mozambique, among others. While elite players initially started careers at the NCAA rungs, helping to "level up" their national teams upon return home, the recruitment of African female players to Europe and France represented the game's growth and development. As FIBA. basketball noted, "this process of exportation to Europe, and particularly France, is the proof that Africa's potential is being recognized."[9] Senegal is also an exporter of male players, and during the 2021–2 season sent twenty-three men to French leagues, including five in ProA; the top professional league also featured players from eleven other African countries.[10]

There are also French NBA players who "rub shoulders" with African basketball. Part Two noted how Boris Diaw, Nicolas Batum, and Evan Fournier contributed to the game in the homeland of their fathers or mothers. A different example is that of Tariq Abdul-Wahad, whose NBA career began in 1997 while Diaw, Batum, and Fournier were still adolescents. Abdul-Wahad's parents were from French Guinea in the Caribbean, not a direct tie to Africa, but growing up and playing around Parisian courts provided first-hand exposure to African basketball, thanks to the capital's melting pot of hoops influences. "Some of my heroes are African players," he said. "It's weird to say, but you play in the playgrounds in France, you grow up with African basketball. These guys get some of the resources and they can work on their game, but what is being done back home for them?"[11]

In 2002, when Abdul-Wahad played for the Dallas Mavericks, he traveled to Senegal with team executive Amadou Gallo Fall to observe a fledgling basketball initiative. The program, SEED Project, fused learning the game with academic studies and life skills education, designed by Fall to provide education and economic opportunities through basketball.[12] The Frenchman enjoyed the trip and the people he met at SEED. Supporting it was an easy decision. "This is a no brainer," he said of why he contributed financially. "Money was put down, but not to get anything back, so it's not an investment to make money. It's an investment in Africa, in Africa's youth," he explained.

Moreover, Abdul-Wahad was sold on SEED's prospects. "It was going to be big. You've got seven footers walking down the street [in Senegal], you put them in the gym, you give them a ball and teach them how to play, it's going to be big." And he credits Fall with SEED's success. "[He] did an outstanding job developing this project," Abdul-Wahad reflected. "Today, it's a factory of talent." SEED graduates include Gorgui Dieng, who parlayed a basketball scholarship at the University of Louisville into a long-term NBA career, and since 2017 serves as a partner for the NBA Academy Africa.[13] Abdul-Wahad wasn't the last Frenchman to be impressed and invest. In 2015, Diaw's foundation Babac'ards teamed up with SEED to launch a girls' academy.[14]

Then there's the example of Joakim Noah. New York-born Noah, who holds French, American, and Swedish nationality, was a product of the American basketball system, a stand-out player with the University of Florida selected ninth by the Chicago Bulls in the 2007 NBA Draft. But the two-time NBA All-Star and 2014 Defensive Player of the Year opted to play for France, notably for EuroBasket 2011. Noah's family ties to sport originated in Yaoundé, Cameroon, where his father, French tennis legend Yannick Noah spent his early childhood years; his grandfather, Zacharie, was a footballer who in 1961 won the Coupe de France with Sedan. Since 2021, Joakim, whose fourteen-year NBA career ended in 2020, is a strategic investor in NBA Africa, the business venture that oversees the NBA's African enterprises, including The BAL. Other strategic investors include former US President Barack Obama and former French international and NBA veteran Ian Mahinmi, who has family ties to Bénin.[15] Throughout The BAL's 2022 season, Noah helped promote the league, placing it in the spotlight for his 495,000 Instagram and 638,500 Twitter followers worldwide.[16]

The Lady Hoops

Another important flow of cultural, technical, and knowledge exchange through basketball occurs as French-born organizers from the African diaspora are working to grow the game in the land of their parents. They are people like Syra Sylla, born in France in 1983 to parents who emigrated from Senegal. As a kid, she was shy and found it difficult to speak in front of a group of people. But things changed once she was eighteen and discovered basketball through a friend. "That's how I fell in love with basketball," she said.[17]

The game became more than just a passion. For Sylla, it helped develop confidence thanks to its cultivation of a team community, teamwork, and how her teammates trusted her on-court when she had the ball. "I think I learned how to be confident in life thanks to what I learned on the court, because of the values of basketball," she said. "I found myself, thanks to basketball."

She found herself, a passion, and a way to help bring the lessons and values of the game to girls in Senegal. Although Sylla grew up in France, every other summer she returned to her parents' hometowns in Senegal to visit family. But her story in African basketball began when, as a twenty-year-old working in basketball journalism, she interviewed Amadou Gallo Fall. Through him, she began to travel more within Senegal to observe and chronicle the game. "Basketball was big in the country," she said. But it was when she started meeting everyday players that she identified a need: basketball shoes.

Sylla began a social action organization to donate basketball sneakers and gear to players in the countryside outside Ranerou, a city in the Ferlo region close to the Mauritanian border. This part of the Senegalese countryside lacks easy access to many things, including water and power. "When it is night-time, nobody can see," she explained of the circumstances. Yet, the city had four basketball courts. "I don't know how or why," she said, but noted "it's almost like they didn't know how to use the hoops." That prompted her to teach some of the girls and young women how to play. She taught them how to practice, how to shoot, and other fundamentals of the game. "They were actually going to the court and trying to improve their game by watching videos on YouTube and everything," Sylla explained of how her young protégés progressed in her absence.

She also noted how basketball became a way for women and girls to engage and interact, an important consideration in a country where football remains king yet dominated by men. "The women didn't have any sports to do there, because they cannot play soccer," she observed. "But with basketball, basketball is a mixed sport. It's for women and for men, it's for young and for older people. So, it's for everybody." In this way, according to Sylla, basketball can empower girls for it provided concrete ways for them to engage in activity outside of the domestic sphere.

> That was always the thinking before: that they are women, so they have to get husbands; when they are kids they have to take care of the house and then when they grow up they have to get married, have children, educate their children, and that's the only way to be. But now with sports, and basketball in particular, it can feel like they are something else, not only housekeepers.

Sylla noted that the girls went from playing basketball four days each year when she visited to playing everyday thanks to now knowing the game, having gear and shoes (thanks to her donations program), and the interest. "They have a team, they have jerseys, so they play games, they have practices. They do everything," she said.

On her travels throughout Senegal, she's noted a distinct change in the growth of basketball and the NBA since 2010. The league's investment in Africa, Canal+ Afrique's broadcasts of NBA games, and documentaries on African players fuels this growth, but so, too, does social media and the NBA's League Pass streaming platform. "You can know literally everything without watching a game," she said. "In Senegal when I see my cousin, they know everything about every player, about their wives, about their lives, about everything, thanks to social media." Moreover, she noted, the storytelling produced and posted through platforms like YouTube make content much easier to access.

Sylla identified as both French and Senegalese, but above and beyond noted, "I think I'm a basketball diplomat." In Senegal, she communicated, represented, and negotiated with the youths of her parents' village to create the basketball team, to explain and impart the game's fundamentals. But she did it back home, too. "I realized I could do it also in France with my peers. There are little girls that are like me, their parents' origins are from Africa, so we have both traditions and both cultures. We are French because we live in France, and we have the French way of life. But we still have our African roots deep inside us, and it's in the way we eat at home with our sisters and brothers. And it's the way we dress when we have weddings and everything," she explained. "We have both of our cultures, French and African."

For Sylla, The BAL can help French and NBA basketball continue to rub shoulders with its African counterpart. She noted that one of the players who signed with Tunisian team US Monastir to play the first BAL season had a long career playing professionally in France but opted to play back home in Tunisia. That's helped flip the script a bit, she said.

> Two years ago, I was dreaming of players from Europe who would wish to go to Africa. So now all the players that are involved in the basketball community here, now everybody is asking, "How can we go there [Africa]? Which are the teams?" So, everybody's looking at [The BAL].

The Basketball Storyteller

Then there's the ways that French of the African diaspora are representing, communicating, and negotiating through basketball at the international level. The story of Youcef Ouldyassia, a former player, journalist, documentary filmmaker, and Associate Vice President and Head of Content for the BAL, provides another angle into the issue at hand.

Ouldyassia was born May 3, 1974, south of Paris in Bretigny-sur-Orge to parents from Algeria. He began playing basketball as a nine-year-old, made his professional debut with Caen in 1993, and played with the French U23 national team at the 1996 European Championship. When in 2000 the Algerian Basketball Federation tapped players of the diaspora to fortify the senior national team, Ouldyassia opted in, as he had not yet played for France at the senior level and was thus eligible under FIBA rules.

He was a bit hesitant, however, unsure how homegrown players would react. Although Ouldyassia visited his grandparents in Algeria as a kid, he worried. "Would they be nice to us? How would they feel about us coming on their territory?"[18] Instead, he was warmly welcomed. "You could tell you are part of a family, that is something that was amazing," he said. "This experience was one of the best in my life."

Ouldyassia was part of Algeria's storied AfroBasket 2001 campaign. The tournament, historically dominated by Senegal,

Egypt, Cote d'Ivoire, and Angola, had long lacked an Algerian imprint; the country last ascended the podium in 1965 when it claimed the bronze medal alongside Tunisia (silver) and host Morocco (gold). But 2001 was different. Les Verts (The Greens), as the team is known, began the tournament with an easy 76–46 win over South Africa, toppled reigning champions Angola 78–70, then lost 58–59 to Nigeria. But it was enough to qualify for the knockout rounds, where they sailed through to the final, a rematch against Angola. This time, however, Les Verts were outmatched 68–78. But their silver medal assured them a first-ever appearance in the following year's FIBA World Cup, during which they tipped off against the United States.

Although Ouldyassia was not part of the post-2001 journey with Les Verts, the experience marked him profoundly. "It was a great honor to represent the country of my parents, and it was also a great honor to represent France," he said of playing for his two cultural heritages. "For me, having the two countries was a big strength and I'm really proud of it. It was something different, and in my opinion, every new experience, good or bad, we learned from it. This was a great one."

After he hung up his sneakers as a professional player, Ouldyassia moved into journalism where for more than a decade he helped introduce francophone audiences to African athletes. Although he was a host with Canal+ and InfoSport+, it was the parent company's Africa-centric division, Canal+ Afrique, which broadcasts to twenty-seven countries, that approached him to lead a new show. The resultant program, "Talent Afrique," was one of the biggest shows on African sports and paved the way for Ouldyassia's onward work with the broadcaster to maximize its rights to televise the NBA in Africa.

Ouldyassia worked to bring the NBA and its African players to francophone African audiences. "We focused on African [players] but we didn't forget that the NBA was also a show," he said of the approach. "We talked about the NBA as regular TV [journalists] should do, talking about Steph Curry, LeBron James, and all those stars. But also focused on the African players."

In this way, Ouldyassia introduced African audiences to the NBA, its culture, and the stories that drive it as a business and social phenomenon. This was foundational work because in Africa people consume basketball differently. The high price of data means that many are not streaming full-length games unless they have access to Wi-Fi. His show helped people watch live games and follow the NBA's news. Moreover, Internet access also facilitated technical and knowledge exchange. "I've been talking to a lot of African coaches, and they told me that they can now work on having the best results, the way maybe Gregg Popovich is coaching, or some other great coaches thanks to tutorials on the Internet," he relayed. The ability to access and watch videos is helping to provide greater access to the coaching and training skills that have often been lacking in Africa. For Ouldyassia, "it's an easy way to learn. If we know we still need to improve in Africa, in a lot of stuff, we can also improve that way."

In addition to his sports journalism work with Canal+ Afrique, Ouldyassia made basketball-centric documentaries. One focused on the Promo Jeune Basket (PJB) club in Goma, Democratic Republic of Congo (DRC). After it aired on Canal+ Afrique, the local French Embassy asked to distribute it country-wide to show the good work that basketball could accomplish. "That's diplomacy for me," he said. Even more beneficial for Ouldyassia was that some of the kids featured earned basketball scholarships to the United States and were doing well.

In 2019, Ouldyassia was named to his position with The BAL, where he focuses on telling the stories of African basketball players and basketball traditions. The BAL is designed to grow the basketball ecosystem on the African continent and provide ways for home grown players to play professionally in an Africa-based NBA league rather than depart for North America or Europe. "The goal is to keep the talent in Africa," Ouldyassia said of The BAL. "This is how we're going to raise Africa."

African Basketball Rubbing Shoulders in France

There is also the flow of basketball exchanges between Africans with formative experience in France who are today helping to grow the game, and the NBA, both in the *métropole* and across Africa. Such stakeholders are agents like Bouna N'Diaye, founder of Comsport agency, born in Gambia but raised in Senegal, who immigrated to France as a fourteen years old. Although he played basketball, in his adult years he's excelled as an agent, brokering contracts for French players in the NBA and WNBA while also helping to grow the game in Senegal.[19] They are grassroots organizers like Victor Samnick, the Cameroonian-born former Georgetown University defensive specialist who, after a professional career in France, is now helping talent in the *hexagone* learn more about and transition to NCAA basketball programs through his association, B Dreamers.

And they are sportspeople like Will Mbiakop who is helping to remake African basketball in part through sports diplomacy. Mbiakop was born in Cameroon in 1980 but grew up in France. He began playing basketball in high school, first on the Parisian outskirts and then in the Picardy region of northern France. "I was not too bad," he said of his teenaged hoops prowess.[20] Coaches agreed, for they selected him to play with higher level clubs. He stopped playing around age seventeen to focus on his academic studies but never lost his passion for the game. Instead, he channeled his energies into organizing basketball camps and events.

One day, a friend invited Mbiakop to help out at a new basketball academy in Yaoundé. It was an invitation to dream big. "We both have the same thought and belief, we believe in the transformative power of sports," Mbiakop explained. "It has helped me a lot as an individual and as a professional, as well. So, I thought that I would help him with his basketball academy." Thus began a career working to develop the game on the African continent, which included seven years with NBA Africa.

It wasn't easy work. "In our continent, there are often issues that are related to war, ethnicity, lack of tolerance, discrimination, and all this stuff," he said.

> I think sports is a powerful vehicle to overcome those challenges, and obviously boost diplomatic efforts. . .I feel like Africa has inherent qualities, assets that the other part of the world may not have. And I'm talking about the intangible assets which can be summarized as values, norms, heritage, customs, education, way of behaving. I feel like sports and diplomacy gets a special boost because in Africa, because of those intangible assets that are part of the African DNA.

Of note is the way that basketball diplomacy in Africa helps boost the creation of identities and communities. As previously discussed, basketball played a role in helping post-independence African countries form identities, create shared histories around their national teams and their exploits, and rally nations together. From Mbiakop's perspective, basketball still plays a role. He pointed to the number of African-born and -trained players who are now in the NBA, which accounted for nearly 10 percent of the international player labor force in 2020. "Kids, they have people and players to relate to," he said. Such success stories create role models and inspire kids, boys and girls alike. That's why WNBA Champions like Senegalese-born Astou N'Diaye, the first African to win a WNBA Championship, are so important.

There has long been a connection between francophone African and French basketball. Members of the French national teams invest in and promote basketball (and other) opportunities in the countries of their parents' or grandparents' births. Yet, today it is ever-more French of the African diaspora and Africans with experience in France who are shaping both French and African hoops, adding yet another layer of complexity into the question of whose basketball empire it anyway.

As longtime basketball journalist Alexander Wolff wrote, "basketball knowledge no longer flows in one direction."[21] Testimonies like that of Ouldyassia and Sylla challenge concepts of whose empire the basketball one belongs to in the larger *Basketball Empire* story. Increasingly in the twenty-first century, perhaps it is far more about fostering a global basketball identity, based on a shared culture, reference points, sense of history, and citizen-community.

Notes

1   FIBA Africa, "Cinquantenaire: Temoignages" (FIBA Africa, n.d.), 6.

2   Michel Rat, Interview with the author, September 24, 2021.

3   "France and the French Union," *The Round Table* 43, no. 169–72 (December 1, 1952): 145–52, https://doi.org/10.1080/00358535208451802.

4   Tony Chafer, "France and Senegal: The End of the Affair?," *SAIS Review (1989–2003)* 23, no. 2 (2003): 155–67.

5   According to Constantino, the rise of streetball deteriorated Senegal's focus on youth formation, as players were less inclined to have mastery of the game's fundamentals; this negatively impacted the

overall approach to building and sustaining national teams. But, he noted, after 1980, there was a push to refocus on a return to the roots of formation. FIBA Africa, "Cinquantenaire: Temoignages" (FIBA Africa, n.d.), 12.

6   For more, see FIBA Africa, "Cinquantenaire: Temoignages" (FIBA Africa, n.d.).

7   Constant Nemale, "L'exode a Meurtri Le Sénégal," *Basket-Ball*, October 1992, 8.

8   Nemale, 9.

9   FIBA, "African Women Creating a Legacy in France," FIBA. basketball, October 7, 2020, http://www.fiba.basketball/news/ african-women-creating-a-legacy-in-france.

10 International Centre for Sports Studies and FIBA, "International Basketball Migration Report (IBMR) 2022" (FIBA, November 2022), 28, https://www.fiba.basketball/documents/ibmr2022.pdf.

11 All Tariq Abdul-Wahad quotes in this chapter, unless specified, from Tariq Abdul-Wahad, Interview with the author, January 21, 2022.

12 J. Simon Rofe and Lindsay Sarah Krasnoff, "Transcript: Interview with Amadou Gallo Fall" (SOAS University of London, May 2020), "Basketball Diplomacy in Africa: An Oral History from SEED Project to the Basketball Africa League (BAL), https://eprints.soas.ac. uk/32957/1/BBDipAF2020%20Amadou%20Gallo%20Fall.pdf.

13 "Gorgui Dieng, SEED Alum, Signs Long-Term Extension with Timberwolves," SEED PROJECT, accessed December 26, 2022, http://www.seedproject.org/blog/2017/2/14/gorgui-dieng-seed-alum- signs-long-term-extension-with-timberwolves; "NBA and SEED Project Officially Open First Academy of Its Kind in Africa," NBA. com: NBA Communications, May 4, 2017, https://pr.nba.com/ nba-academy-africa-opening/.

14 "Boris Diaw and SEED Project to Launch Girls Academy in Senegal," FIBA.basketball, February 3, 2015, https://www.fiba.basketball/news/ boris-diaw-and-seed-project-to-launch-girls-academy-in-senegal.

15 "Former President Barack Obama Joins NBA Africa as Strategic Partner," NBA.com, accessed December 26, 2022, https://www.nba. com/news/former-president-barack-obama-joins-nba-africa-as- strategic-partner.

16 "Joakim Noah (@JoakimNoah) / Twitter," Twitter, accessed December 26, 2022, https://twitter.com/JoakimNoah; "Joakim Noah (@stickity13) Instagram Photos and Videos," accessed December 26, 2022, https:// www.instagram.com/stickity13/.

17 All Syra Sylla quotes in this chapter, unless otherwise noted, are from Syra Sylla, Syra Sylla Transcript, Interview by J. Simon Rofe and Lindsay Sarah Krasnoff (London: Self-Published Research Output, May 14, 2020), Basketball Diplomacy in Africa: An Oral History from SEED Project to the Basketball Africa League (BAL), https://eprints. soas.ac.uk/32901/.

18 All Youcef Ouldyassia quotes in this chapter, unless specified, are from Youcef Ouldyassia, Youcef Ouldyassia Transcript, Interview by J. Simon Rofe and Lindsay Sarah Krasnoff, May 14, 2020, Basketball Diplomacy in Africa: An Oral History from SEED Project to the Basketball Africa League (BAL), https://eprints.soas.ac.uk/32959/.

19 Yann Casseville, "Moi, Je. . .Bouna Ndiaye," *Basket Le Mag*, September 2017.

20 All Will Mbiakop quotes this chapter, unless specified, from Will Mbiakop, Will Mbiakop Transcript, Interview by J. Simon Rofe and Lindsay Sarah Krasnoff (London: Self-Published Research Output, May 14, 2020), https://eprints.soas.ac.uk/32907/.

21 Alexander Wolff, *Big Game, Small World: A Basketball Adventure*, 20th Anniversary Edition (Duke University Press, 2022), xxxii.

14

Contributions to the NBA and WNBA

After France won the 2018 FIFA World Cup, stars Paul Pogba and Antoine Griezmann procured NBA Championship-style rings for each of their Les Bleus teammates. According to ESPN.com, the two NBA fans desired to replicate the US tradition of commemorating a championship title with a diamond-encrusted bauble. The resultant ring, designed by Jason of Beverly Hills, the go-to jeweler for such NBA rings, featured the Gallic cock with two World Cup stars centered over a replica of the tricolor flag in sapphires, white diamonds, and rubies.[1] Paid for by Pogba, with contributions from Griezmann, it was a bling-bling example of how the NBA's culture and traditions had cross-pollinated French football stars, some of the world's best. Yet, thanks to how the country has helped internationalize and globalize the NBA, this example isn't necessarily an Americanization of French culture; rather, it's a demonstration of today's global NBA.

The twenty-first-century league with its French accent has navigated this catechism despite a history of French disdain towards American culture and perennial anxieties over the Americanization of basketball. The rise of Michael Jordan in the 1990s was viewed as part of the "new global capitalism" founded on US culture, a continuity from postwar influences.[2] The NBA was critiqued by the press, and French Basketball Federation (FFBB) officials were conflicted for how to best react to and, perhaps at times grudgingly, engage with it for there was no doubt the league drove the sport's overall growth, even as some feared for the future of French basketball.[3]

But increasingly, for many players, the NBA was viewed as the ideal of what entertainment-driven basketball could be. As longtime *Sports Illustrated* basketball reporter Alexander Wolff wrote in 2002, "the NBA came to be regarded less as a force of cultural imperialism than as an elite version of something essentially familiar."[4] That's because basketball was born global.[5] The appeal for some of the most competitive French basketballers by the 2000s was to play with and hold their own against some of the world's best players, who were in the NBA and WNBA. As the *hexagone* became a main pipeline of talent, they began to influence the leagues' evolutions as part of the larger international cohort. Thus, once France began to inscribe itself within NBA and WNBA history, it became more difficult to villainize their contributions as "American," particularly as so many played for the national teams and gave back to the domestic game.

This chapter focuses on how the sports diplomacy snapshots examined in previous chapters began to mark the NBA and WNBA. It points to how the league's globalization and internationalization began to create a more global entity in the twenty-first century. The evolutions within the WNBA were slightly different, given its smaller size and less significant financial and media footprint, but also embraced a global basketball identity and are an area for further study. Basketballers produced in France helped build a certain cultural cachet in the North American leagues, a story still in the making, but already pointing towards ever-closer links.

Evolving the NBA

The first international player in the NBA was Henry Biasatti, an Italian-born Canadian who played in the fledgling league's first-ever match on November 1, 1946, but it wasn't until the 1980s and 1990s that the NBA began to become more global.[6] Veteran sports communications professional Terry Lyons had a front-row seat to the internationalization of the league's labor force thanks to a twenty-five-year stint with the NBA, including as Director of Media Relations (1989–93) and Vice President of International Communications (1992–2008). While television was the single most important factor in growing the NBA's international popularity, including the springboard of the 1992 Summer

Olympics, the success of international players is critical. "Tony Parker's ability to turn from a second-round diamond in the rough draft pick to a world-class point guard for the NBA Champion San Antonio Spurs becomes the next piece in that puzzle in a relatively short period of time," he said.[7]

That's why he considers players and labor pipelines as the only way to truly measure impact. While the next wave of great international NBA players can come from anywhere, for Lyons, the key to success for an NBA player is not the entertainment value on-court or the flashy ways they can score, but in their ability to defend. "That is so often overlooked," he said.

> People will look at the stats and see the player scoring points or his ability to shoot the ball from a technical standpoint, but how often are they looking at his technical skills and ability to defend?. . .There's a lot of team defense in the NBA, and people don't realize how strong that is, and that's the reason a guy will make it or not.[8]

The French, alongside international and particularly European players, contributed to the NBA's overall twenty-first-century evolution in three ways. First, they helped broaden its labor force. Season over season, the country continues to send young men to the world's elite professional championship. The below numbers paint a portrait over time, based on the number of international players on Opening Night rosters; it does not account for players who sign two-way contracts or who are signed to an NBA contract during the season. According to NBA International, as of July 2022 France had contributed thirty-nine players to the league all-time, leading all other countries as the NBA's main pipeline except for Canada, who had sent forty-seven players. The addition of Moussa Diabate (Los Angeles Clippers) and Ousmane Dieng (Oklahoma City Thunder) to the league as of October 2022, notches France's total to forty-one players all-time.

Second, French players have contributed to the changing game. NBA International Associate Vice President and Head of Elite Basketball Operations Chris Ebersole, who lived in France for a year during high school, noted that by the 2000s, the post-Dream Team influx that included Parker, Boris Diaw, and Ronny Turiaf began to imprint the NBA's domestic game with its emphasis on

TABLE 14.1 *French and African players on NBA opening night rosters, 2005–22*

Season	International Players	Countries Represented	Players From France	% of International Players from France	Players From Canada	Players From Serbia	Players From Africa
2005–06	82	32	5	6%	2	8	6
2006–07	83	37	7	8%	2	8	6
2007–08	76	31	8	12%	4	7	6
2008–09	77	32	9	12%	4	6	6
2009–10	83	36	10	12%	4	6	3
2010–11	84	38	11	13%	4	4	6
2011–12	77	36	9	12%	6	3	6
2012–13	84	37	10	12%	8	N/A	N/A
2013–14	92	39	10	11%	8	2	6
2014–15	101	37	10	10%	12	1	6
2015–16	100	37	10	10%	12	3	10

2016–17	113	41	10	9%	11	3	14
2017–18	108	42	10	9%	11	5	12
2018–19	108	42	9	8%	11	5	13
2019–20	108	38	8	7%	16	6	12
2020–21	107	41	9	8%	17	6	14
2021–22	109	39	7	6%	18	5	13
2022–23	120	40	9	8%	22	5	16

Source: NBA International

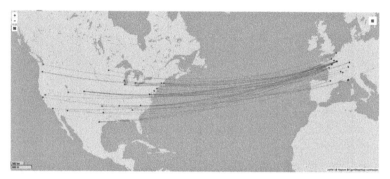

FIGURE 14.1 *French players, from formation clubs to first NBA team all-time (through July 2022). Source: NBA International.*

team-focused play. "There was definitely an influence that came from the European game into the NBA," he said. "Players from international backgrounds share[d] the ball and did not play an isolation-heavy-style coming up in their basketball careers."[9]

The San Antonio Spurs were one of the first franchises to benefit from this influx and helped foment greater openness to the success that international players, particularly Europeans, could provide to NBA teams. General Manager R. C. Buford and Coach Gregg Popovich are often credited with the Spurs' ability to foster a team culture that took into account their international players and their styles.[10] Oklahoma City Thunder General Manager Sam Presti was one of Popovich's protégés in the early 2000s, and is often credited with convincing the veteran coach to give Parker a closer look in scouting. As Presti later told the *Washington Post*, the Spurs' formula rested on the team's ability not just to scout and recruit international talent, but to build an ecosystem to help them shine. "Certainly, they not only did an excellent job in identifying players, but also in creating an environment and a system where those players would want to play and would be capable of thriving," he said.[11] The results paid off, as the Spurs won the NBA Championship four times in the new millennium with a roster that reflected this ethos (which included Parker).

But the Spurs weren't the only team that took advantage of the coming-of-age of the generation inspired by the 1992 US Dream Team. Many other teams did, too, with varying degrees of success.

As Presti noted of this shift in 2015, "the role of the French player, and international players in general, continues to build in importance as the NBA game begins to mirror many of the best traits of the European game."[12]

It's an evolution for which he's had a front-row seat. In 2007 he was hired by the Thunder, then one of the youngest general managers in US professional sports. "The presence of the French player has steadily grown in the NBA and in [the] recent Drafts since the early 2000s," he told CNN International in 2015. But thanks to the earlier Parker generation, league officials like Presti kept an eye on the French pipeline. As he explained, "when a strong core of young players is developing in unison, as was the case in INSEP or the French Junior National teams, there will be a greater importance placed not only on seeing the present-day prospects, but also forecasting future generations."[13]

Since then, several young French players have suited up for Oklahoma City, including Joffrey Lauvergne, Timothé Luwawu-Cabarrot, Jaylen Hoard, Théo Maledon, Olivier Sarr, and most recently, Ousmane Dieng (2022-present). Some arrived to the organization with US experience already under their belts, whether in the NCAA, G-League, or NBA itself. But for others, such as Maledon or Dieng, Oklahoma City was their first step in building their own American hoop dreams.

As Presti noted in 2015, the transition can be tricky even for the most mature young players. "As with any international player, the transition is not just one of playing or competition but also cultural and lifestyle," he explained.

Imagine moving not only into the most competitive work environment you can in your given profession, but also having to move to a new country where you don't speak the language primarily. The NBA has gotten much smarter about orientating international players over the years, and this has only been possible by observation, analysis and implementation.[14]

For Evan Fournier, who in March 2022 became the Knicks' single-season leader for three-point shots made, international players have made a strong imprint. "I think we changed the NBA tremendously, with positive and negative things," he reflected. Although he acknowledged that European players made it much more common to flop on NBA hardcourts, more positive European contributions comes from an increased focus on teamwork and improvements in the league's shot game. European players, he noted, are long used to shooting from everywhere on the floor, including long three-point shots, a trait they brought across the Atlantic. "That was something that was only in Europe for a long time, and now it's here," he noted.[15] Indeed, the NBA's three-point shot revolution since the mid-2010s has significantly altered the game.[16]

The subsequent technical and knowledge exchanges that flourish around the league have created another impact. The NBA hasn't just been a one-way style exchange, as Ebersole pointed out. "There's really been a convergence," of the blending of basketball styles.

> I think European basketball has incorporated some of the isolation and pick-and-roll heavy styles that were sort of American basketball staples in the 90s and early 2000s. And vice versa, I think the NBA has also adopted more and more European concepts in terms of movement without the ball and cutting off the ball, those sorts of things.

This has all blended together in interesting ways on NBA hardcourts. "Now you end up with teams in the NBA who look a lot more like what we would consider those European styles," Ebersole said, pointing to the Golden State Warriors and San Antonio Spurs. As NBA Deputy Commissioner and Chief Operating Officer Mark Tatum observed, "international players, and particularly European players, have had a profound impact on the brand of basketball being played today, which is as exciting as it has ever been."[17]

In turn, these international players helped bring the wider world to their local franchise fan bases. Former NBA Commissioner David Stern, who brought the NBA to the far corners of the planet, noted the importance of international players for NBA teams. "You learn a little bit more and you experience a little bit of internationalization by virtue of your association with [foreign players]," he said. "The San Antonio Spurs are a walking advertisement for the internationalization of our sport."[18]

But the benefits can work in other ways, as evidenced by the NBA Global Games. Since their launch in 1984, the league has played eighty-four preseason and thirty-four regular season games abroad as of January 2023. In 2016, Stern noted the importance of the NBA Global Games for the league's international players. "When we travel," he said, "the players from the country to which we're going delight in taking their teammates out and showing them the best local culture, the food and drink and other things."[19]

It's a two-way exchange of information, ideas, and more that's also left a mark on the NBA's executives. As Deputy Commissioner Tatum observed, "we've seen firsthand the power of sports in creating connections among people of different cultures and backgrounds. The game has taken me all over the world, and sports have always served as an entry point to finding commonality."[20] It's a unique form of informal sports diplomacy.

Lastly, French and international players were part of the league's cultural shift into even more of a fashion trend-setting enterprise than just sneakers and baggy shorts of earlier eras. The NBA's dress code, set by Stern in 2005 to require "business casual" attire when team members are officially representing their franchise or the league itself, was originally controversial. Critics argued it unfairly targeted Black players and the gold chains, throwback jerseys, and do-rags closely associated with hip-hop culture which had fused with the larger player culture.

Yet, players have since made the most of the regulations. They converted the walk from their cars or team bus into the arena into a catwalk, fueled by fashion houses, amplified on social media accounts like Instagram's League Fits, and launched a new industry.[21] For Fournier, the dress code and the overall league player codes of conduct, including fines for foul language, were a welcome move. "The NBA does a really good job of making sure we have a good image," he confided. "Now, the NBA's probably the league the fans appreciate the most, I think."

Evolving the W

The number of French players in the WNBA is one way of measuring the country's impact, even as those numbers are far smaller given that there are just twelve teams in the league—144 roster slots per season—compared to thirty men's franchises with around 450

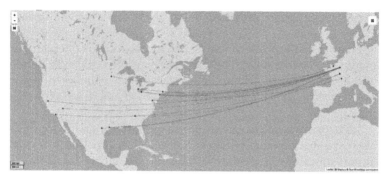

FIGURE 14.2 *French players, from formation clubs to first WNBA team all-time (through July 2022). Source: WNBA.*

players. Since the W's maiden 1997 season, fourteen Frenchwomen have played on its hardcourts, a ratio very close to that of Frenchmen into the NBA.

Because so many WNBA players, American or otherwise, compete overseas during the off-season, it's a league whose DNA is infused with and enhanced by overseas experience. For example, according to the league, sixty-six of their players under contract as of November 2, 2022, signed to play overseas in Australia, Czech Republic, France, Greece, Hungary, Israel, Italy, Poland, Spain, Tunisia, and Turkey.[22] Notably absent on this list: China, which had yet to lift its zero COVID policies, and Russia as W players opted out of contracts following Moscow's February 24, 2022 invasion of Ukraine and 294-day wrongful detention of longtime star and Team USA stalwart Brittney Griner. Thus, there's a far less stark delineation in terms of how its international players contribute to the game style and culture than on the men's side as there's already significant global migration into and by WNBA players.

French players have been part of the overall changes to the WNBA's game style and culture, although due to their smaller numbers, not as visible. The league began to build its identity on- and off-court during its first decade, as the eight original franchises who contested the 1997 season grew to twelve. More rookies infused rosters, and by 2007 the game was faster and more athletic thanks in part to the 2006 introduction of the twenty-four-second shot clock.[23] By the early 2010s, the WNBA style was more distinct from its

NCAA counterpart, ever-faster, and more offense-orientated; movement of the three-point line to a FIBA standard twenty-two feet also impacted the game. But it was the three-point shot revolution of the mid-2010s that by 2018 produced a more exciting, faster product all while players became more versatile.[24]

The culture has changed, just as the W has become more of a phenomenon off the hardcourt. During the 2010s, the league emerged at the forefront of a renewed athlete activism in the United States, one that came to a head in the aftermath of George Floyd's wrongful death in May 2020 and sparked athlete activism globally. From advocating against domestic violence and in support of the Black Lives Matter and pro-democracy movements to the effort to get people to vote in the 2020 elections and more, the social activism of the WNBA and its players is peerless and has influenced the work of other athletes, teams, and leagues.[25] Once Griner was freed by Russia in a prisoner swap on December 8, 2022, her WNBA colleagues vowed to continue to fight for the release of others who are wrongfully detained abroad.

Then there's the fashion. Since 2018, the players have become known for greater fashion style as the game continued to mix hoops with lifestyle and fashion. Digital platforms like MadeForTheW and League Fits have been at the forefront of this trend, while Jordan Brand partnerships further fuel the mix.[26] WNBA players have also become more standard fixtures at sports industry events, no longer merely the obligatory token. All of this was facilitated by the rise of social media and the ability of players to use their individual platforms to call attention to their civic work and causes.

Impact Players Back Home

Many French NBA and WNBA players return home, give back to basketball, and impact the next generation. For French Basketball Federation President Jean-Pierre Siutat, player contributions come in different forms. Some play with the national team and are used in the sport's overall marketing. "We take their image and the fact they play in the NBA to promote our basketball, all the products of the national team, but also programs for kids," he explained. It's the sort of contribution that can prod more youths to begin playing or decide to pursue the game to its highest levels and thus help feed the development pipeline.

Other contributions center around investment in the game in some way, shape, or form. Some invest in teams, like Parker at ASVEL Lyon-Villeurbanne, Boris Diaw at Bordeaux, or Nicolas Batum at Le Mans. Others are invested in helping to promote and maintain ties with the youth programs or academies that formed them, such as Rudy Gobert with Cholet. Then there's those like Fournier, who invested in entities like Hoops Factory that provided access and opportunity to play the game.[27] For Siutat, players' different types of involvement "is very important because they try to give back what French basketball gave to them." He also noted how players from Martinique, Guadeloupe, and French Guinea give back in similar ways there, including running camps for kids in their old neighborhoods. Thus, French NBA and WNBA players are helping to sustain the pipeline and the game.

Longtime NBA journalist for *L'Équipe* Arnaud Lecomte witnessed the evolving relationship between France and the United States through basketball prism. "The NBA has a small French accent now in the last fifteen years thanks to Tony [Parker], Boris [Diaw], and Nicolas Batum," he said.[28] The teenager currently projected to be the number one NBA draft pick in June 2023, if he remains healthy, will add greater emphasis on that accent.

Victor Wembanyama is often described by the French press as a "unicorn" for his unique mix of athleticism, height, technique, skill, and style. He was born January 4, 2004, into a hoops family: his mother Elodie de Fautereau is a former player and coach while grandfather Michel de Fautereau played with Paris Université Club (PUC) in the 1960s. Victor grew up following his mother around the court, just as Diaw and Tariq Abdul-Wahad cut their teeth in the game through their mothers' basketball careers. Formed by the academy at Nanterre, Wembanyama played two seasons with Lyon-Villeurbanne, Parker's team, where he was part of the 2022 championship-winning team.

He then transferred to Parisian-based team Boulogne-Levallois Metropolitans 92. Some said it was to play fewer highly competitive matches (Lyon is in EuroLeague, and thus includes games of greater frequency and intensity) in the year before his likely departure for the NBA. Others said it was to be closer to his family in nearby Le Chesnay. But according to Wembanyama, it was specifically because the club was willing to construct the team around him, a rarity.[29] At Mets 92, Wembanyama is coached by Vincent Collet, who once again found himself preparing a basketball prodigy for the NBA, and dominates the league. At the end of December 2022, Wembanyama led ProA in scoring, averaging 22.9 pts, and rebounding, 9.6, per game.[30]

He is a unicorn in other ways. This season, Mets 92 games are sold out, both home and away, as crowds clamor to see him play. Stars such as French national team footballer Randal Kolo Muani and Hollywood actor Michael Douglas have shown up courtside to watch "Wemby" in person.[31] Of greater importance is that kids are turning out in force with their parents in tow, often for their first live professional game, to catch a glimpse of the teen some call a rock star. "Victor has become an icon for youth interested in basketball," Collet told *L'Équipe* of the phenomenon that's made Mets 92 tickets an ultra-hot commodity. "I receive a lot of requests [for tickets], but the difference with other years is that there are no more available."[32]

The effect is global, too. The NBA began to stream Mets 92 matches on its NBA League Pass app in October 2022, part of the US-based league's strategy of making their digital platform "an all-in-one destination for everything basketball," according to Deputy Commissioner Tatum. The reason for including this French team in their offerings was simple. "As a projected top pick in the 2023 NBA Draft, Wembanyama has already garnered an incredible following in the U.S and around the world," he said. "We want NBA fans to get to know him better and familiarize themselves with his talent, and the response from fans has been incredible."[33] The first Mets 92 game featured on the platform was the highest-performing non-NBA event of the season to date, with Instagram numbers via the NBA Europe channel providing an additional 2.2 million video views for that match.[34]

Notes

1   Julien Laurens, "Inside Story of France's NBA-Inspired World Cup Rings," ESPN.com, March 21, 2019, https://www.espn.com/soccer/club/france/478/blog/post/3805817/inspired-by-the-nba-paul-pogba-and-antoine-griezmann-deliver-world-cup-rings-to-france.

2   Walter LaFeber, *Michael Jordan and the New Global Capitalism* (W.W. Norton, 1999).

3   For in-depth analysis on the NBA, Jordan, and the 1990s, see Cathal Kilcline, *Sport and Society in Global France : Nations, Migrations, Corporations* (Liverpool University Press, 2019).

4   Alexander Wolff, *Big Game, Small World: A Basketball Adventure*, 20th Anniversary Edition (Duke University Press, 2022), 319.

5   Lindsay Sarah Krasnoff, "How Basketball Became the World's Second-Biggest Sport," *Washington Post*, August 16, 2018, https://www.washingtonpost.com/news/made-by-history/wp/2018/08/16/how-basketball-became-the-worlds-second-biggest-sport/.

6   Jordan Ritter Conn, "Is the NBA Done Drafting International Players?," *Grantland* (blog), 88566, https://grantland.com/features/evan-fournier-not-necessarily-surprising-dearth-foreign-prospects-2012-nba-draft/.

7   All Terry Lyons quotes in this chapter, unless specified, from Terry Lyons, Interview with the author, October 22, 2015.

8   Lyons.

9   All Chris Ebersole quotes in this chapter from Chris Ebersole, Interview with the author, March 11, 2021.

10 Joel Gunderson, *The (Inter) National Basketball Association: How the NBA Ushered in a New Era of Basketball and Went Global* (Sports Publishing, 2020).

11 Jason Reid, "San Antonio Spurs Provide a Blueprint for NBA's Small-Market Teams," *Washington Post*, June 10, 2013, sec. Wizards/NBA, https://www.washingtonpost.com/sports/wizards/san-antonio-spurs-provide-a-blueprint-for-nbas-small-market-teams/2013/06/10/7b9137de-d1f9-11e2-8cbe-1bcbee06f8f8_story.html.

12 Sam Presti to Lindsay Sarah Krasnoff, "Sam Presti for CNN International," October 22, 2015.

13 Lindsay Sarah Krasnoff, "NBA: France's Love Affair with Basketball—on and off Court," CNN, November 24, 2015, https://www.cnn.com/2015/11/24/sport/france-basketball-nba-parker/index.html.

14 Presti to Krasnoff, "Sam Presti for CNN International," October 22, 2015.

15 All Evan Fournier quotes in this chapter, unless specified, from Evan Fournier, Interview with the author, part 2, May 19, 2016.

16 Mike Prada, *Spaced Out: How the NBA's Three-Point Revolution Changed Everything You Thought You Knew About Basketball* (Triumph Books, 2022).

17 Mark Tatum, Written interview for the author, via email, December 27, 2022.

18 David Stern, Interview with the author, interview by Lindsay Sarah Krasnoff, Telephone, March 17, 2016.

19 Stern.

20 All Mark Tatum quotes in this chapter, unless specified, from Mark Tatum, Written interview for the author, via email, December 27, 2022.

21 Zack Graham, "How David Stern's NBA Dress Code Changed Men's Fashion," *Rolling Stone*, November 4, 2016.

22 WNBA, "Signings by WNBA Team and by Overseas Country for 2022–23 as of November 2, 2022," November 2, 2022.

23 WNBA, "How Has the WNBA Changed in Ten Years?," WNBA. Com, accessed September 19, 2022, https://www.wnba.com/archive/wnba/history/10thann_leaguechanges.html.

24 Howard Megdal, "The WNBA Is Evolving Right before Our Eyes," Fansided.com, August 22, 2018, https://fansided.com/2018/08/22/wnba-evolving-pace-space-candace-parker/.

25 Chantel Jennings, "Inside the WNBA's Evolution from a League of Activists to Organizers," *The Athletic*, October 15, 2020, https://theathletic.com/2137508/2020/10/15/inside-the-wnbas-evolution-from-a-league-of-activists-to-organizers/; Sarah Kearns, "WNBA Players Reflect on the League's Evolution," HYPEBEAST, March 31, 2022, https://hypebeast.com/2022/3/wnba-players-reflect-on-league-interview.

26 Khristina Williams, "'Women Are Changing the Game': The WNBA's Fashion Evolution," *Just Women's Sports*, September 8, 2021, https://justwomenssports.com/women-are-changing-the-game-the-wnbas-fashion-evolution/.

27 In December 2020, the FFBB acquired Hoops Factory, which was in financial difficulty as a result of the pandemic. Alexandre Bailleul, "Evan Fournier et Rudy Gobert Investissent dans le Futur Centre Indoor de Basket 'Hoops Factory,'" SportBuzzBusiness.fr, September 25, 2015, https://www.sportbuzzbusiness.fr/evan-fournier-et-rudy-gobert-investissent-dans-le-futur-centre-indoor-de-basket-hoops-factory.html; Sacha Rutard, "La FFBB Reprend à Son Compte les Hoops Factory Basket Europe," *BasketEurope* (blog), December 22, 2020, https://www.basketeurope.com/livenews-fr/528565/la-ffbb-reprend-a-son-compte-les-hoops-factory/.

28 Messiah Wambo Fiase, "Voice 26 Arnaud Lecomte," FranceAndUs, accessed November 25, 2022, https://www.franceussports.com/voices/026-arnaud-lecomte.

29 Pascal Giberné, "Victor Wembanyama Is the French Cheat Code Coming to Shake Up the NBA," *SLAM*, October 3, 2022, https://www.slamonline.com/the-magazine/victor-wembanyama-slam-240/.

30 "LNB ProA Stats Center," Betclic ELITE, accessed December 27, 2022, https://www.lnb.fr/elite/.

31 Yann Ohnona, "Portés par Victor Wembanyama, les Metropolitans 92 Remplissent les Salles de France," *L'Équipe*, December 27, 2022, https://www.lequipe.fr/Basket/Article/Portes-par-victor-wembanyama-les-metropolitans-92-remplissent-les-salles-de-france/1371716.

32 Ohnona.

33 Tatum, Written interview for the author, via email.

34 Tatum.

15

La Vie en Bleu

Ahead of the 2020 Tokyo Games, WNBA Champion and longtime Les Bleues offensive leader Sandrine Gruda shared with FIBA basketball her belief that France could go all the way at the Olympics.

> Honestly, yes. We're probably the only team that can challenge the Americans from an athletic standpoint. That's first. The French team has never had as much talent as today. Finally, the game is also played on the mental level. If we happen to be stronger mentally, I am convinced that we can challenge them and, in a game, anything is possible. We shouldn't be any less ambitious because of a fear of failing. It makes everyone panic; everyone is afraid to say what they think. I'm not. I want to win a gold medal at the Tokyo Olympics."[1]

That hunger nearly paid off, although it was prolonged one year by the COVID-19 pandemic that tore across the globe in early 2020. When the pandemic-delayed Games finally got underway in July 2021, Gruda and Les Bleues were ready. France toughed it out through the group stage with one win and two losses, then beat Spain in the quarterfinals 67–64. Despite Gruda's 18 points in the semifinal against Japan, France lost 71–87, then rebounded on August 7 with a bronze medal win against Serbia 91–76. It wasn't the gold that Gruda hungered for, but it was an Olympic podium finish, something to be proud of.

One day earlier, their male counterparts nearly won their own gold medal in a nail-biting contest against the United States. It was a rematch of the teams' encounter barely two weeks earlier in group play, one Les Bleus decisively won, 83–76. France still had the thrilling high of triumph following their tightly contested semifinal against Slovenia, a game that boiled down to the final seconds as captain Nicolas Batum made arguably the biggest play in team history when he denied Slovenia's last-minute scoring attempt. The move, immortalized by video clips and reprinted on posters and t-shirts, sealed France's 90–89 victory and set up their date with Olympic history.

The August 6 final was hard fought. France was within three points of the Americans in the game's last ten seconds. Then, two seconds later, a pair of free throws from US star Kevin Durant secured the game for Team USA 87–82. It was an excellent performance for the newly crowned Olympic vice champions, despite the disappointment of being within reach of the dreamed-of gold medal.

Basketball at the Tokyo Games illustrated France's growth as a global basketball power through two medals and a fourth-place finish in women's 3x3 basketball. The images of French Olympians at the medal ceremonies helped cultivate soft power and projected images about the modern-day country. France's ability to contest the world's top hoops countries, including the United States, reveals the power of the forces at work in *Basketball Empire* that have helped make France a basketball breeding ground. In the twenty-first century, the French national teams have become intimately acquainted with US basketball, its style, tactics, and culture, because so many of their players have experience playing in the United States, know-how augmented by going toe-to-toe with female Americans in French or European league competition during the WNBA off season. It's a recipe rife with informal sports diplomacy that's helped pay dividends in formal sports diplomacy engagements, such as in FIBA-sanctioned competition. In the process, it's enticing more kids to basketball, one that will benefit from the knowledge, culture, and technicalities of the game passed down to the next generation.

Realizing the Legacies of Sydney

In some ways, the 2020 Tokyo Games were a natural conclusion that realized the legacies planted two decades earlier. The 2000

Sydney Games were the first time that both French national teams competed at the Olympic basketball tournament, with fifth place (women) and second place (men) finishes. France has since built generation after generation of talent whose international performances have kept the country among the top of FIBA's world rankings.

After Sydney, Les Bleues made history in a new way when they won EuroBasket 2001. That year's team featured several players with US experience, including the first two Frenchwomen to play in the WNBA, Isabelle Fijalkowski and Laure Savasta (1997), the Washington Mystics' Audrey Sauret (2001), and Yannick Souvré, who contested the 1989–90 NCAA season with Fresno State. Another key component on that championship team was future WNBA stalwart Edwige Lawson-Wade who, from 2005 until 2010, lived her US hoops dream.

That championship title provided a taste of victory that drove the team and subsequent generations of players. After suboptimal performances at the next several EuroBasket tournaments, Les Bleues roared back to win it all again in 2009 thanks to a 57–53 victory over Russia. That version of the team included Gruda, Emile Gomis, and Emmeline Ndongue, who all had accumulated WNBA experience by that point, as legend-in-the-making Céline Dumerc later did (Atlanta Dream, 2014). France won bronze in the 2011 tournament, and since 2013 have reigned as European Vice Champions. Their FIBA World Cup record is less notable, with their best twenty-first-century finish to date fifth place (2006, 2018).

Results were different at the Olympics when Les Bleues returned in a big way at the 2012 London Games. That summer, they fought the United States for gold after posting a 5–0 group play record, which included two overtime victories, and two decisive wins in the knockout rounds. France was familiar with many of Team USA's players thanks to being teammates in the NCAA, WNBA, or in Europe. As Gruda told Agence France Presse, "when we play basketball, we aren't scared of any team. This is a good group. We know how to fight."[2]

The Americans took their opponent seriously. Assistant Coach Doug Bruno told media not to underestimate France. "They are a very good team that has solid experience," he said. "They have all the main ingredients a team needs to be really, really good. And then they are getting some good scoring off of the bench. . .They've played two overtime games and a lot of close games, but I don't think they are getting lucky."[3] US superstar Sue Bird cautioned France wouldn't be easy. "They're a team nobody really talked about heading into the tournament," she told the Associated Press. "But personally, I knew that was going to be a team we might have to face...I've played with all their girls and know how talented they are."[4]

France was the tournament's sleeper team. As coach Pierre Vincent told the Associated Press, "nobody talks about us. We don't exist in the Olympic Village. The only way to exist is to win. I told the girls in the locker room, if we win, we will exist."[5] Unfortunately, France was outclassed on the court by Team USA 50–86. Despite going up 13–10 in the game's early minutes, the second half proved fatal as Candice Parker ignited a 14–5 run that changed the game's momentum.

The team four years later had a slightly different mission. At Rio in 2016, France finished in fourth place, but they played for more than just a chance to medal. A series of terrorist events on French soil that began with the January 2015 *Charlie Hebdo* attacks rattled the nation and sport, particularly the national teams, was one way to forge solidarity. As Gruda told the Associated Press, "we show pride in our country with the flag and we hope these next few weeks can help heal."[6]

The continued successes of Les Bleues reflects the investment given to women's basketball. As FFBB President Jean-Pierre Siutat noted, "we have for many years the politic to promote women's basketball, more than football or rugby."[7] Successes also fuel the larger popularity of the women's game. The national team in turn is fed by the professional clubs. That's why it's the number one team sport for women in France.[8] While their male counterparts cannot make such a statement, they, too, have won accolades since Sydney that similarly infuse the hoop dreams of the next generation.

Performances on the European stage were uneven in the immediate turn of the century as a new generation, the Tony Parker generation, rejuvenated national team ranks. As more of the country's top players dribbled for a living in the NBA, the FFBB found it difficult to cover the high insurance payments NBA teams mandated to protect players.

Les Bleus won bronze at EuroBasket 2005, silver in 2011, and in 2013 they won the European title for the first time. It was a major milestone. Led by the Parker generation, which included fellow NBA veterans Ronny Turiaf and longtime Les Bleus captain Boris Diaw, the team included Mickael Gelabale (Minnesota Timberwolves), Batum (Portland Trailblazers), Johan Petro (Atlanta Hawks), and Nando de Colo (San Antonio Spurs). Victory finally realized the team's potential, talent, and captivated the country along the way for a time. "It symbolizes the champions who constructed the team," coach Vincent Collet later told *Basket Le Mag*. "They showed their force of character."[9]

The 2015 EuroBasket was an important one for France as defending champion and last-minute co-host. That year's tournament, originally scheduled to be hosted by Ukraine, was relocated following the Russian takeover of Ukraine's Crimea region in March 2014. FIBA Europe divided hosting duties between France, Croatia, Germany, and Italy. Playing on home soil was important for stoking awareness of the game, its popularity, and, it was hoped, homecourt advantage. Camille Eleka recalled how his childhood friend, Batum, called him after one of the team's big victories. "Nicolas told me that the atmosphere was incredible because it was in front of more than 26,000 spectators. That's never been seen before," Eleka said.[10]

The tournament was an important turning point in how it rallied French fans to the team. While its normal for a nationalistic atmosphere filled with pride amongst French football fans when supporting the national team, for basketball that's not always been the case. But on this night, that changed. The fans in the bleachers sang *La Marseillaise* and chanted together constantly throughout the match. "This is very, very rare," Eleka relayed.[11] But it was a bonding point for the team as well, despite their eventual bronze medal finish. As of press time, France are the reigning European vice champions after EuroBasket 2022.

Similarly, Les Bleus' FIBA World Cup record was uneven in the 2000s but improved and was sustained in the 2010s. As Siutat told *Sud Ouest* in 2010, "the French team is on all the podiums at the youth level, but we don't have results at the senior level, despite the quality of our formation."[12] Despite elimination from the 2010 tournament in the Round of Sixteen, France regrouped, and the 2014 World Cup in Spain proved pivotal. With Parker absent as Team France's clutch playmaker, Batum stepped up and into a new role as he led Les Bleus to the bronze medal, eliminated the host (and fierce rival) in an epic quarterfinal, and was named to FIBA's All-Tournament team.

The experience helped cultivate the taste for more at the global level. At the 2019 World Cup France retained its bronze medal after knocking Team USA out of the tournament entirely. France's 89–79 win over the Americans in the quarterfinals, the first US team defeat in fifty-eight non-exhibition games, rippled across the world as it snapped Team USA's FIBA world title streak held since 2006. It proved to the basketball world that the US team was beatable, and for France the feat was a phenomenal mental game changer. Thus, when they tipped off against the United States twice at Tokyo 2020, despite disappointing Olympic performances in 2012 and 2016, it was with a far different team and mentality than twenty years earlier.

Of course, it isn't just the 5×5 teams that have accumulated FIBA accolades. Since the introduction of 3×3 competitions in 2010, French teams have crescendoed in performance. The women's 3×3 team won the 2022 FIBA World Cup title, silver in 2012, and bronze at the 2018 and 2019 tournaments while the men won silver in 2021 and bronze in 2017 and 2022. On the continental level, Les Bleues won the 2018, 2019 and 2022 Europe Cup and bronze in 2021, while Les Bleus won silver in 2019. France's women's 3X3 team placed fourth at Tokyo 2020, the first time 3×3 was an official Olympic sport. National team head coach Karim Souchu is no stranger to the informal sports diplomacy exchanges that happen in and around the court. From 1999 until 2003, he crafted an NCAA career with the Furman University Paladins, where he was just one of six players in the program's history with a career record of more than 1,200 points, 600 rebounds, 150 assists, and 100 steals.[13]

National team duty is more than just an obligation. For Batum, as with other players, it's a source of pride. "For us, people like Boris Diaw, Tony Parker, all those guys, every summer we come back and play for the national team."[14] As formal sports diplomats with the Les Bleus and Les Bleues, the country's elite basketballers communicate, represent, and negotiate to the world about the country today, which goes beyond amassing medals. Mickaël Gelabale, who served from 2005 through the 2016 Olympics, described how he and teammates always stopped to take photos with fans, took their headphones off before descending from the team bus so as to be open to the people who waited, and spent time with their supporters to show how they appreciated their public. Such actions were not dictated by the FFBB; rather, they developed among the players, notably led by their captain, Diaw.[15]

The teams also allowed their communications and media colleagues to follow them around in the lead-up to major tournaments, beginning in 2014. Ahead of that summer's World Cup, the federation created a YouTube series that brought fans inside the world of the Les Bleus to highlight the seriousness of preparations, as well as the humor and personalities involved in building team chemistry and representing France. Similar unscripted video series documenting "behind the scenes" were made for both national teams every year since then, allowing the public to better know their representatives. These videos were blueprints for other federations, who saw the ways that such candid content could engage fans, help them better understand what playing for France entailed and meant, and stimulate interest in the sport.[16] These sorts of vignettes serve the dual purpose of helping the basketballers serve as ambassadors of the game to the French public, not just as a representative of France.[17]

The Flying Osteopath

But what is it like to be an insider and observe the national teams' evolutions, understanding the sometimes competing cultural and professional obligations at hand? Fabrice Gautier, the "Flying Osteopath," has had a front-row seat to French basketball's twenty-first-century revival. Born October 1973 in the Val d'Oise, the suburbs just north of Paris, basketball took him from a player in the greater Parisian region to an osteopath who works with the hoops world in Los Angeles. Gautier moved stateside in 2002 and built a practice whose clientele includes international athletes like NBA and WNBA players Candice Parker, Tony Parker, Ronny Turiaf, Boris Diaw, LeBron James, and Rudy Gobert.

Along the way he's engaged in different types of diplomacy. From representing the osteopath field, which was not as developed stateside when he first arrived, to representing the French approach to physical therapy, Gautier translates the cultural differentiators between France and the United States to those around him. Especially so within basketball.

In 2009, Gautier joined Les Bleus' medical staff, a post he held through EuroBasket 2013. "What I could see from inside, from my little seat at the table, was a maturation of the mentality," he explained of the evolution he witnessed first-hand. For Crawford Palmer, who served as the FFBB's liaison with US based players for several years until he stepped down in 2012, the lack of a huge desire to win was a source of frustration. "The NBA guys came back with that kind of 'we play in the NBA, and we can turn it on when we want, so when we want to engage, we can,'" he relayed. But that attitude wasn't enough to win medals at the international level. "I think it's one of the reasons that, despite the reservoir [of talent], the results really weren't there."[18]

Gautier pointed to the changing approach in the 2010s. He noted Tony Parker as a team leader who led a change in mentality, particularly for EuroBasket 2011. That summer, the two worked together for three months to prepare. "He was so driven to make [winning] happen, coming back, working out for it," Gautier said.[19]

The addition of Chicago Bulls' Joakim Noah that year reinforced this hard-nosed winning mentality. "Suddenly, we had a second guy that was all about business, that was all about intensity, and winning," Gautier recalled. Noah's first practice with the team illustrated this perfectly.

> The intensity went up to the point where Coach Collet said, "Oh, we're not going to be able to go at that pace, otherwise we won't have any more players left for the Euro." Joakim brought another side into that team, an intensity that, with Tony's, just took us somewhere else.

For the osteopath, Parker and Noah brought an American trait of the taste of victory, something that he said was a somewhat taboo cultural trait back home. "We were brainwashed with the importance of participation," he said. "We participate. We're the good loser. We had to overcome that mentality to go a step further."

Part of the formula also involved a change in leadership when Vincent Collet took over as head coach in 2009, a position he still holds today. Upon his arrival, Collet focused on changing the culture around the team, reinforcing the winning mentality, and around the sport, too.[20] Gautier also credits the team's improved results to players' overseas experiences. "I think it was the guys playing in the States, they slowly brought back more examples of successful athletes that win," he said. "They don't just win, but they dominate their sports."

In 2019, Gautier resumed his work with Les Bleus and pointed to how close the team has come to winning gold. Whether at the World Cup or Olympics, the notion isn't so far-fetched, he argued. "Three points and maybe one missed call at the beginning of the game," Gautier noted were all that stood between France and the 2020 Olympic gold medal. "Hopefully, if we beat [Team USA], if we win the World Cup, if we win the Olympics, that will maybe start putting some seriousness into [how people see] French sports."

"I'm Playing for My Country, for Its Pride"

One of the next generation players maturing into Les Bleues leadership and helping to put seriousness into how people view French sports is Gabby Williams. Born in Reno, Nevada, in 1996, Williams grew up in the United States running track and field and playing basketball but remained connected with her mother's family back in the *hexagone*. At the University of Connecticut, she stood out on court and helped the Huskies to four NCAA Women's Basketball Final Fours, two of which the team won as back-to-back national championships titles. Williams was selected fourth in the 2018 draft by the Chicago Sky and like so many other WNBA players, played professionally in Europe during the offseason, a move facilitated by her dual citizenship.

Once she moved to France to play with Basket Lattes Montpellier Agglomération (BLMA) in 2019, she began to feel at home, both with herself and her second homeland. Williams improved her French, got to better know her family, began to become less of an introvert, and learned more about the country itself. "I didn't realize how multicultural it was," she said. Moreover, the basketball was an eye-opener. "The physicality really took me by surprise. My body definitely went through a lot that year," she said of being pushed to the limits. "I got on so much better, I improved so much."[21]

In spring 2021, she received an invitation to participate in Les Bleues' Toulouse-based training camp as it prepared for the EuroBasket and Olympic campaigns. It was the realization of an idea that percolated since her first encounter with the team during college. When France lost to the United States in a friendly at Newark, New Jersey, on July 27, 2016 (62–84), Williams was in attendance. She was there to support her Huskies teammates and coach on Team USA but was impressed by the visiting side and its leaders Dumerc and Gruda. "They really stuck in my head," Williams recalled. "I was like, 'Damn, they've got some game.' The little Frenchie in me was rooting for them."

It was an influential moment, one that led her to reach out to the FFBB upon graduation in 2018 and let them know that she would love to play for France. "I made it clear that if I am ever called to the national team, I'm going to go," she said.

En route to Toulouse, questions swirled in her head. Would the others accept her and understand her accent? Would she be able to understand what they said in French? If she made the team, would they be mad at her for taking a spot from someone they had likely played with coming up the ranks on the youth teams? It was helpful that not all the faces were new; two of her BLMA teammates, captain Diandra Tchatchouang and Alix Duchet, were among the national team stalwarts at training camp.

Williams impressed, won her spot on Les Bleues' roster, and embarked upon a summer that realized her earlier dreams of playing for France. Her family was thrilled, particularly her (French) grandmother, and Williams soaked it all in. She was also dazzled that her roommate in Tokyo was a player she long admired: Gruda. "'I've been a big fan of you since 2016," Williams admitted to her teammate. "After you won the WNBA championship, playing with you was a dream come true for me."

With Les Bleues, Williams enjoyed herself on-court, too, and had fun. As she explained,

> I don't think I've ever felt like that with basketball. Basketball is always something I did because I was good at it, it was something that pays the bills. But I wasn't thinking about money. I was just focused on how there was so much to lose, there's so much at stake for every single game. I love that. I could feel every single

emotion, good and bad. I was happy that I could feel those emotions, it reminded me of how special it really was.

Moreover, the experience empowered her to better understand that playing for something bigger, the country, could be transformative. "I never understood what it meant to represent your country," she said. "I've always known what it's like to be a player that gets paid and does their job for the club. That's business. But it was the first time I was playing for something bigger than basketball. I'm playing for my country, for its pride."

Towards Paris 2024

On August 8, 2021, some 60,000 people flooded the Trocadéro as the nation celebrated its Olympic medal-winning team sports.[22] There were the Olympic champion women's and men's handball and men's volleyball teams, the Olympic vice champion men's basketball and bronze-winning women's basketball teams. It was a different scene from the one so many of them, notably Evan Fournier, recalled of the first time the country went wild for a national team, the 1998 FIFA World Cup champions. "It was really crazy," he said a bit wistfully of that moment. "Basketball, to be honest, I don't know if we can have such an impact on the people. But if we could, that would be great because we have such a mix in our national team. I think it represents France a lot."[23]

In hosting the Paris 2024 Summer Games, the hope is that basketball can indeed have such an impact. Many players have enacted career strategies to enable eligibility for national team selection at an Olympiad on home soil. Their gold medal hoops hopes in the 2020s are very realistic thanks to improved results aided by the generations of informal basketball diplomacy between French, American, and African players in and around the court.

The major obstacle to both teams realizing these objectives is likely to be the United States. The familiarity bred from the cultural, technical, and knowledge exchange of transatlantic hoops experiences translates into legitimate French challenges to Team USA on-court. It's helped to create a little bit of a friendly basketball rivalry that, while not as vicious as that with Spain, promises to captivate. As Batum pointed out, "the last three times we played [the United States], it's been exciting games. We won twice, but they beat us in the [Olympic] final. So, it can be [a rivalry]."[24] Off-court, things are already percolating, given the questions that swirl as to whether NBA defensive sensation Joel Embiid, who took French and American citizenship in 2022, will play for France or the United States in 2024.

It is anticipation fed by the symbolism of the 2020s Summer Olympic cycle. When the International Olympic Committee awarded hosting rights to Paris (2024) and Los Angeles (2028) in August 2017, it mandated the two cities proactively build a bridge-like connective tissue between the two sporting mega-events. Fittingly, the 250th anniversary of the Franco-American alliance in February 2028 will set up these two allies as friendly foes on the court.

France has contributed to globalizing and internationalizing the NBA and WNBA. At the same time, the cultural, technical, and knowledge exchange players gain from their US experiences has contributed to amelioration of Team France results. The performances and medal accolades of Les Bleues and Les Bleus have in the twenty-first century helped the country build a new position within the international order through the soft power and cultural cachet of sports diplomacy. It's an evolution built on the foundations of the Franco-American and French–African relationships, as well as Antillean contributions. Although messy and at times acrimonious, they are inextricably linked when it comes to basketball.

Notes

1   "France Start Gruda: 'We Can Win Gold at the Olympics,'" *Impact News Service*, April 21, 2020.

2   "Olympics: French Dance into Olympic Women's Hoop Final," *AFP*, August 9, 2012.

3   Rich Elliott, "UConn Women's Basketball: Bruno Provides His Take on US/France Match-Up," *UConn Women's Basketball* (blog), August 10, 2012.

4   Doug Feinberg, "US–France Meet in Women's Hoops for Olympic Gold," Associated Press, August 10, 2012.

5   Ibid.

6   Doug Feinberg, "France, Turkey Use Hoops to Heal Their Nations after Attacks," Associated Press, August 6, 2016.

7   Jean-Pierre Siutat, Interview with the author, October 19, 2016.

8   Yann Casseville, "Pourquoi le Basket Est le Sport Collectif Féminin No.1," *Basket Le Mag*, June 2017.

9   Yann Casseville, "Moi, Je. . .Vincent Collet," *Basket Le Mag*, May 2020, 61.

10 Camille Eleka, Interview with the author, September 13, 2015.

11 Eleka.

12 Frédéric Cormary, "On Forme pour la NBA," *Sud Ouest*, December 27, 2010.

13 "Furman Basketball: A Look Back at the 2020–21 Campaign," Furman University, accessed December 21, 2022, https://furmanpaladins.com/news/2021/3/19/mens-basketball-furman-basketball-a-look-back-at-the-2020-21-campaign.aspx.

14 Nicolas Batum, Interview with Nicolas Batum, February 4, 2015.

15 Mickaël Gelabale, Interview with the author, April 18, 2017.

16 Gelabale.

17 Gelabale.

18 Crawford Palmer, Interview with the author, interview by Lindsay Sarah Krasnoff, December 8, 2021.

19 All Fabrice Gautier quotes in this chapter, unless specified, from Fabrice Gautier, Interview with the author, October 1, 2018; Fabrice Gautier, Interview with the author, November 14, 2022.

20 "Batum Says Collet Is the Right Coach for France" (FIBA.com, October 27, 2016).

21 All Gabby Williams quotes in this chapter from Krasnoff.

22 Léa Leostic, "Les Médaillés Olympiques Avaient Rendez-Vous avec le Public Place du Trocadéro à Paris," *L'Équipe*, August 9, 2021, https://www.lequipe.fr/Escrime/Article/Les-medailles-olympiques-avaient-rendez-vous-avec-le-public-place-du-trocadero-a-paris/1277333.

23 Evan Fournier, Interview with the author, part 2, May 19, 2016.

24 Nicolas Batum, Interview for the author, interview by Los Angeles Clippers Communicatons, December 14, 2022.

Epilogue

Wet snowflakes flecked the skies above Accor Arena on January 19, 2023, as the NBA returned to Paris for the first time since the COVID-19 pandemic. The heavily anticipated matchup featured one of the league's classic rivalries: the Chicago Bulls versus the Detroit Pistons. Although neither side vied for the Eastern Conference's top rungs, Chicago was in tenth place while Detroit's 12–36 record was worst in the East, they each had ties to the host country. For the Bulls, it was an opportunity to honor and pay homage to their retired longtime hoops hero Joakim Noah, who also played for Les Bleus. The last time the team played in the City of Light, two pre-season games in 1997, Michael Jordan still dominated the world and just one in fourteen NBA players were born and trained overseas. It was a far different scenario that January 2023 evening when nearly one in three league basketballers were international.[1] The Pistons featured one of those players as their sophomore French guard Killian Hayes prepared to play in front of family and friends.

There was a sense of symmetry with the first NBA regular season match in 2020. Traffic was similarly snarled thanks to a country-wide labor strike to protest the government's proposed pension reforms. Advertisements and activations around the city again abounded, from posters and digital billboards in the *métro* to NBA-themed television specials and the return of NBA House, and interactive fan zone where earlier that afternoon French NBA legends Tony Parker and Noah played 3×3 with attendees. By 9 p.m. local time, despite travel difficulties, the sell-out crowd of 15,885 was in place for tipoff.

FIGURE E.1 *The NBA Paris Game 2023, where the Chicago Bulls won over the Detroit Pistons, 126–108. Credit: Lindsay Sarah Krasnoff.*

The First Half

There was a noticeable buzz in the air. On court, Parker welcomed the crowd and introduced the Bulls' French-speaking Montenegrin Nikola Vučević and Hayes, who both expressed their gratitude to fans *en français*. There was a big cheer for the Piston, despite his difficult history with the French Basketball Federation (FFBB). A product of the Cholet youth academy, with Team France Hayes was the U16 European Champion in 2017 and U17 World Cup vice champion the following year. But the federation suspended him for six weeks in 2019 for violating protocol when he refused call-up for the U20 team and instead prepared for his next professional season. The controversial move did not significantly dim the audience's support for Hayes in 2023, but they did not *fête* him like they did Les Bleus captain Nicolas Batum throughout the NBA Paris Game 2020.

Tipoff released the week's build-up of anticipation and sports diplomacy efforts. Since their January 16 arrival on French soil, the

Pistons and Bulls engaged in a multitude of activities that imparted French culture, heritage, and hoops. They took in the city's sites, cuisine, and posed for the obligatory photos by the Eiffel Tower. There were practices but also several youth outreach initiatives organized around the city, sometimes in conjunction with FFBB coaches. Through a variety of programing during their stay, including Jr. NBA and NBA Cares events, the NBA impacted around one thousand youths.[2]

There were more personal implications for some players. Detroit forward Isaiah Livers discovered a new appreciation and love for live opera.[3] Fellow Piston Hamidou Diallo, winner of the 2019 NBA All-Star Weekend Slam Dunk contest, visited the Paris Saint-Germain youth academy and furthered the cross-discipline influences that simmer between the NBA and some of the world's best football clubs and stars. Although Hayes previously introduced the Detroit locker room to French musicians and rappers like Ninho, he admitted that this trip was special. "It's a blessing to be able to come out here in the middle of the season and get to introduce my culture, the French culture, to my teammates," Hayes told NBA.com reporters.[4]

Throughout the half, the announcer and Instagram documented the stars in the crowd. Sitting courtside were former French NBA and national team stars Parker, Ronny Turiaf, Mickaël Piétrus, and Noah, the first generation to significantly mark NBA and FIBA hardcourts with championship titles that contributed to building French soft power through sports. Legendary WNBA champion Sandrine Gruda and her former Les Bleues teammate Diandra Tchatchouang were in attendance, as were fellow French international and WNBA players Gabby Williams and Marine Johannès, reminders that cultivation of French cultural cachet is equally due to women's basketball. Collectively, these men and women represented the various French-American, French-Antillean, and French-African influences at work in the larger *Basketball Empire* story.

The culture of celebrity often infused around NBA hardcourts was also on display. Musician Pharrell Williams, supermodel Naomi Campbell, and Paris Saint-Germain midfielder Marco Verratti lent their star power to the spectacle. So did NBA legends like the Pistons' Richard Hamilton and Ben Wallace, and former Los Angeles Laker Magic Johnson, who received thundering applause from the audience. Potential NBA legend-in-the-making Victor Wembanyama, the nineteen-year-old French phenomenon presumed to be the June 2023 NBA Draft number one pick, also received love from the crowd.

The French–Africa–NBA connection was represented. Noah noted that it was a "full circle moment" for him as, in addition to his Chicago ties, he was there in his capacity as a Basketball Africa League (BAL) ambassador and NBA Africa investor.[5] Four days earlier, the thirteen-season NBA veteran was on site for The BAL's two-day Paris combine, where thirty players invited from the United States, Europe, and Africa tried out for the league's last Season Three roster spots. He was joined by fellow ambassador, investor, former French international and NBA stalwart Ian Mahinmi who, influenced by his parents' ties to Bénin, similarly translated a post-playing career into promotion of basketball, the NBA, and the BAL in Africa.

The next generation was also present. Wembanyama brought his fifteen-year-old brother and fellow player Oscar to the game. Upcoming basketballer Laura Kechichian, founder of the Quai 54-winning iCanPlay 3x3 team, and French-American basketballer-artist Anaia Hoard, whose work was highlighted by the NBA's 2022 Creator Series campaign, were among the crowd. So, too, was a group of U16 players from the NBA Academies as part of a week-long basketball exchange and scrimmages with counterparts at French sports school INSEP. The players hailed from the various Academies worldwide, two of who represented NBA Academy Africa. From the youngest to the oldest attendees, everyone watched the action on and off court as the first half ended with Chicago in the lead 65–56.

The Second Half

The teams reemerged onto the court with renewed resolve, but the Pistons could not convert goodwill and the mental aspect of a "home" game into a triumphant performance. Detroit struggled and the crowd's energy lagged, despite NBA-style entertainment that included break dancers, the Pistons dance team, youth dribble-and-shoot contests, and more. Chicago's Zach LaVine, whose great grandfather immigrated to the United States from France, posted 30 points in the Bulls' 126–108 win.[6]

The NBA Paris Game 2023 demonstrated how France is today a basketball breeding ground, even as the on-court action was dominated by two American teams. Since 1997, the United States' oldest ally has become a key pipeline of talent that has internationalized the NBA, helped it to globalize, and contributed to the WNBA's growth and diversification. But it took time and a variety of different methods through which to devise a French response to the sport's globalization and changing styles of play.

One of the most visible ways that Gallic hoops evolved was to embrace basketball migration and immigration, often at the behest of local basketball officials. The young men (and later, women) who pursued their passion for the game as players and coaches, whether from the United States, the Antilles, or Africa, made the *hexagone*'s hardcourts far more cosmopolitan and brought a variety of attributes that helped evolve the game after 1950. They shared their home hoops cultures, technical aspects, and *savoir faire*, a variety of different informal sports diplomacy exchanges that ultimately benefited French basketball. By the mid-1980s, the flow of player migration began to feature more regularly those from France to the United States, including female players, into the NCAA and, starting in 1997, the WNBA and NBA. Their US hoop dreams enriched their game thanks to different cultural approaches towards mental tenacity, leadership, and understandings of teammates' roles. This knowledge was passed down to subsequent generations and enriched the basketball empire.

A far less visible French response to the game's global growth is the country's youth development system. The youth basketball development system was implemented to detect and train top talent for the national teams that could help achieve wins at international competitions. The focus on "education" in its more holistic humanistic sense infused this approach, particularly within the federal system that features the Federal Basketball Center (CFBB) at INSEP as its apex. The professional clubs' youth academy system evolved and contributed to broadening and enriching the basketball empire. This *formation à la française* system is not perfect. It can overlook promising youths due thanks to a variety of factors from human fallibility to prejudices and biases, while those who wish to leave the system early can face a range of difficulties and complications. But since the 1980s, France has produced results and today informs the NBA's own approach to elite youth development through its NBA Academies.

This system isn't due to an Americanization of French basketball. Instead, it is a French response to globalization. Like its musical and touristic counterparts, basketball borrowed influences and blended it with a richness of cosmopolitan players to produce young talent for the NBA and WNBA through its approach to youth development. Today French players contribute to the leagues, and as part of the international cohort, have helped them evolve. Their US experiences enabled them to fine-tune their hoops skills and knowhow, which in turn has enriched Team France. Since 1997, the national senior teams have garnered three gold, eleven silver, and six bronze medals between EuroBasket, FIBA World Cup, and the Olympics. All of this helped France cultivate soft power through the cultural cachet of basketball.

Several key aspects underpin the basketball diplomacy illuminated in *Basketball Empire*. First, the women's game played an important role. For decades, female and male players and coaches have interacted and influenced each other, from the 1970s camps of Clermont Université Club star Jacky Chazalon and US player-coach Carmine Calzonetti to the more recent basketball bonds between Lisieux natives Batum and Johannès. Frenchwomen and men also played together on playground courts, forging ties that carried into careers in and outside of the game.

Moreover, many in the NBA were raised in the bosom of the women's game. The first Frenchman to play the league, Tariq Abdul-Wahad, grew up in awe of his mother's teammate, US Basketball Hall of Famer Denise Curry. NBA Champion and longtime Les Bleus captain Boris Diaw was born with a basketball in his hands thanks to his mother, legendary center Élisabeth Riffiod-Diaw, while Wembanyama's mother, Elodie de Fautereau, was herself a former player and now coach. Thus, men's and women's basketball inform each other, even as they operate in separate realms.

Second, discussion about "French" basketball naturally encompasses the Antilles as integral components of post-colonial France. Players from Guadeloupe, Martinique, and French Guiana are critical parts of the story, from Jacques Cachemire and Patrick Cham to Gruda and beyond. The islands' geographic proximity to the United States, as well as their climate, have shaped their culture, as have attitudes about the ways that sport could help reinforce ties with the mainland. It's a complicated relationship, but one that since the 1960s served as a basketball backbone.

Third, French and African basketball have long "rubbed shoulders" thanks to complex colonial and post-colonial relationships. Earlier efforts by French officials and tacticians to maintain ties and influence with African counterparts in the early 1960s may well be considered through a neocolonial lens, or to edge out growing US and Soviet attempts to cultivate influence in postcolonial African through sports.[7] But a variety of initiatives, particularly between French technicians and FIBA Africa, appear to have evolved into more collaborative partnerships since then. In the twenty-first century, French of the African diaspora contribute to building basketball throughout the *métropole*, as well as in their parents' or grandparents' homelands, while Africans with formative experience on the *hexagone*'s hardcourts are also helping to forge a new era for basketball. This relationship merits further study, particularly as The BAL continues to drive attention, funding, and interest in basketball in different parts of the continent.

Fourth, the interplay between French and US basketball is one that over time has ebbed and flowed, mirroring at times the strains and closeness of the diplomatic relationship. There are longstanding sensitivities by some over perceptions of an "American colonization" of French hardcourts. That the number of US players on team rosters can prohibit young homegrown talent from the chance to snag a spot and develop. Or that the NBA would take over basketball and cause the demise of the domestic leagues. Tensions have eased over time, particularly since French players entered the NBA, made it a little more global, helped translate cultural sensitives to each side, and began to enter post-playing positions in basketball administration, investment, and development. Concerns still exist, but they are more muted since the NBA began to sport a little French accent.

Lastly, basketball can be a site of unease and clashes as France grapples with its twenty-first-century self, place in international affairs, and comes to terms with its complex colonial past. The sport can highlight tensions between the global and the domestic, urban and rural, elite and working class, native and immigrant, club and playground, republican ideals of assimilation that anyone can become "French" and the realities of discrimination, racism, and xenophobia that target "the other." Yet, it's also a space in which the republic's ideals can be represented, communicated, and negotiated to the rest of the world on and off the court.

The stories highlighted in *Basketball Empire* show how basketball served as a means for a modern, global France to play an important role in the worldwide game. The generations of cultural, technical, and knowledge exchanges between France, the United States, and Africa that feed the story show how informal sports diplomacy has elevated the game and made competitions far more competitive. *Basketball Empire* spotlights the role of individuals in informal sports diplomacy, particularly how everyday citizens can communicate, negotiate, and represent about their home country, culture, and hoops.

Post-Game

Hayes admitted disappointment in his performance during the post-game press conference when he noted, "it just wasn't my day."[8] Yet, the game capped a successful week of sports diplomacy with the ultimate act made public just hours earlier as the NBA announced a new partnership with the FFBB and French government. The agreement to elevate basketball on French and African soil was the result of a meeting between NBA Commissioner Adam Silver and French President Emmanuel Macron. Concrete details were not available when this book went to print but promised to consist of a knowledge exchange between the NBA and its French counterpart around best practices, joint work on grassroots and youth basketball development programs ahead of the Paris 2024 Games, and shared investment in African basketball infrastructure.

Left unsaid was the NBA's respect for the French system. As NBA Deputy Commissioner and Chief Operating Officer Mark Tatum acknowledged three weeks earlier, "France has an incredibly strong and sophisticated basketball infrastructure that encourages participation at the youth level and helps develop talent at the elite and professional levels."[9] Thus, the new partnership was not designed as an NBA takeover of French basketball, but rather for the two partners to walk alongside each other in encouraging the game's growth at all levels.

Officials' laudatory remarks were notably diplomatic. Macron, known for his use of sports in foreign and domestic affairs, expressed delight about "the NBA's choice to make France and Paris one of its privileged playgrounds in the world" and the "special and long-standing relationship that France has with the NBA." FFBB President Jean-Pierre Siutat noted how the partnership built upon a long working relationship with the NBA. "Our national teams are doing great and basketball in France is growing fast," he said. "It is time now to go forward at a higher level and we think there is momentum for our sport." Silver stated the honor of working with Macron, the FFBB, and the Ligue National de Basketball (LNB). "President Macron strongly believes in the power of basketball to inspire and connect people everywhere," he said. "We see enormous potential to grow the game and drive economic opportunity around sport in France and Africa."[10]

This one week in Paris illustrated the various themes at work in how France helped globalize and internationalize the NBA and WNBA. What emerges is a sense that the basketball empire can be used as a tool in multifaceted ways. It cultivates French soft power through on-court results of Les Bleues and Les Bleus, as well as the work of its players in the world's best leagues and their engagement with fans, colleagues, and the media. At the same time, the basketball empire empowers francophone basketball more broadly to flex its muscle globally, within and outside of the NBA.

These ongoing evolutions circle back to the larger question posed earlier: whose empire is this anyway? Geographically, this story centered around the former French empire, but culturally things are a bit different. The NBA is now part of a global heartbeat and lifestyle, even though its American accent has dissipated somewhat as the league globalized and the WNBA became more diverse. Thus, it may be ever more about a global basketball empire underpinned by a broader hoops identity, culture, lifestyle, community, and sense of citizenship. Not a French-, American-, or NBA-specific one.

That's not to say that national pride is moot. Rivalries remain strong on the hardcourts in Olympic, World Cup, and FIBA competition. But as Team USA has shown its fallibility, notably at the hands of France, a new type of friendly clash is emergent between the United States and its oldest ally as the Summer Olympic cycle of Paris 2024–Los Angeles 2028 swings into high gear ahead of the 250th anniversary of the Franco-American alliance in 2028.

For Les Bleus captain and fifteen-season NBA veteran Batum, the sport's evolution at home, in the United States, and worldwide benefits everyone. "The thing that's changed is that the basketball world got better," he said. "The United States has always been the target, but after 2000 things started shifting as the NBA opened the gates. International players became MVPs and All-Stars, and they got better. The United States didn't get worse, but the rest of the world got better."[11]

Notes

1   NBA, "Transcript: Adam Silver NBA Paris Game 2023 Press Conference—NBA Media Central" (NBA, January 19, 2023), https://mediacentral.nba.com/transcript-adam-silver-nba-paris-game-2023-press-conference/.

2   NBA.

3   James L. Edwards III, "Isaiah Livers' Paris Diary: Behind-the-Scenes Look at the Pistons Forward's Trip Abroad," The Athletic, January 22, 2023, https://theathletic.com/4112566/2023/01/22/pistons-isaiah-livers-diary/.

4   Pistons Practice: Killian Hayes on Being Back in Paris, 2023, https://www.nba.com/watch/video/kayes-full-intv?plsrc=nba&collection=nba-paris-games-2023.

5   Spencer Davies, "Joakim Noah Q&A: NBA Paris Game, Investing in BAL, Basketball's Growth," January 18, 2023, https://www.basketballnews.com/stories/nba-chicago-bulls-florida-gators-joakim-noah-qa-2023-paris-game-investing-in-bal-growth-africa-international-basketball-france-french-players-killian-hayes-bol-bol-retirement.

6   Tim Reynolds, "Chicago Bulls vs Detroit Pistons Jan 19, 2023 Game Summary" (NBA, January 19, 2023), https://www.nba.com/game/0022200678.

7   Pascal Charitas, "A More Flexible Domination: Franco-African Sport Diplomacy during Decolonization, 1945–1966," in *Diplomatic Games: Sport, Statecraft, and International Relations since 1945*, ed. Heather L. Dichter and Andrew L. Johns (University of Kentucky Press, n.d.); Pascal Charitas and David-Claude Kemo-Keimbou, "The United States of America and the Francophone African Countries at the International Olympic Committee: Sports Aid, a Barometer of American Imperialism? (1952–1963)," *Journal of Sport History* 40, no. 1 (2013): 69–91.

8   "Killian Hayes (Detroit Pistons) après la défaite contre Chicago à
    Paris : 'Ce n'était juste pas mon jour,'" *L'Équipe*, accessed January 27,
    2023, https://www.lequipe.fr/Basket/Actualites/Killian-hayes-detroit-
    pistons-apres-la-defaite-contre-chicago-a-paris-ce-n-etait-juste-pas-
    mon-jour/1375721.

9   Mark Tatum, Written interview for the author, via email, December
    27, 2022.

10 NBA, "France and NBA Announce Comprehensive Collaboration to
    Elevate Basketball in France and Africa," January 19, 2023, https://pr.
    nba.com/france-nba-collaboration/.

11 Nicolas Batum, Interview with Nicolas Batum, July 31, 2019.

SELECTED BIBLIOGRAPHY

Primary Sources

French Ministry of Youth and Sport Archives, French Foreign Ministry Archives, NBA Media Archives, NBA Statistics, US Department of State Records (US National Archives)

Media Archives: *Basket-Ball, Basket Hebdo, Basket Le Mag*, ESPN, *L'Équipe Basket, L'Équipe, L'Équipe Magazine, Maxi Basket, 5 Majeur, Le Monde, Le Figaro, Le Parisien, The New York Times, Ouest France, Sports Illustrated, The Athletic*

Oral history interviews and journalistic interviews for published media pieces with: Tariq Abdul-Wahad, Christian Baltzer, Nicolas Batum, Gérard Bosc, Jacques Cachemire, Bill Cain, Carmine Calzonetti, Patrick Cham, Vincent Collet, Philippe Desnos, Boris Diaw, Jean-Pierre Dusseaulx, Chris Ebersole, George Eddy, Paoline Ekambi, Camille Eleka, Martin Feinberg, Henry Fields, Isabelle Fijalkowski, Katia Foucade-Hoard, Evan Fournier, Fabrice Gautier, Mickael Gélabale, Rudy Gobert, Kenny Grant, Sandrine Gruda, Marine Johannès, Arthur Kenney, Pascal Legendre, Terry Lyons, Olivier Mazet, Frank Ntilikina, Crawford Palmer, Sam Presti, Johan Rat, Michel Rat, Élisabeth Riffiod-Diaw, Jean-Pierre Siutat, David Stern, Mark Tatum, Diandra Tchatchouang, Gabby Williams.

Selected interviews from the SOAS University of London Basketball Diplomacy in Africa Oral History Project: Carmine Calzonetti and Kenny Grant, Amadou Gallo Fall, Will Mbiakop, Youcef Ouldyassia, Syra Sylla.

Parker, Tony. Beyond All of my Dreams. Triumph Books, 2020.

Secondary Sources

Archambault, Fabien, Loic Artiaga, and Gérard Bosc, eds. *Le Continent Basket: L'Europe et Le Basket-Ball Au XXème Siècle*. Peter Lang, 2015.

Artiaga, Loic, and Fabien Archambault. *Double Jeu: Histoire Du Basket-Ball Entre France et Amériques*. Paris: Vuibart, 2007.

Berjoan, Thomas. *Americain Dream: L'épopée des Français en NBA.* Solar Editions, 2016.

Blanchard, Pascal, S. Lemaire, Nicolas Bancel, D.R.D. Thomas, and A. Pernsteiner. *Colonial Culture in France Since the Revolution.* Indiana University Press, 2014.

Bondy, Filip. *Tip Off: How the 1984 NBA Draft Changed Basketball Forever.* New York: Da Capo Press, 2007.

Bosc, Gérard. *Une Histoire du Basket Français. . .Tome 2: 1966–90.* Paris: Presses du Louvre, 2002.

Bosc, Gérard. *Une Histoire Du Basket Français. . .Tome 3, 1990–2000.* Presses du Louvre, 2002.

Boucheron, Patrick, and Stephane Gerson. *France in the World: A New Global History.* Other Press, 2019.

Castan-Vicente, Florys, Anaïs Bohuon, Pia Henaff-Pineau, and Nicolas Chanavat. "French Pioneers in International Women's Sport: Alice Milliat and Marie-Thérèse Eyquem, between Medical Supervision and Militant Separatism." *Staps* 125, no. 3 (December 10, 2019): 31–47.

Cazaban, Philippe, and Daniel Champsaur. *Géants: Toute l'histoire du Basket-Ball.* Éditions Chronique, 2015.

Chafer, Tony. "France and Senegal: The End of the Affair?" *SAIS Review (1989–2003)* 23, no. 2 (2003): 155–67.

Charitas, Pascal. "A More Flexible Domination: Franco-African Sport Diplomacy during Decolonization, 1945–1966." In *Diplomatic Games: Sport, Statecraft, and International Relations since 1945,* edited by Heather L. Dichter and Andrew L. Johns. University of Kentucky Press, n.d.

Charitas, Pascal, and David-Claude Kemo-Keimbou. "The United States of America and the Francophone African Countries at the International Olympic Committee: Sports Aid, a Barometer of American Imperialism? (1952–1963)." *Journal of Sport History* 40, no. 1 (2013): 69–91.

Curé, Gérard. *Cholet Basket.* Hérault Editions, 1988.

Descamps, Yann, and Ismaël Vacheron. "Où le ghetto (se) joue. Playground, basket-ball et culture afro-américaine." *Géographie et cultures,* no. 88 (December 1, 2013): 169–89.

Doppler-Speranza, François. "'Shooting Hoops with Foreign Teams' Basketball Ambassadors on US Military Bases in France (1916–1961)." In *Beyond Boycotts: Sport during the Cold War in Europe,* edited by Philippe Vonnard, Nicola Sbetti, and Grégory Quin, 135–56. De Gruyter Oldenbourg, 2017.

Doppler-Speranza, François. *Une Armée de Diplomates, Les Militaires Américains et La France, 1944–1967.* Presses Universitaires de Strasbourg, 2021.

Dubois, Laurent. *Soccer Empire: The World Cup and the Future of France*. University of California Press, 2010.

Dumont, Jacques. *Sport et Formation de La Jeunesse à La Martinique: Le Temps Des Pionniers (Fin XIXe Siècle-Années 1960)*. L'Harmattan, 2006.

Dumont, Jacques. "Sport, Culture et Assimilation dans les Antilles Françaises, des Colonies aux Départements d'outre-Mer." *Caribbean Studies* 35, No. 1 (June 2007): 87–106.

Dusseaulx, Jean-Pierre. *Les Dessus du Panier: Les Clubs Qui Font la Gloire du Basket Français*. Solar Editeur, 1971.

Dusseaulx, Jean-Pierre. *Cinq Majeur: Gilles, Staelens, Bonato, Gasnal, Fields*. Solar Editeur, 1972.

Eddy, George. *Mon Histoire Avec La NBA*. Talent Sport, 2019.

Edelman, Robert, and Christopher J. Young. *The Whole World Was Watching: Sport in the Cold War*. Stanford University Press, 2019.

Goudsouzian, Aram. *King of the Court: Bill Russell and the Basketball Revolution*. University of California Press, 2010.

Green, Ben. *Spinning the Globe: The Rise, Fall and Return to Greatness of the Harlem Globetrotters*. Amistad, 2005.

Gunderson, Joel. *The (Inter) National Basketball Association: How the NBA Ushered in a New Era of Basketball and Went Global*. Sports Publishing, 2020.

Henry, Benjamin. *Made in France: Ces Français à l'assaut u Rêve Américain*. Hugo Sport, 2021.

Keys, B.J. *The Ideals of Global Sport: From Peace to Human Rights*. Pennsylvania Studies in Human Rights. University of Pennsylvania Press, 2019.

Kilcline, Cathal. *Sport and Society in Global France: Nations, Migrations, Corporations*. Liverpool University Press, 2019.

Krasnoff, Lindsay Sarah. *The Making of Les Bleus: Sport in France, 1958–2010*. Lexington Books, 2012.

Krasnoff, Lindsay Sarah. "Developing Athletic 'Atomic Armaments': The Role of Sports Medicine in Cold War France, 1958–1992." *Performance Enhancement & Health* 2 (2013): 8–16.

Krasnoff, Lindsay Sarah. "Devolution of Les Bleus as a Symbol of a Multicultural French Future." *Soccer & Society* 18, no. 2–3 (April 16, 2017): 311–19.

Kuisel, Richard. *Seducing the French: The Dilemma of Americanization*. University of California Press, 1993.

LaFeber, Walter. *Michael Jordan and the New Global Capitalism*. W.W. Norton, 1999.

Le Bescon, Armel. *Tony Parker: une vie de basketteur*. Mareuil Éditions, 2017.

Legendre, Pascal, and David Piolé. *MSB: 20 Ans d'émotions*. Éditions Libra Diffusio, 2013.

Murray, Stuart. *Sports Diplomacy: Origins, Theory and Practice*. Routledge New Diplomacy Studies. Taylor & Francis, 2018.

Murray, Stuart, and Geoffrey Allen Pigman. "Mapping the Relationship between International Sport and Diplomacy." *Sport in Society* 17, no. 9 (October 21, 2014): 1098–118.

Poisuil, Bernard. *Canal+: L'aventure Du Sport*. Éditoria, 1996.

Pruneau, Jérome, Jacques Dumont, and Nicolas Célimène. "Voiles Traditionnelles Aux Antilles Françaises: 'Sportivisatoin' et Patrimonialisation." *Ethnologie Française* T36, no. 3 Iles Réelles (September 2006): 519–30.

Rebillard, Franck. "La Presse Basket en France. Évolutions et Diversifications des Magazines Consacrés au Basket-Ball (1982–2002)." In *L'Aventure Des "grands" Hommes. Études Sur l'histoire Du Basket-Ball*, 205–26. Presses Universitaires de Limoges, 2003.

Rofe, J. Simon. *Sport and Diplomacy: Games within Games*. Manchester University Press, 2019.

Stark, Douglas. *Breaking Barriers: A History of Integration in Professional Basketball*. Rowman & Littlefield, 2019.

Stovall, Tyler. *Transnational France: The Modern History of a Universal Nation*. Taylor & Francis, 2015.

Surdam, David George. *The Rise of the National Basketball Association*. Kindle. University of Illinois Press, 2012.

Thomas, Damion L. *Globetrotting: African American Athletes and Cold War Politics*. University of Illinois Press, 2012.

Wolff, Alexander. *Big Game, Small World: A Basketball Adventure*. 20th Anniversary Edition. Duke University Press, 2022.

INDEX